The Latin American Studies Book Series

Series editors

Eustógio Wanderley Correia Dantas, Departamento de Geografia, Centro de Ciências, Universidade Federal do Ceará, Fortaleza, Ceará, Brazil
Jorge Rabassa, Lab Geomorfología y Cuaternar, CADIC-CONICET, Ushuaia, Tierra de Fuego, Argentina
Andrew Sluyter, Louisiana State University, Conference of Latin Americanist Geographers, Baton Rouge, LA, USA

The Latin American Studies Book Series promotes quality scientific research focusing on Latin American countries. The series accepts disciplinary and interdisciplinary titles related to geographical, environmental, cultural, economic, political and urban research dedicated to Latin America. The series publishes comprehensive monographs, edited volumes and textbooks refereed by a region or country expert specialized in Latin American studies.

The series aims to raise the profile of Latin American studies, showcasing important works developed focusing on the region. It is aimed at researchers, students, and everyone interested in Latin American topics.

Submit a proposal: Proposals for the series will be considered by the Series Advisory Board. A book proposal form can be obtained from the Publisher, Juliana Pitanguy (juliana.pitanguy@springer.com).

More information about this series at http://www.springer.com/series/15104

Ezequiel Luis Bistoletti

The Power Struggles over the Post-neoliberal Social Security System Reforms in Venezuela and Ecuador

 Springer

Ezequiel Luis Bistoletti
Berlin, Germany

Dissertation: University of Kassel Faculty of Social Sciences

Disputation: 14 December 2016

ISSN 2366-3421   ISSN 2366-343X   (electronic)
The Latin American Studies Book Series
ISBN 978-3-319-98167-3   ISBN 978-3-319-98168-0   (eBook)
https://doi.org/10.1007/978-3-319-98168-0

Library of Congress Control Number: 2018950780

This Springer imprint is published by the registered company Springer Nature Switzerland AG
The registered company address is: Gewerbestrasse 11, 6330 Cham, Switzerland

Acknowledgements

This research could not have been carried out without the enormous help of my family, my friends and my colleagues. My special thanks to: Roxana Edit Velázquez, Luis Carlos Bistoletti, Anna Jahnke, Darío Maldonado, Francisco González, Alejandra Espinosa, René Behm, Friedrich Bossert, Jenny Jungehülsing, Sebastian Matthes, Paul Hecker, Philip Fehling, Nico Weinmann, Jenny Simon, Timm Schützhofer, Céleo Arias, Matthias Ebenau, Sarah Hackfort, Alke Jens, Shuwen Bian, Elaine Hui, Ahmed Kamel, Anne Tittor, Zeljko Crncic, Christian Möllmann, Christoph Scherrer, Elisabeth Tuider, and Hans-Jürgen Burchardt. My sincere gratitude to my sponsors: the Heinrich-Böll-Stiftung and the STIBET program.

Contents

Abbreviations

ABB	Agenda alternativa bolivariana: una propuesta patriótica para salir del laberinto
ACHPE	Asociación Nacional de Clínicas y Hospitales Privados del Ecuador
AD	Acción Democrática
AFP	Administradora de Fondos de Pensiones
ANL	Asamblea Nacional Legislativa
AP	Alianza PAIS
APAFP	Asociación de Promotores de Administradoras de Fondos de Pensiones
ASI	Alianza Sindical Independiente
AV	Avanza
BANAVIH	Banco Nacional de Vivienda y Hábitat
BCE	Banco Central del Ecuador
BCV	Banco Central de Venezuela
BIESS	Banco del Instituto Ecuatoriano de Seguridad Social
CCANC	Comisión Constitucional de la Asamblea Nacional Constituyente
CDS	Comisión de Derechos Sociales y de la Familia
CDTSS	Comisión de los Derechos de los Trabajadores y Seguridad Social
CEAP	Comisión de Estudios de Postgrado de la Facultad de Ciencias Económicas y Sociales de la Universidad Central de Venezuela
CIRLSS	Comisión Interinstitucional para la Reforma de la Ley de Seguridad Social
CJE	Confederación de Jubilados del Ecuador
CMDMC	Colegio de Médicos del Distrito Metropolitano de Caracas
CNE	Consejo Nacional Electoral
CODESA	Confederación de Sindicatos Autónomos de Venezuela

CONAIE	Confederación de Nacionalidades Indígenas del Ecuador
CONAM	Comisión Nacional de Modernización del Estado
CONAPRI	Consejo Nacional de Promoción de Inversiones
CONESUP	Consejo Nacional de Enseñanza Superior
CONINDUSTRIA	Confederación Venezolana de Industriales
CONSECOMERCIO	Consejo Nacional del Comercio y los Servicios
COPEI	Comité de Organización Política Electoral Independiente
CPDSI	Comisión Permanente de Desarrollo Social Integral
CPF	Comisión Permanente de Finanzas
CPSS	Comisión presidencial para la Elaboración del Proyecto de Ley Orgánica de Seguridad Social
CTV	Confederación de Trabajadores de Venezuela
CUTV	Central Unitaria de Trabajadores de Venezuela
EOSSO	Estatuto Orgánico del Seguro Social Obligatorio
FAPUV	Federación de Asociaciones de Profesores Universitarios de Venezuela
FBT	Fuerza Bolivariana de Trabajadores
FCME	Fondo de Cesantía del Magisterio
FEDECAMARAS	Federación de Cámaras y Asociaciones de Comercio y Producción de Venezuela
FEDEINDUSTRIA	Federación de Industriales, Pequeños, Medianos y Artesanos
FENACLE	Federación Nacional de Trabajadores Agroindustriales, Campesinos e Indígenas Libres del Ecuador
FEUNASSC	Federación Única Nacional de Afiliados al Seguro Social Campesino
FMV	Federación Médica Venezolana
FONDEN	Fondo de Desarrollo Nacional
FUTPV	Federación Unitaria de Trabajadores del Petróleo, del Gas, sus Similares y Derivados de Venezuela
G.O.	Gaceta Oficial de la República Bolivariana de Venezuela
G.O.E:	Gaceta Oficial Extraordinaria de la República Bolivariana de Venezuela
GV	"Gran Viraje"
IESS	Instituto Ecuatoriano de Seguridad Social
ILO	International Labour Organization
IMF	International Monetary Fund
INECE	Instituto Nacional de Estadística y Censos del Ecuador
INEV	Instituto Nacional de Estadística de Venezuela
ISSFA	Instituto de Seguridad Social de las Fuerzas Armadas
ISSPOL	Instituto de Seguridad Social de la Policía Nacional
IVSS	Instituto Venezolano de los Seguros Sociales
LOC	Ley Orgánica de Comunicación
LOE	Ley Orgánica Electoral

LOJL	Ley Orgánica para la Justicia Laboral y Reconocimiento del Trabajo en el Hogar
LOPCYMAT	Ley Orgánica de Prevención, Condiciones y Medio Ambiente de Trabajo
LOSP	Ley Orgánica del Servicio Público
LOSSSE	Ley Orgánica del Sistema de Seguridad Social (Ecuador)
LOSSSI	Ley Orgánica del Sistema de Seguridad Social Integral
LOSSSV	Ley Orgánica del Sistema de Seguridad Social (Venezuela)
LPPRPM	Ley de Partidos Políticos, Reuniones Públicas y Manifestaciones
LRLSS 2009	Ley Reformatoria a la Ley de Seguridad Social, a la Ley de Seguridad Social de las Fuerzas Armadas y a la Ley de Seguridad Social de la Policía Nacional
LRLSS 2010	Ley Reformatoria a la Ley de Seguridad Social
LRLSS 2014	Ley del Banco del Instituto Ecuatoriano de Seguridad Social para la Administración de los Fondos Complementarios Previsionales Cerrados
LRPE	Ley del Régimen Prestacional de Empleo
LRPVH	Ley del Régimen Prestacional de Vivienda y Hábitat
LSSE	Ley de Seguridad Social
LSSO	Ley del Seguro Social Obligatorio
LSSV	Ley de Servicios Sociales
MFY	Movimiento Futuro Ya
MIR	Movimiento de Izquierda Revolucionaria
MPD	Movimiento Popular Democrático
MPPEF	Ministerio del Poder Popular de Economía y Finanzas
MUPP	Movimiento de Unidad Plurinacional Pachakutik
MVR	Movimiento V República
OAEF	Oficina de Asesoría Económica y Financiera
OPS	Organización Promotora de Salud
PDVSA	Petróleos de Venezuela
PEP	Plan de Enfrentamiento a la Pobreza
PGMP	Plan de Gobierno del Movimiento PAIS 2007-2011
PJ	Primero Justicia
PP	Polo Patriótico
PPT	Patria para Todos
PRIAN	Partido Renovador Institucional de Acción Nacional
PSC	Partido Social Cristiano
PSP	Partido Sociedad Patriótica
RED	Red Ética y Democracia
REDIUP	Coordinadora de Redes por una Seguridad Social Pública y Solidaria
RSSS	Rectoría del Sistema de Seguridad Social
SENPLADES	Secretaría Nacional de Planificación y Desarrollo

SINDUOIESS	Sindicato Nacional Único de Obreros del Instituto Ecuatoriano de Seguridad Social
SNVH	Sistema Nacional de Vivienda y Hábitat
SSC	Seguro Social Campesino
SSS	Sistema de Seguridad Social
SSSS	Superintendencia del Sistema de Seguridad Social
SUO	Seguro Universal Obligatorio
TSJ	Tribunal Supremo de Justicia
TSSS	Tesorería del Sistema de Seguridad Social
UCAE	Unión de Organizaciones Campesinas del Ecuador
UN	United Nations
UNAPETROL	Unión Nacional de Trabajadores Petroleros
UNE	Unión Nacional de Educadores
UNO	Una Nueva Opción
WB	World Bank

List of Tables

Prologue

During the first decade of the twenty-first century, Latin America came under a "pink tide", as left-wing governments took over power in most countries. Far from a circumstantial streak, this "pink tide" carried over for around 15 years, until a resurrection of the right broke out in the region by the end of 2015. Thereafter, in only 6 months, right-wing political forces took over power in Argentina (November 2015) and Brazil (May 2016),[1] and brought about victories in the parliamentary elections in Venezuela (December 2015) and in the constitutional referendum in Bolivia (February 2016).

Based on these recent events, numerous political analysts have promptly predicated the "end of the cycle" of the left-wing governments in Latin America and the beginning of a right-oriented political cycle in the region. However, this conclusion comes across as hasty because of two reasons. First, left-wing governments carry through to the present in Bolivia, Uruguay, and Venezuela (despite the crisis in the latter). Besides, the new right-wing governments have come under severe difficulties since their accession to power, as the current political crisis in Brazil and the frustrating economic results in Argentina bring out.

In truth, the present political situation in Latin America should not be characterized as the end of the cycle of the left-wing governments but rather as a "hegemonic tie",[2] in which left and right political forces can hold back the imposition of each other's political projects, while at the same time they cannot carry through their own.

---

[1] Even though the right-wing governments in Argentina and Brazil correspond to each other in political, economic, and ideological terms, they must certainly be differentiated with regard to their coming. In the case of Argentina, the government of President Mauricio Macri took over power through a free and fair democratic election, whereas in the case of Brasil, the government of Michel Temer took over power through a parliamentary coup.

[2] Based on the Gamscian concept of hegemony, the notion of "hegemonic tie" was brought out by Portantiero in the early 1970s (Portantiero 1973), in order to conceptualize the political situation in Argentina between 1995 and 1973.

This hegemonic tie materializes in very different ways depending on the country at issue. Venezuela, Ecuador, and Argentina represent three very good examples of this enormous divergence. In the case of Venezuela, the hegemonic tie currently comes out as a "tragic tie", in which both poles violently contravene each other in no holds barred struggle. In the case of Ecuador, the hegemonic tie materializes as the political confrontation between incumbent President Lenín Moreno and former President Rafael Correa. In the case of Argentina, the hegemonic tie comes about as the massive social protests against the neoliberal policies promoted by the right-wing government.

What factors have brought about these differences? Why does this hegemonic tie materialize in Venezuela, Ecuador, and Argentina—and in all other countries associated with the pink tide—so differently?

To some extent, the different form assumed by the hegemonic tie in each country can be made out as the result of its specific historical, economic, and cultural context. To a much larger extent, however, this divergence is associated with the very different performances achieved by the left-wing governments during their administrations. And in this regard, despite the overwhelming generalizations of both left- and right-leaning political analysts, the experiences of the left-wing governments in Latin America have divaricated enormously.

This research represents a modest contribution to the comparative study of the Latin American left-wing governments and, more specifically, to the study of the Venezuelan and Ecuadorian left-wing governments. It breaks down the reforms of the social security systems in Venezuela and Ecuador under the left-wing governments of Hugo Chávez and Rafael Correa. Almost identical in their conceptions, these reforms undertook to establish universal social security systems in both countries for the first time in history, but they came out with very different results. In the case of Venezuela, the implementation of the reform sanctioned by Chávez' government in 2002 has broken down to this day, whereas in the case of Ecuador, the reform announced by Correa's in 2007 has come along despite manifold obstacles. What factors have determined this contrasting outcome? In order to puzzle out this question, this investigation carries out a comparative analysis of the power struggles over the reforms in both countries.

The focus on the reforms of the social security systems does not come about by chance. As explained in detail below, the expansion of social policy represents one of the most distinctive features of the Latin American left-wing governments. Moreover, social policy is inherently associated with the construction of their political bases. Besides, both in Venezuela and Ecuador the conception, sanction and (non)implementation of these reforms came about in the context of ferocious struggles for hegemony between the government and the opposition. For this reason, the analysis of the reforms is carried out from the perspective of the power struggles, falling back upon a groundbreaking theoretical approach which commingles the Gramscian concept of hegemony as developed by Poulantzas with the concept of power resources as developed by Esping-Andersen.

The results of this research, which materialized over several years and presupposed many months of fieldwork in both countries, not only represent a contribution to puzzle out the similarities and differences between the Venezuelan and Ecuadorian left-wing governments, but they also bring about several hints to make out the current political situation in Venezuela, Ecuador, and throughout Latin America.

Reference

Portantiero JC (1977) Economía y política en la crisis argentina: 1958–1973. Rev Mex Sociol 39 (2) (Universidad Nacional Autónoma de México, México)

Chapter 1
Introduction

Between 1999 and 2015 Latin America came under the rule of left-wing governments (Sader 2008; Figueroa Ibarra 2008, 2009; Figueroa Ibarra and Cordero Díaz 2011; Stolowickz 2011; Dávalos 2014). In effect, during that period governments regarded as left-wing have taken over power in Argentina, Bolivia, Brazil, Chile, Ecuador, Nicaragua, Paraguay, Uruguay and Venezuela (Figueroa Ibarra and Cordero Díaz 2011; Stolowickz 2011).

Beyond their particularities, these governments were characterized by a handful of common elements. First, they repudiated the neoliberal policies implemented since the 1970s in Latin America under the auspices of the International Monetary Fund (hereinafter IMF) and the World Bank (hereinafter WB) (Borón 2003; Sader 2008). Second, their coming to power represented the consequence of the social, economic and political crisis caused by the implementation of neoliberalism throughout the region (Figueroa Ibarra 2008, 2009). Third, they brought about policies which, to a greater or lesser extent, contravened neoliberal policies and could be broadly categorized as left-wing. Fourth, they established the reduction of poverty and inequality among their highest priorities, because of which they carried out a quantitative and qualitative expansion of social policies (Figueroa and Cordero Díaz 2011; Dávalos 2014).

© Springer Nature Switzerland AG 2019
E. L. Bistoletti, *The Power Struggles over the Post-neoliberal Social Security System Reforms in Venezuela and Ecuador*, The Latin American Studies Book Series,
https://doi.org/10.1007/978-3-319-98168-0_1

Table 1.1 Average public social expenditure of the left-wing governments

	Average public social expenditure as share of GDP (%)	Average public social expenditure as share of public expenditure (%)
1990	9.83	39.35
1995	11.97	42.21
2000	14.45	47.51
2001	15.29	47.86
2002	15.27	50.20
2003	15.22	48.66
2004	15.19	50.91
2005	15.44	50.89
2006	16.47	50.68
2007	17.17	54.21
2008	17.29	53.67
2009	18.68	56.37
2010	15.50	58.10
2011	16.68	56.79

Source Prepared by the author based on CEPAL (2013) and CEPALSTAT (2015)

Figures concerning public social expenditure clearly substantiate this latter point (CEPAL 2010, 2011, 2012, 2013, 2014). Between 1990 and 2009, the average public social expenditure as a share of the gross domestic product branched out from 9.83 to 18.68%, and the average public social expenditure as a share of the total public expenditure branched out from 39.35 to 56.37% in those Latin American countries ruled by left-wing governments (CEPAL 2013; CEPALSTAT 2015), as Table 1.1 brings out (Table 1.1).[1]

Although the conditional cash transfers to the poor represented their most prominent social programs,[2] the Latin American left-wing governments actually carried through a much wider range of social programs comprising education, health, old age, housing, food, unemployment, recreation, etc. (Figueroa and Cordero Díaz 2011). Beyond their particularities, these programs were associated with a general reconceptualization of social policy initiated during the 2000s in the Latin American

---

[1]These figures correspond with the following countries: Argentina, Bolivia, Brazil, Ecuador, Nicaragua, Uruguay and Venezuela.

[2]The conditional cash transfers initiated or expanded by the left-wing governments bring about the Asignación Universal por Hijo implemented in Argentina in 2009, the Bono Juancito Pinto and the Bono Madre Niño-Niña respectively implemented in 2006 and 2009 in Bolivia, the Bolsa Família implemented in 2003 in Brazil, the Bono de Desarrollo Humano implemented in 2003 in Ecuador, the Red de Protección Social implemented from 2000 to 2006 in Nicaragua, the Tekoporá and the Abrazo both implemented in 2005 in Paraguay, and the Asignaciones Familiares implemented in 2008 in Uruguay

academia.[3] In very broad terms, this reconceptualization brought out the intrinsic relation among social policy, labor market and citizenship, therefore advocating the universalization of social policy.

Against this background, the left-wing governments of Argentina, Bolivia, Ecuador and Venezuela undertook social security system reforms in order to bring about universal social security (Mesa-Lago 2009; Mesa-Lago and Ossio Bustillos 2012). In the cases of Argentina and Bolivia these reforms were basically circumscribed to the pension systems, maximizing the old-age pension coverage in order to take over the elders excluded from the existing pension systems.[4] In the cases of Ecuador and Venezuela, however, the initiated reforms branched out over the entire social security systems, as they undertook to establish universal and unified pension, health, employment and labor risks systems which commingled both the contributory and the non-contributory pillars of social security.

The social security system reforms initiated by the left-wing governments in Venezuela and in Ecuador (hereinafter referred to as "post-neoliberal reforms"[5]) corresponded to each other almost exactly. In the first place, both reforms acknowledged the universal right to social security and consequently brought forward a universal social insurance for everyone. Moreover, both reforms corresponded with the principles of basic universalism listed by Filgueira (2014): (1) guarantee of basic income for children, (2) guarantee of basic income for the elder, (3) basic income in case of unemployment, (4) universal education coverage of the obligatory cycle of schooling, (5) guarantee of universal health package, and (6) universal care services and family policies. With the obvious exception of universal education coverage, which is naturally closed out from the scope of social security, the post-neoliberal social security systems in Venezuela and Ecuador predicated all the aforementioned points. In the second place, both reforms established a unified and integrated public social security system, co-financed by the state, the workers (formal and informal) and the employers. In the third place, the post-neoliberal social security system reforms in Venezuela and Ecuador came about after a strikingly similar history, for in both countries the neoliberal social security system reforms promoted by the previous governments could not be carried through due to the political and judiciary opposition to them.[6]

---

[3]The specifics of this reconceptualization of social policy are particularized in Chap. 2.

[4]In Argentina this was accomplished through the expansion of the already existing minimum old-age pension in 2005 and 2014, which brought about the incorporation of the elders who had not completely carried out the required payments for an old-age pension (Mesa-Lago 2009; Lombardía and Rodríguez 2015). In Bolivia this was carried out through the introduction of a universal minimum pension for the elders over 60 years of age called Renta Dignidad (English: dignity income), implemented in 2007 (Mesa-Lago and Ossio Bustillos 2012).

[5]The "post-neoliberal" label points out the fact that these social security system reforms superseded the neoliberal reforms of the social security systems undertaken during the 1990s. Falling back upon another term to bring out the same point, Mesa-Lago characterizes these reforms as "re-reforms" instead (Mesa-Lago 2009).

[6]The failure of the neoliberal social security system reform promoted by Rafael Caldera's government in Venezuela is particularized in Chap. 4, while the failure of the neoliberal social security system reform promoted by Jamil Mahuad's government in Ecuador is particularized in Chap. 5.

In addition to these similarities, which are particularized below, the social security reforms initiated by the left-wing governments in Venezuela and Ecuador brought out an even more significant resemblance. For both reforms came across analogous obstacles which, eventually, determined the reform's stalemate in the case of Venezuela and the reform's reformulation in the case of Ecuador, even though the governments promoting the reforms had accumulated extraordinary power resources since their coming to power.

In the case of Venezuela, the post-neoliberal social security system reform started out with the introduction of the universal right to social security into the new constitution of 1999. Subsequently, the National Assembly brought about the Ley Orgánica del Sistema de Seguridad Social (English: Organic Law of the Social Security System) (hereinafter LOSSSV) in December 2002. The LOSSSV represented the core of the social security system reform proposed by Hugo Chávez' government, for it established the general principles and the institutional structure of the new universal and unified social security system. However, after the sanction the LOSSSV the assembly did not bring out the required regulatory laws concerning the health and pension systems afterwards, even though the government party took over its control in 2000 (Salcedo González 2006; PROVEA 2007; Coromoto Montilla 2009). Without the sanction of these fundamental regulatory laws, the implementation of the social security system reform initiated in 2002 by the Chávez' government has broken down to this day (Fernández 2012; PROVEA 2013; Méndez Cegarra 2015).

In the case of Ecuador, Rafael Correa's government promulgated its intention to carry out a comprehensive social security system reform aimed at universalization in 2007, when the Plan Nacional de Desarrollo 2007–2010 (English: National Plan of Development 2007–2010) came out (SENPLADES 2007: 72). One year later, the new Constitution established the "right of all persons" to social security, explicitly including homemakers, land workers, self-employed and unemployed workers (Constitución Ecuador 2008). In July 2012 the government circulated around governmental offices a draft bill for the social security system reform under the name of Ley Orgánica del Sistema de Seguridad Social (English: Organic Law of the Social Security System) (hereinafter LOSSSE). Basically, the LOSSSE determined the suppression of the existing social security system in order to bring about a new, universal and unified social security system. However, after the LOSSSE leaked out to the media, Correa's government did not hand it over to the assembly for consideration, even though the government party took over its control in 2013. Instead, the government carried out successive partial reforms to the existing social security system since 2014. Although these partial reforms did not establish a new, universal and unified social security system as originally intended, they have increasingly brought about the universalization and the unification of the existing social security system.

This research undertakes to puzzle out why, despite the striking similarities between both social security system reforms, the reform initiated by Chávez' government in Venezuela has broken down since the sanction of the LOSSSV in 2002, whereas the reform initiated by Correa's government in Ecuador has come along in spite of the obstacles since 2007.

For that purpose, this investigation carries out a comparative analysis of the power struggles over the post-neoliberal social security system reforms in Venezuela and Ecuador falling back upon a new theoretical and methodological approach to social policy. This approach correlates social policy with the struggles for hegemony as suggested by Poulantzas (1973). This way, it deracinates the shortcomings of the existing approaches to social policy when confronted with social policy in the Global South in general and in Latin America in particular.

1.1   Research Structure

The research is broken down into five argumentatively accumulative chapters. Thus, the content of Chap. 2 presupposes the content of chap. 1, the content of Chap. 3 presupposes the content of Chap. 2, and so on.

Chapter 1 delineates the research object of the investigation and brings forward the research question on which the investigation is predicated. In addition, this chapter breaks down how the research is structuralized.

Chapter 2 brings forward the theoretical and methodological approaches of the research. This chapter is structuralized into eight parts. The first part delineates the conceptual definitions utilized throughout the investigation with regard to social policy, social protection, social security and informal labor. The second and third parts break down the two interrelated debates on social policy which represent the theoretical starting point of the research. Based on these debates, the fourth part brings forward a complementary approach to social policy which commingles the Poulantzian and the political class struggle approaches to social policy. The fifth part basically delineates the research methods definitions utilized throughout the investigation. The sixth part points out why the post-neoliberal social security system reforms in Venezuela and Ecuador are singled out as research cases. The seventh part particularizes the strategies used for the collection of data. Finally, the eight part basically recapitulates the theoretical and methodological approaches of the research.

Chapters 3 and 4 carry out the analyses of the power struggles over the social security system reforms in Venezuela and Ecuador respectively, following the complementary approach brought forward in Chap. 2. Both chapters are broken down into three parts. The first part contextualizes the power struggles over the reform, for which it brings about a detailed reconstruction of the reform process and its social, economic and political context. The second part operationalizes the power struggles over the reform falling back on the concept of power resources, which is transubstantiated for the analysis of the reform in Venezuela and Ecuador. Both, the contextualization and the operationalization are structuralized into the four analytical dimensions explained in Chap. 2, symbolized by the questions "where," "what," "who" and "how". Finally, the third part recapitulates the findings of the analyses of both research cases.

Chapter 5 carries through the comparative analysis of the power struggles over the social security reforms in Venezuela and Ecuador based on the findings obtained in

Chaps. 3 and 4. In order to accomplish a "structured focus comparison" as explicated in Chap. 2, the comparative analysis is structuralized into the four aforementioned analytical dimensions. The chapter is broken down into six parts. The first, second, third and fourth parts respectively bring out the similarities and divergences with regard to the "where," "what," "who" and "how" questions. The fifth part delineates the conclusions of the comparative analysis and establishes why, despite the striking similarities between both social security system reforms, the reform initiated by Chávez' government in Venezuela has broken down, whereas the reform initiated by Correa's government in Ecuador has come along in spite of all obstacles. Finally, the sixth part deliberates the prospects of the complementary approach to social policy brought forward in this research with a view to the comparative study of social policy in Latin America and the Global South.

References

Borón A (2003) El pos-neoliberalismo: un proyecto en construcción. In: Sader E, Gentili P (eds) La trama del neoliberalismo. Mercado, crisis y exclusión social. Consejo Latinoamericano de Ciencias Sociales, Buenos Aires

CEPAL (Comisión Económica Para América Latina y el Caribe) (2010) Social panorama of Latin America. Comisión Económica para América Latina y el Caribe, Santiago de Chile

CEPAL (Comisión Económica Para América Latina y el Caribe) (2011) Social panorama of Latin America. Comisión Económica para América Latina y el Caribe, Santiago de Chile

CEPAL (Comisión Económica Para América Latina y el Caribe) (2012) Social panorama of Latin America. Comisión Económica para América Latina y el Caribe, Santiago de Chile

CEPAL (Comisión Económica Para América Latina y el Caribe) (2013) Social panorama of Latin America. Comisión Económica para América Latina y el Caribe, Santiago de Chile

CEPAL (Comisión Económica Para América Latina y el Caribe) (2014) Social panorama of Latin America. Comisión Económica para América Latina y el Caribe, Santiago de Chile

Coromoto García Mantilla M (2009) La seguridad social en el marco de la Constitución de la República Bolivariana de Venezuela. Vadell Hermanos Editores, Caracas

Dávalos P (2014) El posneoliberalismo: apuntes para una discusión. In: Revista Encuentros Latinoamericanos, vol 3, no 2. Centro de Estudios Interdisciplinarios Latinoamericanos, Montevideo

Fernández ME (2012) La protección social frente a la vejez en Venezuela. In: Anuario de derecho, vol 29, no 29. Universidad de los Andes, Mérida

Figueroa Ibarra C (2008) América Latina, en el umbral del posneoliberalismo. In: Revista Metapolítica, vol 12, no 59. Benemérita Universidad Autónoma de Puebla, México

Figueroa Ibarra C (2009) La crisis mundial: naturaleza y perspectivas. In: Bajo el Volcán, vol 8, no 14. Benemérita Universidad Autónoma de Puebla, México

Figueroa Ibarra C, Cordero Díaz BL (eds) (2011) ¿Posneoliberalismo en América Latina? Los límites de la hegemonía neoliberal en la región. Juan Pablos Editor, México

Filgueira F (2014) Hacia un modelo de protección social universal en América Latina. Comisión Económica para América Latina y el Caribe, Santiago de Chile

Lombardía ML, Rodríguez K (2015) La experiencia argentina en políticas de transferencias monetarias durante la última década. Secretaría de Política Económica y Planificación del Desarrollo, Buenos Aires

Méndez Cegarra A (2015) Desconocimiento de la ley. http://absalonmendezcegarra.blogspot.de/2015/05/desconocimiento-de-la-ley.html

Mesa-Lago C (2009) Re-reform of Latin American private pensions systems: argentinean and Chilean models and lessons. In: The Geneva papers, no 34. The International Association for the Study of Insurance Economics, Zurich

Mesa-Lago C, Ossio Bustillos L (2012) Pension re-reform in Bolivia. In: Zeitschrift für ausländisches und internationales Arbeits- und Sozialrecht, vol 26, no 3. Verlag Müller, Heidelberg

Poulantzas N (1973) Political power and social classes. New Left Books, London

PROVEA (Programa Venezolano de Educación-Acción en Derechos Humanos) (2007) Situación de los derechos humanos en Venezuela: informe anual 2007. Programa Venezolano de Educación—Acción en Derechos Humanos (PROVEA), Caracas

PROVEA (Programa Venezolano De Educación-Acción En Derechos Humanos) (2013) Situación de los derechos humanos en Venezuela: informe anual 2013. Programa Venezolano de Educación—Acción en Derechos Humanos (PROVEA), Caracas

Sader E (2008) Refundar el estado. Posneoliberalismo en América Latina. Instituto de Estudios y Formación de la Central de Trabajadores de la Argentina, Buenos Aires

Salcedo González AM (2006) Consideraciones sobre la reforma de la seguridad social en Venezuela. Comisión de Estudios de Postgrado, Facultad de Ciencias Económicas y Sociales, Universidad Central de Venezuela, Fondo Editorial Tropykos, Caracas

SENPLADES (Secretaría Nacional de Planificación y Desarrollo) (2007) Plan nacional de desarrollo 2007–2010. Planificación para la revolución ciudadana. Secretaría Nacional de Planificación y Desarrollo, Quito

Stolowicz B (2011) El 'posneoliberalismo' y la reconfiguración del capitalismo en América Latina. In: Estrada Álvarez (ed) América Latina en disputa. Bogotá, Espacio Crítico Centro de Estudios, Jairo

Constitutions, Laws, Decrees and Regulations

Ecuador
Constitución de la República del Ecuador (2008)

Statistical Databases

CEPALSTAT (2015). http://estadisticas.cepal.org/cepalstat/WEB_CEPALSTAT/Portada.asp?idioma=e

Chapter 2
Theoretical and Methodological Approaches

This chapter brings forward the theoretical and methodological approaches of the research. It is broken down into eight parts.

The first part delineates the conceptual definitions utilized throughout the investigation regarding social policy, social protection, social security, and informal labor.

The second and third parts break down the two interrelated debates on social policy, which represent the theoretical starting point of the research. The first debate is predicated on the inability of the predominant theoretical approach in social policy research to puzzle out the determinants of social policy in the Global South, in general, and in Latin America, in particular. The second debate is associated with the reconceptualization of social policy occurred in the Latin American academia since the early 2000s, which brought about the reflection on the structural and political determinants of social policy and consequently advocated its universalization.

Based on these debates, the fourth part brings forward a complementary approach to social policy, which commingles the Poulantzian and the political class struggle approaches to social policy.

The fifth part basically delineates the research methods definitions utilized throughout the investigation.

The sixth part points out why the post-neoliberal social security system reforms in Venezuela and Ecuador are singled out as research cases.

The seventh part particularizes the strategies used for the collection of data.

Finally, the eighth part basically recapitulates the theoretical and methodological approaches of the research.

© Springer Nature Switzerland AG 2019
E. L. Bistoletti, *The Power Struggles over the Post-neoliberal Social Security System Reforms in Venezuela and Ecuador*, The Latin American Studies Book Series,
https://doi.org/10.1007/978-3-319-98168-0_2

2.1 Conceptual Definitions: Social Policy, Social Protection, Social Security, and Informal Labor

Social policy has been conceptualized in countless ways (Skocpol and Amenta 1986; Huber and Stephens 2001). To a great extent, the proliferation of definitions correlates with the fact that social policy has permanently metamorphosed over time, what naturally brings about the constant redefinition of the concept. In order to circumvent this problem, this research conceptualizes social policy in very broad terms. Hence, social policy represents the public actions taken in response to social deprivations and risks considered as socially unacceptable within society at a given time and place (Norton et al. 2001: 7). Beyond minor disagreements, most scholars would countenance this definition due to its willingly broad conceptualization of social policy. The "public" character of the actions commingles both state and non-state actions (and their combination). This does not presuppose the equalization of state and non-state actions, as the state represents the ultimate responsible for the responses to the aforementioned depravations and risks (Cecchini and Martínez 2011: 20). The reference to this these two (deprivations and risks) purposes to comprise both the actions taken against actual social depravations and the actions taken against eventual social risks. Because of the staggering variety of possible depravations and risks (Arrow 1963), social policy comprises a very broad scope of actions, ranging from education to housing policies, just as examples. Finally, the allusion to the time- and place-related social (un)acceptance acknowledges the historically and geographically determined character of social policy, which inherently associates social policy with the historical development of social rights.

Based on the very broad definition proposed above, social policy dates back to antiquity. However, in the context of modern nation states social policy commenced in the early nineteenth century with the inception of state mass education, the sanction of state health regulations and the provision of non-state charity (Skocpol and Amenta 1986; Cecchini and Martínez 2011).

Since the early 2000s, the concept of social policy has been increasingly super-seded by the concept of social protection in the academia. The growing adoption of the concept of social protection is associated with the reconceptualization of social policy initiated in response to the neoliberal concept of social security preponder-ating during the 1990s.[1] In general terms, the concept of social protection does not essentially divaricate from the preceding definition of social policy, but it concate-nates it with the labor policy (Cecchini y Martínez 2011: 18–19). Against this back-ground, scholars have brought forward the concept of social-labor policy in order to accentuate the interrelation between both spheres (Ruiz Viñals 2004; Weinmann and Burchardt 2010; Burchardt 2012).

---

[1] Since this process of reconceptualization of social policy represents one of the two theoretical starting points of this research, it will be broken down in detail below. For now, it is only anticipated that this reconceptualization of social policy correlates it with the labor market and the economic, social, and cultural rights.

While subscribing to the reconceptualization of social policy which has brought about the increasing use of the term "social protection" in the academia, this research holds out on using the term "social policy" for two reasons. First, because social protection not only represents an array of public actions but also an approach to them, as it was wisely pointed out by Shepherd (2004; Artigas 2005). Second, because the incorporation of the term "social protection" precludes the theoretical comparison with theoretical approaches to social policy brought out before.

Social security represents a part of social policy. Concretely, social security subsumes the actions in response to sickness, maternity, children, disability, old age, death, occupational accidents, occupational diseases, and unemployment. Social security can be categorized in two main groups based on its funding: non-contributory and contributory. Non-contributory social security is subsidized by the state through fiscal revenue, receiving the name of social assistance. Contributory social security is disbursed by individuals who carry out contributions to an insurance scheme. Accordingly, contributory social security receives the name of social insurance. In turn, contributory social security can be categorized in two subgroups: compulsory contributory and voluntary contributory. In the case of compulsory contributory social security individuals must obligatorily carry through contributions to an insurance scheme, whereas in the case of voluntary contributory social security can willingly disburse contributions to a social security scheme. Social insurance represents the biggest part of social security by far. For this reason, in everyday language social security and social insurance often come out as synonyms. Nonetheless, modern social security comprises both social assistance and social insurance.

The history of social security dates back to the late nineteenth century, when German chancellor Otto von Bismarck established a compulsory insurance scheme covering old age, disability, and death which soon spread out over Europe (Mesa-Lago 2007). However, modern social security was actually brought forward by William Beveridge in his report Social Insurance and Allied Services published in 1942, which advocated the implementation of a "social security plan" integrating social assistance, compulsory social insurances, and voluntary insurances (Beveridge 1942).

Figure 2.1 graphically delineates the scope of social policy, social protection, and social security (Fig. 2.1).

Informal labor is conceptualized as employment without formal contracts, and therefore excluded from labor regulation and contributory social security (Chen 2005: 7). Informal labor comprises a vast constellation of labor relations which can be categorized in two big groups: (1) self-employment in informal businesses, including employers, own account operators, and unpaid family workers, and (2) wage employment in informal jobs, including employees of informal businesses, unregistered employees of formal businesses, unregistered domestic workers, casual or temporary workers, and unregistered outworkers. As Fig. 2.2 brings out, informal labor does not exclusively come about in the informal sector (informal businesses) but also in the formal sector (formal businesses) (Fig. 2.2).

In addition, whereas men are overrepresented in the higher part of the figure, women are overrepresented in the lower part of the figure (Fig. 2.3)

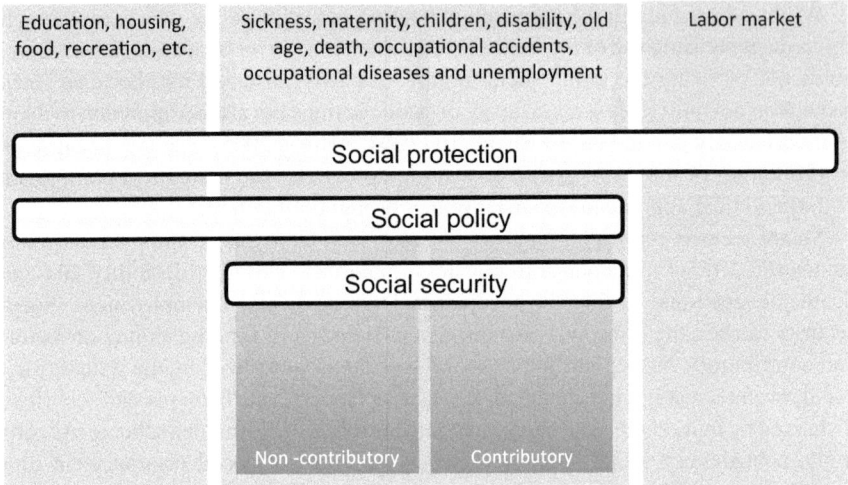

Fig. 2.1 Scope of social policy, social protection, and social security. *Source* Prepared by the author

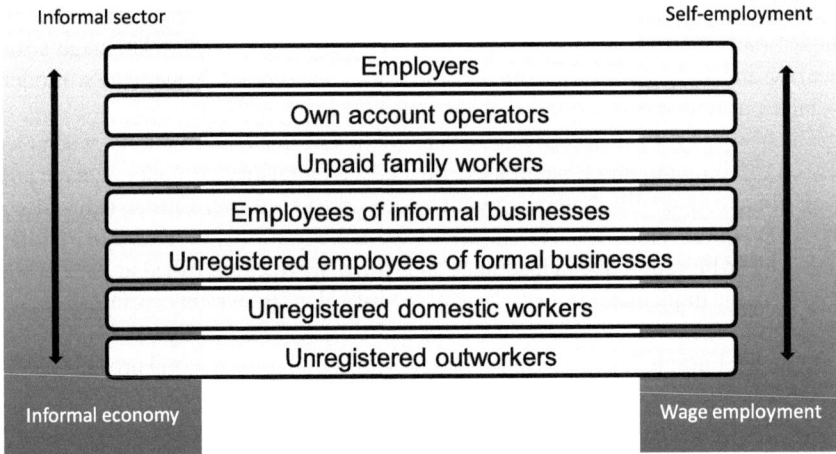

Fig. 2.2 Definition and segmentation of informal labor. *Source* Prepared by the author based on Chen (2005)

2.2 Theoretical Approaches in Social Policy Research

While most social policy scholars would countenance the definition of social policy proposed above, under no circumstance would they ever come around concerning the causes and effects of social policy, nor concerning the relations between social policy, economy, and politics (Skocpol and Amenta 1986: 132). In fact, the differences with

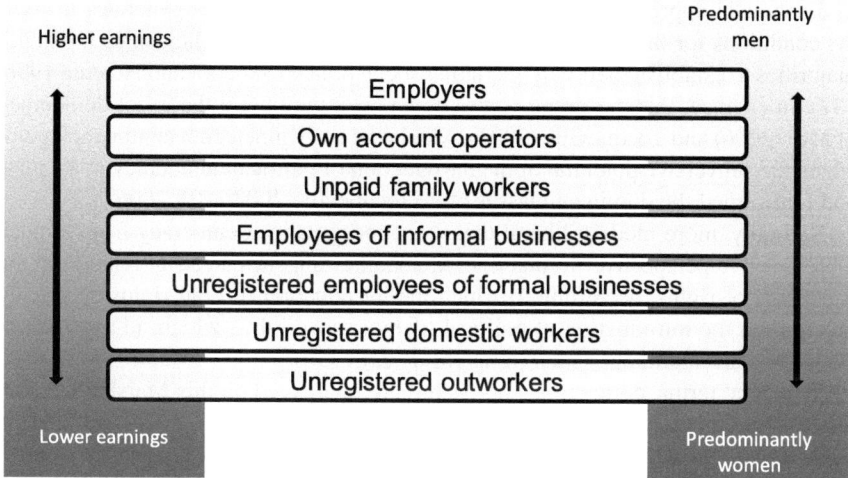

Fig. 2.3 Gender segmentation of informal labor. *Source* Prepared by the author based on Chen (2005)

regard to these matters have brought about impassioned debates and the emergence of diverging theoretical approaches to social policy. These theoretical divergences cannot be looked down upon as mere academic blabbering, for they determine how present social policy is broken down and, on this basis, how future social policy is carried out. All in all, theoretical approaches to social policy can be categorized in three groups depending on their explanatory emphases: "democratic", "structuralist", and "political power struggles" approaches (Skocpol and Amenta 1986, 1994; Huber and Stephens 2001, 2012).

Notwithstanding their differences, democratic, structuralist, and political class struggle approaches presuppose a common ground, for they associate the emergence of social policy with the processes of industrialization and democratization which commenced in the Global North during the nineteenth century and spread out throughout the world after Second World War with the establishment of the welfare state. The following parts recapitulate the main characteristics of democratic, structuralist, and political class struggle approaches to social policy with regard to their theoretical postulates, operationalization strategies, and criticisms.

2.2.1   Democratic Approaches

Democratic approaches basically predicate that the unfolding of democracy precipitates the expansion of social policy. Hewitt (1977: 451) and Myles (1984: 82) characterize democratic approaches as "simple democratic" since it does not accentuate the class basis of the political forces which bring about social policy. According to democratic approaches, the existence of liberal democracies generates in itself the conditions for the emergence and development of social policy since it enables majorities to establish their will, including social policy (Skocpol and Amenta 1986: 137). In essence, this reasoning comes down from the liberal theory of democracy of Mill (2006) and Tocqueville (2003), who in the early nineteenth century acknowledged the subversive potential of the introduction of political democracy in advance and forewarned the dominant classes of it (Tocqueville 2003; Mill 2006).

Naturally, more modern liberal theorists conceptualize democracy from a much more positive perspective. In this line, Marshall establishes a causal relation in the expansion of rights, according to which the introduction of civil rights eventually precipitates the introduction of political (democratic) rights, which, in turn, brings about the introduction of social rights (Marshall 1950).

In general terms, democratic approaches are predicated on this Marshallian postulate. Nevertheless, they branch out into three different variants with regard to the concrete way in which the establishment of democracy brings about the development of social policy. The first variant, the institutional approach, predicates that the introduction of democratic institutions such as universal suffrage, secret ballot competitive elections, elected executives, and political rights precipitates the expansion of social policy (Cutright 1967; Wilensky 1975; Hewitt 1977; Flora and Alber 1981; Myles 1984). The second variant, the electoralist approach, asseverates that the electoral competition predisposes elected politicians competing for office to maximize social policy during election years (Tufte 1978; Frey and Schneider 1978). The third variant, the popular protest approach presupposes that popular aspirations are not canalized by representative institutions and electoral processes. For this reason, social policy is only countenanced by the elites when "disruptive" protests (such as riots, strikes, or demonstrations) represent a real threat to their privileged situation (Piven and Cloward 1971, 1977; Piven 2006).

Due to its uncomplicated theoretical approximation to social policy, the operationalization of democratic approaches does not come across significant difficulties as in the case of structural and political class struggle approaches. In order to determine the existence of democracy, both the institutional and the electoralist approaches capitalize on indicators concerning democratic institutions such as the enforcement of the universal suffrage, the implementation of the secret ballot, the fulfillment of competitive elections, the magnitude of electoral participation, and the compliance of political rights. For the operationalization of the development of social policy both approaches fall back upon the same indicators, examining the level of public social spending and the expansion of social insurances (especially health and old-age insurances). The only difference between both approaches is associated with the timing of the analysis, since the institutionalist approach breaks down the development of these indicators in the long-run whereas the electoralist approach looks upon its development during the election years. Based on this operationalization, both approaches correlate the development of democracy with the development of social policy in order to authenticate their hypothesis. In the case of the popular protest approach, the operationalization is carried out through the socio-historical analysis of the "disruptive" protests and their consequences in terms of social policy (Piven and Cloward 1977; Piven 2006).

Despite its uncomplicated operationalization (or precisely because of it), democratic approaches have come under inexorable criticisms concerning the deficient empirical support of its hypothesis (Skocpol and Amenta 1986: 137–139). Rather than the absence of empirical evidence in support of its allegations, criticisms against democratic approaches accentuate the proliferation of empirical evidence against it (Golden and Poterba 1980; Massad 1978; Griffin et al. 1983; Achenbaum 1983). These criticisms comprise the institutional approach (Skocpol and Amenta 1986), the electoralist approach (Golden and Poterba 1980; Griffin et al. 1983) and the democratic popular protest approach (Massad 1978; Achenbaum 1983; Skocpol and Ikenberry 1983).

Because of this, democratic approaches, in general, have backed away from the spotlight in social policy research since the 1980s.

2.2.2   Structural Approaches

Despite their commendable attempt to coalesce politics into the usually economy-focused debate on social policy, democratic approaches contravene the historic fact that the earliest social policy initiatives materialized before democracy under Bismarck in Germany and under Taaffe in Austria (Esping-Andersen 1990: 15). Besides, social policy was held back where liberal democracy came about early: United States, Switzerland, and Australia. This contradiction can only be circumvented resorting to economic structure and social class. According to Ditch, early democratic countries were characterized by an agrarian economic structure and a political system dominated by small property owners who repudiated the rise of taxes associated to social policy, whereas nondemocratic countries were subordinated to a powerful governing class which could effectively establish high taxes on an unwilling population (as cited in Esping-Andersen 1990: 15–16).

Structural approaches conceptualize social policy holistically. From the structuralist perspective, social policy represents a functional requisite for the reproduction of society and economy. Structuralist approaches presuppose two variants. The first variant is structuralized around a "logic of industrialism" and it is, therefore, categorized as industrialist approach. The second variant is structuralized around a "logic of capitalism" and it is, therefore, categorized as Marxist approach.

2.2.2.1   Industrialist Approaches

Industrialist approaches predicate that industrialization invariably brings about social policy regardless of the existing political regime. According to industrialist approaches, industrialization deracinates the preindustrial modes of social reproduction, such as the family, the church, the guild solidarity, etc. (Pryor 1968; Flora and

Alber 1981). Since the market does not supersede the "welfare function" which the preindustrial institutions formerly accomplished, the state appropriates the care for the disabled, the ill, the elderly, and the unemployed. Concomitantly, the economic development which accompanies industrialization generates the material resources for the expansion of social policy (Kerr et al. 1964). This process is accelerated by two complementary consequences of industrialization: the aging of the population, and the development of a modern centralized bureaucracy which advances its own growth (Cutright 1967; Wilensky 1975, 1987). In more refined version, industrialist approaches asseverate that the convergence of social policy in industrialized countries only materializes up to a point beyond which sociocultural variations are carried over (Williamson and Fleming 1977; Coughlin 1979).

In order to operationalize its hypothesis, industrialist approaches look upon social and economic indicators such as social security spending, housing spending, higher education enrollment, military spending, gross national product, gross domestic per capita, etc.

In spite of its pioneering contribution to the comparative analysis of social policy in industrialized countries, industrialist approaches could never puzzle out why social policy came about 50 or even 100 years before preindustrial modes of social reproduction effectively dematerialized (Esping-Andersen 1990: 13). Besides, industrialist approaches bring forward a bird's eye perspective on social policy which completely brushes away geographic and historical differences among countries and regions. As Haggard and Kaufman pointed out:

> [...] industrial growth and social modernization certainly contributed to the emergence of the modern welfare state. But these are highly general processes, and if we have learned one thing about modern capitalism it is the absence of a single model. (Haggard and Kaufman 2008: 6)

Due to their incapacity to particularize the determinants of social policy beyond its broad connection with the process of modernization, industrialist approaches have been practically abandoned since the 1970s.

2.2.2.2 Marxist Approaches

Due to their functional reasoning, Marxist approaches bring out striking similarities to the industrialist approach. However, Marxist approaches do not establish the focus on the transition from agrarianism to industrialism as the industrialist approach. Instead, they break down the transition within the capitalist mode of production from the "competitive" capitalism of the nineteenthcentury to the "monopoly" capitalism of the twentieth century (Skocpol and Amenta 1986: 134). Unlike "competitive" capitalism, "monopoly" capitalism presupposes the active intervention of the state for its reproduction. In this context, the capitalist state reciprocates the functional demands of advanced capitalism for "social reproduction" through state policies aimed at two objectives: the accumulation of capital and the democratic legitimation of the system (O'Connor 1973; Gough 1975, 1979; Marklund 1982; Offe 1984;

Mishra 1984). These policies comprise the preparation of skilled and motivated wage workers, the regulation of goods and services for the daily and intergenerational reproduction of the labor force, the care of the disabled (sick, injured, or elder), and the preservation of political and economic order against possible discontent. Depending on the accentuated factor, Marxist approaches based on "the logic of capitalism" can be categorized in three subgroups.

The first group is exclusively structuralized around the functional requirements of capital accumulation (Müller and Neussüs 1978; Altvater 1978; Blanke et al. 1978). Theorists supporting this approach are commonly characterized as "state derivationists", since they conceptualize the state (and therefore social policy) as the derivative from the capitalist relations of production (Holloway and Picciotto 1978: 2).

Müller and Neussüs' represent the main exponents of this perspective. Based on their reading of the works of Marx and Engels, they establish a linear and nonmediated relation between capitalist accumulation and state action, including state social policy. Underneath its "social" appearance, the capitalist state carries out the reproduction of the social conditions which bring about the surplus-value production and appropriation.

> Since the direct aim of production is not social subsistence but surplus-value production, and since the process of production is therefore driven on by laws which are concealed from the conscious will of individuals and are implemented behind their backs although by means of their own actions, there is a real need for such a particular social institution which confronts productive society. This ex post facto and makeshift supervision by the state of the natural pattern of the social production process is necessary for the maintenance of surplus-value production, which is the particular form of appropriation of the surplus-labour of one class by another class. (Müller and Neussüs 1978: 38)

On this basis, Müller and Neussüs denounce the "welfare-state illusion" (so the title of their best-known article on the subject) and its actual counterproductive character for the real emancipation of the working class.

> 'Social policy' (i.e. state activity intervening ex post facto in society and seeking to resolve its 'social problems') thus has the characteristics, down to its smallest details, of a process of paternalistic supervision, control or 'welfare' of the producer. [...] Hence, however much state social policy offers individual producers a certain security in the event of their partial or total inability to, work, social policy can never provide a conscious and planned care for the maintenance, renewal and improvement of the social working capacity of the collective worker, the associated producers themselves. (Müller and Neussüs 1978: 38–39)

The second group of approaches commingles both the economic and the political functional requirements of advanced capitalism (O'Connor 1973; Offe 1984).

Offe's approach represents a perfect example of this perspective. Offe conceptualizes social policy as an economic and political requirement of advanced capitalism. In this sense, Offe looks upon social policy as the "state's manner of effecting the lasting transformation of non-wage labourers into wage-labourers" (Offe 1984: 72). According to Offe, the process of proletarization, which necessarily antecedes the development of capitalism, does not naturally come about as a result of the progressive elimination of the preexisting conditions of labor derived from the undermining

of agrarian labor and agrarian life, the continual introduction of labor-saving technical changes and the impact of cyclical crises. Besides, the process of proletarization
under no means determines the contention of workers in the wage–labor relation,
as modern industrial capitalism increasingly strikes down a significant part of the
already incorporated labor force from the wage–labor market.

For these reasons, capitalist states must actively advance both the proletarization
and the contention of wage–labor workers in order to bring about the availability of
the labor force in the wage–labor market. This is accomplished through three main
lines of action: (1) the incorporation of the labor power into the supply side of the
labor market, which comprises manifold functions ranging from the socialization,
instruction, and motivation of the workers to the repression and criminalization of
alternate modes of subsistence different from the wage–labor relationship, (2) the
conservation of the wage–labor relation over time, including the creation of "catch-
ment areas" outside the labor market, "in which labor power can be accommodated
either permanently (old-age pensions, payments for disabled workers) or temporarily (institutions of health care and further education)" (Offe 1984: 98), and (3) the
regulation of the supply and demand in the labor market.

Defined in these terms, social policy carries out an economic and a political
function. The economic function of social policy is associated with the production
and reproduction of the socioeconomic conditions without which the process of
accumulation cannot be accomplished. The political function of social policy is
correlated with the domination required for the political sustention of the process
of accumulation. In modern capitalist societies, this political function does not only
presuppose the repressive function of the state but also the ideological function of
the state aimed at the legitimation of the economic and political order within the
framework of liberal democracy (Offe 1975: 303).

Based on this, Offe points out the existing tension between the structural function
of social policy (or any policy of the capitalist state) and the demands of organized
social groups regarding social policy in the context of liberal democracy. Offe for-
mulates this contradiction in the following terms:

> [...] the pattern of development of the strategies and innovations of state social policy is
> determined through treatment of the 'meta-problem' that may be summed up by this question:
> how can strategies of social policy be developed and existing institutions modernized so that
> there can be a satisfaction of both the political demands 'licensed' in the context of the
> prevailing political rights of the working class and the foreseeable exigencies and labour and
> budgetary prerequisites of the accumulation process? (Offe 1984: 104)

Clearly, the "meta-problem" alluded by Offe presupposes the fundamental question of the power struggles over social policy among contending social actors. However, Offe does not advance beyond this point, brushing this essential issue away.
Instead, influenced by Luhmann's systemic theory Offe conjectures that the answer
to this "meta-problem" is associated with the internal process of rationalization of
the capitalist state. From this perspective, social policy represents more and more
the product of internal structural problems of the state apparatus. In consequence,
the analytical focus of Offe's approach ultimately revolves around the integration
strategy of the state (Offe 1975, 1984).

The third group of approaches accentuates the political requirements of capitalism, focusing on the conflicts and the compromises between capital and labor and within them (Poulantzas 1973; Abraham 1981).

Poulantzas' approach represents the main exponent of this perspective. Poulantzas conceptualizes social policy within the context of the power struggles over hegemony among contending social groups.[2] On this basis Poulantzas predicates that the state action, including social policy, ultimately purposes to establish the hegemony of the dominant classes over the dominated classes.

> The capitalist state, characterized by hegemonic class leadership, does not *directly* represent the dominant-classes' economic interests, but their *political interests*: it is the dominant classes' political power centre, as the organizing agent of their political struggle. (Poulantzas 1973: 190)

In this context, the capitalist state carries out two main political functions: (1) it advances the political organization of the dominant classes through the cancelation of their economic isolation and (2) it holds back the organization of the dominated classes though the maintenance of their economic isolation and the universalization of the interest of the dominant classes as the general interests of the people or the nation.

> [...] in performing its political function the state presents a characteristic ambivalence, depending on whether it is dealing with the dominant or the dominated classes. [...] With regard to the dominated classes the function of the capitalist state is to prevent their political organization which would overcome their economic isolation. [...] the capitalist state maintains the political disorganization of the dominated classes, by presenting itself as the unity of the people-nation, composed of political-persons/private-individuals. [...] On the other hand, with regard to the dominant classes, the capitalist state is permanently working on their organization at the political level, by cancelling out their economic isolation [...]. (Poulantzas 1973: 188–189)

Since Poulantzas correlates the social policy of the capitalist state with the process of hegemony construction of the dominant classes he disbelieves that the dominated classes could capitalize on social policy in order to accomplish their emancipatory goals. In this regard, despite his focus on the political dimension on social policy Poulantzas does not completely deracinates the functionalist logic which characterizes all structuralist approaches.

> So this 'social policy', though it may happen to contain real economic sacrifices *imposed* on the dominant class *by the struggle of the dominated classes*, cannot under any circumstances call into question the capitalist type of state, so long as it operates *within* these limits. (Poulantzas 1973: 194)

---

[2]Based on Gramsci, Poulantzas conceptualizes hegemony as the prevalence of the interests of a social group throughout society. This prevalence represents the outcome of the confrontation among social groups in which "one of them, or at least a single combination of them, tends to prevail, to gain the upper hand, to propagate itself over the whole social area—bringing about not only a unison of economic and political aims, but also intellectual and moral unity, posing all the questions around which the struggle rages not on a corporate but on a 'universal' plane, and thus creating the hegemony of a fundamental social group over a series of subordinate groups" (Gramsci 2000: 205).

However, Poulantzas' approach presupposes a fundamental advantage over the aforementioned structuralist approaches. As pointed out above, Poulantzas contextualizes social policy within the power struggles over hegemony among contending social groups. These struggles extremely divaricate depending on innumerable factors: historical, geographical, social, economic, political, cultural, etc. For this reason, by correlating social policy with the power struggles over hegemony, Poulantzas inherently associates social policy with the specific social, economic, and political context in which it materializes. Because of this, Poulantzas' approach comprises an original perspective for the analysis of social policy in historically and geographically diverging contexts.

Unfortunately, Marxist approaches very rarely substantiate their overarching theoretical reflections with contrastable empirical analysis. The national-level studies carried out by O'Connor for the case of the United States (O'Connor 1973), by Offe for the case of Western Germany (Offe 1975, 1984), and by Gough for the case of the United Kingdom (Gough 1979) represent the only exceptions to the general scarcity of empirical analysis. No comparative studies were carried through except from the cross-national study made by Marklund (1982).

O'Connor, Offe, and Gough bring forward different strategies to operationalize their national-leveled studies. O'Connor mostly looks upon fiscal indicators of the United States, such as state debt, social investment, state enterprises, taxation, budgetary control, etc. (O'Connor 1973). Offe capitalizes on the systemic concept of "integration" as a yardstick to take apart the (failed) process of reform of the vocational educational law in West Germany in 1969. On this basis, Offe demarcates the political positions of labor unions and employer's organizations with regard to the reform in order to determine to what extent they advance or hold back the integration strategies of the capitalist state. The mapping of the positions of both labor unions and employer's organizations is carried out through the analysis of their official documents regarding the reform. Similarly to the political class struggle approach, Gough looks over the public social spending in the United Kingdom. As a matter of fact, Gough's operationalization resembles the operationalization of the political class struggle approaches in most parts, since it breaks down the public social spending of the United Kingdom from a quantitative perspective (Gough 1979).

Unfortunately, Marklund's comparative study does not provide any groundbreaking hints for the operationalization of Marxist approaches to social policy. Instead, Marklud commingles indicators used by the industrialist approach concerning economic growth, industrialization, and urbanization with indicators used by the political class struggle approach such as redistributive effect of taxes, social security coverage, social spending compared to gross domestic product, amount of strikes, and strike involvement.

Without doubt, the incapacity of Marxist approaches to operationalize their theoretical cogitations represents their most substantial debility (Skocpol and Amenta 1985, 1986: 135; Therborn 1986: 135). Besides, Marxist approaches come under criticism due to their rigid functionalism (Mann 1984: 185; Esping-Andersen 1990: 14), which often precludes the identification of the real social actors who participate in the shaping of social policy (Skocpol 1986: 136; Therborn 1986: 135). This criticism is especially associated with the derivationist approach because of its functionalist reductionism, but it can be extrapolated to the dual approaches of O'Connor and Offe as well (O'Connor 1973; Offe1984). Even though the Poulantzian approach partially counterbalances this criticism though the incorporation of the concept of "relative autonomy of the state", significant questions regarding the state's autonomy are not puzzled out: "how autonomous is the state?", "from whom is it autonomous?", and so on (Miliband 1973: 86; Block 1977: 9; Portantiero 1988: 107).

Finally, Marxist approaches come under another relevant criticism regarding their specificity. Put briefly, the Marxist approaches accentuate the systemic function of social policy as labor control in capitalism, but they do not particularize the specific functional requirements of advanced capitalism as such in opposition to the functional requirements of extinct state-socialism (Bell 1978; Skocpol and Amenta 1986, Esping-Andersen). In this regard, the historical comparison brings out significant resemblances among industrialized societies under different modes of production.

Because of their shortcomings (insufficient empirical foundation, unyielding functionalism, and exclusive focusing on advanced capitalism), Marxist approaches to social policy have been superseded by political class struggle approaches since the early 1990s.

2.2.3 Political Class Struggle Approaches

Political class struggle approaches partially commingle with Marxist approaches as they all presuppose the class structure of capitalist societies (Korpi 1983). However, political class struggle approaches repudiate the functionalist perspective of structuralist approaches and look upon social classes as the main agents of change. They predicate that the development of social is brought about by the unfolding of working-class-based organizations which successfully accumulate state power through parliamentary democracy. On this account, class struggles are canalized from the industrial to the political arena and the democratic state comes along as a nonmarket instrument to share out income and services away from the economically privileged (Hewitt 1977; Hollingsworth and Hanneman 1982; Korpi 1978, 1980; Stephens 1979). From this perspective, conventional social policy (regarding health, old age, disability, unemployment, housing, education, social insurance, welfare transfers, etc.) cannot be dissociated from macro- and microeconomic policies aimed at full employment, minimum wages, unionization, etc. (Skocpol and Amenta 1986: 140).

Political class struggle approaches are commonly characterized as social democrat approaches for they presuppose that social democratic (or labor) parties represent the political organizations *par excellence* of the working class. For this reason, social democrat approaches asseverate (and partially substantiate) that disruptive protests (including industrial strikes) represent relatively irrelevant means for workers to condition policy outcomes when social democrat (or labor) parties have taken over power (Hibbs 1978; Korpi and Shalev 1980).

Due to the historic political hegemony of the social democratic party in Swedish politics (uninterruptedly governing from 1936 to 1976, from 1982 to 1991, and from 1994 to 2006) and the extended role of the Swedish state regarding social assistance and inequality equalization, social democrat approaches conceptualize Sweden as the archetypical model of this path. Despite this "Swedocentrism" (Shalev 1983), political class struggle approaches represent the predominant theoretical approach in social policy research since the early 1990s. The reason of their predominance is associated with the publication of Esping-Andersen's pathbreaking comparative analysis of the Northern industrialized welfare regimes "The Three Worlds of Welfare Capitalism" in 1990 (Esping-Andersen 1990).

Compared to "competing" approaches (and even compared to previous political class struggle studies on social policy), the main advantage of Esping-Andersen' research revolves around its capacity to consistently operationalize its main hypothesis. The operationalization proposed by Esping-Andersen actually capitalizes on the very same indicators as previous political class struggle studies (reviewed in detail below) concerning the power of the working class. However, Esping-Andersen additionally correlated the conventional indicators regarding the power of the working classes with multiple indicators measuring the level of decommodification of labor and the type of social stratification in their countries. The concept of decommodification conceptualizes the loosening of the status of labor as a pure commodity, due to which decommodification is naturally associated with the granting of universal social rights (Esping-Andersen 1990: 22). Esping-Andersen demarcates the difference between the loosening and the eradication of labor as a commodity in the following terms:

> [...] decommodification should not be confused with the complete eradication of labor as a commodity; it is not an issue of all or nothing. Rather, the concept refers to the degree to which individuals, or families, can uphold a socially acceptable standard of living independently of market participation. In the history of social policy, conflicts have mainly revolved around what degree of market immunity would be permissible; i.e. the strength, scope, and quality of social rights. (Esping-Andersen 1990: 37)

Against this background account Esping-Andersen carried out a very solid comparative analysis in both, theoretical and methodological terms, which corroborated the positive relation between the power of the working class-led coalitions in the Northern industrialized countries and the development of their welfare regimes. Based on the successful operationalization of the long-existing but never before proven hypothesis behind the political class struggle approach, Esping-Andersen successfully established three ideal types of welfare regimes depending on the combination of state, market, and family in the social provision: liberal, conservative-corporatist, and social democratic. Liberal welfare regimes are mainly structuralized around the market, conservative-corporatist mainly around the family and social democratic mainly around the state (Esping-Andersen 1990: 26–28).

This simple, didactic, and very appealing typology also brought about the generalized acceptance of Esping-Andersen's political class struggle approach among social policy scholars. In fact, since the publication of "The Three Worlds of Welfare Capitalism" complementary (or even alternative) typologies of the welfare regimes of the Northern industrialized countries have proliferated in the academia (Arts and Gelissen 2002). Leibfried brought forward a typology consisting of Anglo-Saxon, "Bismarck", Scandinavian, and "Latin Rim" welfare regimes (Leibfried 1992), Castles and Mitchell advanced a typology comprising liberal, conservative, "non-right hegemony", and radical welfare regimes (Castles and Mitchell 1993), Siaroff advocated a more gender-sensitive typology encompassing Protestant social democratic, Protestant liberal, advanced Christian democratic, and "female mobilization" welfare regimes (Siaroff 1994), Ferreira brought forward a typology similar to Liebfried's consisting of Anglo-Saxon, Bismarck, Scandinavian, and southern welfare regimes (Ferrera 1996), Bonoli advanced a typology comprising British, continental, Nordic, and southern welfare regimes (Bonoli 1997), and Korpi and Palme advocated a typology composed of basic security, corporatist, encompassing, targeted, and voluntary state subsidized welfare regimes (Korpi and Palme 1998).

Due to the widespread predominance of political class struggle approaches in social policy research, cross-country studies on social policy in Latin America have been carried through from this perspective as well. The first attempt to extrapolate Esping-Andersen's approach to Latin America was carried out by Filgueira, who brought forward a specific typology for the welfare regimes in Latin America based on Esping- Adersen's (amplified and modified) approach (Filgueira 1998). Filgueira categorized three types of welfare regimes in Latin America: universal stratified, dual, and excluding welfare regimes. After Filgueira's research, several scholars purposed to generate specific typologies for the welfare regimes in Latin America. Gough and Wood advanced a broader typology of the welfare regimes in less industrialized countries (including Latin America) which accentuated the role of "informal" welfare provision (Gough and Wood 2004). Unlike "formal" welfare provided by the state and the formal labor market, informal welfare is mainly associated with the families and the communities because of the absence of state social policies and extended formal labor markets. Barrientos further particularized this typology for the Latin American countries, pointing out the transition from "conservative-informal" to "liberal-informal" welfare regimes in the region as a result of the neoliberal reforms during the 1990s (Barrientos 2004). From a slightly different perspective, Rudra categorized welfare regimes in less industrialized countries in two classes: productive regimes and protectionist regimes (Rudra 2007). Just as Filgueira, Gough and Wood and Barrientos, Rudra mostly broke down public spending in order to establish this typology. However, Rudra not only looked upon the level of public spending but also how public spending was shared out. Whereas productive regimes canalize public spending toward the promotion of market development, protectionist regimes canalize it toward the protection of individuals from the market. In Rudra's analysis most Latin American regimes are categorized either as productive or dual regimes (a combination between productive and protectionist regimes). In line with Rudra, Pribble carried through an assessment of the quality of the public spending in Chile and Uruguay (Pribble 2006). Pribble's originality revolved around the inclusion of the gender perspective into the analysis, which purposed to determine to what extent public spending in both countries maximized the sexual division of labor. Franzoni further advanced with this line of research, extending the scope of the analysis to 18

Latin American countries. Based on indicators regarding commodification, decommodification, and defamilialization, Franzoni established three ideal types of Latin American welfare regimes: state-targeted, state-stratified, and informal-familialist (Franzoni 2008).

Regarding operationalization, political class struggle approaches are provided with a consistent operational framework for the empirical examination of national cases and their comparison. As pointed out above, this framework is structuralized around the assessment of the power resources of the working class, measured by an array of indicators concerning the quantity and quality of worker's unions and worker's parties. Power resources represent characteristics of the actors (individual or collective), which bring about the capacity to establish punishments and rewards to other actors.

> What, then, are power resources? Power resources are characteristics which provide actors - individuals or collectivities -with the ability to punish or reward other actors. These resources can be described in terms of a variety of dimensions. (Korpi 1983: 15)

The possession and the control over the means of violence, the means of production, and the capital comprise, according to this perspective, essential power resources. However, since these are successfully monopolized by the state and the capitalist classes, the analytical focus of political class struggle approaches is established on the associational power resources, which basically correspond with the capacity of social actors to bring about organizations the defense of their interests (Korpi 1983: 16–17). More recently, scholars from the field of labor studies have branched out the scope of power resources of the working class, introducing the notion of structural power resources (Wright 1994; Brinkmann et al. 2008; Schmalz et al. 2013). In essence, structural power resources are predicated on the structural characteristics of the economic system (Wright 1994).

The variables used to operationalize power resources conventionally comprise multiple indicators concerning class mobilization (unionization, unity, or division of the labor confederations, density of the labor unions), political mobilization (share of the electorate voting for left parties, share of the electorate voting for religious parties, type of constituting cleavages in the party system, share of left parties in the cabinet), electoral participation (class electoral participation, political interest, party identification) party preferences (share of left voters by social group) and industrial conflict (amount of labor conflicts—strikes and lockouts—,amount of workers involved in labor conflicts, amount of man-days idle of labor conflict, and relative involvement of workers in labor conflicts).

Despite its flaws (tackled in detail below), the operational framework of political class struggle approaches presupposes substantial advantages with respect to the operational frameworks of democratic and structural approaches, for it brings about the possibility to carry out empirical and comparative research. Without doubt, the widespread predominance of political class struggle approaches since the early 1990s is associated with the soundness of their operational framework (Skocpol and Amenta 1994; Huber and Stephens 2001, 2012).

Notwithstanding the foregoing, political class struggle approaches have come under severe criticisms. On the first place, the assumption that the parliament represents a real instance of decision-making is repudiated by corporatist scholars, who predicate that power increasingly breaks away from parliaments to neocorporatist institutions of interest intermediation (Schmitter and Lembruch 1979). On the second place, the exclusive focus on social democratic parties is repudiated because the capacity of social democratic parties to bring about social policy is circumscribed by the relative power of conservative political parties (usually Christian democratic) (Castels 1978, 1982). On the third place, it is pointed out that Christian democratic parties effectively mobilize large fractions of the working class in Holland, Italy, and Germany, where they advocate social policies similar to the social policies of the social democratic parties (Wilensky 1981; Schmidt 1982). On the fourth place, due to its tendency to conceptualize the development of social policy on the basis of the rather extraordinary Swedish experience, the political class struggle approach is regarded as "Swedocentric" (Shalev 1983; Esping-Andersen 1990).

All these criticisms can be subordinated to a fundamental objection. Social democrat approaches revolve around a linear conception of power which presupposes that a quantitative expansion of the worker's organizations (in terms of unionization or parliamentary representation) automatically brings about more social policies (Esping-Andersen 1990: 17). Scholars supporting social democratic approaches reciprocated this fundamental objection by expanding the focus of their research. In this line, they reaccommodated their analytical focus toward the class coalitions between urban workers and farmers and between blue collar workers and white collar workers (Esping-Andersen 1985, 1990; Weir and Skocpol 1985; Gourevitch 1986). Despite the unequivocal advantages of this enhancement, "expanded" political class struggle approaches presuppose a linear conception of power as well, primarily focusing on the urban working class and its coalitions.

Finally, political class struggle approaches have come under criticism because of the uncritical proliferation of typologies which supervened after the publication of Esping-Andersen's "The Three Worlds of Welfare Capitalism" in 1990 (Esping-Adersen 1990). Since then, social policy research based on political class struggle approaches has overwhelmingly revolved around the development of complementary or alternative ideal typologies of welfare regimes. In this context, academic discussions on social policy deliberate on how to break down social spending (quantitatively or qualitatively, gender-blindly or gender-sensitively, focused on social transfers or social services, etc.) in order to establish ideal types of welfare regimes. However, these discussions completely relegate the social, economic, and political processes underlying welfare regimes. Since these historically and geographically situated processes determine the shape and scope of welfare regimes, they should actually represent the main research subject of political class struggle approaches. In fact, Esping-Andersen admonished this before he capitulated himself to the uncritical proliferation of typologies following the publication of "The Three Worlds of Welfare Capitalism":

[…] our task is to reintegrate the welfare-state debate into the intellectual tradition of political economy. This serves to bring into sharper focus the principal theoretical questions involved. On this basis we will be in a better position to specify the salient characteristics of welfare states. The convention of conceptualizing welfare states in terms of their expenditures will no longer do. In a sense, our ultimate goal is to 'sociologize' the study of welfare states. (Esping-Andersen 1990: 2)

The proliferation of typologies not only characterizes research on social policy in the Global North. As Wehr pointed out, political research on social policy in the Global South carries over a strong orientation toward the generation of ideal types as well (Wehr 2009), what necessarily diminishes its capacity to contemplate the divergences among countries (Rieger 1998; Weinmann and Burchardt 2010).

Due to the often tremendous divergences between Northern more industrialized countries and Southern less industrialized countries in terms of their social, economic, and political conditions, the extrapolation of political class struggle approaches into the research on social policy in the Global South comes across recurrent problems. Because of this, political class struggle approaches should carry through a substantial modification of their theoretical premises before undertaking the study of social policy in the Global South. This pressing need was openly acknowledged by manifold scholars, who carried out researches on social policy in southern countries using Esping-Andersen's analytical categories (Gough and Wood 2004, 2006; Rudra 2007; Haggard and Kaufmann 2008). In this manner, Gough and Wood pointed out the need to look upon the historic differences among northern and southern countries for the comparative analysis of their social policies (Gough and Wood 2004, 2006), Rudra brought out the structural differences between the labor markets in northern countries and the largely informal labor markets in southern countries (Rudra 2007), and Haggard and Kaufmann advocated the inclusion of additional explanatory factors beyond worker's organizations and class coalitions such as varieties of capitalism and political institutions (Haggard and Kaufmann 2008). Scholars specialized in the study of social policy in Latin America such as Filgueira, Barrientos, and Franzoni overtly advocated these criticisms as well (Filgueira 1998; Barrientos 2004; Franzoni 2008). Unfortunately, the same scholars who come out for the incorporation of the historical and structural differences among northern and southern countries within political class struggle approaches rarely bring them forward in their own analysis (Haggard and Kaufman being an important exception) (Wehr 2009).

Political class struggle approaches come across another obstacle when tackling social policy in Latin America. Wehr brought forward this issue with reference to postcolinonalism, calling it the problem of the postcolonial stateness (Wehr 2009). According to Wehr, political class struggle studies of social policy in southern countries completely leave out the heritage of postcolonial state-building, which structurally predetermines the development of social policy. While the contention concerning the postcolonial character of the state cannot be generalized to all Latin American countries, Wehr's argument definitively comes across when it points out that the study of social policy in southern countries systematically brushes away the existence of distinctive relationships between society and state. This is often dissimulated through the commonplace notions of deficient or peripheral stateness.

Unfortunately, Wehr does not come out with many hints on how to circumvent this obstacle, which not only characterizes political class struggle approaches but also structural approaches. All in all, the criticisms against social policy research in Latin America based on political class struggle approaches comprise three fundamental and interrelated points: (1) the historical differences between the development of welfare regimes in Latin American countries and the development of welfare regimes in northern countries, (2) the structural divergences among Latin American and northern countries with regard to their productive structures, labor markets and integration into the world market, (3) and the differences regarding the relationship between society and state in Latin American and northern countries.

Despite all these criticisms, political class struggle approaches represent the predominant theoretical approach in social policy research since the 1990s, comprising both the Global North and the Global South. The predominance of political class struggle approaches, however, under no circumstance contravenes the urgent need to restructuralize their underlying assumptions in order to puzzle out the determinants of social policy in the Global South, in general, and in Latin America, in particular. This need for reform represents the first theoretical starting point of this research.

2.3 Reconceptualization of Social Policy in the Latin American Academia

In parallel to the criticisms regarding the shortcomings of political class struggle approaches when dealing with social policy in Latin America, the concept of social policy commenced to be reconceptualized in the Latin American academia during the 2000s. This reconceptualization of social policy came about in the context of the political turn to the left in the region known in the English-speaking world as the "pink tide" (Moraña 2008), which brought about the rise of diverse left-wing governments in most Latin American countries. Scholars supporting this reconceptualization repudiated the two main premises underlying the neoliberal reform of social policy implemented in Latin America under the supervision of the IMF and the WB, which basically established that (1) poverty and inequality represented the inevitable side effect of modern societies and (2) social policy carried out a palliative function aimed at ameliorating poverty and inequality but not deracinating them (Álvarez Leguizamón 2005, 2008; Cimadamore and Cattani 2008). In opposition to this, they undertook the study of the conditions which generated and regenerated poverty and inequality, which expectedly brought about the reflection on the economic and political dimensions of social policy (Álvarez Leguizamón 2005, 2008; Cimadamore and Cattani 2008; CEPAL 2006, 2010, 2012, 2013, 2014).

This determined two consequences. First, it brought out the relation between social policy and labor market, bringing up the issue of the structural limits of the Latin American economies regarding their high exposure to international crisis and their largely informal labor markets.[3] Second, it brought out the relation between social policy and citizenship, as social policy not only maximized social fragmentation but ultimately brought about a citizenship gap between those who participated in the contributory social insurance system, and those who participated in the non-contributory social assistance system (Huber 2006; Lo Vuolo 2009; Cecchini and Martínez 2011).

Against this background, several proposals were brought forward in the academia in order to close down the citizenship gap and effectively materialize the enjoyment of social rights for everyone. While some of them simply advocated technical solutions such as the increment of the contributions of both formal and informal workers to the social security systems (Ribe et al. 2010) or the improvement of the institutional coordination of contributory and non-contributory social policy (Acosta and Ramírez 2004), other purposed to circumvent the structural limits of the Latin American economies through the universalization of social policy (Filgueira et al. 2006; Huber 2006; Molina 2006; Tokman 2006; Lo Vuolo 2009).

The most audacious proposals brought forward the intervention of the state as an employer of last resort, which provides employment to anyone requiring it through a government-run program (Cibils and Lo Vuolo 2004), and the implementation of a differential universal income, unconditional for the children and the elderly and conditional for the unemployed (Isuani 2006), in line with the proposals of a basic income introduced in the Global North since the late 1970s (Kuiper 1976; Meyer et al. 1981 [1978]; Schmid 1984; Mitschke 1985; Gorz 1985; McKay and Vanevery 2000). The least audacious proposals advocated the universalization of social assistance in line with the principles for social policy recommended by CEPAL since the early 2000s: universalism, solidarity, and efficiency (CEPAL 2000). Within this framework, the proposals comprised the universalization of the access to health care and education (Medici 2006; Tobar 2006; Opertti 2006), and the expansion toward universalization of the conditional cash transfer programs to poor families with children (Aguiar and Araújo 2002; Simões 2006). Finally, an intermediate line of proposals advanced the universalization of social security in order to decrease the gap between the contributory and the non-contributory pillars of social security (Huber 2006; Filgueira 2007). The tax system reform required for the implementation of these proposals was broken down as well in order to financially substantiate them (Rezk 2006).

Considering the aforesaid regarding the reconceptualization of social policy, the proposals aimed at the universalization of social security presuppose several advantages. In the first place, the universalization of social security correlates social policy

---

[3] Actually, the reincorporation of labor into the discussions on poverty and inequality represented no novelty, since the study of the "deviations" of the Latin American labor markets and their consequences on the social structures had determined the beginning of the scientific sociology in Latin America during the 1950s (Germani 1962). Nonetheless, this "comeback" of labor into the discussions on poverty and inequality brought about an innovative perspective on the role of labor beyond its economic dimension, for it conceptualized labor not only as the income source par excellence for most people (Medina and Galván 2008), but also as a fundamental factor for social and political integration (Cimadamore and Cattani 2008; CEPAL 2007).

and labor market, for it closes down the gap between the formal and the informal labor markets in two complementary ways: (1) spreading out the provision of social services to informal workers, and (2) incorporating informal workers into the universe of contributors to the system, as proposed by Ribe, Robalino, and Walker (Ribe et al. 2010). In the second place, the universalization of social security decreases the foregoing citizenship gap between those who participate in the contributory social insurance system and those who participate in the non-contributory social assistance system, for it acknowledges the immanent right of everyone to social security. In the third place the universalization of social security smoothes out the costs of institutional incoordination and disintegration, as requested by Acosta and Ramírez (Acosta and Ramírez 2004) because it establishes a unified and integrated system of social security.

On account of this, several left-wing governments undertook thoroughgoing social security system reforms since the 2000s in order to universalize social security. The reconceptualization of the social policy in the Latin American academia which accompanied these reforms represents the second theoretical starting point of this research.

2.4 Taking In the Good and Leaving Out the Bad: The Complementary Approach

Based on the above, this research comes out from two interrelated theoretical starting points. The first revolves around the inability of the predominant theoretical approach in social policy research to puzzle out the determinants of social policy in the Global South, in general, and in Latin America, in particular. The second is associated with the reconceptualization of social policy in the Latin American academia since the 2000s, which brought about the reflection on the economic and political determinants of social policy and consequently advocated its universalization.

Against this background, this research brings forward a theoretical approach to social policy which undertakes to deracinate the aforementioned flaws of political class struggle approaches with regard to social policy in Latin America and acknowledge the economic and political determinants of social policy at the same time. This approach basically commingles the Poulantzian and the political class struggle approaches into a complementary approach which capitalizes on the analytical strengths of both approaches while precluding their analytical weaknesses.

As explained above, the Poulantzian and the political class struggle approaches bring about advantages and disadvantages. On the one side, the Poulantzian approach to social policy brings forward a comprehensive and adaptable conceptual framework, which correlates social policy with the power struggles over hegemony among contending social groups, which inextricably associates social policy with the historical, social, economic, and political conditions in which it materializes. However, the Poulantzian approach comes across severe difficulties regarding its operationalization, because of which practically no empirical analysis of social policy was carried out (not even by Poulantzas) from this perspective. On the other side, political class struggle approaches are provided with a sound operational framework based on the quantification of power resources in possession of social classes (with special focus on the working class), which brings about the possibility to carry out empirical and comparative analysis of social policy. Because of this, political class struggle approaches represent the predominant theoretical approach in social policy research since the 1990s, including the study of social policy in the Global South. However, political class struggle approaches come across recurrent problems when dealing with social policy in the Global South because its theoretical premises divaricate from the historical, social, economic, and political conditions beyond the Global North.

In this context, the complementation of the Poulantzian and the political class struggle approaches brings about an enormous potential for the research on social policy in Latin America. The "compatibility" required for the complementation of both approaches is substantiated by the fact that, despite their differences, the Poulantzian and the political class struggle approaches are predicated on a common theoretical premise, according to which social policy represents the outcome of power struggles among contending social groups.

Based on the respective strengths of both approaches, the complementary approach commingles the conceptual framework of the Poulantzian approach and the operational framework of the political class struggle approaches, bringing about a two-stepped analytical approach which circumvents their respective weaknesses. The first step contextualizes the power struggles over social policy resorting to the comprehensive perspective of the Poulantzian approach. On this basis, the second step operationalizes the power struggles over social policy utilizing the operation framework of the political class struggle approach.

Naturally, the complementation of the Poulantzian and the political class struggle approaches does not preclude them from modifications in order to accommodate to the historical, social, economic, and political conditions of Latin America, or anywhere else for that matter. The way in which the two consecutive steps (contextualization and operationalization) are accomplished is broken down below.

2.4.1 Contextualization Based on the Poulantzian Approach

The use of the conceptual framework of the Poulantzian approach for the contextualization is predicated on its overall theoretical perspective, which conceptualizes social policy within the context of the construction of hegemony. In doing so, the Poulantzian approach automatically associates social policy with the historical, social, economic, and political conditions in which social policy materializes. For this reason, the Poulantzian approach represents a powerful devise for the contextualization of the power struggles over social policy in historical and geographical contexts, which divaricate from those assumed by political class struggle approaches.

Far from a superficial account of divergences with respect to a "universal" model (as in the case of political class struggle studies on Latin America's social policy), the contextualization based on the Poulantzian approach presupposes an in-depth submersion into the social, economic, and political processes, which have brought about the emergence of social policy in a particular historical and geographical context. To accomplish this, the contextualization must carry out a detailed reconstruction of these processes. Concretely, this reconstruction must clearly make out four explanatory questions concerning four fundamental dimensions of the power struggles over social policy, simplified as "where", "what", "who", and "how".

The first question, boiled down as the "where" question, establishes the focus on the structural dimension of social policy. Thus, the "where" question revolves around two essential elements of social policy: (1) the economic structure, which represents the material basis of social policy, and (2) the role of the state, which is predicated on the economic structure.

The "where" question presupposes the questioning of the economic structure assumed by political class struggle approaches. Based on this questioning, the "where" question undertakes to delineate the real foundations of the economic structure of the country under examination. In the case of Ecuador and Venezuela, this redefinition redirectionalizes the analytical focus from the effects of industrial relations on social policy (Korpi 1983; Esping-Andersen 1990), to the impacts of the rent-based economies of both countries on the development of their social actors and the function of their social policies.

The "where" question also presupposes the questioning of the role of the state and its relation to society. This questioning is predicated on the acceptance of three Gramscian postulates. First, the state realm percolates the other realms of social relations (Gramsci 2000: 235). Second, society does not represent a preexisting and pre-organizational domain in which social classes antecede political confrontations. On the contrary, social classes are catalyzed by their political confrontations in which the state carries out a preponderant role (Portantiero 1985: 282). Third, the relation between state and society is associated with the construction of hegemony (Gramsci 2000: 205).

The second question, summarized as the "what" question, breaks down the concrete sticking points around social policy. The "what" question undertakes to bring out the concrete points of contention around which the struggles over social policy are structuralized. These conflicts presuppose two dimensions. The first dimension is directly associated with the specific realm of social policy, as in the hypothetical case of the struggle between the rich and the poor over the implementation of a social program which provides assistance to the latter with resources extracted from the former. The second dimension is rather associated with the process of construction of hegemony within which social policy materializes. In this case, the struggles over social policy are not directly predicated on the material consequences of the implementation of a specific social program, but they are brought about by the broader struggles over two contending models of society. The struggles over the commoditization of social services or the instauration of universal social rights represent a good example of this.

The concrete forms assumed by the conflicts represent a central issue for the analysis of the power struggles over social policy, since they determine the scope of the actors who can participate in the struggles, the relations which the actors can establish among them (adversaries, allies, and neutral), the positions which the actors can advocate, and so on.

The third question, boiled down as the "who" question, establishes the focus on the real actors involved in the struggles over social policy. Naturally, the "who" question presupposes the questioning of the main actors assumed by political class struggle approaches which, as explained before, correlates the industrial working class with the subaltern classes and conceptualizes labor unions and social democratic parties as the archetypical economic and political representation of the working class. In the case of Ecuador and Venezuela, these premises openly contravene the historic development of social classes, since the absence of a thoroughgoing process of industrialization held back the emergence of a powerful industrial working class which could take over the leadership among subaltern classes, including the peasantry, the indigenous movement (very important in Ecuador because of its size), and the informal urban workers. Besides, the political representation of the heterogeneous subaltern classes through social democratic political parties never materialized in Ecuador and completely dematerialized in Venezuela with the practical extinction of Acción Democrática by the end of the 1990s.

For these reasons, the questioning of the main social actors assumed by political class struggle approach (and most structuralist Marxist approaches) brings about the extrapolation of the analytical focus from labor unions and class political parties to the entire spectrum of social, economic, and political actors involved in the struggles over social policy. In the case of the struggles over the social security system reforms in Venezuela and Ecuador, the actors involved commingle not only the labor unions and labor parties, but also employers' organizations, professional associations, pensioners' associations (including the pensioners of the police and military forces), social movements demanding their incorporation into social security, and the government itself.

The fourth question, summarized as the "how" question, breaks down the channels through which the struggles over social policy are canalized. The "how" question undertakes to make out the different arenas in which the previously identified conflicts over social policy materialize. Since these conflicts are correlated with the process of construction of hegemony, they come out through manifold channels of expression which, just as the process of construction of hegemony, are determined by specific historical, geographical, social, economic, and political conditions.

In consequence, the "how" question presupposes the questioning of the channels through which the power struggles over social policy are canalized according to political class struggle approaches. As pointed out above, political class struggle approaches preconceive that parliaments represent the actual realm where power struggles among contending social classes are determined. On this account political class struggle approaches predicate that parliamentary democracy can circumvent the hegemony of the dominant classes and contravene their essential interests.

[…] it is held that parliaments are, in principle, effective institutions for the translation of mobilized power into desired policies and reforms. Accordingly, parliamentary politics is capable of overriding hegemony, and can be made to serve interests that are antagonistic to capital. (Esping-Andersen 1990: 16)

The questioning of the channels assumed by political class struggle approaches necessarily takes down this premise. Moreover, the questioning implied in the "how" question presupposes to conceptualize parliamentary democracy (or for that matter presidential democracy) as an essential component of the process of construction of hegemony (Gramsci 2000: 211–212).

Accordingly, the "how" question brings about the extrapolation of the analytical focus from the parliamentary struggles over social policy to all relevant arenas in which the power struggles over social policy materialize. In the case of the post-neoliberal social security system reforms in Venezuela and Ecuador this redirectionalizes the analytical focus from the parliamentary relation of forces regarding the reforms to the complex entanglement of struggles which determined the development of the reforms, both inside the parliament and outside of it, in the overall context of all-out hegemonic struggles between government and opposition.

All in all, the contextualization based on the Poulantzian approach provides the contextual groundwork for the analysis of the power struggles over the social security system reforms in Venezuela and Ecuador. Based on a detailed reconstruction of the struggles, the contextualization breaks down the structural dimension underlying the struggles over the reforms (the "where" question), the concrete points of contention over the reforms (the "what" question), the real actors involved in the struggles over the reforms (the "who" question), and the manifold channels through which the struggles over the reforms are canalized (the "how" question). In a nutshell, the contextualization based on the Poulantzian approach brings out where (in what structural context) the struggles come about, over what points of contention the struggles materialize, who (what social, economic and political actors) participates in the struggles, and how (through what channels) the struggles are carried out.

Put in these terms, it comes across as obvious that no research on the power struggles over social policy can be carried through without fully making out these contextual questions.

2.4.2 Operationalization Based on Political Class Struggle Approaches

Based on the contextualization, the second step operationalizes the power struggles over social policy resorting to the political class struggle approaches. As pointed out above, the recourse to the political class struggle approaches for the operationalization is predicated on their sound operational framework, which is structuralized around the concept of power resources.

Essentially, the concept of power resources purposes to break down the distribution of power among social actors. To this end, political class struggle approaches conceptualize power as the capacity of social actors to establish punishments or rewards over others. Following this logic, power resources represent anything providing this capacity. The ownership and the control over the means of violence, the means of production and the capital comprise, according to this perspective, essential power resources. However, since these are successfully monopolized by the state and the capitalist classes, the analytical focus of political class struggle approaches is established on the associational power resources. In essence, associational power resources revolve around the capacity of social groups to establish organizations for the defense of their interests (Korpi 1983: 16–17).

As explained before, this perspective presupposes labor unions and left-wing political parties (typically social democratic) on the one side, and employer's organizations and right-oriented political parties (typically Christian democratic) on the other side, as the main social actors and the main holders of power resources. Accordingly, the confrontation of these two social actors determines the development or underdevelopment of social policy.

> Finally, the proponents of a "political class struggle" or "power resources" approach identify the distribution of organizational power between labor organizations and left parties on the one hand and center and right-wing political forces on the other hand as primary determinants of differences in the size and distributive impact of the welfare state across countries and over time. (Huber and Stephens 2001: 15)

While useful for the empirical analysis of social policy in the Northern industrialized countries, these premises divaricate from the real struggles over social policy in Ecuador and Venezuela. For this reason, the concept of power resources must be accommodated to the social, economic and political reality of both countries.

As pointed out above, the analytical broadening of the concept of power resources aiming at the study of social policy in peripheral countries has been brought forward by several scholars before (Gough and Wood 2004, 2006; Rudra 2007; Haggard and Kaufmann 2008). While praiseworthy, their theoretical proposals are associated with a macroanalytical perspective, which mainly purposes to categorize peripheral countries in clusters. Besides, their theoretical proposals carry out the analytical broadening of the concept of power resources from top to bottom, determining their analytical focus before approaching their cases of study.

On the contrary, the adaptation of the concept of power resources proposed in this research contravenes this logic, proceeding from bottom to top. To this aim, the definition of the concept of power resources is maximized beyond the capacity of actors to establish punishments or rewards to other actors. Instead, power resources are conceptualized as any resources which capacitate their possessors to advance their interests, even (but not necessarily) against the interests of others. This way, power resources comprise both the idea of "power over" and the idea of "power to".[4]

---

[4]This way, the concept of power resources corresponds with both the view of power initially proposed by Lukes (2005)[1974], which presupposes the exercise of power of A over B ("power over"), and the view of power advanced by Lukes' critics, which accentuates the ubiquitous nature of

On this basis, the adaptation of the concept of power resources basically capitalizes on the previously elaborated contextualization based on the Poulantzian approach. Concretely, the adaptation of the concept of power resources proposed in this research is structuralized into the four questions used for the contextualization. As explained above, these questions are associated with: (1) the structural dimension of social policy (the "where" question), including the economic structure behind it and the function of the state derived from it, (2) the concrete points of conflict over social policy (the "what" question), (3) the actors involved in the conflicts over social policy (the "who" question), and (4) the channels through which the conflicts over social policy are canalized (the "how" question).

Since power resources cannot be conceptualized without the social, economic, and political contexts in which power struggles among social actors materialize, the redefinition of power resources proposed in this research correlates them with these four questions.

In the case of the first question ("where"), which establishes the focus on the structural dimension of social policy, the analysis of the productive structure of Ecuador and Venezuela brings out: (1) the extraordinary importance of oil exportation for both the economy and the state, and (2) the enormous magnitude of informal labor in the economy.[5] In this context, oil resources and informal labor represent fundamental sources of power, and more so when considered with relation to social policy. For this reason, both elements are conceptualized as structural power resources for the operationalization of the power struggles over social policy in Ecuador and Venezuela. As mentioned above, structural power resources are predicated on the structural characteristics of the economic system (Wright 1994; Brinkmann et al. 2008; Schmalz et al. 2013).

The ownership of oil resources can be easily operationalized through the analysis of the legislation on the oil sector and its changes. This analysis comprises the legislation concerning the extraction, processing (refining and dressing), and commercialization of the oil resources, giving special attention to any changes in the legal regulations.

---

power ("power to") (Lukes 2005). In a very practical compilation, Hradil recapituales the manifold variations of both views of power (Hradil 1980).

[5] Academic discussions on the causes of the high level of labor informality in Latin American labor markets date back to the 1950s. In general terms, the proposed explanations can be categorized in three groups. The first group accentuates the "segmented" character of Latin American labor markets, in which informal labor represents the only alternative to unemployment for workers deprived of formal labor (Lewis 1954; Beccaria and Groisman 2015). The second group points out the "integrated" character of Latin American labor markets, in which workers and employers willingly carry out their activities in the informal labor market in order to circumvent the restrictions imposed by the formal labor market (Maloney 2004). The third group brings out the "induced" character of Latin American labor markets, in which workers are capacitated for formal labor markets but they are circumscribed to the informal labor market due to the high entry costs of formal markets (De Soto 2000). In any case, this research does not purpose to determine why the labor markets are characterized by a high level of labor informality in Ecuador and Venezuela, but rather how a high level of labor informality advantages or disadvantages the contending actors involved in the power struggles over the social security system reforms in both countries.

Additionally, the analysis breaks down the effective control of oil resources, including the control of strategic managerial positions in the oil sector, the control of the labor unions in the oil sector, the mandatory accountability of the oil resources, and the distribution of the oil revenues among the national, provincial, and municipal governments. Even though this effective control cannot be as easily operationalized as the ownership of oil resources, it can still be dimensioned through the reconstruction of the struggles over the oil resources. The relevance of the analysis of the effective control of oil resources is associated with its vital importance for the non-state social actors, especially labor unions and employer's organizations.

Finally, the analysis of the control of oil resources is concatenated with an examination of the changes in the absolute and relative magnitudes of these resources.

Though counterintuitive, informal labor represents a fundamental power resource in Ecuador and Venezuela, as its magnitude determines the relative power of several actors, including labor unions, employers' organizations, political parties, and the government itself. The way in which informal labor delineates the relative power of social actors divaricates depending on the actors at stake. Informal labor can scale down the relative power of the social actors whose membership is predicated on formal workers, such as professional organizations, labor unions, and left-wing parties related to labor unions. In turn, informal labor can maximize the relative power of the social actors who are unshackled from the labor legislation associated to formal labor, such as employers' organizations and the government, or because it exacerbates the dependence of informal workers from their assistance policies, as in the case of the governments.

The absolute and relative magnitude of informal labor can be operationalized with ease through labor indicators such as the total amount of workers in informal employment, the total amount of workers in the informal sector, the total amount of workers in informal employment outside the informal sector, the share of informal workers within the labor force, the share of informal workers within the salaried labor force, the amount of informal workers living below the poverty line, and so on.

In the case of the second question ("what"), which revolves around the concrete points of contention over social policy, the analysis of the struggles over the social security system reforms in Ecuador and Venezuela brings out that the main conflicts are associated with the participation of the profit-making private sector in the pension system, the maintenance or elimination of the already existing "special regimes" of social security, and the orientation of the state contribution to the pension system.

Even though these two issues cannot be directly transubstantiated into specific forms of power resources, they predetermine the context in which social actors mobilize their power resources. The extraordinary importance of this context for the mobilization of power resources can be made out when comparing the struggles over the social security system reforms in the northern industrialized countries with the struggles over the social security system reforms in Ecuador and Venezuela. In the case of the Northern industrialized countries, the struggles revolved around the increasing costs of social security systems for the state and the taxpayers in the context of aging populations (Esping-Andersen 1990). For this reason high earners advocated the reduction of the public social security systems and the inception of private social security services according to their individual needs. On the contrary, in the case of Ecuador and Venezuela the struggles were associated with the privatization of social services, the elimination of preexisting special social security regimes and the orientation of the state contribution to the social security system. For this reason, high earners organized in professional organizations repudiated the privatization of social security services as it would bring about the loss of their state subsidized special social security regimes.

In the case of the third question ("who"), which establishes the focus on the actors involved in the struggles over social policy, the analysis brings out: (1) the existence of an entanglement of social actors involved in the struggles over the social security system reforms in Venezuela and Ecuador, much more complex than the social actors presupposed by the political class struggle approach, comprising professional associations, expert groups, military and policy forces, feminist organizations, pensioners' associations, lobby groups, nongovernmental organizations, bureaucratic groups, indigenous and peasant organizations, etc., (2) the extraordinary importance of the government as social, economic, and political actor due to its prerogative over the oil sector, and (3) the dissociation of labor unions and class parties from the popular classes[6] (O'Donnell 1977: 524) in both countries.

Although these three issues cannot be directly transubstantiated into specific forms of power resources either, they predetermine the context in which power resources are mobilized as well. Based on these three issues, the social actors involved in the struggles over the reforms are categorized in two different categories depending on their scope, as elaborated by Li (2012).

The first category subordinates the macro actors who can commingle a nationwide organizational structure with the disposal of two or more types of power resources. Most of these actors are looked upon by the political class struggle approach: labor unions, employers' organizations and political parties. However, due to the aforementioned extraordinary importance of the government as social, economic, and political actor in both countries, the national government is comprised in this category too.

The second category subordinates the meso actors who do not accomplish the two aforementioned characteristics of macro actors (a national organizational structure and the disposal of two or more types of power resources). This category comprises a complex of organizations with very diverse characteristics, such as military and police forces, professional associations, expert groups, nongovernmental organizations, lobby groups, feminist organizations, indigenous and peasant groups, pensioners' associations, bureaucrat groups, etc. Some of these actors fall back upon a nationwide organizational structure and sometimes even one type of power resources (but not two), as in the case of the military and police forces.

The social actors involved in the struggles over the social security system reforms in Venezuela and Ecuador are delineated in Table 2.1.

---

[6]As explained by O'Donnell and Portantiero, the concept of popular classes conceptualizes the economically marginalized sectors which are usually not represented by the conventional labor organizations (O'Donnell 1975, 1977; Portantiero 1973, 1977)

Table 2.1 Social actors involved in the struggles over the social security system reforms in Venezuela and Ecuador

Category	Type	Venezuela	Ecuador
Macro	Governments	Venezuelan Government	Ecuadorian Government
	Political parties	MVR/PSUV, PCV, PPT, AD, COPEI, MAS, UNT, PJ	MPD/UP, MUPP, AP, AV, RED, UNO/CREO, PSC/MCMG, PRIAN, PSP
	Labor unions	CTV, CODESA, CGT, CUTV, FBT	FUT, PLE, CUT
	Employers' organizations	FEDECAMARAS, CONSECOMERCIO, CONINDUSTRIA, FEDENAGA, FEDEAGRO	CCG, CGQ, AMCHAM, CCAP, CEE
Meso	Military and police forces	FANB, Provincial Police Forces (24), Municipal Police Forces (99)	FAE, PNE
	Professional associations,	FAPUV, FMV, CMDMC	
	Lobby and expert groups	APAFP, REDIUP	
	Nongovernmental organizations	PROVEA	
	Feminist organizations		Mujeres por la vida
	Indigenous and peasant organizations		CONAIE, FEI, FENOCIN, FEINE
	Pensioners' associations		CJE, CCP, AMSP, FEUNASSC, CONFEUNASSC

Source Prepared by the author

In the case of the fourth question ("how"), which revolves around the channels through which the contending actors canalize their struggles over the reforms, the analysis of the concrete struggles brings out that: (1) the struggles over the reforms are not dissociated from the more general struggles for hegemony, which came about in manifold ways, (2) in light of the aforementioned, the struggles over the reforms in the National Assembly cannot be broken down excluding several other parallel clashes which determine the development of the reforms just as much as the specific struggles over the reforms in the National Assembly, (3) the organizational capacity of the social actors (related to the magnitude of their memberships) does not necessarily correlate their relative power, (4) in a context of political radicalization, the institutional channeling of conflict became less and less relevant as conflict is increasingly canalized through street mobilization, and (5) the decrease of institutional politics and the increase of street politics maximizes the political role of mass media.

As pointed out above, political class struggle approaches operationalize power through the assessment of the associational power resources of social groups. In this research, associational power resources are broken down into two types of power resources: (1) corporative associational power resources and (2) political associational power resources. Corporative associational power resources revolve around the capacity of social groups to establish organizations for the defense of their interests outside the realm of party politics, including social groups gathered around economic interests such as labor unions, employers' organizations, professional associations, pensioners' associations, as well as social groups gathered around social interests such as indigenous and peasant movements, feminist organizations, nongovernmental organizations, etc. In contrast, political associational power resources revolve around the capacity of social groups to establish organizations for the defense of their interests inside the realm of party politics.

As explained above, political class struggle approaches operationalize associational power resources through indicators concerning the level of unionization, the composition of labor confederations, the density of labor unions, the amount of labor conflicts (including strikes and lockouts), the amount of workers involved in labor conflicts, the duration of labor conflicts, the share of the electorate voting for left- and right-oriented political parties (associating social democrat and communist parties to the former and Christian democratic and liberal to the latter), the share of assembly members belonging to left- and right-oriented political parties, the share of Cabinet members belonging to left- and right-oriented political parties, the party identification by social group, etc. In this research, the assessment of both corporative and political associational power resources is carried out in a very similar way. The only differences are predicated on the absence of available information on the aforementioned indicators.

However, in opposition to political class struggle approaches the assessment of associational power resources is not dissociated from the process of construction of hegemony. On the contrary, the assessment is carried out with reference to the struggles for hegemony which in both countries come about in parallel to the social security system reforms. The reason for this is associated with the foregoing contextualization of the power struggles over the reforms, which relativized the centrality of both corporative and political power resources and, instead, brought out the growing importance of street politics and mass media communication.

Given this transposition of political conflict, which carries over from the conventional channels of institutional politics into the alternative channels of street politics, the assessment additionally breaks down the mobilizational power resources the contending actors. Unlike associational power resources, which are associated with the capacity of social groups to establish massive organizations and carry through large scale labor conflicts (either as strikes or lockouts), mobilizational power resources revolve around the capacity of the social groups conglomerate people (regardless of their formal affiliation) to participate in political mobilizations. Mobilizational power resources are operationalized through indicators such as the amount of massive political mobilizations carried out, the amount of protesters participating in massive political mobilizations, the characteristics of massive political mobilizations in term of goals, use of violence, social composition, etc.

Finally, due to the extraordinary role played by mass media throughout both reform processes, the assessment of the power resources of the contending actors looks upon their communicational power resources as well. Communicational power resources are predicated on the control of the mass media, because of which they are operationalized through indicators concerning their ownership.

All in all, the operationalization of the power struggles over the social security system reforms in Ecuador and Venezuela comprises four types of power resources: structural, associational, mobilizational, and communicational. As pointed out above, these four types of power resources correlate the four questions ("where", "what", "who", and "how") utilized for the contextualization of the analysis. The indicators used for the operationalization of structural, associational, mobilizational and communicational power resources are recapitulated in Table 2.2.

2.5   Methodological Definitions

Following the contemporary methodological development of social sciences (Goodin and Klingemann 1996; Van Evera 1997; George and Bennett 2005; Lauth et al. 2009; Kaiser 2014), this research commingles multiple research methods.

First and foremost, this investigation falls under case study research. As defined by George and Bennett, case study research is characterized by the detailed examination of a research object in order to generate or corroborate explanations which can be generalized to other research objects (George and Bennett 2005: 5). While circumscribed to a small number of research of cases, case study research outdistances statistical research in the attainment of high conceptual validity, the examination of causal mechanisms and the treatment of causal complexity, such as path dependence, tipping points, multiple interactions effects, selection effects, disproportionate feedback loops, equifinality, and multifinality (George and Bennett 2005: 19). Based on this, case study research exceedingly advances theory development. Since case study research represents a type of qualitative research (George and Bennett 2005: 18–19), this research falls under qualitative research as well.

In order to break down the social security system reforms in Venezuela and Ecuador, this investigation capitalizes on the process-tracing method. As defined by Collier, process-tracing represents the "close processual analysis of the unfolding of events over time within the research case" (Collier 1993: 115). This analysis is systematically carried through and the evidence broken down "in light of research questions and hypotheses posed by the investigator" (Collier 2011: 823). Basically, process-tracing undertakes to establish links between possible causes and observed outcomes (George 1979; George and Bennett 2005). To this aim, the unfolding of

Table 2.2 Power resources

Type	Dimension	Indicators on exports of goods and services (V4)(E4)
Structural	Ownership of oil resources	Oil production and oil prices (V4)(E4)
		Fiscal revenue (V9)(E2)
		Oil legislation (E2)
	Control of oil resources	Public and private oil production share (V5)(E5)
	Informal labor	Labor force (V5)(E5)
		Labor situation (V5)(E6)
		Informal labor (V4)(E6)
Associational	Corporative	Structure of the government cabinet (V2)(E2)
		Nationalized and renationalized companies (V)
		Legislative electoral results (V3)
		Endorsements and active members of the national political parties (E3)
		Labor confederations in 2001 (V4)
		Union members under collective bargaining in 2004 (V)
		Union density (V4)(E4)
		Members and regional organizations of the national indigenous organizations (E2)
		Members of the police and military forces (E4)
	Political	Composition of the legislative power (V8)(E8)
		Results of the voting on the legislation regarding the social security system reform (E4)
		Position of the political parties in the voting on the legislation regarding the social security system reform (E4)
		Composition of the government cabinet (V)(E)
Mobilizational		Progression of public protests (V3)

(continued)

Table 2.2 (continued)

Type	Dimension	Indicators on exports of goods and services (V4)(E4)
		Public mobilizations of national scope (V3)(E3)
Communicational		National TV networks (V4)(E4)
		Table 5.26 National newspapers (E4)

Source Prepared by the author

events is structuralized into a chronological sequence so that links between causes and outcomes can be brought out (Bennett 2010: 208–209).

Throughout this research, the chronological sequence is brought about through the detailed reconstruction of the social security system reforms in Venezuela and Ecuador. Following Collier (2011), the reconstruction of the reforms is systematically carried through on the basis of the four explanatory questions described in this Chapter: "where", "what", "who", and "how".

After the analysis of both research cases, a comparative analysis is carried out. Therefore, this investigation falls under comparative case study research. Comparative case study research presupposes manifold advantages with respect to other comparative methods such as controlled comparison, qualitative comparative analysis, and positive and negative comparative methods, which preclude the close processual of the research cases which characterizes case study research (George and Bennett 2005: 18–19). These advantages revolve around the capacity of comparative case study research to acknowledge qualitative variables, individual actors, decision-making processes, historical and social contexts, and path dependencies (George and Bennett 2005: 9).

In order to carry out the comparative analysis, this research capitalizes on the structured focused comparison method. Structured focused comparisons comprise two main characteristics. First, they carry through "structured" comparisons, as they bring forward general questions defined by the scholar, which are carried over the research cases in order to systematize the findings and the comparison among them (Geroge and Bennett 2005: 67). Naturally, these general questions must correspond with the research's objective in order to bring about relevant results. Second, they carry out "focused" comparisons, as they establish the analytical focus on specific aspects of the research cases (George and Bennett 2005: 67). Again, these specific aspects must correspond with the research's objective.

In this investigation, the structured focused comparison of the social security systems in Venezuela and Ecuador is predicated on the four explanatory questions described above: "where", "what", "who", and "how". The comparison is carried through following a "most similar cases" research design.

   Originally contrived by Mill (2011), most similar cases research designs purpose to resemble experimental research designs. In most similar cases designs, the scholar singles out research cases which ideally correspond in all their aspects except for one. Accordingly, the diverging outcomes among the research cases can be correlated with their only divergent aspect (Przeworski and Teune 1970: 32–34). In practice, since no research cases divaricate in only one aspect, the diverging outcomes among the research cases are usually associated with several aspects, what naturally debilitates the causal relationship between the independent and the dependent variables. Against this problem, process-tracing represents a powerful method to counterbalance erroneous inferences, for it brings out the causal relations within research cases (George and Bennett 2005: 254).

2.6 Research Cases Selection

The social security system reforms carried out by President Chávez in Venezuela and President Correa in Ecuador are singled out as research cases based on the most similar cases research design. Accordingly, the selection of both research cases is associated with their similarities which, moving from the more general to the more specific, can be categorized into three levels: structural, conjunctural, and reform-related. Since all of them (structural, conjunctural, and reform-related similarities) are meticulously broken down throughout this research, they are only briefly delineated in the following, dispensing with overall statistical figures.

   On the structural level, Venezuela and Ecuador are characterized by the archetypical features of Andean countries concerning their strong colonial heritages (García Canclini 1990; Coronil 1997; Mignolo 1999), extractivist economies and rentier states (Gudynas 2009, 2013; Acosta 2012; Lander 2014). According to the United Nations (hereinafter UN), both countries correspond in terms of human development, ranking in the middle among the countries with high human development (UN 2015).

   On the conjunctural level, Venezuela and Ecuador undertook a political turn to the left in the context of the "pink tide" in Latin America, which started out with the coming to power of President Hugo Chávez in Venezuela in February 1999 and subsequently spread out over the region, including the coming to power of President Rafael Correa in Ecuador in January 2007 (Moraña 2008). As explained above, beyond their particularities these left-wing governments were characterized by two common elements: (1) they repudiated the neoliberal policies implemented in Latin America between the 1970s and 1990s under the supervision of the IMF and the WB, and (2) their coming to power represented the consequence of the complete failure of the neoliberal polices implemented in the region (Sader: 2008; Figueroa Ibarra 2009). Among the left-wing governments, the Venezuelan and Ecuadorian governments are additionally categorized, along with the Bolivian government, into the subgroup of the "revolutionary" governments (Stolowicz 2007; Dirmoser and Merkel 2007; Bistoletti 2009).

On the reform-related level, Venezuela and Ecuador carried out social security system reforms under the Chávez' and Correa's governments which, in very similar terms, undertook to establish universal social security systems. In both cases, however, the reforms came across analogous obstacles involving similar social actors. This resemblance represents the most significant parallelism with a view to this research, forasmuch as it revolves around the power struggles over the social security system reforms in both countries.

In the case of Venezuela, the post-neoliberal social security system reform started out with the introduction of the universal right to social security into the new constitution of 1999. Subsequently, the Venezuelan National Assembly brought about the Ley Orgánica del Sistema de Seguridad Social (English: Organic Law of the Social Security System) in 2002, which established the general principles and the institutional structure of the new social security system, providing the legal framework for the universalization of social security in Venezuela. However, the assembly did not bring out the required regulatory laws concerning health care and pensions afterward, even though the government party took over its control in 2000 (Salcedo González 2006; PROVEA 2007; Coromoto Montilla 2009). Without the sanction of these fundamental regulatory laws, the implementation of the social security system reform passed in 2002 has broken down to this day (Fernández 2012; Méndez Cegarra 2015; PROVEA 2013).

In the case of Ecuador, the first official reference to the government's plan to carry out a social security system reform aimed at the universalization of social security came out in the Plan Nacional de Desarrollo 2007–2010 (English: National Plan of Development 2007–2010) published in September 2007, 9 months after its coming to power (SENPLADES 2007: 72). One year later, the new Constitution established the "right of all persons" to social security, explicitly including homemakers, landworkers, self-employed, and unemployed workers (Constitución Ecuador 2008). In July 2012, the government circulated around governmental offices a draft bill for the social security system reform under the name of Ley Orgánica del Sistema de Seguridad Social (English: Organic Law of the Social Security System) (LOSSSE). Basically, the LOSSSE determined the suppression of the existing social security system in order to bring about a new, universal, and unified social security system. However, after the LOSSSE leaked out to the media, Correa's government did not hand it over to the assembly for consideration, even though the government party took over its control in 2013. Instead, the government carried out successive partial reforms since 2014 which did not undertake to establish a new, universal and unified social security system as originally intended, but rather to bring about the universalization and the unification of the existing social security system.

2.7 Data Collection

With regard to the data collection, this research capitalizes on multiple methods, including the analysis of primary and secondary sources, the conduction of interviews and the participant observations made during the field researches (Lauth et al. 2009; Pickel et al. 2009).

The analysis of primary sources comprises the examination of newspapers, (not scientific) magazines, official and unofficial documents (such as documents formulated by the governments, political parties, labor unions, employers' organizations, professional associations, peasant and indigenous organizations, etc.), draft bills, bills, laws and decrees, surveys, and statistical data banks. The analysis of secondary sources comprises the examination of scientific journals (printed and online) and scientific books (printed and online).

In addition, this research capitalizes on 39 qualitative expert interviews conducted during two field research trips of 3 months each in Venezuela and Ecuador (Meuser and Nagel 2009; Kaiser 2014). As noticed by Lauth, Pickel and Pickel, expert interviews represent a very useful procedure for the reconstruction of social, economic, and political processes (Lauth et al. 2009). The experts who participate in the interviews are associated with the social security system reforms, including government officials; assembly members; leaders of political parties, labor unions, and employers' organizations; members of professional associations, nongovernmental organizations, and pensioners associations; leaders of peasant and indigenous organizations and feminist organizations; scholars, professors, and technicians.[7] Following Kaiser, the interviews are carried through as "semi-structured" interviews (Kaiser 2014), in which a personalized interview guideline slightly structuralizes the conversation without holding it back.

Finally, the participant observations made throughout the field researches, duly registered, represent an additional source of information for this research (Lauth, Pickel and Pickel 2009; Kaiser 2014).

2.8 Summary

In terms of theory, this research comes out from two interrelated starting points. The first revolves around the shortcomings of political class struggle approaches when confronted with social policy in the Global South. The second is associated with the reconceptualization of social policy in the Latin American academia initiated during the 2000s, which establishes the focus on the economic and political determinants of social policy and consequently advocates its universalization.

Against this background, this research brings forward a theoretical approach to social policy aimed at two goals: (1) to deracinate the shortcomings of political class struggle approaches when confronted with social policy in Latin America, and (2) to acknowledge the economic and political determinants of social policy at the same time. This approach basically commingles the Poulantzian and the political class struggle approaches into a complementary approach which capitalizes on the

[7]The names and positions of the interviewees are particularized in Notes. Due to their extensive length, the transcriptions of the interviews accompany this research in electronic format.

analytical strengths of both approaches while striking off their analytical weaknesses. The "compatibility" between both approaches is substantiated by their common theoretical premise, according to which social policy represent the outcome of power struggles among contending social groups.

The complementary approach concatenates two parts. The first part carries through a detailed reconstruction of the power struggles over social policy based on the Poulantzian approach. The use of the Poulantzian approach for the reconstruction is predicated on its comprehensive theoretical framework, which correlates social policy with the construction of hegemony. By doing so, the Poulantzian approach inherently associates social policy with the historical, social, economic, and political conditions in which it materializes. The second part carries out the operationalization of the power struggles over social policy resorting to the useful operational framework of political class struggle approaches, which is associated with the concept of power resources. However, this concept is not reduplicated in its original form, but it is completely transubstantiated in order to circumvent its shortcomings when dealing with social policy in Latin America.

In order to acknowledge the economic and political determinants of social policy and deracinate the shortcomings of political class struggle approaches, both the contextualization and the operationalization are broken down into four consecutive questions: "where", "what", "who", and "how". The "where" question revolves around the structural dimension of social policy, the "what" question is associated with the concrete points of conflict over social policy, the "who" question correlates the social, economic, and political actors involved in the conflicts over social policy (the "who" question), and the "how" question revolves around the channels through which the conflicts over social policy are canalized. These questions represent the basis for the comparison of both research cases, following the method of comparative case studies known as "structured, focused comparison", as defined by George and Bennett (George and Bennett 2005: 67).

In terms of methodology, this research commingles multiple research methods, following the contemporary methodological development of social sciences (Goodin and Klingemann 1996; Van Evera 1997; George and Bennett 2005; Lauth et al. 2009; Kaiser 2014).

First and foremost, this investigation comes under case study research. Case study research represents the detailed examination of a research object in order to generate or substantiate explanations which can be generalized to other research objects (George and Bennett 2005: 5). Case study research is characterized by the attainment of high conceptual validity, the examination of causal mechanisms and the treatment of causal complexity, such as path dependence, tipping points, multiple interactions effects, selection effects, disproportionate feedback loops, equifinality, and multifinality (George and Bennett 2005: 19. Forasmuch as case study research represents a type of qualitative research (George and Bennett 2005: 18–19), this research comes under qualitative research as well.

In order to break down the social security system reforms in Venezuela and Ecuador, this investigation capitalizes on the process-tracing method. As defined by Collier, process-tracing represents the "close processual analysis of the unfolding of events over time within the research case" (Collier 1993: 115). To this aim, the unfolding of events is structuralized into a chronological sequence, so that links between causes and outcomes can be brought out (Bennett 2010: 208–209).

Throughout this research, the chronological sequence is brought about through the detailed reconstruction of the social security system reforms in Venezuela and Ecuador. As explained above, the reconstruction of the reforms is systematically carried through on the basis of the four explanatory questions: "where", "what", "who", and "how".

After the analysis of both research cases, a comparative analysis is carried out. To this aim, this research capitalizes on the structured-focused comparison method. Structured-focused comparisons are characterized by two main features. First, they carry through "structured" comparisons, as they bring forward general questions defined by the scholar, which are carried over the research cases in order to systematize the findings and the comparison among them (George and Bennett 2005: 67). Second, they carry out "focused" comparisons, as they establish the analytical focus on specific aspects of the research cases (George and Bennett 2005: 67). In this investigation, the structured-focused comparison of the social security systems in Venezuela and Ecuador is predicated on the four explanatory questions described above: "where", "what", "who", and "how".

The comparison between both research cases is carried through following a "most similar cases" research design. Based on this research design, the social security system reforms carried out by President Chávez in Venezuela and President Correa in Ecuador are singled out as research cases. The selection of both research cases is associated with their remarkable similarities at all levels: structural, conjunctural, and reform-related.

With regard to the data collection, this research capitalizes on multiple methods, including the analysis of primary and secondary sources, the conduction of interviews and the participant observations made during the field researches (Lauth et al. 2009; Pickel et al. 2009).

References

Abraham D (1981) Corporatist compromise and the re-emergence of the labor/capital conflict in Weimar Germany. Polit Power Soc Theory 2 (JAI Press, London)

Achenbaum A (1983) Shades of gray: old age, American values, and federal policies since 1920. Little, Brown and Company, Boston

Acosta A (2012) Breve historia económica del Ecuador. Corporación Editora Nacional, Quito

Acosta OL, Ramírez JC (2004) Breve historia económica del Ecuador. Comisión Económica para América Latina y el Caribe, Santiago de Chile

Aguiar M, Araújo CH (2002) Bolsa-escola: educación para enfrentar la pobreza. Organización de las Naciones Unidas para la Educación, la Ciencia y la Cultura, Brasilia

Altvater E (1978) Some problems of state interventionism. In: Holloway J, Picciotto S (eds) State and capital: a Marxist debate. Edward Arnold, London

Álvarez Leguizamón S (2008) La producción de la pobreza masiva y su persistencia en el pen-
    samiento social latinoamericano. In: Cimadamore A, Cattani AD (eds) Producción de pobreza y
    desigualdad en América Latina. Siglo del Hombre Editores, Bogotá
Arrow K (1963) Uncertainty and the welfare economics of medical care. Am Econ Rev 53(5)
Artigas C (2005) Una mirada a la protección social desde los derechos humanos y otros contextos
    internacionales. Santiago de Chile, Comisión
Arts W, Gelissen J (2002) Three worlds of welfare capitalism or more? A state-of-the-art report. J
    Eur Soc Policy 12(2)
Blanke B, Jürgens U, Kastendiek H (1978) On the current Marxist discussion on the analysis of
    form and function of the bourgeois state. In: Holloway J, Picciotto S (eds) State and capital: a
    Marxist debate. Edward Arnold, London
Barrientos A (2004) Latin America: towards a Liberal-Informal Welfare Regime. In: Gough I,
    Wood G (eds) Insecurity and welfare regimes in Asia, Africa, and Latin America: social policy
    in developmental contexts. Cambridge University Press, Cambridge
Beccaria L, Groisman F (2015) Informalidad y segmentación del mercado laboral: el caso de la
    Argentina. In: Revista CEPAL, no 117. Comisión Económica para América Latina y el Caribe,
    Santiago de Chile
Bell D (1978) The cultural contradictions of modern capitalism. Basic Books, New York
Bennet A (2010) Process tracing and causal inference. In: Brady H, Collier (eds) Rethinking social
    inquiry. Rowman & Littlefield Publishers, Lanham
Beveridge W (1942) Social insurance and allied services. Her. Majesty's. Stationery Office, London
Bistoletti EL (2009) Unterschiedliche Wege, gemeinsames Ziel. Schweizer Personalvorsorge 3
    (VPS Verlag Personalvorsorge und Sozialversicherung, Luzern)
Block F (1977) The ruling class does not rule: notes on the Marxist theory of the state. In Socialist
    revolution, no 33
Bonoli G (1997) Classifying welfare states: a Two-dimension approach. J Soc Policy 26(3) (Cam-
    bridge University Press, Cambridge)
Brinkmann U, Choi HL, Detje R, Dörre K, Holst H, Karakayali S, Schmalstieg C (2008) Strategic
    Unionism. Aus der Krise zur Erneuerung? Umrisse eines Forschungsprogramms. VS Verlag für
    Sozialwissenschaften, Wiesbaden
Burchardt HJ (2012) Las reformas sociolaborales en América Latina. Una Propuesta para un nuevo
    acercamiento analítico. In: Revista de Ciencias Sociales, no 135. San José, y Rica
Castles FG (1978) The social-democratic image of society. Routledge and Kegan Paul, London
Castles FG (ed) (1982) The impact of parties: politics and policies in democratic capitalist states.
    Sage, London
Castles FG, Mitchell D (1993) Worlds of welfare and families of nations. In: Castles FG (ed)
    Families of nations: patterns of public policy in western democracies. Dartmouth Publishing,
    Aldershot
Cecchini S, Martínez R (2011) Protección social inclusiva en América Latina. Una mirada integral,
    un enfoque de derechos. Comisión Económica para América Latina y el Caribe, Santiago de
    Chile
CEPAL (Comisión Económica Para América Latina y el Caribe) (2000) Equidad, desarrollo y
    ciudadanía. Comisión Económica para América Latina y el Caribe, Santiago de Chile
CEPAL (Comisión Económica Para América Latina y el Caribe) (2006) La protección social de
    cara al futuro: acceso, financiamiento y solidaridad. Comisión Económica para América Latina
    y el Caribe, Santiago de Chile
CEPAL (Comisión Económica Para América Latina y el Caribe) (2007) Cohesión social: inclusión
    y sentido de pertenencia en América Latina y el Caribe. Comisión Económica para América
    Latina y el Caribe, Santiago de Chile
CEPAL (Comisión Económica Para América Latina y el Caribe) (2010) La hora de la igualdad:
    brechas por cerrar, caminos por abrir. Comisión Económica para América Latina y el Caribe,
    Santiago de Chile

CEPAL (Comisión Económica Para América Latina y el Caribe) (2012) Eslabones de la desigualdad: heterogeneidad estructural, empleo y protección social. Comisión Económica para América Latina y el Caribe, Santiago de Chile

CEPAL (Comisión Económica Para América Latina y el Caribe) (2013) Social panorama of Latin America. Comisión Económica para América Latina y el Caribe, Santiago de Chile

CEPAL (Comisión Económica Para América Latina y el Caribe) (2014) Pactos para la igualdad: hacia un futuro sostenible. Comisión Económica para América Latina y el Caribe, Santiago de Chile

Chen MA (2005) Rethinking the informal economy: linkages with the formal economy. United Nations University, Helsinki

Cibils A, Lo Vuolo R (2004) El estado como empleador de última instancia. Centro Interdisciplinario para el Estudio de Políticas Públicas, Buenos Aires

Cimadamore A, Cattani AD (2008) Producción de pobreza y desigualdad en América Latina. Siglo del Hombre Editores, Bogotá

Collier D (1993) The comparative method. In: Finifter A (ed) Political science: the state of the Discipline II. American Political Science Association, Washington

Collier D (2011) Understanding process tracing. Polit Sci Polit 44(4) (American Political Science Association, Washington)

Constitución de la República del Ecuador (2008)

Coronil F (1997) The magical state: nature, money, and modernity in Venezuela. The University of Chicago Press, Chicago

Coughlin R (1979) Social policy and ideology: public opinion in eight rich countries. Comp Soc Res 2 (University of New Mexico, Albuquerque)

Cutright P (1967) Income redistribution: a cross-national analysis. Soc Forces 46(2) (Oxford University Press, Oxford)

De Soto H (2000) The mystery of capital: why capitalism triumphs in the west and fails everywhere. Black Swan, Berkshire

De Tocqueville A (2003)[1835] Democracy in America and two essays on America. Penguin Books, London

Dirmoser D, Merkel W (2007) Lateinamerika: die Linke, die Demokratie und die soziale Frage. In: Neue Gesellschaft – Frankfurter Hefte, no 12. Friedrich-Ebert-Stiftung, Berlin

Esping-Andersen G (1985) Politics against markets. Princeton University Press, Princeton

Esping-Andersen G (1990) The three worlds of welfare capitalism. Princeton University Press, Princeton

Fernández ME (2012) La protección social frente a la vejez en Venezuela. In: Anuario de derecho, vol 29, no 29. Universidad de los Andes, Mérida

Ferrera M (1996) The 'southern model' of welfare in social Europe. J Eur Soc Policy 6(1) (Sage Publications, Thousand Oaks)

Figueroa Ibarra C (2009) La crisis mundial: naturaleza y perspectivas. In: Bajo el Volcán, vol 8, no 14. Benemérita Universidad Autónoma de Puebla, México

Filgueira F (1998) El nuevo modelo de prestaciones sociales en América Latina eficiencia, residualismo y ciudadanía estratificada. In: Roberts B (ed) Ciudadanía y política social latinoamericana. Facultad Latinoamericana de Ciencias Sociales, San José

Filgueira F (2007) Cohesión, riesgo y arquitectura de protección social en América Latina. Comisión Económica para América Latina y el Caribe, Santiago de Chile

Filgueira F, Gerardo MC, Papadópulos J, Tobar F (2006) Universalismo básico: una alternativa posible y necesaria para mejorar las condiciones de vida. In: Molina CG (ed) Universalismo básico: una nueva política social para América Latina. Banco Interamericano de Desarrollo, Washington

Flora P, Alber J (1981) Modernization, democratization, and the development of welfare states in Western Europe. In: Flora P, Heidenheimer A (eds) The development of welfare states in Europe and America. Transaction Publishers, New Brunswick

Franzoni J (2008) Welfare regimes in Latin America: capturing constellations of markets, families, and policies. Lat Am Politics Soc 50(2) (University of Miami, Miami)

Frey B, Schneider F (1978) An empirical study of politico-economic interaction in the United States. Rev Econ Stat 60(2) (The MIT Press, Cambridge)

George A (1979) Case studies and theory development: the method of structured, focused comparison. In: Lauren PG (ed) Diplomatic history: new approaches. Free Press, New York

George A, Bennett A (2005) Case studies and theory development in the social sciences. The MIT Press, Cambridge

Germani G (1962) Política y sociedad en una época de transición. De la sociedad tradicional a la sociedad de masas. Editorial Paidós, Buenos Aires

Golden D, Poterba J (1980) The price of popularity: the political business cycle reexamined. Am J Polit Sci 24(4) (Midwest Political Science Association, Bloomington)

Goodin R, Klingemann HD (eds) (1996) A New handbook of political science. Oxford University Press, Oxford

Gorz A (1985) L'allocation universelle: version de droite et version de gauche. In: La Revue Nouvelle, no 81

Gough I (1975) State expenditure in advanced capitalism. New Left Rev 1(92) (New Left Review, London)

Gough I (1979) The political economy of the welfare state. Macmillan, London

Gough I, Wood G (eds) (2004) Insecurity and welfare regimes in Asia, Africa, and Latin America: social policy in developmental contexts. Cambridge University Press, Cambridge

Gough I, Wood G (2006) A comparative welfare regime approach to global social policy. World Polit 34(10) (Cambridge University Press, Cambridge)

Gourevitch P (1986) Politics in hard times. Cornell University Press, Ithaca

Gramsci A (2000)[1948] The Antonio Gramsci reader: selected writings 1916–1935. New York University Press, New York

Griffin L, Devine J, Wallace M (1983) On the economic and political determinants of welfare spending in the post-war era. Polit Soc 13 (SAGE Publications, Thousand Oaks)

Gudynas E (2009) Diez tesis urgentes sobre el nuevo extractivismo: contextos y demandas bajo el progresismo sudamericano actual. In: Schuldt J, Acosta A, Barandiarán A, Folchi M, Bebbington A, Alayza A, Gudynas E (eds) Extractivismo, política y sociedad. Centro Andino de Acción Popular, Centro Latinoamericano de Ecología Social, Quito

Gudynas E (2013) Extracciones, extractivismos y extrahecciones: un marco conceptual sobre la apropiación de recursos naturales. In: Observatorio del Desarrollo, no 18. Centro Latino Americano de Ecología Social, Montevideo

Haggard S, Kaufman R (2008) Development, democracy and welfare states: Latin America, East Asia, and Eastern Europe. Princeton University Press, Princeton

Hewitt C (1977) The effect of political democracy and social democracy on equality in industrial societies: a cross-national comparison. Am Sociol Rev 42 (American Sociological Association, Washington)

Hibbs D (1978) On the political economy of long-run trends in strike activity. Br J Polit Sci 8(2) (Cambridge University Press, Cambridge)

Hollingsworth R, Hanneman R (1982) Working-class power and the political economy of western capitalist societies. Comp Soc Res 5 (JAI Press, London)

Holloway J, Picciotto S (eds) (1978) State and capital: a Marxist debate. Edward Arnold, London

Hradil S (1980) Die Erforschung der Macht. Eine Übersicht über die empirische Ermittlung von Machtverteilungen durch die Sozialwissenschaften. Verlag W. Kohlhammer, Stuttgart

Huber E (2006) Un nuevo enfoque para la seguridad social en la región. In: Molina CG (ed) Universalismo básico: una nueva política social para América Latina. Banco Interamericano de Desarrollo, Washington

Huber E, Stephens J (2001) Development and crisis of the welfare state: parties and policies in global markets. The University of Chicago Press, Chicago

Huber E, Stephens J (2012) Democracy and the left: social policy and inequality in Latin America. The University of Chicago Press, Chicago

Isuani EA (2006) Importancia y posibilidades del ingreso ciudadano. In: Molina CG (ed) Universalismo básico: una nueva política social para América Latina. Banco Interamericano de Desarrollo, Washington

Kaiser R (2014) Qualitative Experteninterviews: Konzeptionelle Grundlagen und praktische Durchführung. Springer Publishing, New York

Kerr C, Dunlop J, Harbison F, Myers C (1964) Industrialism and industrial man. Oxford University Press, New York

Korpi W (1978) The working class in welfare capitalism: work, unions and politics in Sweden. Routledge and Kegan Paul, London

Korpi W (1983) The democratic class struggle. Routledge and Kegan Paul, London

Korpi W, Palme J (1998) The paradox of redistribution and strategies of equality: welfare state institutions, inequality, and poverty in the western countries. Am Sociol Rev 63(5) (American Sociological Association, Washington)

Korpi W, Shalev M (1980) Strikes, power and politics in the western nations, 1900–1976. Polit Power Soc Theory 2 (JAI Press, London)

Kuiper JP (1976) Arbeid en Inkomen: Twee Plichten en Twee Rechten. Sociaal Maandblad Arbeid 9 (Amsterdam)

Lander LE (2014) Venezuela: ¿crisis terminal del modelo petrolero rentista?. In: SinPermiso. http://www.sinpermiso.info/textos/venezuela-crisisterminal- del-modelo-petrolero-rentista

Lauth HJ, Pickel G, Pickel S (2009) Methoden der vergleichenden Politikwissenschaft: eine Einführung. VS Verlag für Sozialwissenschaften, Wiesbaden

Leguizamón SÁ (ed) (2005) Trabajo y producción de la pobreza en Latinoamérica y el Caribe: estructuras, discursos y actores. Consejo Latinoamericano de Ciencias Sociales, Buenos Aires

Leibfried S (1992) Towards a European welfare state: on integrating poverty regimes in the European community. In: Ferge Z, Kolberg JE (eds) Social policy in a changing Europe. Campus Verlag, Frankfurt

Lewis W (1954) Economic development with unlimited supplies of labour. In: The Manchester School, vol 22, no 2. Wiley, New Jersey

Li B (2012) From a micro–macro framework to a micro–meso–macro framework. In: Christensen S, Mitcham C, Li B (eds) Engineering, development and philosophy. Springer Publishing, New York

Lo Vuolo R (2009) Social exclusion policies and labour markets in Latin America. In: Hujo K, Mcclanahan S (eds) Financing social policy mobilizing resources for social development. Springer Publishing, New York

Lukes S (2005)[1974] Power: a radical view. Palgrave Macmillan, Basingstoke

M Coromoto García Mantilla (2009) La seguridad social en el marco de la Constitución de la República Bolivariana de Venezuela. Vadell Hermanos Editores, Caracas

Mac Kay A, Vanevery J (2000) Gender, family, and income maintenance: a feminist case for citizen's basic income. Soc Polit 7(2) (Oxford University Press, Oxford)

Maloney W (2004) Informality revisited. World Develop 32(7) (Elsevier, Amsterdam)

Mann M (1984) The autonomous power of the state: its origins, mechanisms and results. Arch Europeennes Sociologie 25 (Cambridge University Press, Cambridge)

Marklund S (1982) Capitalisms and collective income protection: a comparative study of the development of social security programs in Europe and the USA 1930–1975. Research reports from the department of sociology, no. 68. University of Umea, Umea

Marshall TH (1950) Citizenship and social class: and other essays. Cambridge University Press, Cambridge

Massad T (1978) Disruption, organization and reform: a critique of Piven and Cloward. Harvard University Press, Cambridge

Medici A (2006) Políticas y acceso universal a servicios de salud. In: Molina CG (ed) Universalismo básico: una nueva política social para América Latina. Banco Interamericano de Desarrollo, Washington

Medina F, Galván M (2008) Descomposición del coeficiente de Gini por fuentes de ingreso: evidencia empírica para América Latina 1999–2005. Comisión Económica para América Latina y el Caribe, Santiago de Chile

Méndez Cegarra A (2015) Desconocimiento de la ley. http://absalonmendezcegarra.blogspot.de/2 015/05/desconocimiento-de-la-ley.html

Mesa-Lago C (2007) Reassembling social security: a survey of pensions and health care reforms in Latin America. Oxford University Press, Oxford

Meuser M, Nagel U (2009) Das Experteninterview—konzeptionelle

Meyer N, Petersen H, Sorensen V (1981)[1978] Revolt from the center. Marion Boyars, London

Mignolo W (1999) Local histories/global designs: coloniality, subaltern knowledges and border thinking. Princeton University Press, Princeton

Miliband R (1973) Poulantzas and the capitalist state. New Left Rev 1(82) (New Left Review, London)

Mill JS (2006)[1859] On liberty and the subjection of women. Penguin Books, London

Mill JS (2011)[1843] A system of logic. Cambridge University Press, Cambridge

Mishra R (1984) The welfare state in crisis: social thought and social change. Saint Martin's Press, New York

Mitschke J (1985) Steuer- und Transferordnung aus einem Guß. Entwurf einer Neugestaltung der direkten Steuern und Sozialtransfers in der Bundesrepublik Deutschland. Nomos, Baden-Baden

Molina CG (ed) (2006) Universalismo básico: una nueva política social para América Latina. Banco Interamericano de Desarrollo, Washington

Moraña M (2008) Negotiating the local: the latin American "pink tide" or what's left for the left? Can J Lat Am Caribb Stud (The Canadian Association for Latin American and Caribbean Studies, Toronto)

Müller W, Neusüss C (1978) The 'welfare-state illusion' and the contradiction between wage labour and capital. In: Holloway J, Picciotto S (eds) State and capital: a Marxist debate. Edward Arnold, London

Myles J (1984) Old age in the welfare state: the political economy of public pension. Little Brown, Boston

Néstor GC (1990) Culturas híbridas. Estrategias para entrar y salir de la modernidad. Editorial Paidós, Buenos Aires

Norton A, Conway T, Foster M (2001) Social protection concepts and approaches: implications for policy and practice in international development. Overseas Development Institute, London

O'Connor J (1973) The fiscal crisis of the state. Saint Martin's Press, New York

O'Donnell G (1975) Reflexiones sobre las tendencias generales de cambio del estado burocrático-autoritario. In: Documento CEDES, núm. 1. Centro de Estudios de Estado y Sociedad, Buenos Aires

O'Donnell G (1977) Estado y alianzas en la Argentina, 1956–1976. Desarrollo Económico 16(64) (Instituto de Desarrollo Económico y Social, Buenos Aires)

Offe C (1975) Berufsbildungsreform. Eine Fallstudie über Reformpolitik. Suhrkamp Verlag, Frankfurt am Main

Offe C (1984) Contradictions of the welfare state. Hutchinson Publishing Group, London

Opertti R (2006) Una nueva agenda de cambios educativos. In: Molina CG (ed) Universalismo básico: una nueva política social para América Latina. Banco Interamericano de Desarrollo, Washington

Pickel S, Pickel G, Lauth HJ, Jahn D (eds) (2009) Methoden der vergleichenden Politik- und Sozialwissenschaft: neue Entwicklungen und Anwendungen. VS Verlag für Sozialwissenschaften, Wiesbaden

Piven F, Cloward R (1971) Regulating the poor: the functions of public welfare. Pantheon Books, New York

Piven F (2006) Challenging authority: how ordinary people change America. Rowman & Littlefield Publishers, Lanham

Piven F, Cloward R (1977) Poor people's movements: why they succeed, how they fail. Vintage Books, New York

Portantiero JC (1973) Clases dominantes y crisis política en la Argentina. In: Braun O (ed) El capitalismo argentino en crisis. Siglo XXI Editores, Buenos Aires

Portantiero JC (1977) Economía y política en la crisis argentina: 1958–1973. Rev Mex Sociol 39(2) (Universidad Nacional Autónoma de México, México)

Portantiero JC (1985) Notas sobre crisis y producción de acción hegemónica. In: Labastida J, Del Campo M (eds) Hegemonía y alternativas políticas en América Latina (Seminario de Morelia). Siglo XXI Editores, México

Portantiero JC (1988) La producción de un orden. Ensayos sobre la democracia entre el estado y la sociedad. Ediciones Nueva Visión, Buenos Aires

Poulantzas N (1973) Political power and social classes. New Left Books, London

Pribble J (2006) Women and welfare: the politics of coping with new social risks in Chile and Uruguay. Latin American Studies Association, Pittsburgh

PROVEA (Programa Venezolano de Educación-Acción en Derechos Humanos) (2007) Situación de los derechos humanos en Venezuela: informe anual 2007. Programa Venezolano de Educación—Acción en Derechos Humanos (PROVEA), Caracas

PROVEA (Programa Venezolano De Educación-Acción En Derechos Humanos) (2013) Situación de los derechos humanos en Venezuela: informe anual 2013. Programa Venezolano de Educación—Acción en Derechos Humanos (PROVEA), Caracas

Pryor F (1968) Public expenditures in communist and capitalist nations. Richard. D Irwin Inc, Homewood

Przeworski A, Teune H (1970) The logic of comparative social inquiry. Wiley, New Jersey

Rezk E (2006) Desafíos de la viabilidad financiera. In: Molina CG (ed) Universalismo básico: una nueva política social para América Latina. Banco Interamericano de Desarrollo, Washington

Ribe H, Robalino D, Ian W (2010) Achieving effective social protection for all in Latin America and the Caribbean. From right to reality. World Bank, Washington

Rieger E (1998) Soziologische Theorie und Sozialpolitik im entwickelten Wohlfahrtsstaat. In: Lessenich S, Ostner I (eds) Welten des Wohlfahrtskapitalismus. Campus Verlag, Frankfurt

Rudra N (2007) Welfare states in developing countries: unique or universal? J Polit 69(2) (Southern Political Science Association, Atlanta)

Ruiz Viñals C (2004) Políticas sociolaborales: un enfoque pluridisciplinar. Editoria UOC, Barcelona

Sader E (2008) Refundar el estado. Posneoliberalismo en América Latina. Instituto de Estudios y Formación de la Central de Trabajadores de la Argentina, Buenos Aires

Salcedo González AM (2006) Consideraciones sobre la reforma de la seguridad social en Venezuela. Comisión de Estudios de Postgrado, Facultad de Ciencias Económicas y Sociales, Universidad Central de Venezuela, Fondo Editorial Tropykos, Caracas

Schmalz S, Dörre K (2013) Comeback der Gewerkschaften? Machtressourcen, innovative Praktiken, internationale Perspektiven. Campus Verlag, Frankfurt

Schmid T (ed) (1984) Befreiung von falscher Arbeit. Thesen zum garantierten Mindesteinkommen. Wagenbach, Berlin

Schmidt M (1982) The role of parties in shaping macro-economic policies. In: Castels FG (ed) The impact of parties: politics and policies in democratic capitalist states. Sage, London

Schmitter P, Lembruch G (eds) (1979) Trends towards corporatist intermediation. Sage, London

SENPLADES (Secretaría Nacional de Planificación y Desarrollo) (2007) Plan nacional de desarrollo 2007–2010. Planificación para la revolución ciudadana. Secretaría Nacional de Planificación y Desarrollo, Quito

Shalev M (1983) The social democratic model and beyond: two generations of comparative research on the welfare state. Comp Soc Res 6 (JAI Press, London)

Shepherd A (2004) Policy paper on social protection. Department for International Development, London

Siaroff A (1994) Work, welfare and gender equality: a new typology. In: Sainsbury D (ed) Gendering welfare states. Sage, London

Simões A (2006) Los programas de transferencia: una complementariedad posible y deseable. In: Molina CG (ed) Universalismo básico: una nueva política social para América Latina. Banco Interamericano de Desarrollo, Washington

Skocpol T, Amenta E (1985) Did Capitalists Shape Social Security? (A comment on Quadagno 1984). Am Sociol Rev 50(4) (American Sociological Association, Washington)

Skocpol T, Amenta E (1986) States and social policies. Ann Rev Sociol 12 (Annual Reviews, Palo Alto)

Skocpol T, Amenta E (1994) Redefining the new deal: world war II and the development of social provision in the United States. In: Skocpol T (ed) Social policies in the United States: future possibilities in historical perspective. Princeton University Press, Princeton

Skocpol T, Ikenberry J (1983) The political formation of the American welfare state in historical and comparative perspective. Comp Soc Res 6 (JAI Press, London)

Stephens J (1979) The transition from capitalism to socialism. Macmillan, London

Stolowicz B (ed) (2007) Gobiernos de izquierda en América Latina. Un balance político. Ediciones Aurora, Bogotá

Therborn G (1986) Karl Marx returning: the welfare state and neo-marxist, corporatist and statist theories. Int Polit Sci Rev 7(2) (Sage, London)

Tobar F (2006) ¿Qué es universalismo básico en salud? In: Molina CG (ed) Universalismo básico: una nueva política social para América Latina. Banco Interamericano de Desarrollo, Washington

Tokman V (2006) Empleo y protección: una vinculación necesaria. In: Molina CG (ed) Universalismo básico: una nueva política social para América Latina. Banco Interamericano de Desarrollo, Washington

Tufte E (1978) Political control of the economy. Princeton University Press, Princeton

UN (United Nations) (2015) Human development report 2015. United Nations, New York

Van Evera S (1997) Guide to methods for students of political science. Cornell University Press, Ithaca

Wehr I (2009) Esping-Andersen travels South: Einige kritische Anmerkungen zur vergleichenden Wohlfahrtsregimeforschung. Peripherie: Zeitschrift für Politik und Ökonomie in der Dritten Welt 29(2) (Westfälisches Dampfboot, Münster)

Weinmann N, Burchardt HJ (2010) Die Reise des jungen Offe – ein Besuchs- und Forschungsprogramm für Lateinamerika? In: Burchardt HJ, Peters S, Weinmann N (eds) Arbeit in globaler Perspektive. Facetten informeller Beschäftigung. Campus Verlag, Frankfurt

Weir M, Skocpol T (1985) State structures and the possibilities for "Keynesian" responses to the great depression in Sweden, Britain, and the United States. In: Evans P, Rueshemeyer D, Skocpol T (eds) Bringing the state back in. Cambridge University Press, Cambridge

Wilensky H (1975) The welfare state and equality: structural and ideological roots of public expenditures. University of California Press, Berkeley

Wilensky H (1981) Leftism, Catholicism and democratic corporatism. In: Flora P, Heidenheimer A (eds) The development of welfare states in Europe and America. Transaction Books, London

Wilensky H (1987) Comparative social policy: theories, methods, findings. In: Dierkes M, Antal A (eds) Comparative policy research: learning from experience. Aldershot, Gower

Williamson J, Fleming J (1977) Convergence theory and the social welfare sector: a cross-national analysis. Int J Comp Sociol 18(3) (Leiden, Brill)

Wright EO (1994) Interrogating inequality: essays on class analysis, socialism and Marxism. Verso, London

Chapter 3
Analysis of the Power Struggles over the Post-neoliberal Social Security System Reform in Venezuela

This chapter breaks down the power struggles over the post-neoliberal social security system reform in Venezuela. The analysis is carried out following the complementary approach brought forward in Chap. 2, which commingles the conceptual framework of the Poulantzian approach and the operational framework of the political class struggle approaches. The chapter is structuralized into three parts.

The first part contextualizes the power struggles over the reform, for which it carries through a detailed reconstruction of the reform process and its social, economic, and political context.

The second part operationalizes the power struggles over the reform resorting to the concept of power resources, which is transubstantiated for the analysis of the reform in Venezuela. Both, the contextualization and the operationalization are structuralized around the four analytical dimensions explained in Chap. 2, symbolized by the questions "where", "what", "who", and "how".

Finally, the third part recapitulates the findings of the analysis.

3.1 Contextualization of the Power Struggles over the Post-neoliberal Social Security System Reform

As explained in Chap. 2, the contextualization of the power struggles over the post-neoliberal social security system reform in Venezuela is carried out on the basis of the Poulantzian approach to social policy. The use of the Poulantzian approach for the contextualization is predicated on its overall theoretical perspective, which conceptualizes social policy within the context of the construction of hegemony. In doing so, the Poulantzian approach automatically associates social policy with the historical, social, economic, and political conditions in which social policy materializes. Following this perspective, the subsequent contextualization carries out a detailed reconstruction of the power struggles over the social security system reform

© Springer Nature Switzerland AG 2019
E. L. Bistoletti, *The Power Struggles over the Post-neoliberal Social Security System Reforms in Venezuela and Ecuador*, The Latin American Studies Book Series, https://doi.org/10.1007/978-3-319-98168-0_3

in Venezuela which delineates the social, economic, and political conditions in which they came about.

The reconstruction undertakes to puzzle out the four "questions" proposed in the first chapter as analytical guidelines for the contextualization: (1) "where", (2) "what", (3) "who", and (4) "how". As pointed out, these questions correlate four analytical dimensions: (1) the structural underpinnings underlying social policy, (2) the concrete points of conflict over social policy, (3) the real actors involved in the struggles over social policy, and (4) the channels through which the struggles are canalized. In order to carry out an intelligible recount of the power struggles over the reform, the reconstruction is chronologically structuralized. However, the four aforementioned questions can be easily acknowledged throughout the reconstruction. In addition, the answers to the "where", "what", "who", and "how" questions are broken down in the summary of the contextualization.

3.1.1   The History of Social Security in Venezuela

The first legal reference to social insurance in Venezuela came out in the Ley del Trabajo (English: Law of Work) (G.O. 19640, 16/07/1936) sanctioned in 1936, which prescribed established that the government would bring about a compulsory social insurance (Zambrano Gutiérrez 2004). In compliance with this, the government promulgated the Ley del Seguro Social Obligatorio (English: Law of the Compulsory Social Insurance) (24/06/1940) (hereinafter LSSO) in 1940, whose implementation came about 4 years later, when the government brought out the Reglamento General de la Ley del Seguro Social Obligatorio (English: General Regulations of the Law of the Compulsory Social Insurance). Thereby, the LSSO established the very first social insurance in Venezuela, comprising sickness, maternity, and labor risks. However, the jurisdiction of the LSSO was circumscribed to the capital city and a part of the state of Miranda. Two years later, in 1946, the congress carried out the first reform of the LSSO, creating the Instituto Venezolano de los Seguros Sociales (English: Venezuelan Institute of the Social Insurances) (hereinafter IVSS) for the management of the existing social insurances (Fernández 2007: 72).

In 1951, the congress struck down the LSSO and promulgated the Estatuto Orgánico del Seguro Social Obligatorio (English: Organic Statute of the Compulsory Social Insurance) (G.O.E. 310, 05/10/1951) (hereinafter EOSSO instead, which determined the inception of the social security system in Venezuela. Next, to the aforementioned protection against sickness, maternity, and labor risks, the EOSSO brought about protection against layoffs. Thus, by the time the Pacto de Punto Fijo (English: Punto Fijo Agreement) was subscribed in 1958, Venezuela had legally established a social security system. In line with this, the preamble of the constitution sanctioned 3 years later, in 1961, predicated that the promotion of social security represented one of the purposes of the new constitution. Furthermore, the constitutional article 94 prescribed the progressive development of a comprehensive social security system including protection against old age (Fernández 2007: 73).

However, as the constitutional reference to the "progressive" development of the social security system brings out, the legal establishment of the social security system was not accompanied by its real development. According to Vifañe, in 1991, the social security system barely comprised 35% of the economically active population (Vifañe 1991). Basically, the underdevelopment of the system was associated with the lack of public institutions with the capacity to bring about the social services prescribed by the law. As a result, in the absence of an effectively functioning social security system, the emergence of special social security regimes rapidly came along among the better-paid workers.

In 1966, the government promulgated the Ley del Seguro Social (English: Law of the Social Insurance) (G.O.E. 1023, 11/07/1966), which finally established the pension system (Vifañe 1991). As the public institution in charge of the social insurances, the IVSS took over the administration of the newly created pension system. Eight years later, in 1975, the Decreto 878 (English: Decree 8 78) prescribed the extension of the (previously limited) pension system to the entire national territory (Fernández 2007).

From its inception, the pension system was characterized by structural flaws due to the low compulsory contributions prescribed by the law. Besides, the discretionary use of the pension funds by the successive governments and the steep devaluation of the national currency in 1983 devastated the pension finances. In consequence, by the time the first retirements came about in 1983, the pension system was already collapsed. In this context, the idea of privatizing the social security system increasingly advanced.

3.1.2 The Privatization of the Social Security System

The first systematically formulated proposal for the privatization of the social security system came out in 1989 in connection with the political program known as the "Gran Viraje" (English: Great Turn) (hereinafter GV), proposed by the president Carlos Andrés Pérez. The GV brought forward the inception of a new development model based in the private economy and the consequent restructuring of the state aimed at ameliorating its efficiency (Alvarado Chacín 2003: 112–113). With regard to the social security system, the GV clearly publicized the introduction of the private sector into the social insurance system (COORDIPLAN 1990: 15–16).

The GV was associated with the Plan de Enfrentamiento a la Pobreza (English: Plan for Fighting against Poverty) (hereinafter PEP) which basically delineated the implementation of focalized social programs according to the guidelines of the IMF in order to ameliorate the (expected) negative social effects of the "Gran Viraje" (D'Elía 2002). The social programs of the PEP were successively carried through, however, the social insurance system reform did not materialize due to the massive popular rejection against the policies of the GV (Méndez Cegarra 2006).

After the destitution of Carlos Andrés Pérez, the government of Rafael Caldera brought forward the Plan de Solidaridad Social (English: Plan of Social Solidarity) and the Plan de Recuperación y Estabilización Macroeconómica (English: Plan of Macroeconomic Recovery and Stabilization) in 1994, which essentially held down the social programs of the PEP with minor modifications (España 1997; Gutiérrez Briceño 2008). However, Caldera also reactivated the social insurance system privatization, as he established a commission called Comisión Reestructuradora (English: Restructuring Commission) in order to break down the existing reform proposals. Exceeding its mandate, the presidential commission brought out its own reform proposal in August 1995, advocating the introduction of the private sector into the social insurance system. However, this proposal was relegated due to the controversial composition of the presidential commission (Méndez Cegarra 2006).

Against this background, in November 1996, Caldera commissioned a tripartite committee comprising representatives of the state, the labor unions (the CTV, the CUTV, the CODESA and the CGT) and the employers' organizations (the FEDECAMARAS) in order to delineate the social security system reform (Hernández Ledezma 2009). The convening of the tripartite committee came about in connection with the "Agenda Venezuela" (AV), the political program which the president Caldera had annunciated a few months before. The AV represented a turnaround in the course of the government, as it openly advanced the neoliberal policies recommend by the IMF which Caldera had previously repudiated (Gutiérrez Briceño 2008). In consonance with the neoliberal orientation of the AV, the tripartite committee brought out its privatization proposal in March 1997. Unlike the previously circulating privatization proposals, the proposal of the tripartite committee purposed the establishment of a completely privatized social insurance system which resembled the Chilean social security system implemented by the military government of Augusto Pinochet in 1980 (Interview Rafael Ríos). For this reason, the CUTV determined to abandon the tripartite committee during the course of its deliberations (Hernández Ledezma 2009: 151).

Once finished, the government restructuralized the reform proposal of the tripartite committee into a bill and handed it over to the congress for its approval. With the support of the political parties Acción Democrática (English: Democratic Action) (hereinafter AD) and Comité de Organización Política Electoral Independiente (English: Independent Political Electoral Organization Committee) (hereinafter COPEI), the bill was brought officially out by the congress after an extremely fast legislative treatment in June 1997. Finally, the government promulgated the Ley Orgánica del Sistema de Seguridad Social Integral (English: Organic Law of the Integral System of Social Security) (hereinafter LOSSSI) on 30 December 1997 (G.O.E. 5199, 30/12/1997).

As an organic law, the LOSSSI delineated the guidelines for the social security system privatization but it did not particularize the specifics for the privatization of its subsystems. To this aim, the LOSSSI established the sanction of six special laws, including one for each of its five subsystems (the pension subsystem, the health subsystem, the unemployment and professional training subsystem, and the recreation subsystem), and one for the liquidation of the IVSS. However, since the legislative period was reduced due to the upcoming presidential election, the congress could not bring out the required laws. For this reason and in line with the extremely fast legislative treatment of the LOSSSI, the congress commissioned the government to legislate through an enabling law (Méndez Cegarra 1998). Accordingly, a few weeks before the presidential election held in December 1990 the government promulgated the Decreto 2744 (English: Decree 2744) (G.O. 36557, 09/10/1998), regulating the liquidation of the IVSS; the Decreto con Rango y Fuerza de Ley 2944 (English: Decree with Status and Force of Law 2944) (G.O. 36568, 27/10/1998), regulating the health subsystem; the Decreto con Rango y Fuerza de Ley 2963 (English: Decree with Status and Force of Law 2963) (G.O. 36575, 05/11/1998), regulating the unemployment and professional training subsystem; the Decreto con Rango y Fuerza de Ley 2992 (English: Decree with Status and Force of Law 2992) (G.O. 36575, 05/11/1998), regulating the housing subsystem; and the Decreto con Rango y Fuerza de Ley 2993 (English: Decree with Status and Force of Law 2993) (G.O. 36575, 05/11/1998), regulating the pension subsystem. Naturally, due to the impending presidential election, the implementation of the LOSSSI carried over into the next government.

3.1.3 The Subject of Social Security in the Electoral Campaign of Hugo Chávez for the Presidential Election of 1998

The first public pronouncement made by Hugo Chávez regarding social security came out in the "Agenda alternativa bolivariana: una propuesta patriótica para salir del laberinto" (English: Alternative Bolivarian Agenda: a patriotic proposal to get out of the labyrinth) (hereinafter ABB), a political manifesto composed by Chávez in 1996. Basically, the ABB delineated the social, economic and political guidelines of the Bolivarian[1] movement led by Chávez. With regard to social security, the ABB repudiated the aforementioned neoliberal program known as "Agenda Venezuela" and its compensatory approach to social policy (Chávez 2007: 36). In opposition to it, the ABB promulgated the priority of social over economic policy and, most important, it annunciated the necessity of a social security system reform for the first time (Chávez 2007: 36–37).

One year later, in 1997, Chávez established the political party Movimiento V República (English: Movement V Republic) (hereinafter MVR) in order to participate in the forthcoming presidential election. In line with this, Chávez congregated a group of experts in order to delineate the electoral program of the MVR for the presidential election of 1998. Whereas relatively few experts participated in the formulation of the general guidelines (El Universal 10/03/2002), numerous experts were congregated for the formulation of the specific sections.

Under the title "La propuesta de Hugo Chávez... para transformar a Venezuela. Una revolución democrática" (English: Hugo Chávez' proposal... to transform Venezuela. A democratic revolution), the program was finally brought out in April

---

[1] Bolivarianism represents a political doctrine inspired by Latin American independence hero Simón Bolívar.

1998. The program comprised five parts, each of which addressed a thematic area aiming at a stable transition. These five parts encompassed the following topics: (1) Equilibrio político (English: Political stability), Equilibrio social (English: Social stability", (2) Equilibrio economic (English: Economic stability), (3) Equilibrio territorial (English: Territorial stability) and (4) Equilibrio mundial (English: World stability). The second part, "Equilibrio social", contained thirteen sections, one of which concentrated on social security. For the composition of this section Juan de Jesús Montilla, one of the experts who participated in the shaping of the entire program, commissioned Absalón Méndez Cegarra, a fellow lecturer of the Universidad Central de Venezuela and a renowned expert on social security (Méndez Cegarra 2005: 67).

Unlike the ABB, the section on social security of the political program for the presidential elections of 1998 brought forward a detailed proposal regarding social security. In its beginning, the program broke down the multiple causes of the crisis if social security system (Chávez 1998: 16).

The program came out in April 1998, only a few months after the promulgation of the Ley Orgánica del Sistema de Seguridad Social Integral (English: Organic Law of the Integral Social Security System) (LOSSSI) promoted by the government of President Caldera. As explained before, the LOSSSI established a neoliberal social security system reform with the creation of the private pension funds known as Administradora de Fondos de Pensiones (English: Pension Funds Administrator) (hereinafter AFP). In this regard, the program characterized the social security system reform as a fraud to the Venezuelan workers and pointed out the financial unviability of the system promoted by Caldera's reform (Chávez 1998: 16).

Further on, the program delineated the guidelines around which the future system of social security should be established. According to the program, the system of social security had to acknowledge the principles of universalism, solidarity, integration, and unity (Chávez 1998: 17). These principles contravened the ongoing neoliberal social security system reform in two main ways. In the first place, they repudiated the commodification of social security by establishing the universal right to social security and the principle of solidarity as the paradigm for its financing. In the second place, they presupposed the suppression of the numerous existing special pension regimes, whose uncontrolled expansion had come about at the expense of the general regime (Chávez 1998: 16).

The rejection of the LOSSI came out openly in Chávez electoral speeches as well. During the presidential campaign of 1998, he harshly criticized the neoliberal orientation of Caldera's social security system reform. Moreover, he undertook to strike down Caldera's reform as soon as he took over the presidency (Méndez Cegarra 2005: 67). Chávez' rejection of Caldera's reform contravened the position of his main competitor for presidency, Henrique Salas Römer, in this regard. During his campaign, Salas Römer openly advocated the introduction of individual capitalization into the pension system (Notitarde 19/10/1998).

In an electoral campaign dominated by the candidates' attempt to personalize the idea of a complete break with past (López Maya 2005; Bistoletti 2011), Chávez successfully came across as the agent of a radical change better than the rest of the presidential candidates. Among other factors, Chávez' rejection of the ongoing privatization of the social security system substantiated this perception. In the presidential election held on 6 December 1998 Chávez accomplished a remarkable victory, receiving 56.20% of the votes. Henrique Salas Römer barely attained 39.97% of the suffrages.

3.1.4 The Struggles over the Formulation and Passing of the Decree-Laws Suspending the Implementation of the LOSSSI

A few days after the presidential election, the outgoing government of Rafael Caldera and the incoming government of Hugo Chávez established the Comisiones de Enlace (English: Liaison Commissions) in order to supervise the governmental transition. The creation of the liaison commissions for the government transition represented a historic custom in Venezuelan politics. In this case, five thematic commissions were established under the coordination of Luis Giordani, who had supervised the aforementioned political program of MVR for the presidential election. The liaison commissions comprised of five working groups: (1) a social commission coordinated by the UCV's professor Hector Navarro, (2) an economic commission, (3) a political commission, (4) a territorial commission, and (5) an international commission (El Universal 13/12/1998). These thematic commissions comprised, in turn, more specific subcommissions. The subject of social security was deliberated by the subcommission of health and social security coordinated by the UCV's rector Luis Fuenmayor Toro.

Even though the subcommission of health and social security was only commissioned to carry out an evaluation of the health sector and the social security system, the existence of contending positions and interests regarding both subjects came out during its work. In this context, the coordinator of the subcommission, Luis Fuenmayor Toro, publicly asseverated that the health and social security laws promulgated by Caldera's government would bring about the privatization of hospitals and pension funds, for which their implementation had to be held over until the passing of new laws (El Universal 31/12/1999).

Another member of the subcommission of health and social security, UCV's professor Absalón Méndez Cegarra advocated this position as well. In one of the meetings of the subcommission, Méndez Cegarra pointed out the urgent need to carry over the imminent implementation of the LOSSSI (prescribed for 31 December 1999). To this end, he advocated the passing of a partial reform law differing the implementation of the LOSSSI until a fully new organic law of social security was promulgated (Méndez Cegarra 2005: 69).

Above all, the necessity of a postponement of the LOSSI was associated with the imminent liquidation of the IVSS, the public state office in charge of social security in Venezuela, prescribed by the LOSSSI for 31 December 1999. Since no social security institution had yet been established in replacement of the IVSS, its liquidation would immediately generate the total collapse of the social security system nationwide.

For this reason, Méndez Cegarra handed over a draft bill for the partial reform of the LOSSSI to the social commission (Méndez Cegarra 2005: 69). This draft bill was concatenated with the report of the social commission, which was finally handed over to Chávez before his assumption. Chávez did not reciprocate it until February 1999, when he requisitioned the sanction of a "ley habilitante" (English: enabling law) to the assembly in order to bring about legislation on several matters, including social security, for a 6 months period. With this request, Chávez indirectly repudiated the proposal of the liaison commission, which advocated the passing of a law to carry over the implementation of the LOSSSI until the sanction of a new organic law of social security.

After several discussions, the National Assembly finally countenanced the president's request almost entirely with the sanction of an enabling law on 22 April 1999. After its promulgation a few days later, on 26 April 1999, president Chávez was capacitated to bring about legislation on several financial, administrative, and social matters, including social security, for the next 6 months.

Once empowered by the enabling law, Chávez promulgated altogether 63 decree-laws during the following 6 months. He did not bring about any specific decree-laws on social security until the very last week of the 6 months period prescribed by the enabling law, when he promulgated four decree-laws modifying the LOSSSI and its regulatory norms. Before that, only one decree-law dictated by Chávez, namely the Decreto con Rango y Fuerza de Ley Orgánica de Reforma de la Ley Orgánica de la Administración Central (English: Decree Law with Status and Force of Organic Law of Reform of the Organic Law of the Central administration) (G.O. 36775, 30/08/1999, Decree Law 369), was loosely associated with the subject of social security, as it established a unified ministry for health and social development. However, since this unified ministry was commissioned to manage the state's social policy, including the social security, it openly contravened the ministerial configuration prescribed by the LOSSSI, which established the administration of the social security under a unified ministry of labor and social security (Méndez Cegarra 2005: 73).

During his last week in possession of legislative powers, Chávez promulgated four decree-laws directly concerning the LOSSSI and its regulatory norms. Despite the formal rejection of the proposal made by the liaison commission, the content of these decree-laws fully corresponded with the content of the proposal of the liaison commission (Méndez Cegarra 2005: 72–74). Altogether, the four decree-laws comprised the following: (1) Decreto con rango y fuerza de Ley de Reforma del Decreto con rango y fuerza de Ley que regula el Subsistema de Paro Forzoso y Capacitación Profesional, el cual pasa a denominarse Decreto con rango y fuerza de Ley que regula el Subsistema de Paro Forzoso y Capacitación Laboral (English: Decree with status and force of Law of Reform of the Decree with status and force of Law that regulates the Subsystem of Layoff and Professional Training which becomes the Decree with the status and force of Law that regulates the Subsystem of Layoff and Labor Training), (2) Decreto con Rango y Fuerza de Ley de Reforma Parcial de la Ley Orgánica del Sistema de Seguridad Social Integral (English: Decree with status and force of Law of Partial Reform of the Organic Law of the Integral Social Security System) (G.O.E. 5398, 25/10/1999, Decree Law 424) (hereinafter Decree Law 424), (3) Decreto con rango y fuerza de Ley de Reforma Parcial del Decreto 2944 de fecha 14 de Octubre de 1998 (English: Decree with status and force of Law of Partial Reform of the Decree 2944 dated 14 October 1998) (G.O.E. 5398, 25/10/1999, Decree Law 425) (hereinafter Decree Law 425), and (4) Decreto con rango y fuerza de Ley de Reforma Parcial del Decreto 2993 de fecha 4 de noviembre de 1998 (English: Decree with Status and Force of Law of Partial Reform of the Decree 2993 dated 4 November 1998) (G.O.E. 5398, 25/10/1999, Decree Law 426) (hereinafter Decree Law 426).

The Decree Law 424 established the partial modification of the LOSSSI. Considering the 79 articles contained in the LOSSSI, the Decree Law 424 modified 50.63%, removed 3.53%, revoked 6.32% and incorporated 11.39% of them. Altogether this accounts for 70.87% of the articles originally included in the LOSSSI.[2] However, as noticed by Méndez Cegarra, most of these changes only represented formal and unsubstantial modifications (Méndez Cegarra 2005: 74). For this reason, the suspension of the imminent liquidation of the IVSS and the confirmation of its continuance as the public institution in charge of social security represented the most important modifications to the LOSSSI contained in the decree (G.O.E. 5398, 26/10/1999, Decree Law 424: 13–14).

In line with the Decree Law 424, the Decree Law 425, and the Decree Law 426 held over the implementation of the health and pension subsystems until 1 January 2001. Both subsystems were established by the LOSSSI and regulated by the Decree Law 2944 and the Decree Law 2993 sanctioned by Caldera in October and November 1998, respectively.

Later on, the Decree Law 424, the Decree Law 425, and the Decree Law 426 would be carried over twice (each time for additional six months) by the National Assembly since no new law replacing the LOSSSI was yet promulgated. These additional deferrals would be promulgated on 9 January 2001 (G.O. 37115, later corrected in G.O. 37125 due to printing errors) for the first time, and 6 months later for the second time.

While the sanction of the decree-laws suspending the implementation of the LOSSSI did not yet bring out the contending positions regarding the content of the social security system reform proposed by Chávez, it established two relevant elements which characterized the context in which the struggles around the reform came about from beginning to end.

The first element was associated to the chaotic development of legal proceedings regarding the reform. In this context, the uncoordinated comings and goings of the government and the assembly, the recurrent deferrals of unwanted legal norms and the continuous delays in the passing of annunciated laws determined a general land-

---

[2]In concrete, the Decree Law 424 restructuralized articles 1, 8, 9, 12, 13, 14, 16, 17, 20, 30, 31, 32, 34, 35, 39, 40, 41, 42, 43, 47, 48, 49, 50, 51, 53, 54, 55, 57, 58, 59, 64, 65, 66, 68, 70, 71 and 79, repositioned the articles 52 and 59, struck down articles 73, 75, 76, 77 and 78, and brought forward articles 63, 64, 65, 66, 67, 68, 69, 79 and 80 (Méndez Cegarra 2005: 74).

scape in which the actions of the actors at stake were strongly circumscribed by the incidental actions effectuated by other actors before. Within this chaotic framework, the sanction of any legal norm (as in the case of the decree-law reforming the structure of the central administration) could easily materialize as a determining factor for the formulation and passing of another unrelated law (as in the case of the LOSSSV).

For this reason, the process of reform in Venezuela could be characterized to a great extent as an "incidental" reform (Méndez Cegarra 2005: 72).

The second element was correlated with the president's propensity to accumulate political decisions in his office. This tendency came out for the first time in the process of reform when Chávez struck down the proposal made by the liaison commission of postponing the implementation of the LOSSSI through the sanction of a law but later promulgated himself a decree law in accordance with the proposal of the liaison commission.

These two elements—the incidental character of the reforms and the tendency toward the concentration of decisions in the presidency—came out for the first time during this initial phase of the social security system reform but they carried over during the entire process of reform. Thus, they composed the general context in which the struggles around the social security system reform came about.

3.1.5   The Struggles over the Formulation and Passing of the Constitutional Articles Concerning Social Security

During his presidential campaign, Chávez had brought forward the convocation of a constituent assembly for the formulation of a new constitution. Consequently, in his presidential inauguration on 2 February 1999 Chávez undertook the oath of office proclaiming the upcoming of a new constitution, after which he officially annunciated the realization of a binding constituent plebiscite through which Venezuelans would countenance or repudiate the formulation of a new constitution. Since Chávez electoral campaign had been predicated on the promise of a constituent assembly (López Maya 2005), the proposal of a constituent assembly received a massive popular approval in the plebiscite held on 25 April 1999, despite high electoral abstention. Due to this massive support, the political opposition determined to participate in the constituent process, nominating its candidates for the constituent assembly. However, in the election of the constituent assembly members held two months later, on 25 July 1999, the opposition parties accomplished catastrophic electoral results, as the governmental coalition took over 100 of the 104 seats at stake for the constituent assembly (El Universal 26/07/1999).

Even though the vast majority of the elected constituents politically countenanced the government either as members of MVR or allied parties, the profound differences among them concerning the subject of constitutional social rights came out as soon as the discussions of the constituent assembly started out. The opposed standpoints of the constituents with regard to the constitutional social rights and, more specifically, with regard to the constitutional rights to social security divaricated so widely that the discussions on the matter almost paralyzed the work of the constituent assembly (Méndez Cegarra 2005: 83). For this reason, the assembly deliberated on the constitutional articles concerning social security until only a few days before it officially subscribed its constitutional proposal and delivered it to the president.

The constituent assembly congregated from early August to late November 1999. Since its inception, the assembly received manifold proposals. Some of these proposals represented integral constitutional drafts, as in the case of the constitutional projects submitted by the president, the governmental coalition Polo Patriótico (English: Patriotic Pole) (hereinafter PP), the political party Patria para Todos (English: Fatherland for All) (hereinafter PPT) and the Comisión Constitucional de la Asamblea Nacional Constituyente (English: Constitutional Commission of the National Constituent Assembly) (hereinafter CCANC). However, most proposals submitted to the constituent assembly only revolved around specific topics (e.g., civil rights, institutional structure of the judiciary, form of government, etc.). In this manner, the Federación de Asociaciones de Profesores Universitarios de Venezuela (English: Federation of Associations of University Professors of Venezuela) (hereinafter FAPUV) brought forward a proposal containing only specific articles regarding the subject of social security.

Altogether, four proposals for the constitutional articles regarding social security were handed over to the constituent assembly: (1) the proposal submitted by President Hugo Chávez "Ideas Fundamentales para la Constitución Bolivariana de la V República" (English: Fundamental Ideas for the Bolivarian Constitution of the V Republic), (2) the proposal submitted by the PP, (3) the proposal submitted by the CCANC, which consecutively handed over two drafts of its proposal due to the incorporation of modifications, and (4) the proposal submitted by the FAPUV.

The four submitted proposals brought out substantial differences concerning essential aspects of social security.

In the first place, they divaricated in the fundamental matter regarding the right to social security whereas the proposals of the president, the CCANC, and the FAPUV explicitly established the right of everyone to social security, the proposal of the PP did not acknowledge it at all. In fact, the proposal of the PP resembled the conceptual approach of the current constitution sanctioned in 1961, which predicated a "progressive development" of social security without any explicit mention to the right to it (Constitución de la República de Venezuela 1961).

Even the proposals acknowledging the right to social security divaricated in the way in which they conceptualized this right. Thus, the proposal of the FAPUV pointed out that the right of "all persons" to social security coalesced both, the Venezuelan nationals and the foreigners legally residing in Venezuela, whereas the proposal of the CCANC associated the right of "all persons" to social security with the declaration of social security as a nonprofit public service. On the contrary, the proposal of the president predicated the right of "all people" to social security in a rather contradictory way, since it established the right to "accessible, universal, integral, equitable and solidary social security", countervailing the principle of universalism, related to the idea of social security for all, with the principle of accessibility, related to the idea of purchased social security.

In the second place, the proposals divaricated in the obligation of the state to materialize the fulfillment of the right to social security. Whereas the proposals of the CCANC and the FAPUV incontestably predicated this obligation, the proposal of the president advocated the obligation of the state to establish a social security system aimed at protecting and incorporating all inhabitants of the republic", and the proposal of the PP did not acknowledge the obligation of the state at all.

In the third place, the proposals contravened the essential question regarding the exclusion of profit from the realm of social security.

This fundamental issue is usually bandied about as the "privatization of social security" in common language, although this expression brings about two conceptual errors. First, the private character of social security does not necessarily presuppose its profit-making nature, as the existence of nonprofit public–private social security organizations (for example, the "obras sociales" of the labor unions in Argentina) corroborates. Second, the allusion to the privatization of social security presupposes the incorporation of profit-making administrators of individual pension funds while it completely brushes away the well-established existence of profit-making providers of health services. For this reason, the reference to the exclusion of profit corresponds much better with the subject at stake.

As explained before, the inclusion or the exclusion of the profit-making administrators of individual pension funds represented the first key point on which the struggles over the social security system reform were predicated. In principle, the constituent assembly was to delineate the general principles of social security in Venezuela without particularizing the specifics of the social security system, for which a specific law should be promulgated in the future. Nevertheless, the issue concerning the incorporation or the exclusion of the AFPs was indirectly brought forward in the constituent debates on social security as some of the proposals explicitly countenanced profit within the social security system.

The proposal of the CCANC repudiated the making of profit within the social security system by declaring social security as a "nonprofit public service" and the proposal of the FAPUV proscribed profit within the social security system as it established that social security represented a "basic and essential public service, not susceptible to commodification with the aim of profit". On the contrary, the proposals of the president and the PP did not exclude profit from the social security system in any way.

In the fourth place, the proposal divaricated on the structure of the social security system. This issue was associated with the elimination of the existing special pension regimes through their incorporation into a unified social security system.

As pointed out above, the elimination of the "special pension regimes" represented the second key point around which the struggles over the social security system reform revolved. The significance of this issue was predicated on the fact that the special pension regimes represented a substantial part of the Venezuelan social security system, even though their total number and their relative size within the social security system represented a complete enigma, even for the government.

They were exclusively associated with the state public sector, including the public administration, the universities, the state companies (PDVSA), the autonomous state institutions (IVSS, BCV), the national, provincial, and municipal police forces, etc.

The proposal of the CCANC established the creation of a "universal, comprehensive, solidarity-based, unitary, efficient and participative" social security system, whereas the proposals of the president, the PP, and the FAPUV did not bring forward any reference to a unitary system. In fact, the proposal of the FAPUV predicated the creation of one unified health care system but three separate pension systems: one for the salaried and autonomous workers of the private sector, one for the salaried workers of the public state sector and one for those unable to work or in social need. This special emphasis on the separation of the pension systems was associated with the fact that the state university professors capitalized on special pension regimes which brought about very high pensions for them. In the case of the UCV, for example, the professors handed over 4.00% of their salaries to social security but received pensions equivalent to 100.00% of their salaries. For this reason, the otherwise very universalistic proposal of the FAPUV carried over the existing special pension regimes of the public state sector.

During the initial phase of the constituent assembly, the legislative work was carried out by thematic commissions. These thematic commissions were commissioned to break down the submitted proposals, deliberate over them and finally bring about their own proposals for the constitution. After this, the proposals of the thematic commissions had to be deliberated by the plenary assembly in a first discussion. If the proposals came under observations in the first discussion, they had to be deliberated by the plenary assembly in a second discussion before countenancing them.

The submitted proposals on social security were deliberated by the Comisión de de Derechos Sociales y de la Familia (English: Commission of Social and Family Rights) (hereinafter CDS), in which the following constituents participated: Alexis Navarro, Lenin Romero, Marelis Pérez, Ángel Landaeta, David Figueroa, Julio César Alviárez, Froilán Barrios, Antonio Briceño, Raúl Esté, Victoria Mata, Sol Musett, Marisabel de Chávez, Pedro Ortega Díaz, José León Tapia, Osear Feo, Cristóbal Jiménez, Braulio Álvarez, Blancanieve Portocarrero, Haydée Machin, and Reina Romero.

After several heated discussions, the DCS finally subscribed to the second draft of the proposal of the CCANC. The proposal of the CCANC prescribed the right of all persons to social security as a nonprofit-making public service, established the obligation of the state to ensure the incorporation of all inhabitants to the social security system, dismissed the making of profit within social security and postulated a unitary system of social security. The second draft did not establish a "single social security system" as the first draft, but it still predicated a "unitary" system. Beyond this, both drafts corresponded quite well. During the first discussion in the plenary assembly the aforementioned contentions about social security, which had been held back within the CS, finally came out in full. The contending positions were represented by two groups: on the one side, a rather silent majority group in favor of a nonprofit-making unified social security system and on the other side a very active minority group in favor of a mixed and disaggregated social security system (Méndez Cegarra 2005: 79).

The speeches of the constituents Alberto Franceschi, Antonio Di Giampaolo, Leopoldo Puchi and Allan Brewer Carías concerning the proposal of the CS on health and social security during the first discussion of the plenary assembly perfectly characterized the position of the minority group. In a nutshell, these constitutents repudiated the "statist" and "anti-private sector" character of the social security system delineated in the draft, and they pointed out that the social security system devised in the draft would financially break down sooner or later due to its universalistic character.

Despite the opposition of the constituents of the minority group, the proposal of the CS was countenanced by the plenary assembly and brought forward for its second discussion.

The methodology of double discussions for the conflicting constitutional proposals looked upon the second discussion as an instance of consensus building. In the case of the constitutional articles on social security, however, the second discussion only maximized the already existing conflicts. The position of the minority group during the second discussion was brought out by the speech of the constituent Leopoldo Puchi, who once again pointed out the financial unsustainability of the social security system devised in the draft and reiterated the claim for the incorporation of private pension funds into the social security system (ANCV 12/1/1999: 59).

Finally, after a long debate, the proposal of the CS was countenanced by the plenary assembly in the second discussion and it was concatenated to the final constitutional proposal of the constituent assembly as the article 90. The article established the right of all people to social security, including social protection in the case of maternity, paternity, family, illness, incapacity, old age, labor risks, unemployment, and housing. Besides, the article acknowledged the obligation of the state in the provision of social security services for everyone, including for those without contributive capacity. Finally, the article delineated the creation of a universal social security system and closed out the private administration of the compulsory contributions to social security (ANCV 12/11/1999: 62).

Once the constituent assembly accomplished its work, its constitutional proposal came under a binding constitutional plebiscite held on 15 December 1999. The proposal of the constituent assembly was massively countenanced by the Venezuelans, who accompanied it with 71.78% of the votes. Finally, the constitution was promulgated by the executive power on 30 December 1999 when it formally came out in the Gaceta Oficial de la República Bolivariana de Venezuela (English: Official Gazette of the Bolivarian Republic of Venezuela (hereinafter G.O.), the official publication of the Venezuelan state, and later again on 24 March 2000 due to formal errors in the first publications (G.O. 36860 310/1271999 and G.O.E. 5453 24/03/2000).

Amazingly, the final text concerning social security was promulgated with several modifications compared to the text approved by the constituent assembly. While some of these modifications only represented stylistic changes, such as substituting "all persons" for "every person", some of these modifications brought about content changes. Without a doubt, the most important content modification was carried out in the passage referred to the administration of the obligatory contributions of workers to social security, which in the constitutional proposal of the constituent assembly explicitly repudiated the private profit-making administration of the contributions (ANCV 12/11/1999: 62).

The promulgated text restructuralized this fundamental passage by removing the reference to the private profit-making administration. Instead, it ambiguously established that the administration of the affiliates' contributions had to be carried out with "social purposes" under the state's supervision (GO 36860 30/12/1999: 312176).

This modification overtly contravened the express will of the constituents, who had clearly undertaken to deracinate the possibility of profit-making from social security. In the end, the resulting text was characterized by an obvious ambiguity, since it neither definitively repudiated nor acknowledged the participation of the private profit-making sector in social security.

Regardless of its institutional implications, this incident perfectly corresponds with the previous clashes around the social security system reform. As pointed out above, these clashes revolved around the participation of the private profit-making sector in the social security system and the continuation of the existing special pension regimes. Besides, the modification of the constitutional article on social security dovetailed with the aforementioned characteristic elements of the context in which the struggles around the social security system reform came about. Just as in the decree-laws suspending the implementation of the LOSSSI, the alteration of the constitutional article on social security brought out the overall chaotic development of the legal proceedings related to the post-neoliberal social security system reform and the fundamental role assumed by President Hugo Chávez in it.

Both, the sticking points around which the reform revolved—the participation of the private profit-making sector and the continuation of the special pension regimes—and the characteristic elements of the context in which the reform came about, carried over into the subsequent process of formulation and passing of the new law of social security recounted in the following section.

3.1.6 The Struggles over the Formulation and Passing of the LOSSSV

The sanction of the new constitution brought about the main guidelines for the social security system reform. Condensed in the article 86, these guidelines established: (1) the right of everyone to social security, (2) the nonprofit-making public service character of social security, (3) the scope of protection of social security (including integral health care; maternity, paternity, adoption, and temporary incapacity paid leaves; permanent partial incapacity, permanent complete incapacity, old age and survival pensions; family allowances and subsidies; housing support; and unemployment financial and professional assistance, (4) the solidary financing of social security (based on direct obligatory contributions from workers and employers, indirect contributions from state, and voluntary direct contributions from workers), and (5) the obligation of the state to carry through the fulfillment of the constitutional right of everyone to social security. Besides the new constitution additionally predicated the right of homemakers to social security (article 88), the right of cultural workers to social security (article 100), and the existence of a separate system of social security for the armed forces (article 328). Based on these premises, the new organic law of social security had to establish the foundation for the new social security system.

The social security system reform was deliberated in three stages (1) the Presidential Commission for the Formulation of the Draft Organic Bill of Social Security; (2) The First Reading of the LOSSSV in the National Assembly; and (3) The First Reading of the LOSSSV in the National Assembly. The following sections break down the struggles over the reform in all of them.

3.1.6.1 The Presidential Commission for the Formulation of the Draft Organic Bill of Social Security

During the first months after the sanction of the new constitution, the government could not undertake effective measures regarding the new organic law of social security because the new national legislative institution prescribed in the constitution, the Asamblea Nacional Legislativa (English: National Legislative Assembly) (hereinafter ANL), had not yet been constituted. Throughout this time, several social, economic, and political actors publicly anticipated that the constitution had not really proscribed the existence of private administrators of individual pension funds, openly promoting the inclusion of AFPs in the forthcoming organic law of social security. Interestingly, this position was not only advocated by the leaders of the Federación de Cámaras y Asociaciones de Comercio y Producción de Venezuela (English: Venezuelan Federation of Chambers of Commerce) (hereinafter FEDECAMARAS) and the Confederación de Trabajadores de Venezuela (English: Confederation of Workers of Venezuela) (hereinafter CTV), which had participated in the neoliberal social security system reform under Caldera's government in 1997 (Méndez Cegarra 2005), but also by members of the government. Minister of Labor Lino Martínez publicly asseverated that the article 86 of the new constitution did not contravene the creation of AFPs (El Universal 23/03/2000). Later, Martínez annunciated in an interview with a national newspaper that the government would bring about a mixed pension system with the participation of private AFPs for the new organic law of social security (El universal 07/08/2000).

Finally on 2 January 2000, exactly one week before the first legislative meeting of the (now unicameral) National Assembly, Chávez established by decree a Comisión presidencial para la Elaboración del Proyecto de Ley Orgánica de Seguridad Social (English: Presidential Commission for the Formulation of the Draft Organic Law of Social Security (hereinafter CPSS) (G.O. 37008 07/08/2000). The commission was supervised by the Vice President Julián Isaías Rodríguez and comprised the Minister of Production and Commerce, Juan de Jesús Montilla, the Miniters of Labor, Lino Martínez, the Minister of Health and Social Develompment, Gilberto Rodríguez

Ochoa, the Minister of Planification, Jorge Giordani, the Attorney General of the Republic, Heitel Alvarado, the Vice President of FEDECAMARAS, Alberto Cudemus, the presbyter José Ignacion Arrieta, three representatives of the civil society, Juan Carlos Uribe, Alberto Yáñez and Pedro Luis Garmendia, and one representative of the ANL, Oscar Feo.

Even though Chávez did not publicly bring out his position regarding the participation of the private sector in social security during this time, he allegedly advocated the establishment of a mixed social security system (Interviews with Absalón Méndez Cegarra, Aurelio Concheso and Rafael Ríos).

FEDECAMARAS, the largest employers' organization, was represented in the commission, whereas no labor union participated in it. Besides, the representatives of the civil society exclusively represented the financial sector. This situation was publicly denounced by CTV's president, Federico Ramírez León, who contemplated the overrepresentation of the financial sector as negative (El Universal 10/08/2000)

The reason for the unbalanced composition of the presidential commission was predicated on two reasons: (1) the aforementioned intention of the government to establish a mixed (public and private) social security system, and (2) the open political confrontation between the government and the labor unions, including the largest CTV, politically allied to the AD, and the smaller but well-established Confederación de Sindicatos Autónomos de Venezuela (English: Confederation of Autonomous Labor Unions of Venezuela) (hereinafter CODESA), politically allied to the COPEI.

Interestingly, CTV and CODESA advocated the establishment of a mixed social security system (Barrios y Camejo 2006), hence their participation in the presidential commission would have not contravened the government's plan in this regard under normal conditions. However, both labor unions and the government repudiated one another to such an extent that no political collaboration among them could come about. On the contrary, the Central Unitaria de Trabajadores de Venezuela (English: Unitary Centra of Workers of Venezuela) (hereinafter CUTV), politically allied to the PCV was not commissioned to participate in the presidential commission, even though it politically accompanied the government in general because it repudiated the incorporation of the private sector into the pension system.

Despite the 3 months' period of work prescribed in the decree, the presidential commission carried over its work for twice as long in order to accomplish its gigantic assignment. During this time, the first postponement of the implementation of the LOSSSI determined, because of which the National Assembly countenanced the repostponement for six extra months, deferring the prescribed implementation again from 1 January 2001 to 1 July 2001.

By the end of February 2001, after 6 months of work, the presidential commission finally brought out its proposal. The proposal clearly contravened the mandate of the president to formulate a draft organic law of social security, since it comprised five separate draft bills: one draft organic law for the social security system and four draft specific laws for the health, pension, unemployment and labor risks subsystems. As it could be anticipated on the basis of the composition of the commission, the proposal established altogether a mixed system of social security. The very short draft organic law contained in the proposal (consisting of only 50 articles) delineated the structure and principles of the social security system. These principles promulgated the universality, solidarity, integrality, unicity, participation, concurrency, efficacy, budget legality, fiscal balance, and efficiency, but they did not point out the nonprofit-making public service character of social security established by the constitution. Instead, the nonprofit-making public service character was acknowledged as an organizational criterion (CPSS 2001: 15).

Besides, the elaboration of the principle of concurrency clearly contravened the nonprofit-making public service character postulated by the constitution (Constitución de la República Bolivariana de Venezuela 1999), since it openly established the participation of the private sector in social security (Méndez Cegarra 2001: 9; CPSS 2001: 17).

As pointed out before, the inclusion of the private sector in the social security system (including the participation of the private sector in the pension system), does not necessarily bring about the incorporation of profit-making, as the existence of nonprofit-making private organizations of social security brings out. The cooperative administrators of collective capitalization pension funds represent an example of this within the pension system.

However, the proposal of the presidential commission did not concentrate on this kind of private participation but it undoubtedly purposed to incorporate the profit-making AFPs into the social security system. In this regard, the draft specific law for the pension system included in the proposal of the presidential commission prescribed a mixed pension system based on three pillars: (1) a basic obligatory PAYG regime administered by the state, (2) a complementary obligatory individual capitalization regime administered by private AFPs,[3] and (3) an additional voluntary insurance regime administered by private insurance companies. The obligatory contributions to the pension system amounted to 3.00% of the worker's gross salary for the first pillar (2.25% paid by the employer and 0.75% paid by the worker), and 10% of worker's gross salary for the second pillar (7.50% paid by the employer and 2.50% paid by the worker).[4]

The draft specific law for the pension systems also delineated the rights and duties of the AFPs and the subcontracted insurance companies in detail, including their respective fees for the administration of the old age pension funds and the provision of the survival, invalidity and incapacity pensions. These fees represented up to 1.6% of the worker's gross salary for the administration of the old age pension funds, and 1.6% of the worker's gross salary for the provision of the survival, invalidity and incapacity pensions. Altogether the fees of the AFPs and the subcontracted insurance companies (3.2% of the worker's gross salary) represented between 25 and 32% of the workers' contributions to them.

---

[3] Actually the second pillar did not only comprise private AFPs but also private insurance companies. The AFPs were commissioned to administer the individual old age pension funds but they were not authorized to provide survival, invalidity or incapacity pensions, for which they had to subcontract a private insurance company.

[4] This amount advanced by 0.5% every year up to 15% in the end.

Due to the blatant contradiction between these fees and the nonprofit-making character of social security established by the constitution, the specific law for the pension system established that the fees assigned to the AFPs simply presupposed a "remuneration" for their services as administrators (CPSS 2001: 107).

In order to substantiate this position, the proposal of the presidential commission was accompanied by an attachment containing an interpretative report of the constitutional article on social security. The report commingled the collaborations submitted to the presidential commission by several interested groups and it had been established by the members of the presidential commission as a road map for their work. It must be pointed out that most of the collaborations included in the report had been made out by renowned law firms such as "Andrade, Casanova & Asociados" or "Torres Plaza & Araujo", which clearly advocated the incorporation of the profit-making private sector into the pension system. Another collaboration included in the report had been made out by former constituent Allan Brewer Carías, who had actively come out for the participation of the private sector in the social security system during the plenary discussions of the constituent assembly on the subject. Not surprisingly, the interpretative report determined that the public service character of social security prescribed by the constitution presupposed that the state had to take over the direction and regulation of the social security system but it did not presuppose that the state had to monopolize the provision of the social security services, which could also be handed out by the private sector under the state's supervision (CPSS 2001: 297).

Further on, the interpretative report acknowledged that due to the nonprofit-making character of social security prescribed by the constitution, the provision of social security services could not generate private profit. However, right after that, the report predicated that the costs of the social security services had to be remunerated (CPSS 2001: 298–299). In the end, the report pointed out that the costs of administration services provided by private institutions had to be remunerated as well (CPSS 2001: 299).

Despite the overrepresentation of the financial sector in the presidential commission, the incorporation of the private sector into the pension system in these terms brought about controversy among its members. Presbyter José Ignacio Arrieta and Assemblyman Oscar Feo, a member of the governing party repudiated the final proposal of the presidential commission casting dissenting votes.

Oscar Feo recapitulated the reasons for his dissenting vote in a brief document send to the presidential commission. In this document, Feo castigated that the draft specific law for the pension system camouflaged the profit-making character of the AFPs and insurance companies, which together drew out 26% of the worker's contributions to the pension system. Furthermore, Feo pointed out that according to the actuarial studies made, after 30 years, more than 50% of the contributing workers would not have accumulated enough funds in their individual capitalization accounts to take back the minimum pension (CPSS 2001: 264).

Juan Ignacio Arrieta broke down his dissenting vote in two separate documents submitted to the presidential commission. The first one revolved around the draft organic law and the second one exclusively particularized on the draft specific law for the pension system. In the first document, Arrieta castigated the overcomplex institutional structure contained in the proposal of the presidential commission, advocating a much simpler structure. Besides, Arrieta pointed out the privatizing bias of the system of labor risks prescribed in the proposal. In the second document, Arrieta characterized the proposed pension system as simply unconstitutional, since it contravened the principles of universality, solidarity and nonprofit-making established by the constitution. He substantiated this assertion with three arguments. First, based on actuarial studies (one of the of the OIT) 65% of the contributing workers would not accumulate enough funds in 30 years to take back the minimum pension. For this reason, the state would have to subsidize their pensions so that they can take back the minimum pension just as any person without contributions to the pension system. In consequence, the proposal of the presidential commission established a contributory pension system which was exclusively capitalized on by only 35% of the contributing workers with the highest income. Second, the prescribed contribution of 3% to the PAYG regime represented a minimal contribution to the solidarity-based system. On the contrary, the draft-specific law accentuated the contribution to the individual capitalization regimen (initially of 10% and finally of to 12% of the worker's gross salary), what obviously deteriorated the solidarity principle. Third, the amount of the fees allowed to AFPs and insurance companies corresponded with the amount of the fees received by AFPs and insurance companies in other countries where profit making in social security was not legally closed out. Accordingly, the fees contained in the proposal obviously camouflaged profit making.

Alberto Yánez, one of the three members of the presidential commission representing the financial sector, documented his viewpoint on the accomplished work as well. In a document submitted to the presidential commission Yánez, a renowned businessman, celebrated the final proposal approved by the majority of the members, repudiated that the proposal had not been countenanced by all the members and candidly acknowledged the professional competence and the capacity for dialogue of the representatives of the government (CPSS 2001: 262–263).

Yánez' document brings out the enormous importance of the issue regarding the participation of the private sector in the social security system during the work of the presidential commission. According to him, the disagreements within the commission revolved around three issues of substance: (1) the participation of the private sector in the activities of the health, pension, employment and labor risks subsystems included in the proposal, (2) the interpretation of the nonprofit-making character of social security prescribed by the constitution, and (3) other social moral issues such as euthanasia, sexual education, and genetic manipulation (CPSS 2001: 259).

The presidential commission finally promulgated its proposal on 23 February 2001. A few days later, on 6 March 2002, the proposal was publicly handed over to President Chávez (Tal Cual 07/03/2001). Chávez did not speak out about the proposal but, according to the interviews conducted with Absalón Méndez and Rafael Ríos, at this point, he sympathized with it in general terms (Interviews with Absalón Méndez and Rafael Ríos).

After receiving the proposal, Chávez handed it over to the "social cabinet" in order to break it down before submitting it into the National Assembly. The social cabinet had been established by President Chávez a few months before as an interministerial body in charge of the government's social policy. It comprised the Minister of Health and Social Development María Lourdes Urbaneja, the Minister of Education Héctor Navarro and the Minister of Environment Ana Elisa Osorio.

After analyzing the proposal of the presidential commission, the social cabinet brought out a very critical document repudiating the mixed system of social security contained in it. Furthermore, with regard to the draft-specific law for the pension system, the document denunciated the absence of financial sustainability, the insufficiency of the coverage and the discrimination of people without contributory capacity (PROVEA 2001b: 10; El Universal 15/06/2001).

The rejection of the proposal by the social cabinet brought out once again the conflicting positions within the government and the governing party regarding the social security system reform. Due to this situation, Chávez determined to straighten out these disagreements before submitting a bill to the National Assembly. However, the conflicting parties within the government and the governing party did not back down from their positions on the matter during the following months despite the pressure of the president and the imminent expiration of the second postponement of the LOSSSI.

3.1.6.2 The First Reading of the LOSSSV in the National Assembly

After 3 months of internal confrontations the government was bamboozled by the opposition assembly member of the political organization (and soon later political party) Primero Justicia (English: Justice First) (hereinafter PJ), which capitalized on the government's internal contentions on this matter and astutely handed over, in June 2001, their own draft organic law of social security to the assembly. The draft of PJ practically represented a duplicate of the draft organic law of the presidential commission rejected by the social cabinet (Méndez Cegarra 2006: 29). However, its content became completely trivial because PJ could not really presuppose that its draft organic law would be countenanced by the assembly members of the governing party holding the absolute majority of the National Assembly. Nonetheless, due to the imminent expiration of the second postponement of the LOSSSI, the National Assembly had to deliberate it as the only submitted draft on the subject. In this context, PJ actually brought out its draft organic law of social security in order to precipitate the government into submitting its own draft which, after the rejection of the social cabinet, had not yet been reaccommodated (El Universal 06/06/2001).

In parallel, the advocates of the incorporation of the AFPs into the pension system generated political pressure against the National Assembly controlled by MVR through different channels. Norma de Dueñas, president of the Asociación de Promotores de Administradoras de Fondos de Pensiones (English: Association of Promoters of Pension Funds Administrators) (hereinafter APAFP) publicly predicated that the deferment of the implementation of the LOSSSI had brought about a loss of 1.6 billon of dollars in internal savings which could have been accumulated if the LOSSSI had been carried through in due time (Tal Cual 13/06/2001). Besides, in an interview with a national newspaper, she asseverated that the postponement of the LOSSSI had closed out the creation of 3500 jobs in the financial sector and the development of a capital market in Venezuela (Tal Cual 13/06/2001).

Legally forced by the setup orchestrated by PJ, president Chávez handed over a pile of documents to the National Assembly containing some unfinished drafts formulated by the government on the basis of the criticisms made by the social cabinet, as well as draft specific law for the pension system formulated by presbyter José Ignacio Arrieta with the assessment of his technical consultants Harald Allheimer and Gerardo Navarro. In addition, the government handed over another draft bill to the assembly in order to hold over the implementation of the LOSSSI again.

Naturally, the legislative trick of PJ also brought about the immediate submission of all the draft organic laws of social security formulated by the social, economic, and political actors involved in the subject. In this manner, the FAPUV, the Comisión de Estudios de Postgrado de la Facultad de Ciencias Económicas y Sociales de la Universidad Central de Venezuela (English: Commission of Postgraduate Studies of the Faculty of Economic and Social Sciences of the Central University of Venezuela) (hereinafter CEAP), and the Colegio de Médicos del Distrito Metropolitano de Caracas (English: College of Physicians of the Metropolitian District of Caracas) (hereinafter CMDMC) handed over their drafts laws to the National Assembly as well.

According to the internal debate code of the National Assembly, the draft bills concerning the same subject received simultaneously had to be processed by the permanent legislative commission with competence in the subject. These commissions were commissioned to break down the received drafts and, based on this, restructuralize and coalesce them into one condensed draft bill which, finally, was handed over to the plenary assembly for its first discussion. In the case of social security this task corresponded with the Comisión Permanente de Desarrollo Social Integral (English: Permanent Commission of Integral Social Development) (hereinafter CPDSI) presided by José Salamat Kahn (MVR) and further composed of Dellis Manzoul Campos (AD), Rafael Ángel Ríos (MVR), Nicolás Maduro (MVR), Luis Eduardo Franceschi (MVR), Tulio Amado Jiménez (MVR), Briccio Urdaneta (MVR), Ángel Rodríguez (MVR), José Armando Salazar (MAS), Héctor Larreal (AD), Julio Borges (PJ), Rafael Parra Barrios (LAPY[5]) and Enrique Márquez (UNT[6]) (CPDSI 2002: 2).

Unlike the presidential commission convocated by Chávez one year before, the CPDSI was circumscribed to assembly members, without any presence of the employers or financial sector. The government party took over the CPDSI, holding seven seats against six seats controlled by opposition parties (two of AD, one of MAS, one of PJ, one of LAPY, and one of UNT). Despite the internal confrontations regarding the social security system reform within the government and the govern-

---

[5]The contraction LAPY represented Lo Alcanzado por Yaracuy (English: The Achieved by Yaracuy). LAPY comprised a local appendage of Convergencia in the Estate of Yaracuy.
[6]The contraction UNT represented Un Nuevo Tiempo (English: A New Time).

ment party, in the case of the CPDSI, all members of MVR advocated a state public social security system and repudiated the creation of a mixed pension system. This univocal stance was probably predicated on the rather left position of the assembly members of MVR who participated in the CPDSI within their own party.

The political trajectories of these assembly members bring out their left political affiliation. José Salamat Kahn, the president of the CPDSI was associated with the labor unionism since he had participated in the labor union of the administrative employers of the UCV (El Mundo Economía y Negocios 14/08/2013). Rafael Ríos, who supervised the work of the CPDSI on the received draft bills, came down from the students' movement politically related to the Movimiento de Izquierda Revolucionaria (English: Movement of Revolutionary Left) (hereinafter MIR), a left revolutionary movement stemming from the AD during the 1960s. Nicolás Maduro had participated as a youngster in the Liga Socialista (English: Socialist League), another revolutionary left political organization came down from the MIR, before coming out as a union leader of the bus drivers of Caracas.

With regard to the second key point concerning the social security system reform, namely the maintenance or elimination of the special pension regimes, the members of the governing party more or less countenanced the idea of their progressive incorporation into the general system, despite some disagreements on the transition period.

In accordance to the internal debate code of the National Assembly, the CPDSI commissioned a Comisión Técnica Asesora (English: Technical Advisory Commission) for the analysis of the received drafts and their conformity with the constitutional articles on social security. This commission was presided by Carlos Eduardo Febres and further composed of Alejandro Cardozo, Absalón Méndez Cegarra, Pedro Sassone, Harald Halheimer, Libertad Polanco, Vilma Hernández, Leopoldo Yanes, Edgar Capriles, Mauricio Vegas and José Contreras. Most of the members of the technical advisory commission publicly advocated a state public pension system and some of them had even participated in the formulation of the drafts bills received by the CPDSI, as in the case of Absalón Méndez Cegarra and Harald Halheimer.

As it could be anticipated, the analysis determined that the submitted drafts contravened the constitutional articles on social security, for which it advocated the formulation of a new draft in conformity with the constitution (El universal 02/08/2001). The CPDSI countenanced the recommendation of the technical advisory commission and undertook the formulation of a new draft with its assistance, incorporating substantial parts of the submitted drafts into a new draft (CPDSI 2002: 29).

To this aim, the CPDSI carried out roundtables with representatives of the International Labour Organization (hereinafter ILO), the WB and the IMF during this period. Besides, it predicated on the assistance of three international experts on social security: Carmelo Mesa-Lago from the University of Pittsburgh, Alejandro Bonilla from the University of Social Sciences of Tolouse and Ernesto Murro from the Uruguayan Bank of Social Welfare (CPDSI 2002: 4). Interviewed by a Venezuelan national newspaper, Murro came out against the participation of the profit-making private sector in the pension system, as he asseverated that social security should be contrived for 100% of the society and not for 10% of it. In line with this, he openly repudiated the incorporation of private individual capitalization funds into the Venezuelan pension system (El Universal 13/10/2001).

Finally, the CPDSI concluded its bill by October 2001. As it could be anticipated, the draft organic law of the CPDSI prescribed a state public PAYG pension system without participation of the private sector (PROVEA 2001a: 11).

The members of the governing party who advocated the introduction of private individual capitalization funds into the pension system did not remain quiet. Following the formal legislative proceeding, the CPDSI handed over its new draft to the Oficina de Asesoría Económica y Financiera (English: Office of Economic and Financial Assessment) (hereinafter OAEF) of the National Assembly in November 2001. As an autonomous entity of the legislative power, the OAEF was commissioned to financially break down the draft bills before they were handed over to the plenary assembly for discussion. The OAEF was commanded by Francisco Rodríguez, a Keynesian who had personally admonished President Chávez on economic matters in the past (El Universal 04/09/2000) Soon after receiving the draft bill of the CPDSI, the OAEF delivered a very critical report on it (El Universal 12/11/2001). In a nutshell, the report basically repudiated the PAYG pension system contained in the draft bill of the CPDSI due to its financial unviability. Instead, the report advanced a mixed pension system (El Universal 17/11/2001).

The disclosure of the draft bill of the CPDSI immediately precipitated the opposition of several assembly members of MVR who repudiated it. The president of the Comisión Permanente de Finanzas (English: Permanent Commission of Finance) (hereinafter CPF) of the National Assembly, Alejandro Armas, publicly characterized the pension system prescribed in the draft bill as not sustainable and advocated not to repudiate any possibility, including the incorporation of the private sector (El Universal 19/11/2001). Supported by the vice president of the CPF, Rodrigo Cabezas, and the leader of the parliamentary fraction of MVR, Ernesto Alvarenga, Armas requisitioned the postponement the already programmed discussion of the draft bill in the plenary assembly. This situation maximized the tension between the group of assembly member of MVR promoting the draft bill of the CPDSI, commanded by Nicolás Maduro, and the group of assembly members of MVR repudiating it, led by Alejandro Armas and Ernesto Alvarenga.

The opposition press caricatured this situation of internal conflict within the governing party, calling it the "rosy soap opera of MVR" (Tal Cual 16/11/2001a). More than that, the opposition press ferociously castigated Maduro and the assembly members of MVR in favor of the draft bill of the CPDSI, calling them "the Talibans of MVR" and describing them as "a bunch of ignorant with their heads full of cobwebs" (Tal Cual 16/11/2001b). These harsh attacks against the left wing of the governing party not only brought out the absolute rejection of the opposition press to the draft bill formulated by the CPDSI but also brought out the radicality of the confrontation between government and opposition.

Above all else, the confrontation between government and opposition revolved around the dispute over the control of the main source of oil revenue, the state oil company Petróleos de Venezuela (English: Petroleum of Venezuela) (hereinafter PDVSA). As explicated above, unlike most Latin American state oil companies,

PDVSA had not been denationalized during the 1990s, formally remaining in possession of the Venezuelan state. However, the penetration of the interests of the multinational oil corporations within its managerial structure had dissociated the control of PDVSA from the national government, bringing about an almost completely autonomous company directed by its own corporate friendly managers (López Maya 2005).

In this context, the confrontation rushingly escalated when Chávez promulgated 49 decree-laws on the very last day of his second temporary entitlement to legislate through enabling powers, including a very resisted one regarding the oil activity. This decree-law, entitled "Decreto con Fuerza de Ley Orgánica de Hidrocarburos (English: Decree with the Force of Organic Law of Hydrocarbons) (GO 37323, 13/11/2001, Decree Law 1510), profoundly restructuralized the oil sector, as it established that the private oil companies could only participate in the oil business as minority partners of the state.

The 49 decree-laws sanctioned by Chávez encompassed another much resisted one concerning land property. This decree-law, entitled Decreto con Fuerza de Ley de Tierras y Desarrollo Agraria (English: Decree with Force of Law of Land and Agrarian Developmnet) (GO 37323, 13/11/2001, Decree Law 1546), regularized the private property of land, distributing idle land among landless peasants.

Expectedly, the sanction of these decree-laws sparked off an escalation in the confrontation between government and opposition which would bring about an "all-or-nothing" violent conflict, including a failed coup against president Chávez a few months later, in April 2002. In the meantime, however, the social security system reform carried through, as the government established a negotiating table with the FEDECAMARAS, its main opponent, in order to preclude a full-scale confrontation.

After several failed attempts, the group of assembly members of MVR supporting the draft bill of the CPDSI finally predominated and managed to put it up for debate on 20 November 2001.

The draft bill of the CPDSI submitted to the plenary assembly for its first discussion comprised altogether 101 articles divided in five sections. The first section of the draft bill, entitled Disposiciones Fundamentales (English: Fundamental Provisions), prescribed the essential principles of the social security system. In accordance to the constitutional articles on social security, this section established the human right to social security, explicitly entitling all inhabitants of Venezuela (Venezuelans and Non-Venezuelans) to social security, as well as Venezuelans residing abroad. For this reason, the report of the Technical Advisory Commission attached to the draft bill pointed out that the draft bill abided by a universal rather than a laborist approach to social security (Fernández 2002: 10). It also prescribed the right to protection against the contingencies enumerated in the constitution: integral health care, maternity, paternity, adoption, and temporary incapacity paid leaves; permanent partial incapacity, permanent complete incapacity, old age, and survival pensions; family allowances and subsidies; housing support; and unemployment financial and professional assistance. Finally, the first section determined the public nonprofit-making character of social security and its consequences for the social security system.

The second section, entitled Estructura Organizativa y Funcional del Sistema de Seguridad Social (English: Organizational and Functional Structure of the Social Security System) established a state public social security system which encompassed five subsystems: (1) Régimen Prestacional de Salud" (English: Benefit Regime of Health), (2) Régimen Prestacional Dinerario (English: Benefit Monetary Regime), (3) Régimen Prestacional de Empleo (English: Benefit Regime of Employment), (4) Régimen Prestacional de Seguridad, Salud de los Trabajadores y Ambiente (English: Benefit Regime of Security, Workers' Health and Working Environment), and (5) Régimen Prestacional de Vivienda y Hábitat (English: Benefit Regime of Housing and Environment).

Without a doubt, the Benefit Monetary Regime represented the key point of the draft bill of the CPDSI, since it concentrated all monetary benefits with the only exception of those related to occupational accidents and diseases (PROVEA 2001a: 11). As such, the Benefit Monetary regime comprised disability, incapacity, survival, orphanage, maternity and paternity pensions, family special needs and unemployment allowances, and, most important, old age pensions. Regarding the latter, the second sections of the draft bill prescribed a solidarity-based pension system which composed of two levels of protection administered by the state.

The first level encompassed the elders without contributory capacity throughout their active lives and it was financed with fiscal and parafiscal resources. This level was structuralized as a universal system of assistance pensions, providing old age pensions equivalent to the urban minimum salary to the elders without contributory capacity during their active lives.

The second level encompassed the elders with contributory capacity throughout their active lives and it was financed with the obligatory contributions of workers and employers. This level was structuralized as a PAYG regime with defined pensions. The amount of the pensions was determined by adding a common basic sum and an individual additional sum related to the contributions made. Additionally, workers could voluntarily contract complementary pension plans from the private sector.

The draft bill of the CPDSI did not particularize the level of the obligatory contributions but the members of the Technical Advisory Commission presupposed an overall contribution (including workers' and employers' contributions) of 27.51% of workers' gross income. This level of contributions clearly outdistanced the level prescribed in the proposal of the presidential commission of 23.75% of workers' gross income.

During its first discussion in the plenary assembly, the draft bill of the CPDSI came under massive objections from both the assembly members of the opposition parties and the assembly members of MVR in favor of a mixed pension system. However, the assembly members of MVR brought about an internal agreement according to which they would jointly countenance the draft bill but, in exchange, the CPDSI would commingle the draft bill and the observations against it into a new draft bill for the second (and definite) discussion (PROVEA 2002a: 1).

This compromise acknowledged all the critical observations made to the draft bill, including those of the assembly members of MVR in favor of a mixed pension system, those of the assembly member of the opposition parties, and those of the social, economic, and political actors opposed to the draft bill, such as the FEDECAMARAS (PROVEA 2002a: 1).

The opposition parties repudiated the bill of the CPDSI, voting as a unified parliamentary bloc against it. However, since the MVR preponderated in the National Assembly with an absolute majority, the role of the opposition parties was circumscribed to bring forward observations to the draft bill and castigate its "statist character" during the plenary discussion.

The opposition press, on the contrary, took over a much more active role in the dispute over the bill of the CPDSI, candidly celebrating that the group of assembly members commanded by Maduro had to countenance a profound modification of the bill. On the next day after the first reading in the assembly, the opposition paper Tal Cual characterized the draft bill of the CPDSI as "too weak", because it could not congregate the necessary support for its approval, not even in the governing party (Tal Cual 21/11/01a). This evaluation was substantiated by the newspaper with the opinions of two "experts" on the subject, María Bernardoni de Govea and Francisco Casanova. Bernardoni, who had participated in the formulation of the LOSSSI under Caldera's government, pointed out that the draft bill of the CPDSI reiterated and aggravated the flaws of the existing social security system. Casanova, who had partaken in the CPSS as a legal advisor, also criticized the draft bill of the CPDSI and reminded the advantages of the proposal of the presidential commission for social security (Tal Cual 21/11/01a).

In the same edition of the newspaper, another article mordaciously recounted the clashes among the assembly members of MVR during the first discussion of the draft bill in the assembly the day before. According to this recount Alejandro Alvarenga, leader of the parliamentary fraction of the MVR and one of the main opponents of the draft bill of the CPDSI within the MVR, asseverated during Maduro's intervention that he had recently come across president Chávez in a meeting in which Chávez had clearly repudiated the draft bill of the CPDSI, characterizing it as "very statist" (Tal Cual 21/11/2001b).

Only a few days later, the financial sector annunciated its rejection to the draft bill approved by the National Assembly in its first discussion, since it brushed aside the recommendations of the OAEF and completely struck down the private sector from the pension system (El Universal 01/12/2001). According to Norma de Dueñas, the draft bill approved by the National Assembly was percolated a discriminatory character, because it brushed aside low-income workers from the access to private individual capitalization funds (El Universal 01/12/2001).

A few days after the first reading of the bill, the short truce in the confrontation between government and opposition over the 49 decree-laws sanctioned by Chávez broke down when the FEDECAMARAS finally repudiated, after several comings and goings, the call for dialogue of the government. On 28 November 2001, the president of the FEDECAMARAS Pedro Carmona Estanga officially convocated a "civic strike"[7] for 10 December 2001, receiving a standing ovation from the audience (El Universal 29/11/2001).

During the next days, the strike received the endorsement of manifold social, economic, and political actors. CTV, the largest labor union in Venezuela, subscribed to the strike in an executive meeting held on 5 December (El Universal 05/12/2001). On this occasion, CTV's president Carlos Ortega anticipated that CTV would convocate a general strike after 10 December 2001 if the government did not respond to the worker's demands (El Universal 05/12/2001).

The strike was finally carried out as annunciated on 10 December with a high level of attendance and mobilization. Even though no major violent incidents were registered, this strike represented a key point in the escalation of the confrontation between government and opposition for four reasons.

First, the strike congregated all opposition forces in a unified space for the first time. Until then, those forces had remained fragmented and uncoordinated despite their common opposition to the government.

Second, the strike catapulted Pedro Carmona as the natural leader of the unified opposition, since he had undertaken the call for strike (López Maya 2005: 263).

Third, due to the massiveness of the mobilization the opposition undertook to take over the control of the streets, which until then had been monopolized by the supporters of the government, known as "Bolivarians".

Fourth, the civic strike held on 10 December represented the first of several massive mobilizations and counter-mobilizations carried out by government and opposition in a context of extreme political polarization. As a matter of fact, after the civic strike of 10 December both government and opposition maximized their stances, rejecting any possibility of dialogue and negotiation. Two weeks after the strike, on 24 December 2001, Chávez designated Efraín Andrade as Minister of Agriculture in order to accelerate the distribution of idle land prescribed in Decree Law 1546.

Against this background, the confrontation between government and opposition became total. The contention over the 49 decree-laws finally eventuated in an open confrontation over the removal of president Chávez. Naturally, in this context, the social security system reform became a secondary issue and the subject was postponed.

On 23 January 2002, the opposition carried through another massive demonstration against the government. On this occasion, the mobilization was not convocated by FEDECAMARAS but it was brought forward by the opposition parties (AD, COPEI, PJ, and MAS), which straightened out their previous internal differences coalescing into a unified political bloc against the government. The demonstration was convocated in "defense of democracy and freedom", and it was symbolically carried out on 23 January 2002 (El Universal 23/01/2002), when the anniversary of the fall of dictator Marcos Pérez Jiménez was commemorated. In turn, the government reciprocated with a massive counter-mobilization through poor neighborhoods of Caracas.

---

[7]Civic strikes basically represented general strikes. However, the opposition brought out the term "civic strike" in order to accentuate the political character of its strikes (García Guadilla 2007).

Something similar came up on 4 February, when the government effectuated a massive mobilization to celebrate the 10th anniversary of the failed coup commanded by Chávez in 1992. In response, the opposition called an "active mourning" for that day.

In this context of extreme polarization and continuous mobilization, the peak of the confrontation would be achieved in April 2002, with the second civic strike of the opposition and the subsequent coup against Chávez government. The events of April 2002 commenced two months before when Chávez removed the president of PDVSA Guaicaipuro Lameda Montero and its entire executive board on December 2001. Lameda Montero had been designated at the head of PDVSA by president Chávez only a few months before (on 15/10/2001) in order to countervail the opposition of PDVSA's managers and finally subordinate the state company to the government's oil policy. However, Lameda Montero did not accomplish this goal and even publicized critical observations of the government's reform of the oil sector (El Universal 07/1272001). For this reason, Chávez determined to substitute him for Gastón Parra, who became PDVSA's fourth president since Chávez' assumption. Parra and the new executive board were harshly discountenanced by PDVSA's managers, who asseverated that their designations disregarded the company's established policy of personnel nominations based on professional merit. In truth, the opposition of PDVSA's managers to the government's nominations was associated with the aforementioned conflict over the control of Venezuela's main source of income. As explicated above, the government undertook to subordinate the state oil company to its political project, whereas the managers of PDVSA advocated an autonomous corporate friendly management of the company (López Maya 2003: 58, 2005: 266–267).

After two months of growing tensions. PDVSA's, managers undertook an indefinite strike on 5 April, partially paralyzing the oil production (El Universal 05/04/2002). Two days later, the president of CTV, Carlos Ortega, annunciated a second civic strike in solidarity with PDVSA's workers for 9 April. FEDECAMARAS, the opposition parties and the Venezuelan Episcopal Conference immediately endorsed the strike, which was carried out on 9 April as planned. After extending the strike another day, Ortega proclaimed an indefinite civic strike and convocated a demonstration aimed at the PDVSA building located in the east side of Caracas for the next day. On 11 April, thousands of supporters of the opposition congregated in front of the PDVSA building. Encouraged by the size of the protest, the organizers redirected the demonstration to the Palacio de Miraflores, Venezuela's government house, in order to "kick Chávez out", as Ortega vociferated in his speech (López Maya 2005: 268). The demonstration was profusely covered by the private TV channels, which advocated the insurrectional mobilization and repeatedly encouraged viewers to participate (López Maya 2005: 268–269). The house of government was massively barricaded by thousands of supporters of the government who had congregated in its defense. When the demonstration of the opposition arrived at downtown Caracas a shootout came about causing several casualties. This incident was capitalized on by a civilian and military alliance which, on the dawn of the next day, removed the

elected government and established a de facto administration led by the president of
the FEDECAMARAS Pedro Carmona.

In his first public announcement, Carmona promulgated the dissolution of the
National Assembly, the supreme court of justice and the national electoral council.
However, after two days Chávez was reestablished in power due to a massive popular
uprising and the realignment of the military (López Maya 2003: 55, 2005: 69).

3.1.6.3 The Second Reading of the LOSSSV in the National Assembly

Astonishingly, soon after Chávez restitution in power the CPDSI of the National
Assembly recommenced its work on the draft bill allowing a greater participation
of the opposition, included CTV and FEDECAMARAS. Against the existing background of extreme confrontation between government and opposition, this "rap-
prochement" concerning the social security system reform was predicated on three
related circumstances.

First, the government undertook a more conciliatory course of action in the after-
math of the failed coup (López Maya 2005: 270), what probably generated a more
suitable context for dialogue between those in favor of the draft bill approved by the
National Assembly in the first discussion (the "left" fraction of MVR) and the actors
against it (the "right" fraction of MVR, the opposition parties, CTV and FEDECA-
MARAS).

Second, the draft bill approved at the first reading was not only repudiated by the
opposition but also by a fraction of the MVR itself. Due to this internal disagreement
within the government party and the absence of a clear definition on the subject
from president Chávez, the opposition (including the opposition parties, the CTV
and the FEDECAMARAS) conjectured that a complete modification of the draft bill
represented a feasible possibility despite the absolute majority of the MVR in the
National Assembly. For this reason, the opposition countenanced to participate in
all the dialogue instances concerning the social security system reform inaugurated
after the failed coup of April 2002.

Third, the introduction of private individual capitalization funds into the pension system represented an enormous business opportunity for the financial sector.
Due to the magnitude of this business opportunity the financial sector in particular
(represented by APAFP) and the employers' sector in general (represented by the
FEDECAMARAS), were predisposed to brush aside their ideological reluctance to
the government and capitalize on any given possibility in order to materialize the
introduction of individual capitalization into the pension systems. Because of this,
both the APAFP and the FEDECAMARAS, which otherwise repudiated the government to the utmost, actively participated in the reformulation of the draft bill after
the failed coup.

The decisions made by the CPDSI after resuming its work corroborated the evaluation of the opposition regarding the actual chances of a substantial modification
of the draft bill approved in the first discussion.

In the first place, the CPDSI established a round of consultations with the social, economic, and political actors involved in the reform (Méndez Cegarra 2006: 33). Throughout these consultations, the actors broke down their positions and recommendations on the subject. The financial sector, represented by APAFP, and the employers' sector, represented by FEDECAMARAS and other organizations such as the Confederación Venezolana de Industriales (English: Venezuelan Confederation of Industrialists) (hereinafter CONINDUSTRIA), the Consejo Nacional del Comercio y los Servicios) (English: National Council for Commerce and Services) (hereinafter CONSECOMERCIO), the Consejo Nacional de Promoción de Inversiones (English: National Council for Investment Promotion) (hereinafter CONAPRI), the Federación de Industriales, Pequeños, Medianos y Artesanos) (English: Federation of Industrialists, Small, Medium, and Artisans) (hereinafter FEDEINDUSTRIA), the Cámara de Comercio de Caracas (English: Caracas Chamber of Commerce) and the Cámara Inmobiliaria (Real State Chamber) partook in the consultation meetings. The labor unions, comprising CTV, CODESA, CUTV, the Alianza Sindical Independiente (English: Independent Labor Alliance) (hereinafter ASI), and the Fuerza Bolivariana de Trabajadores (English: Bolivarian force of Workers) (hereinafter FBT) participated in the meetings too. Additionally, some professional associations such as FAPUV and the Federación Médica Venezolana (English: Venezuelan Medical Federation) (hereinafter FMV) partook in the consultations as well.

After the consultations, the CPDSI reassembled the Technical Advisory Commission in order to process the observations made during the first discussion in the National Assembly and the recommendations gathered throughout the consultations (Méndez Cegarra 2006: 33).

Besides, the CPDSI congregated a Comisión Técnica Actuarial (English: Technical Actuarial Commission) presided by Libertad Polanco in order to carry out an actuarial analysis of the pension system prescribed in the draft bill of the CPDSI approved in the first discussion. Based on its actuarial analysis the Technical Actuarial Commission delivered two reports in May 2002: "Valuación Actuarial del Proyecto de Ley Orgánica del Sistema de Seguridad Social" (English: Actuarial Assessment of the Draft Organic Law of the Social Security System) and "El Financiamiento de la Seguridad Social y en especial de las Pensiones de Vejez" (English: The Financing of Social Security and the Old-Age Pensions in particular). Both documents substantiated that the social security systems (including the pension system) prescribed by the draft bill approved in the first discussion was quite solidly underpinned from the actuarial perspective (PROVEA 2002a: 10). This conclusion ruled out the actuarial objections previously made by the OAEF of the National Assembly.

Throughout the month of May, the Technical Advisory Commission processed the observations and recommendations received during the first discussion in the National Assembly and in the consultations of the CPDSI. According to Méndez Cegarra, the Technical Advisory Commission deliberated more than 30 draft bills before submitting its proposal to the CPDSI by the end of May (Méndez Cegarra 2006: 33). Subsequently, the CPDSI circulated this proposal among the involved actors in order to receive their opinions.

The draft bill circulated by the CPDSI in May (hereinafter draft bill of May) brought out several modifications compared to the draft bill approved in the first discussion. Some of these modifications had been subscribed to by (almost) all involved actors, such as (1) the creation of special regimes for homemakers, informal workers and disables peoples, (2) the incorporation of workers' and employers' representatives into the lead institution of the social security system, (3) the improvement of the regulation concerning the already existing special pension regimes, guaranteeing both the acquired rights of their members and the purpose of progressive unification of the social security system, and (4) the incorporation of the "principle of progressive development", enabling the state to advance in the expansion of the social security system in consecutive stages.

Regarding the main issue in discussion, namely the incorporation of private individual capitalization funds, the draft bill of May established an intermediate model, which carried over the main structure of the draft bill approved in the first discussion, consisting in a first state public level of social assistance for those without contributory capacity, a second state public level of obligatory social insurances for those with contributory capacity, and a third private level of voluntary social insurances. However, the draft bill of May broke down the second state public level into two sublevels. The first level was structuralized as a PAYG system funded by the contributions of all members based on a contributory basis of up to five minimum salaries. The second level was structuralized as an individual capitalization system administered by the state funded by the contributions corresponding to the income over five minimum salaries.

The level of obligatory contributions came out unchanged, amounting to 27.51% of the members' income, including both workers' and employers' contributions. Two-quarters of the contributions (75%) were disbursed by to the employers and one-quarter of the contributions (25%) to the workers, just as in the draft bill approved in the first discussion. The contributions to the PAYG pension system amounted to 10% of the members' income up to five minimum salaries (7.5% paid by the employers and 2.5% paid by the workers) and the contribution to the individual capitalization pension system added up to 2.76% of the members' income over five minimum salaries (2.07% paid by the employers and 0.69% paid the workers) (El Universal 10/07/2002).

As it could be anticipated, this intermediate model was repudiated by both parties in dispute, those against and those in favor of the incorporation of private administrators of individual pension funds into the pension system.

The position of the actors against the participation of the profit-making private sector was perfectly recapitulated in a document submitted to the CPDSI by the Coordinadora de Redes por una Seguridad Social Pública y Solidaria (English: Coordinator of Networks for Public and Solidary Social Securtiy) (hereinafter REDIUP) (PROVEA 2002a: 12–13). In this document, REDIUP persevered in its rejection of the third level of voluntary private insurances. Additionally, REDIUP repudiated the introduction of individual capitalization for workers with an income higher than five minimum salaries, since it diminished the amount of contributions to the solidary PAYG system (REDIUP 2002: 2). Finally, REDIUP deprecated the lowering of the maximal contributory basis for the obligatory social insurances from twenty to ten minimum salaries, which would bring about the strengthening of the third private level of voluntary (REDIUP 2002: 2).

On the contrary, the actors in favor of the participation of the private profit-making sector in the pension system repudiated that the participation of the AFPs was held down to the third level of voluntary insurances and therefore advocated the introduction of the AFPs into the second level of obligatory insurances.

Norma de Dueñas, president of APAFP, positively acknowledged that the CPDSI had commissioned all interested actors to participate in the consultations on the draft bill, revising the "strong statist bias" of the draft bill approved at first reading (Tal Cual 01/07/2002). However, she asseverated that the PAYG pension system experienced a major crisis worldwide for which she advocated for the inclusion of the AFPs into the obligatory pension system (Tal Cual 01/07/2002).

Aurelio Concheso, an employers' leader specialized in social security, spoke out in similar terms, as he publicly petitioned for the introduction of an individual capitalization pension system administered by AFPs (Cobertura 2002: 10, El Universal 03/07/2002).

León Arismendi, social security consultant of CTV, pointed out that the draft bill of May prioritized the PAYG regime over the individual capitalization regime (El Universal 03/07/02). For this reason, he advocated that workers could determine for themselves what pension regime they wanted (El Universal 03/07/2002).

The truce in the confrontation between government and opposition after the failed coup of April 2002, during which the opposition parties could reestablish dialogue over the social security system reform, commenced to collapse by mid-August 2002, when the (extremely politicized) Tribunal Supremo de Justicia (English: Supreme Court of Justice) (hereinafter TSJ) publicly annunciated its verdict of not guilty on the military officers who had perpetrated the failed coup of April (López Maya 2005: 271). After this incomprehensible decision, the confrontation between government and opposition continuously escalated throughout the remaining months of the year.

In October the opposition, led by FEDECAMARAS and CTV, convocated to a third civic strike for 21 October. Unlike the two previous civic strikes, this one was not masqueraded with economic demands such as salary increases or financial deregulation, but it openly advocated the president's resignation. The third civic strike was not massively accompanied as the two previous civic strikes, however, together with the aforementioned decision of the TSJ it successfully reactivated the insurrectionary atmosphere. One day after the strike, 11 high military officers, including some of those who had been exonerated for their command of the failed coup, took over the Plaza Francia in the east side of Caracas, pronouncing it "liberated territory" (Lander 2004: 17). While most military officers repudiated the rebellion on this occasion, this ongoing local insurrection maximized the radicalization of the conflicting parties.

In early November, Rafael Ríos, one of the members of the CPDSI, brought forward a new draft bill al the CPDSI. This new draft bill established a PAYG pension system without individual capitalization, which overtly contravened the draft bill of May formulated by the Technical Advisory Commission and still under discussion with all involved actors (El Universal 06/11/2002). One week later, the members of the CPDSI belonging to MVR finally determined to countenance this new draft bill, which was handed over to the plenary assembly for the second reading (El Universal 14/11/2002).

By the end of November, the opposition convocated a fourth civic strike for 2 December. Devised as the final confrontation against the government, the fourth strike not only advocated the renounce of President Chávez as the previous one, but it was additionally annunciated as "of indefinite duration" until the fall of the government (Lander 2004: 18).

On 3 December 2002, during the second day of the fourth civic strike of indefinite duration, the draft bill of the CPDSI was deliberated at second reading in the plenary assembly. The draft bill, which comprised 182 modifications to the draft bill approved at first reading, was finally countenanced by the assembly members who politically accompanied the government on 6 December 2002 (G.O 37600, 30/12/2002). In a context of extreme political radicalization and insurrectional demands, the assembly member of the opposition determined to abandon the plenary and did not participate in the discussion of the draft bill (Arrieta 2003: 245).

Due to the ongoing political situation, the definitive sanction of the draft bill of the CPDSI, entitled Ley Orgánica del Sistema de Seguridad Social (English Organic Law of the System of Social Security) did not bring about the attention of the press or the public opinion at all (PROVEA 2002b: 10, 2003: 95).

The fourth civic strike completely paralyzed the Venezuelan economy for weeks, completely hamstringing the crucial oil sector for the first time: Because of this, the press characterized the strike "paro petrolero" (English: oil strike). With the passing of the weeks, however, the intensity of the oil strike eventually diminished until it was officially struck down on 3 February 2003. In the end, the government took over the control of the PDVSA and throw out the managers who had participated in the lockout. In spite of this, the oil strike brought about tremendous consequences in economic and social terms. The economy deteriorated by 27% during the first quarter of 2003 and the unemployment rate skyrocketed from 15.4 to 20.3% in only 4 months (López Maya 2005: 274).

3.1.7   The (Non-)Implementation of the LOSSSV

In accordance with the constitutional articles on social security, the LOSSSV established the right of all Venezuelans and non-Venezuelans legally residing in Venezuela to social security. In order to accomplish this right, the LOSSSV established a "universal, integral, efficient, solidarity-based funded, unitary, and participatory" social security system called Sistema de Seguridad Social (English: System of Social Security) (hereinafter SSS) which was to provide services and benefits for the following contingencies: disease, accident, discapacity, special need, maternity, paternity, family, involuntary loss of employment, unemployment, occupational training,, old age, widowhood, orphanage, and housing.

The SSS was structuralized into three subsystems: (1) the Sistema Prestacional de Salud (English: System of Health), (2) the Sistema Prestacional de Previsión Social (English: System of Social Welfare), and (3) the Sistema Prestacional de Vivienda y Hábitat (System of Housing and Habitat). In turn, these three subsystems were compartmentalized in six regimes. The System of Health comprised the Régimen Prestacional de Salud (English: Regime of Health); the System of Social Welfare comprised the Régimen Prestacional de Servicios Sociales al Adulto Mayor y Otras Categorías de Personas (Regime of Social Services for the Elderly and other Categories of Persons), the Régimen de Empleo (English: Regime of Employment), the Régimen de Pensiones y Otras Asignaciones Económicas (English: Regime of Pensions and Other Economic Allowances) and the Régimen de Seguridad y Salud en el Trabajo (English: Regime of Safety and Health at Work); and the System of Housing and Habitat comprised the Régimen Prestacional de Vivienda y Hábitat (English: Regime of Housing and Habitat).

For each of these six regimes, the LOSSSV established an institution in charge. Thereby, the Regime of Health was to provide health services through the Sistema Público Nacional de Salud (English: Public National System of Health), the Regime of Social Services for the Elderly and Other Categories of Persons was to deliver social services through the Instituto Nacional de Servicios Sociales (English: National Institute of Social Services), the Regime of Employment was to advance the reincorporation of the unemployed workers to the labor market through the Instituto Nacional de Empleo (English: National Institute of Employment), the Regime of Pensions and Other Economic Allowances was to disburse the economic benefits established by the LOSSSV through the the Instituto Nacional de Pensiones y Otras Asignaciones Económicas (English: National Institute of Pensions and Other Economic Allowances), the Regime of Safety and Health at Work was to supervise the labor conditions through the Instituto Nacional de Prevención, Salud y Seguridad Laborales (English: National Institute of Labor Prevention, Health and Safety) and carry out training and recreation programs through the Instituto Nacional de Capacitación y Recreación de los Trabajadores (English: National Institute of Workers' Training and Recreation), and the Regime of Housing and Habitat was to facilitate the access to housing through the Sistema Nacional de Vivienda (English: National System of Housing), which comprised the Banco Nacional de Vivienda y Hábitat (English: National Bank of Housing and Habitat).

Besides, the LOSSSV established three institutions at the top of the structure of the SSS: (1) the Rectoría del Sistema de Seguridad Social (English: Governing Body of the System of Social Security) (hereinafter RSSS), the Tesorería del Sistema de Seguridad Social (English: Treasury of the System of Social Security) (hereinafter TSSS), and the Superintendencia del Sistema de Seguridad Social (English: Superintendence of the System of Social Security) (hereinafter SSSS). The RSSS represented an intermediate body between the government and the SSS, and it was to advance the development of the SSS. The TSSS was commissioned with the financial administration of the SSS, including the collection and the investment of the funds of the SSS. Finally, the SSSS was to supervise the financial administration of the funds of the SSS. Both, the TSSS and the SSSS were explicitly acknowledged as autonomous institutions by the LOSSSV.

Last, the LOSSSV established the liquidation of the IVSS and its substitution by the institutions of the SSS.

According to the LOSSSV, this complex institutional structure had to be established within the next five years after its sanction. However, the LOSSSV did not determine in detail the specific characteristics of the six prescribed regimes and their corresponding institutions, but it only delineated their guiding principles and overall structures. For this reason, the LOSSSV commissioned the national assembly to bring about one specific law for each of the regimes. In consequence, the effective implementation of the SSS established by the LOSSSV was subordinated to the sanction of six specific laws by the assembly which particularized the guiding principles and overall structures delineated in the LOSSSV.

During 2003 and 2004, none of these specific laws was brought about by the assembly, even though the government party had taken over the absolute majority of the assembly seats in the legislative elections held in July 2000. However, this deferment was reasonably predicated on the extremely turbulent ongoing political situation which precluded the legislative labor of the national assembly.

The oil strike represented a watershed in the struggles between government and opposition, for it determined the end of the "hegemonic tie" (Portantiero 1973, 1977; O'Donnell 1975, 1977) between them in favor of the government (López Maya 2005: 275). The tremendous economic and social consequences of the oil strike clearly debilitated the opposition, however, it did not back down. Almost immediately after the end of the strike, the opposition annunciated that it would advance a recall election in compliance with the new constitution in order to bring down President Chávez. To this aim, the opposition undertook a nationwide campaign with the active support of the mass media opposed to the government to accumulate the 2.4 million signatures required by the electoral law. The collected signatures were handed over to the Consejo Nacional Electoral (English: National Electoral Council) (hereinafter CNE), the highest electoral authority, in December 2003, but CNE repudiated the validity of 1.5 million of them. Finally, after the validity of these signatures was corroborated through a second signature collection campaign, the CNE countenanced the realization of the presidential recall election in June 2004. The recall election was carried out on 15 August 2004, reconfirming Hugo Chávez as president with almost 60% of the votes (59.1% against his destitution and 40.6% for his destitution).

The electoral defeat in the recall election devastated the opposition, which forcedly backed down in its attempts to strike down the government. This brought about the appeasement of the political tensions and reactivated the legislative labor of the national assembly. In this context, the assembly brought about four of the six specific laws required for the implementation of the SSS throughout 2005: (1) the Ley del Régimen Prestacional de Vivienda y Hábitat (English: Law of the Regime of Housing and Habitat) (hereinafter LRPVH), (2) the Ley Orgánica de Prevención, Condiciones y Medio Ambiente de Trabajo (English: Organic Law of Prevention, Conditions and Environment of Labor) (hereinafter LOPCYMAT), (3) the Ley de Servicios Sociales (English: Law of Social Services) (hereinafter LSSV), (4) the Ley del Régimen Prestacional de Empleo (English: Law of the Regime of Employment) (hereinafter LRPE).

The LRPVH received the sanction of the assembly at a second discussion on 12 April 2005 and it was promulgated on 9 May 2005 (G.O. 38182, 09/05/2005 reprinted due to errors G.O. 38204, 08/06/2005). The LRPVH regulated the Regime of Housing and Habitat, for which it established the Banco Nacional de Vivienda y Hábitat (English: National Bank of Housing and Habitat) (hereinafter BANAVIH) as prescribed by the LOSSSV. The LOPCYMAT was brought out by the assembly two months later, on 30 June 2005, and it was promulgated on 26 July 2005 (G.O. 38236, 26/07/2005). The LOPCYMAT legislated the Regime of Safety and Health at Work, for which it prescribed the creation of the National Institute of Labor Prevention, Health and Safety and the National Institute of Workers' Training and Recreation. On 26 July 2005, the assembly brought about the LSSV. Promulgated on 12 September 2005 (G.O. 38270, 12/09/2005), the LSSV regulated the Regime of Social Services for the Elderly and other Categories of Persons, for which it established the National Institute of Social Services. Finally, the assembly brought about the LRPE at a second discussion on 29 August 2005. Promulgated on 27 September 2005 (G.O. 38281, 27/09/2005), the LRPE regulated the Regime of Employment, for which it established the National Institute of Employment.

Nevertheless, the assembly did not bring about the two specific laws concerning the Regime of Health and the Regime of Pensions and Other Economic Allowances, which represented the most important components of the SSS. A bill for the health regime entitled Ley Orgánica de Salud (English: Organic Law of Health) was in fact deliberated by the assembly at first discussion in December 2014. However, its legislative treatment broke down and never started out again.

The "organic" character of both specific laws, which presupposed a two-thirds majority for their approval, probably held back their sanction during 2005, when the LRPVH, the LOPCYMAT the LSSV and the LRPE were promulgated. However, this obstacle dematerialized after the legislative elections held in December 2005, when the government party took over 68.2% of the seats in the assembly. Besides, the rest of the political parties taking over seats in the assembly were politically associated with the government, as the opposition parties had determined not to participate in the legislative elections in order to delegitimize them. This strategy, which was predicated on the intransigence of the opposition, brought about its further weakening and maximized the political power of the government and its political allies.

Despite this, the government has not countenanced the two specific laws required for the implementation of the LOSSSV since 2006. As pointed out above, these laws should legislate the health and pension systems, which represent the main core of the universal social security system prescribed by the LOSSSV. Instead, the assembly and the government carried out two partial reforms of the LOSSSV which in part contravened its original text.

The first partial reform was promulgated under the title "Ley de Reforma Parcial de la Ley Orgánica del Sistema de Seguridad Social" (English: Law of Partial Reform of the Organic Law of the Social Security System) (G.O.E 5867, 28/12/2007) two days before the 5 years deadline established by the LOSSSV culminated. First, it completely removed the deadline without replacing it with a new one. Second, it recomposed the article concerning the substitution of the IVSS with the institutions devised in the LOSSSV, and prescribed the "transformation" of the IVSS through the new institutions of the LOSSSV.

The second partial reform was brought about by the government through an enabling law in July 2008 (G.O.E 5891, 31/07/2008) which took out the housing regime, including the BANAVIH, form the social security system. Additionally, the enabling law commissioned the BANAVIH with the administration of the obligatory contributions of the affiliates to the housing regime. This way, the obligatory contributions would not be canalized to the autonomous treasury of the SSS and supervised by the autonomous superintendence of the SSS, as prescribed by the LOSSSV, but they would be supervised by the BANAVIH, which was subordinated to the ministry of housing.

The sluggishness in the implementation of the LOSSSV divaricated from the expeditious development of a parallel structure of social policy initiated in 2004. This structure revolved around the programs known as Misiones Bolivarianas (English: Bolivarian Missions) and later Grandes Misiones (English: Great Missions), which comprised manifold areas such as health, pensions, employment, education, and housing, including those embraced by the LOSSSV.

The Misiones Bolivarianas started out in Caracas in March 2003, a few weeks after the end of the oil strike. The missions were associated with two main objectives. First, they undertook to ameliorate the dramatic social situation derived from the oil strike. Second (and without detriment of the first), they undertook to maximize the political base of the government in view of the forthcoming presidential recall election.

The missions rashly accomplished both because of which the government determined to maximize their extension and scope. Based on the remarking increase of the fiscal oil revenues experienced since 2003, the missions extraordinarily branched out between 2003 and 2008, decelerated due to the international crisis between 2009 and 2010, and recommenced its expansion in 2011, following the general trend of public expenditure (Aponte Blank 2006, 2010, 2015) (Table 3.1). As a result, poverty and inequality steeply decreased during this period, as Table 4.2 substantiates (Table 3.2).

The first and probably most significant mission, the Misión Barrio Adentro (English: Mission Inside the Neighborhood) was established in March 2003. The Misión Barrio Adentro initially provided primary health care in poor neighborhoods where no health facility had been established before. Soon, the program branched out to provide secondary, tertiary, and quaternary health care through the Misión Barrio Adentro II (initiated in 2005), the Misión Barrio Adentro III (inaugurated in 2005), and the Misión Barrio Adentro IV (started in 2006), as well as odontological and ophthalmological care through the Misión Sonrisa (initiated in 2003) and the Misión Milagro (inaugurated in 2005).

In this regard, the complex of the Misión Barrio Adentro I, II, III, and IV became a *sui generis* public health system comparable to the SPNS devised by the LOSSSV (PROVEA 2008). However, since Misión Barrio Adentro I, II, III, and IV were not subordinated to the autonomous Superintendence of Social Security and Treasury

Table 3.1 Public expenditure

	Public social expend as share of GDP (%)			Public expend as share of GDP (%)
	Central Government	General Government	Restricted public sector	Restricted public sector
1998	8.2	12.5		29.0
1999	9.5	14.1		26.0
2000	11.0	16.7		27.8
2001	12.2	18.0		31.6
2002	11.3	18.0		30.7
2003	12.2	17.7		32.0
2004	11.9	17.1	18.6	31.9
2005	11.6	16.0	18.0	33.2
2006	13.9	19.3	22.4	38.9
2007	13.0	18.1	21.7	35.7
2008	13.3	17.9	19.2	34.1
2009	13.2	17.7	18.4	32.7
2010	11.9	15.2	17.6	30.8
2011	13.6	17.0	21.4	37.9
2012	14.6	18.1	21.1	

Source Aponte Blank (2015)

Table 3.2 Poverty and inequality

	National poverty by income (%)	National extreme poverty by income (%)	Gini coefficient	Theil coefficient
2006	37.60	16.89	0.540	
2007	36.74	16.45	0.551	0.630
2008	35.09	15.69	0.515	0.562
2009	36.03	15.37	0.504	0.491
2010	32.76	13.09	0.505	0.512
2011	28.64	11.61	0.473	0.461
2012	27.31	11.18	0.477	0.455
2013	25.55	8.61	0.485	0.460
2014	22.49	7.65	0.467	0.428

Source INEV (2015)

of Social Security prescribed by the LOSSSV, they were not supervised by them. Instead, Misión Barrio Adentro I, II, III, and IV were formally subordinated to the Fundación Misión Barrion Adentro (English Foundation Mission Inside the Neighborhood), an ad hoc public foundation which was in turn subordinated to the ministry of health and whose executive board was determined by the president.

Additionally, the financing of the Misión Barrio Adentro I, II, III, and IV divaricated from the financing of the SPNS of the LOSSSV. Whereas the SPNS was financially predicated on the contributions of both, the state and the affiliates with financial capacity of the health regime, the Misión Barrio Adentro I, II, III, and IV exclusively received funds from the state and, principally, from PDVSA.

Given the deficient housing situation, the government undertook the Gran Misión Vivienda Venezuela in order to provide housing in February 2011. Following the LRPVH sanctioned in 2005, the Gran Misión Vivienda Venezuela established the Sistema Nacional de Vivienda y Hábitat (English: National System of Housing and Habitat) (hereinafter SNVH) which comprised all the housing institutions, including the aforementioned BANVIH. However, the SNVH was not supervised by the autonomous controlling institutions devised by the LOSSSV, but it was subordinated to the Órgano

Superior del Sistema Nacional de Vivienda y Hábitat (English: Superior Body of the National System of Housing and Habitat) which, in turn, was subordinated to the ministry of housing.

Unlike the Misión Barrio Adentro, the financing of the Gran Misión Vivienda Venezuela comprised the contributions of both, the state and the affiliates of the general social security regime. However, the contributions of the affiliates (regarded as compulsory savings) represented a small fraction of the funding, whereas a substantial fraction of the funding was subsidiated by PDVSA and public debt (Transparencia Venezuela 2013: 12).

Finally, the government commenced the Gran Misión en Amor Mayor (English: Great Mission in Higher Love) in December 2011. The Gran Misión en Amor Mayor provided old age pensions for the elders excluded from the pension system. As in the cases of the Misión Barrio Adentro and the Gran Misión Vivienda Venezuela, the Gran Misión en Amor Mayor was subordinated to the IVSS, which was subordinated to the ministry of labor, instead of being supervised by the autonomous controlling institutions prescribed by the LOSSSV.

In this case, the financing corresponded with the contributions of both, the state and the members of the IVSS, but it struck down the contributions of the affiliates of the countless special pension regimes excluded from the general pension regime. As pointed out above, the affiliates of the special regimes were characterized by the highest salaries. Besides, the implementation of the Gran Misión en Amor Mayor brought about an inequitable leveling of the old age pensions perceived by the newly incorporated affiliates, and the old age pensions received by the affiliates who had carried out the obligatory contributions, regardless of the amount of their contributions.

In this context, the development of the structure of the missions brought about the stagnation of the implementation of the LOSSSV, bringing about the coexistence

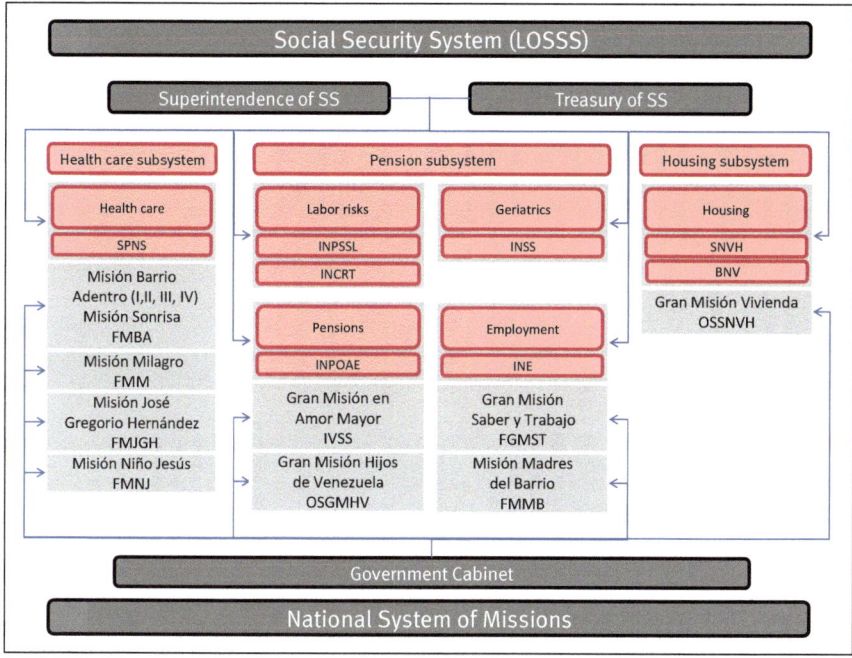

Fig. 3.1 Institutional structures of the social security system and the national system of missions. SPNS: Sistema Público Nacional de Salud. INPSSL: Instituto Nacional de Prevención, Salud y Seguridad Laborales. INCRT: Instituto Nacional de Capacitación y Recreación de los Trabajadores. INPOAE: Instituto Nacional de Pensiones y Otras Asignaciones Económicas. INSS: Instituto Nacional de Servicios Sociales. INE: Instituto Nacional de Empleo. SNVH: Sistema Nacional de Vivencia y Hábitat. BANAVIH: Banco Nacional de Vivienda y Hábitat. FMBA: Fundación Misión Vivienda. FMM: Fundación Misión Milagro. FMJGH: Fundación Misión José Gregorio Hernández. FMNJ: Fundación Misión Niño Jesús. IVSS: Instituto Venezolano de los Seguros Sociales. OSGMHV: Órgano Superior de la Gran Misión Hijos de Venezuela. FMMB: Fundación Misión Madres del Barrio. OSSNVH: Órgano Superior del Sistema Nacional de Vivienda y Hábitat. *Source* Prepared by the author

of two parallel structures: on the one side, the implemented institutional structure of the LOSSSV and on the other side the ad hoc structure of the missions. Figures 3.1 and 3.2 delineate both structures in detail (Figs. 3.1 and 3.2).

The surprising creation of the TSSS and the SSSS by the government in May 2012 brought about the accentuation of the aforementioned parallelism. The appointment of Rafael Ríos and Julio César Alviárez as treasurer and superintendent, two lifelong activists for the universalization of social security, was congratulated by members of the government and the opposition alike (Interview with Aurelio Concheso). However, both the TSSS and the SSSS have not yet been commissioned to carry out the duties assigned to them by the LOSSSV, carrying out secondary duties so far.

All in all, only three institutions delineated by the LOSSSV fully carry out their prescribed duties at present: the INSS, the INPSSL, and the INCRT. However, these

Contingencia	Sistema de Seguridad Social					Misiones Bolivarianas y Grandes Misiones	
	Régimen	Ley regulatoria	Unidad de gestión	Estado	Adscripción	Programa	Unidad de gestión
Enfermedad / Discapacidad / Maternidad	Régimen Prestacional de Salud	Pendiente. Ley del Régimen Prestacional de Salud tratada en primera discusión (14/12/2004)	Sistema Público Nacional de Salud	Pendiente	Pendiente	Misión Barrio Adentro (1, 2, 3 y 4) / Misión Milagro / Misión Sonrisa / Misión José Gregorio Hernández / Misión Niño Jesús	Fundación Misión Barrio Adentro / Fundación Misión Milagro / Fundación Misión Barrio Adentro / Fundación Misión José Gregorio / Fundación Misión Niño Jesús
Vejez	Régimen Prestacional de Servicios Sociales al Adulto Mayor y	Ley de Servicios Sociales (GO 38270, 12/09/2005)	Instituto Nacional de Servicios Sociales	Funcionando	Ministerio del Poder Popular del Despacho de la Presidencia y		
Pobreza y marginalidad						Misión Negra Hipólita	Comisión Presidencial Misión
Asignación jubilar / Asignación familiar	Régimen Prestacional de Pensiones y Otras Asignaciones	Pendiente	Instituto Nacional de Pensiones y Otras Asignaciones Económicas	Pendiente	Pendiente	Gran Misión En Amor Mayor / Gran Misión Hijos de Venezuela	Instituto Venezolano de los Seguros / Órgano Superior de la Gran Misión Hijos
Desempleo	Régimen Prestacional de Empleo	Ley del Régimen Prestacional de Empleo (GO 38281, 27/09/2005)	Instituto Nacional de Empleo	Pendiente	Pendiente	Misión Madres del Barrio / Misión Che Guevara / Gran Misión Saber y Trabajo	Fundación Misión Madres del Barrio / Fundación Misión Che Guevara / Fundación Gran Misión Saber y
Riesgos laborales / Capacitación laboral / Recreación	Régimen Prestacional de Seguridad y Salud en el Trabajo	Ley Orgánica de Prevención, Condiciones y Medio Ambiente de Trabajo (GO 38236, 26/07/2005)	Instituto Nacional de Prevención, Salud / Instituto Nacional de Capacitación y Recreación de los Trabajadores	Funcionando / Funcionando	Ministerio del Poder Popular para el / Ministerio del Poder Popular para el Trabajo y Seguridad Social (MPPPTSS)		
Vivienda	Régimen de Vivienda y Hábitat	Ley del Régimen Prestacional de Vivienda y Hábitat (GO 38182 09/05/2005)	Sistema Nacional de Vivienda y Hábitat	Desacoplado del Sistema de Seguridad Social (GOE 5889, 5890, 5891, 5892, 31/07/2008)		Gran Misión Vivienda	Órgano Superior del Sistema Nacional de Vivienda y Hábitat

Fig. 3.2 Institutional anchoring of the social security system and the national system of missions. *Source* Prepared by the author

institutions had been established before the sanction of the LOSSSV, which in fact only restructuralized them.

The INE was promulgated by the LRPE sanctioned in 2005 but it has not yet been established.

The SNVH devised by the LOSSSV has been brought about in the context of the Gran Misión Vivienda Venezuela, dissociated from the social security system.

The SPNS has been established *sui generis* in the context of the Misión Barrio Adentro I, II, III, and IV, disconnected from the social security system as well. No specific law for the health regime has yet been promulgated. In fact, the legislative treatment of a bill composed to this aim broke off after its first discussion in the assembly in December 2004.

The INPOAE has not materialized at all because no specific law for the pension regime has yet been promulgated. However, the government maximized the coverage of the pension system through the Gran Misión en Amor Mayor administered by the IVSS (Fernández 2012: 211). For this reason, the IVSS has not been taken down as prescribed by the LOSSSV but, instead, it has clearly branched out.

The government has not provided an official explanation concerning the truncated implementation of the LOSSSV after more than 10 years since its sanction. Nonetheless, the fact that the government has not accomplished the implementation of the LOSSSV under extraordinary advantageous political and economic conditions clearly brings out its lack of political will in this regard. Moreover, the concurrent development of the parallel structure of the missions since 2004 points out that the struggles over the social security system reform completely metamorphosed after the government took down the opposition between 2003 and 2004. This way, the main sticking point concerning the reform, which revolved around the privatization (total or partial) of the pension system, suddenly became meaningless as the struggles over the reform came down to the implementation of the LOSSSV sanctioned in December 2002 or the development of a parallel structure of social policy which dovetailed with the political project of the government.

3.2   Operationalization of the Power Struggles over the Post-neoliberal Social Security System Reform

As explained in Chap. 2, the operationalization of the power struggles over the post-neoliberal social security system reform in Venezuela is carried out on the basis of the concept of power resources devised by political class struggle approaches to social policy. However, this concept is not reduplicated in its original form, but it is completely transubstantiated in order to deracinate its shortcomings when dealing with the social policy of the Global South.

The operationalization of the power struggles in Venezuela correlates the four analytical dimensions ("where", "what", "who", and "how") included in the previous contextualization of the Venezuela case. As pointed out, these four dimensions comprise (1) the structural underpinnings underlying social policy, (2) the concrete points of conflict over social policy, (3) the real actors involved in the struggles over social policy, and (4) the channels through which the struggles are canalized.

As noticed before, the incorporation of these multiple analytical dimensions to the study of power struggles brings about as a natural consequence the increase of both the actors involved in the struggles and the power resources used by the actors. Unlike the associational and electoral power resources used by political class struggle approaches, which can be usually correlated with all (or almost all) contending actors, many types of power resources examined below do not correspond with all contending actors, and sometimes they even correlate with only one of them. For this reason, the operationalization of the different types of powers resources presented in the following sections initially breaks down the particular characteristics of the specific type of power resources under examination in order to bring out how they advantage the actors controlling them and disadvantage the actors deprived of them.

3.2.1 Operationalization of the "Where" Question

The reconstruction of the power struggles over the post-neoliberal social security system reform in Venezuela brought out the centrality of two structural factors which predetermined the clashes on the intended reform: (1) the oil resources and (2) the labor informality. According to the definitions given in Chap. 2, both oil resources and labor informality represent power resources, for they advantage their possessors by providing them with the capability to determine outcomes according to their preferences, even over the preferences of others. More specifically, oil resources and labor informality represent structural power resources, since they are predicated on the structural characteristics of the economic system.

3.2.1.1 Oil Resources as Power Resources

As power resources oil resources resemble "conventional" power resources (economic, associational, etc.), for their possession brings about a relational power which advantages their possessor(s) over their non-possessor(s). Following this logic, the bigger the possession of oil resources, the bigger the relational power of its possessor and vice versa. Considered as power resources, oil resources are usually associated with the government. However, private oil companies may capitalize on oil resources as well if they successfully take over their control.

The availability of oil resources as power resources commingles two interrelated dimensions: (1) the ownership of oil resources per se, and (2) the control of oil resources. The ownership of oil resources presupposes the ownership of the oil revenue derived from them. In turn, the control of oil resources brings about the free availability of the oil resources and, consequently, the free availability of the oil revenue for its owner. For the government, the control of oil resources is usually

Table 3.3 Exports of goods and services

	Total exports (millions of USD FOB)	Oil exports (millions of USD FOB)	Oil exports share of total exports (%)	Non-Oil exports (millions of USD FOB)
2000	34,711	27,874	80.30	6837
2001	28,043	21,745	77.54	6298
2002	27,794	21,532	77.47	6262
2003	28,108	22,029	78.37	6079
2004	40,809	32,871	80.55	7938
2005	56,829	48,069	84.59	8760
2006	67,122	57,972	86.37	9150
2007	72,062	63,232	87.75	8830
2008	98,240	89,305	90.90	8935
2009	60,658	54,447	89.76	6211
2010	68,731	62,567	91.03	6164
2011	95,655	88,393	92.41	7262
2012	100,033	93,844	93.81	6189
2013	90,965	85,991	94.53	4974
2014	61,750	58,365	94.52	3385

Source BCV (2015)

associated with the possible limitations to its discretionary use. These limitations could materialize as coercive restrictions, such as the stoppages to the oil exploitation imposed by labor unions and employers' organizations, as well as legal restrictions, such as the mandatory accountability of the oil resources and the prescribed distribution of the oil revenue among the national, provincial and municipal governments.

Oil resources represent a crucial factor for the Venezuelan economy, state and government, as Table 4.4 brings out (Table 3.3). Since 2000 the oil exports have represented between 77.47 and 94.53% of the total exports, consolidating Venezuela's historical dependence on the oil revenue. This tendency has been maximized by the extraordinary increase of the oil revenue experienced since 2003. Non-oil exports, on the contrary, have decreased in both absolute and relative terms since 2007. Due to the very high apportionment of imports in Venezuela's domestic consumption, the capacity of consumption of the Venezuelan economy is completely subordinated to the oil exports. As a result, any fluctuation in the oil exports brings about immediate effects on the domestic economy.

Before the reform of the oil sector undertaken by Chávez' government in 2001, private oil companies had taken over de facto the control of oil resources, even though the state held over de jure the ownership of oil resources. As pointed out above, the Venezuelan oil sector was not formally denationalized during the 1990s, as the ownership of the state oil company PDVSA was not taken away from the state. However, the government was increasingly dissociated from the real control of PDVSA since 1992, when the process known as "apertura petrolera" (English: oil opening) commenced. In this context, the control of PDVSA was factually taken over by its upper management, who was associated with the international oil companies. This situation brought about the minimization of the oil revenue captured by the state, the maximization of the oil revenue captured by the private oil companies and the strengthening of the Venezuelan employers' organizations, most specially FEDECAMARAS.

The following sections break down the ownership and control of oil resources.

Ownership of Oil Resources

In order to contextualize the development of Venezuela's oil revenue since 2000, Table 3.4 delineates an outline of the evolution of the Venezuelan oil production and the international oil prices since then (Table 3.4).

Table 3.4 brings out two things (Table 3.4). First, the crude oil production did not come under substantial changes from the late 1990s until the late 2000s, as the annual production revolved around 800 million o barrels—the oil strike exceptionally brought about a slight reduction of the annual production between 2002 and 2003. Since 2009, however, the production has decreased to a lower level, fluctuating around 720 million barrels a year. The production of oil derivatives has continuously diminished since the late 1990s until now. Second, the crude oil prices have skyrocketed since 2004, increasing from 31.08 USD and 28.85 USD per barrel (WTI and Brent, respectively) during 2003 to 97.98 USD and 108.56 per barrel during 2013 (WTI and Brent, respectively). Based on this extraordinary increase of the oil crude prices, the fiscal revenue has been notably maximized since 2004 in spite of the unchanged oil production and even despite the decreased oil production since 2009. Table 3.5 clearly substantiates this (Table 3.5).

From 2004 to 2011 (latest published figure), the fiscal revenue brought about a permanent increase, only interrupted in 2010. As pointed out above, this increase was associated with the extraordinary increase of the oil prices, which maximized the fiscal non-tributary revenue (mostly composed of oil revenue), as shown in Table 3.5 (Table 3.5). The fiscal tributary revenue (mostly composed of non-oil revenue) has advanced since 2004 as well, but this increase has come about at a lower rate. Besides, the tributary fiscal revenue barely represented 11.1% of the GDP between 2000 and 2011. In addition to this, the fiscal tributary revenue in Venezuela is mostly associated with the value-added tax, a highly regressive indirect tax.

The government could capitalize on the extraordinary increase of the crude oil prices due to the reform of the oil sector sanctioned by President Chávez in 2001. Basically, the reform of the oil sector brought about three main changes. First, it reestablished the control of the government over PDVSA, displacing the upper management who in practice had taken over its control in the early 1990s. Second, it restructuralized the oil taxes to the oil companies, replacing the existing income taxes with oil royalties. This change purposed to decrease the high tax evasion of the

Table 3.4 Oil production and oil prices

	Crude oil (thousands of barrels)	Oil derivatives (thousands of barrels)	Annual average oil price WTI (USD per barrel)	Annual average oil price brent (USD per barrel)
1997	813,000	295,000	20.61	19.11
1998	835,000	299,000	14.42	12.76
1999	725,000	302,000	19.34	17.9
2000	787,000	290,000	30.38	28.66
2001	830,000	243,000	25.98	24.46
2002	747,000	220,000	26.18	24.99
2003	726,000	179,000	31.08	28.85
2004	799,000	232,000	41.51	38.26
2005	845,000	224,000	56.64	54.57
2006	853,000	223,000	66.05	65.16
2007	807,000	211,000	72.34	72.44
2008	813,000	244,000	99.67	96.94
2009	737,000	242,000	61.95	61.74
2010	696,000	188,000	79.48	79.61
2011	702,000	201,000	94.88	111.26
2012	759,000	186,000	94.05	111.63
2013	706,000	179,000	97.98	108.56
Average production 1997–2008	798,333	246,833		
Average production 2009–2013	720,000	199,200		

Source BCV (2015) and US EIA

oil companies. Third, it established the majority shareholding of the state in the oil mixed companies.

As recounted above, the reform of the oil sanctioned by the government of President in 2001 sparked off the violent rejection of the opposition, becoming the main issue around which the struggles for hegemony between government and opposition revolved. In this context, the opposition carried out the failed coup perpetrated in April 2002, the oil strike sustained between December 2002 and February 2003 and the presidential recall referendum held in August 2004, which conclusively determined the total control of PDVSA by the government and the displacement of the upper management aligned with the opposition.

The fulfillment of the reform of the oil sector provided the government with the unrestricted ownership of the oil resources, what naturally maximized its structural power resources and decreased the structural power resources of the opposition, particularly of the FEDECAMRAS and the CTV. The availability of the extraordinary

Table 3.5 Fiscal revenue

	Tributary (mostly non-oil) (millions of constant VEF)	Variation (%)	Share of GDP (%)	Non-tributary (mostly oil) (millions of constant VEF)	Variation (%)	Share of GDP (%)	Total	Variation (%)	Share of GDP (%)
2000	7,433,776		9.3	18,612,769		23.4	26,046,545		32.7
2001	7,830,469	5.1	9.6	14,474,856	−22.23	17.7	22,305,325	−14.36	27.3
2002	7,244,036	−8.1	10.0	14,067,112	−2.82	19.5	21,311,148	−4.46	29.5
2003	9,021,498	19.7	10.3	19,217,903	36.62	22.0	28,249,842	32.56	32.3
2004	16,011,766	43.7	11.4	32,281,073	67.97	23.0	48,298,736	70.97	34.4
2005	25,874,902	38.1	12.1	54,627,064	69.22	25.5	80,522,581	66.72	37.6
2006	39,466,228	34.4	12.2	82,324,349	50.70	25.5	121,797,017	51.26	37.7
2007	52,825,722	25.3	12.8	85,735,059	4.14	20.8	138,560,782	13.76	33.7
2008	53,551,180	1.4	11.5	95,189,806	11.03	20.4	148,740,986	7.35	31.9
2009	79,976,620	33.0	12.4	80,276,441	−15.67	12.4	160,253,061	7.74	24.8
2010	56,229,512	−42.2	10.2	60,383,005	−24.78	11.0	116,612,517	−27.23	21.2
2011	109,707,136	48.7	11.3	152,667,338	152.83	15.7	262,374,474	125.00	26.9

Source MPPEF (2015)

Table 3.6 Public and private oil production share

	Crude oil (thousands of barrels)	Public companies (thousands of barrels)	Private companies (thousands of barrels)	Public share (%)	Private share (%)
2000	787,000	720,000	67,000	91.49	8.51
2001	830,000	735,000	95,000	88.55	11.45
2002	747,000	622,000	125,000	83.27	16.73
2003	726,000	560,000	166,000	77.13	22.87
2004	799,000	601,000	198,000	75.22	24.78
2005	845,000	612,000	233,000	72.43	27.57
2006	853,000	633,000	220,000	74.21	25.79
2007	807,000	609,000	198,000	75.46	24.54
2008	813,000	813,000	0	100.00	0.00
2009	737,000	737,000	0	100.00	0.00
2010	696,000	696,000	0	100.00	0.00
2011	702,000	702,000	0	100.00	0.00
2012	759,000	759,000	0	100.00	0.00
2013	706,000	706,000	0	100.00	0.00

Source BCV (2015)

oil resources received since 2004 represented the structural basis on which the government effectively established the parallel structure of social policy of the Misiones Bolivarianas.

Control of Oil Resources

With regard to the control over the oil resources, the reform of the oil sector initiated in 2001 brought about three main changes.

First, the reform established that the extraction of crude had to be carried out by the state or, eventually, by mixed oil companies with the state as the majority holder. For this reason, the share of PDVSA in the oil sector significantly branched out, as Table 3.6 corroborates (Table 3.6). The state share of the oil production came up from 72.43% in 2005 to 100.00% in 2008, which naturally brought about an increased control over the oil resources by the national government.

Second, the reform additionally brought about the ouster of the upper managers of PDVSA who participated in the oil strike against the government. After the end of the oil strike, the upper managers were superseded with military officers subordinated to the government (López Sánchez 2012). Likewise, the government took over the control of the oil labor unions, for which it took down the Unión Nacional de Trabajadores Petroleros (English: Nation Union of Oil Workers) (hereinafter UNAPETROL), an oil labor union allied to the CTV which actively participated in the oil strike, from the collective bargaining, and advantaged the Federación Unitaria de Trabajadores del Petróleo, del Gas, sus Similares y Derivados de Venezuela (English: Unitary Federation of Oil, Gas and Derivatives Workers) (hereinafter FUTPV), an oil labor union which repudiated the oil strike. This way, the government effectively subordinated the managers and the workers of PDVSA to the president of the company and minister of oil and mining, who was in turn subordinated to the president.

Third, the reform of the oil sector was accompanied by the reform of the central bank sanctioned in 2005, which prescribed that the surplus funds of PDVSA had to be canalized to a special fund called Fondo de Desarrollo Nacional (English: National Development Fund) (hereinafter FONDEN) instead of being deposited in the central bank. Since the FONDEN was subordinated to the central government, the reform to the central bank capacitated the government to determine the use of surplus funds of PDVSA obtained from the oil exports with even less accountability than before.

In a nutshell, the control exercised by the government over the oil resources significantly advanced after the reform of the oil sector due to the (1) expansion of the share of the state oil company PDVSA in the oil production, (2) the subordination of the managers and workers of PDVSA to the government, and (3) the lessening of the accountability of the government for its use of the oil revenue.

3.2.1.2 Labor Informality as Power Resource

As a power resource, labor informality is characterized by extraordinary features compared to the "conventional" power resources. First, it is not correlated with its possession, for labor informality does not represent something "possessable". On the contrary, labor informality predetermines the possibilities of social, economic, and political actors to accumulate other power resources (associational, institutional, mobilizational, etc.). For this reason, labor informality is usually conceptualized as a contextual factor which determines the development of the power resources of the contending actors instead of a power resource itself (Filgueira 1998, 2007; Huber and Stephens 2005; Pribble 2006; Segura-Ubiergo 2007). However, this approach presupposes that labor informality represents a structurally given condition to which labor-related actors are inevitably subordinated. This assumption may correspond with the situation of the labor unions, around which political class struggles approaches revolve. However, as soon as the analytical scope is maximized in order to come across the remaining actors involved in the conflict (especially the government and the employers' organizations), labor informality materializes as the result of the very conscious actions of the social, economic, and political actors, who capitalize on labor informality as a resource in order to accomplish their goals. In this sense, though not "possessable" as conventional power resources, labor informality clearly represents a type of power resource available to some of the contending actors. Second, labor informality brings about dissimilar effects depending on the social, economic, and political actors in question. No doubt, high labor informality decreases the potential power of labor unions and working-class political parties in terms of their associational, institutional, and mobilizational power resources and vice versa (Boffi 2015). However, high labor informality maximizes the potential power resources of nonlabor related social organizations and nonlabor related political parties and vice versa. Employers' organizations definitely capitalize on the relative weakening of labor unions and working-class political parties, but high labor informality does not necessarily advance their own power resources. The effect of labor informality on the power resources of the government divaricates depending on several factors. In principle, informal workers circumvent taxes (Chen 2005: 6), what naturally diminishes the tax revenue collected by the government. Additionally, informal workers do not disburse social security contributions and receive the social services of the noncontributory pillar of the social security system. In this regard, labor informality rather decreases the potential economic power resources of the government. Nevertheless, precisely for these reasons informal labor brings about the context for the clientelistic use of social policy by the government, in which case the beneficiaries of the social services provided by the government must reciprocate them with their political support. Under these circumstances, the increase of labor informality can eventually bring about the potential increase of the government's associational, electoral, and mobilizational power. However, this situation cannot be presupposed in advance, since it is determined by the way in which the government and the popular sectors typically associated to the informal labor correlate with one another.

As pointed out above, the economy of Venezuela is characterized by a high level of labor informality (ILO 2011), defined as unregistered and unprotected labor, including both self-employed and waged employed workers (Chen 2005). In fact, the subject of the universalization of social security in Venezuela is inextricably associated with the high level of labor informality, which precludes the majority of the population from social security.

In order to contextualize the labor situation in Venezuela since 2000, Tables 3.7 and 3.8 bring out a compendium of fundamental labor indicators (Tables 3.7 and 3.8).

Tables 3.7 and 3.8 substantiate that the labor situation in Venezuela substantially ameliorated since Chávez' coming to power in 1999 (Tables 3.7 and 3.8). General unemployment came down from 14.50% in 2000 to 6.70% in 2014, approaching full employment. Despite a slightly worse situation, female unemployment diminished between 2000 and 2014 as well, coming down from 16.10 to 7.70%, respectively. The labor participation rate advanced from 55.05% in 2000 to 60.09% in 2015 and the female participation ameliorated as well, increasing from 36.89 to 46.06 during the same period. The nominal minimum salary has remarkably accelerated since 2000, as Table 3.8 brings out (Table 3.8). Nonetheless, due to the elevated inflation registered the real minimum salary advanced to a lesser extent.

In this context, the informal labor accompanied the positive development of the labor situation, decreasing around twelve percentage points since between 2000 and 2014 (Table 3.9). According to the INEV, the informal labor rate (including domestic labor) came down from 53.0% in 2000 to 41.6% in 2014, and the female informal labor rate diminished from 52.9% in 2000 to 38.2% in 2014.

Table 3.7 Labor force

	Total population	Working age population	Economically active population	Labor participation (%)	Female labor participation (%)
2000	24,183,007	15,984,803	8,862,015	55.05	36.89
2001	24,627,099	16,432,475	9,150,709	55.39	37.56
2002	25,072,822	16,878,958	9,441,329	55.72	38.19
2003	25,518,258	17,285,364	9,734,037	56.06	38.80
2004	25,962,781	17,749,525	10,029,423	56.41	39.42
2005	26,405,604	18,253,996	10,326,957	56.77	40.05
2006	26,845,759	18,693,110	10,625,580	57.15	40.69
2007	27,282,416	19,112,242	10,924,842	57.52	41.32
2008	27,714,508	19,526,361	11,223,731	57.88	41.94
2009	28,140,883	19,942,923	11,521,132	58.23	42.55
2010	28,560,293	20,353,798	11,816,253	58.56	43.15
2011	28,971,448	20,766,473	12,107,447	58.89	43.73
2012	29,374,449	21,172,017	12,398,210	59.21	44.33
2013	29,772,739	21,578,165	12,688,450	59.52	44.92
2014	30,165,900	21,881,807	12,976,957	59.81	45.50
2015	30,553,587	22,112,737	13,263,389	60.09	46.06

Source INEV (2015) and CEPALSTAT (2015)

While certainly significant, the reduction of informal labor achieved since 2000 has not fully correlated the remarking decrease of unemployment accomplished during the same period. The persistence of a high level of informal labor brings out the structural character of labor informality in Venezuela (ILO 2011) and reciprocates the difficulties experienced by all Latin American countries in reducing labor informality below a predetermined threshold (ILO 2011).

For this reason, the reduction of labor informality achieved since 2000 did not bring about a relevant increase of the associational, institutional, and mobilizational power resources of the labor unions and the working class political parties. Likewise, it did not presuppose a substantial increase in the tax revenues collected by the government.

3.2.2 Operationalization of the "What" Question

The reconstruction of the power struggles over the post-neoliberal social security system reform in Venezuela brought out that the conflicts revolved around (1) the introduction of individual capitalization pension funds managed by private administrators and (2) the continuity of the existing special pension regimes.

Table 3.8 Labor situation

	Unemployment rate (%)	Female unemployment rate (%)	Minimum salary (VEF)	Variation (%)	Inflation rate (%)
1999	14.50	16.10	120.00	20.00	20.0
2000	13.20	14.40	144.00	20.00	13.4
2001	12.80	14.60	158.40	10.00	12.3
2002	16.20	18.80	190.08	20.00	31.2
2003	16.80	20.30	247.10	30.00	27.1
2004	13.90	16.40	321.24	30.00	19.2
2005	11.40	13.00	405.00	26.07	14.4
2006	9.30	11.10	512.33	26.50	17.0
2007	7.50	8.10	614.79	20.00	22.5
2008	6.90	7.40	799.23	30.00	31.9
2009	8.10	9.00	959.08	20.00	26.9
2010	8.50	9.40	1223.89	27.61	27.4
2011	7.80	9.10	1548.21	26.50	29.0
2012	7.40	8.40	2047.52	32.25	19.5
2013	7.50	8.70	2973.00	45.20	52.7
2014	6.70	7.70	4889.11	64.45	64.7

Source INEV (2015)

Table 3.9 Informal labor

	Formal labor rate (%)	Informal labor rate 1 (%)	Female informal labor rate (%)	Domestic labor rate (%)
2000	47.0	53.0	52.9	2.1
2001	50.1	49.9	52.6	2.1
2002	48.6	51.4	53.5	2.6
2003	47.3	52.7	54.4	2.9
2004	51.1	48.9	49.5	2.6
2005	53.3	46.7	47.1	2.4
2006	54.7	45.3	45.1	2.1
2007	56.0	44.0	43.8	2.0
2008	56.6	43.4	42.5	1.7
2009	55.9	44.1	42.5	1.5
2010	55.7	44.3	41.6	1.4
2011	56.1	43.9	41.1	1.2
2012	57.9	42.1	39.4	1.4
2013	59.1	40.9	38.0	1.5
2014	59.2	41.6	38.2	1.5

Source INEV (2015)

The fact that the struggles over the reform were principally associated with the reform of the pension system was predicated on two circumstances. First and foremost, as pointed out above the introduction of private pension funds represented a billion-worth business opportunity for the banking sector. In addition, the assimilation of the existing special pension regimes into private pension funds would maximize the profit of the private administrators. Second, the reform of the pension system represented an all-or-nothing dispute, since it either established private pension funds or completely precluded them. In contrast, the health system reform did not hold back the private provision of health services through optional prepaid health insurances.

Even though both points of contention (the introduction of private pension funds and the continuity of the existing special pension regimes) initially generated internal divisions within the government and the opposition, the radicalization of the hegemonic struggles between them brought about the end of the struggles over the social security system reform when the government abruptly promulgated the LOSSSV on 30 December 2002, in the midst of the oil strike. Paradoxically, the radicalization of the struggles for hegemony between government and opposition also brought about the development of a parallel ad hoc structure of social security by the government, which eventually precluded the implementation of the LOSSSV.

The power struggles over the continuity of the preexisting special social security regimes and the orientation of the state contribution to the pension system cannot be directly extrapolated into specific forms of power resources. However, due to their specific characteristics, these struggles are associated with particular forms of power resources (structural, associational, institutional, etc.).

3.2.2.1   The Struggles over the Introduction of Individual Capitalization Pension Funds Managed by Private Administrators

The introduction of individual capitalization pension funds managed by private administrators, commonly referred as the privatization of the pension system, had been undertaken by the previous government of President Rafael Caldera. However, the implementation of the privatization reform broke down when President Hugo Chávez took over power in 1999. Chávez had openly repudiated the complete privatization of the pension system proposed by Caldera during his electoral campaign, however, he had not clearly brought out what kind of pension system he actually purposed. The reason of the impreciseness was predicated on the existence of conflicting positions within the MVR between those who advocated an exclusively state public pension system and those who advocated a mixed pension system with the participation of private pension administrators. For this reason, once in power Chávez promulgated the suspension of the privatization reform promoted by Caldera's government but he initially did not carry out modifications to the existing pension system.

After this, the struggles over the introduction of the private sector into the pension system commenced, facing the sector of the government which repudiated it with the opposition and the sector of the government which advocated it. The struggles among these actors comprised three subsequent phases: (1) the struggles in the constituent assembly over the constitutional articles regarding social security, (2) the struggles within the government over the formulation of the draft bill for the social security system reform before its introduction in the national assembly, and (3) the struggles in the national assembly over the bill for the social security system reform at first and second reading

The conflicting positions over the introduction of private individual capitalization funds came clearly out in the constituent assembly for the first time. The constitutional articles on social security were firstly deliberated in the Commission of Social and Family Rights which after long and heated internal discussions finally handed over its draft to the plenary assembly. The draft of the commission explicitly precluded the participation of the profit-making private sector in the administration of the obligatory contributions of the affiliates to the social insurances, what was fiercely repudiated by a group of constituents in the plenary assembly. Most of these constituents were politically associated with the political parties opposed to the government, however, a sector of the constituents of the MVR led by Leopoldo Puchi. In the end, the majority of the constituents subscribed to the draft proposed by the commission which prescribed the prohibition of the private profit-making administration of the obligatory contributions.

Nevertheless, the final constitutional text promulgated in the official gazette incredibly comprised a modified article on this matter, superseding the explicit prohibition of the private administration of the obligatory contributions of the affiliates, as sanctioned by the constituent assembly, with an ambiguous passage which established that the administration of the obligatory contributions had to be carried out with "social purposes" under the state's supervision. The distortion of the constitutional article approved by the constituent assembly corroborated the internal dispute within the government on this matter. As pointed out above, whereas one sector of the government party purposed a state public pension system, another sector of the government advocated a mixed system, in accordance with the opposition.

In this initial phase of the struggles over the introduction of individual capitalization pension funds administered by private administrators, the power resources mobilized by the contending actors were circumscribed to their political associational power resources. However, the aforementioned alteration of the constitutional text finally promulgated brought out the utilization of surreptitious actions which could only be acknowledged through the detailed reconstruction of the power struggles over the reform.

The disagreement within the government carried over into the formulation of the draft bill of organic law of social security. After the sanction of the new constitution, Chávez established a presidential commission in order to bring about the draft bill for the social security system reform. The commission mostly comprised ministers, technicians, and representatives of the employers' organizations who openly advocated the participation of private pension administrators in the pension system. Expectedly, the presidential commission brought about a draft bill which advanced the introduction of individual capitalization pension funds administered by private pension administrators. Chávez delivered the draft bill to the "social cabinet" of the government, composed by the minister of environment, the minister of education and the minister of health and social development, in order to receive their feedback on the draft bill before presenting it to the national assembly. The ministers of the social cabinet repudiated the draft bill because of its privatization bias, what stalemated the formulation of the draft bill.

In this phase, the power resources mobilized by the contending actors comprised the corporative associational, the political associational and marginally the communicational power resources as well. The sectors of the government for and against the introduction of private pension administrators capitalized on their political associational power resources, using their positions in the cabinet in order to advance their stances, and the FEDECAMARAS mobilized its corporative associational power resources in order to participate in the presidential commission as the legitimate representation of the employers. Additionally, the FEDECAMARAS continuously advanced the introduction of private pension administrators through the mobilization of their communicational power resources, advertising for it in its allied printed and broadcasted media.

Finally, the struggles over the introduction of the private pension administrators carried through to the national assembly, where the treatment of the submitted bills for the social security system reform commenced before the government could resolve its internal dispute on this matter. The sector of the government party which repudiated the participation of the private pension administrators in the pension system preponderated in the plenary assembly and in the commission in charge of the formulation of the bill. However, the sector of the government party in favor of the introduction of private pension administrators actively contravened the bill formulated by the assembly commission through the assembly office for financial assessment under its political control. In addition, the assembly members of the government party in favor of the private pension administrators denounced the bill delivered by the assembly commission as financially unsustainable in the plenary discussion at first reading. The opposition parties represented in the assembly repudiated the bill of the assembly commission at first reading as well, characterizing it as "too statist". However, due to its minority position in the assembly, the role of the opposition parties was circumscribed to pointing out observations to the bill. On the contrary, the non-parliamentary actors in favor of the private pension administrators took over a much more active role in the dispute over the bill of the assembly commission. The FEDECAMARAS and the recently created APAFP, a lobby group promoting private pension administrators, carried out a very intense media campaign against the exclusion of the private sector from the pension system.

Soon after the first reading, the legislative activity broke down as the conflict between government and opposition over the reforms of the oil and agriculture sectors escalated into an open confrontation, in which the contending actors subordinated their corporative and political power resources and mobilized their mobilizational and communicational power resources in an all-or-nothing confrontation. The peak of the conflict came about when the opposition perpetrated a coup which removed President Chávez from the government for two days after which he took over power again thanks to the massive popular mobilizations demanding his restitution and the support of a loyal sector of the military forces.

From then on, the struggles over the introduction of individual capitalization pension funds managed by private administrators were more and more dovetailed with the struggles between government and opposition for hegemony, in which the reforms of the oil and agriculture sectors represented the main points of contention. In this contest, the use of corporative and political associational power resources decreased and the contending actors increasingly mobilized their mobilizational and communication power resources. The radicalization of the hegemonic struggles between government and opposition also brought about the weakening of the sector of the government party which advocated a mixed pension system.

Against this background, the legislative treatment of the bill for the social security system reform recommenced during a truce in the struggles between government and opposition after the failed coup. Once more, the contending actors mobilized their corporative and political power resources in order to advance their positions in the commission in charge of reformulating the bill. The non-parliamentary actors supporting the introduction of private pension administrators comprised the employers' organization FEDECAMARAS, the lobby group APAFP and the labor unions CTV and CODESA, whereas the non-parliamentary actors against the private pension administration comprised the labor unions CUTV, FBT, and the lobby group REDIUP. All of them participated in the consultations convocated by the commission. After the consultations the commission circulated a draft bill containing an intermediate pension system which was repudiated by all contending actors alike, retracing the process of reformulation to the beginning. Nonetheless, the legislative bargaining did not completely break down until the truce between government and opposition collapsed and the hegemonic struggles commenced anew. In this context, the opposition parties broke away from the national assembly in the context of the oil strike and the assembly commission brought out a reformulated bill for the second hearing which deracinated the private administration of the obligatory contributions to the social security system. In this context of political radicalization, all the assembly members of the government party, including the assembly members who had repudiated the bill approved at the first hearing, subscribed to the bill reformulated for the second hearing, sanctioning it on 6 December 2002 in absence of the opposition.

In this final phase, the power resources mobilized by the contending actors initially comprised the corporative associational, the political associational and the communicational power resources. However, in the context of escalating political radicalization, the struggles over the introduction of private pension administrators into the pension system increasingly coalesced with the hegemonic struggles between government and opposition. Against this background, the actors involved in the struggles over the introduction of private pension administrators increasingly mobilized their mobilizational and power resources.

In a nutshell, the struggles over the introduction of individual capitalization pension funds managed by private administrators comprised three subsequent phases: (1) the struggles in the constituent assembly over the constitutional articles regarding social security, (2) the struggles within the government over the formulation of the draft bill for the social security system reform before its introduction in the national assembly, (3) the struggles in the national assembly over the bill for the social security system reform at first and second reading. Throughout the first and second phases, the contending actors exclusively mobilized their corporative and political power resources. In the third phase, the struggles over the introduction of the private administrators increasingly dovetailed with the struggles between government and opposition for hegemony, in which the reforms of the oil and agriculture sectors represented the main points of contention. As the hegemonic struggles escalated the actors mobilized their communicational and mobilizational power resources more and more, including insurrectional attempts. In the end, the radicalization of the hegemonic struggles brought about the strengthening of the sector of the government against the private pension administrators, which could finally countenance its bill. The sanction of the LOSSSV in December 2002 determined the definitive defeat of the attempt of privatization of the pension system. Paradoxically, however, the radicalization of the hegemonic struggles between government and opposition brought about the establishment of a parallel structure of social security by the government as well, which contravened the implementation of the system of social security prescribed by the LOSSSV.

3.2.2.2 The Struggles over the Continuity of the Existing Special Collective Capitalization Pension Funds

The special pension regimes represent a substantial part of the Venezuelan social security system, even though their actual number and size are not certainly established, as the government acknowledges (Interview with Alviárez 2013). According to the latest available estimation, the total number of special pension regimes approximates 400 (Salcedo González 2006), however, this figure is not corroborated. In any case, the fact that even the employees of the IVSS participate in a special pension regime brings out the scope of their expansion within the pension system.

As mentioned above, the special pension regimes are exclusively associated with the state public sector, including the national, provincial, and municipal public administration, the public universities, the state companies (PDVSA), the autonomous state institutions (IVSS, BCV), the national, provincial, and municipal police forces, etc. Only the military forces are precluded, as they are provided with their own social security system.

In general, the special pension regimes are structuralized as private collective capitalization funds initiated with seed capital from the state. In spite of this, they receive regular state funding as well. The special pension regimes are characterized by high replacement rates, ranging between 80 and 100% and low contributions rates, ranging between 4 and 6%.

The special regimes were established in order to provide pensions to the workers of the state public sector in the absence of a unified pension system. Accordingly, they did not purpose to generate a universal and unified pension system but only to disburse the highest possible pensions to their affiliates. For this reason, the special pension regimes openly contravened the main objective of the social security system reform intended by the government, namely the creation of a universal and unified social security system.

The struggles over the existing special pension regimes concatenated two consecutive phases: (1) the struggles in the constituent assembly over the constitutional articles regarding social security and (2) the struggles in the national assembly over the bill for the social security system reform at first reading. The actors involved in the struggles over the existing special pension regimes comprised all the actors who participated in the struggles over the introduction of private pension administrators: the government, the political parties, the labor unions, the employers' organizations, the lobby groups, the professional associations, and the NGO's. However, one actor, in particular, participated very actively in the struggles over the special pension regimes: the FAPUV, which congregated the professors of the public universities. Since the university professors were associated to special pension regimes with extraordinarily good conditions, the FAPUV naturally advocated their continuity. This position contravened the unification of the pension system proposed by the sector government which purposed a universal state public PAYG pension system. However, the FAPUV also repudiated the establishment of a mixed pension system proposed by a sector of the government and the opposition, which presupposed the elimination of the special pension regimes as well.

In the first phase of the struggles over the special pension regimes, the FAPUV mobilized their corporative associational power resources in order to advance its interests within the constituent assembly, presenting its own constitution proposal for the constitutional articles concerning social security. Smartly, the proposal of the FAPUV established a universal and non-unified PAYG pension system in which the special pension regimes were carried over. The proposal was finally renunciated but, in the end, the FAPUV and the sector of the government promoting a universal PAYG pension system came around with a tacit compromise according to which the special pension regimes would be concatenated with the general pension regime only when the new unified pension system was completely established, preserving the value of the pensions already paid to the pensioners of the special pension regimes.

After the constituent assembly both, the professional associations defending the continuity of the special pension regimes and the sector of the government promoting a universal state public pension system were precluded from the presidential commission convocated by President Chávez to devise the draft bill for the social security system reform. For this reason, the second phase of the struggles over the maintenance or elimination of the existing special pension regimes came about when the national assembly commenced the legislative treatment of the bill for the social security system reform at first reading.

In the second phase of the struggles, the actors carried over their foregoing positions regarding the special pension regimes. The FAPUV mobilized its corporative associational power resources again, participating in the assembly commission in charge of the formulation of the bill for the first reading. Despite some differences regarding the transition period, the FAPUV could successfully reestablish the compromise agreement reached in the constituent assembly with the sector of the government party which advocated a state public PAYG pension system. Thus, the bill submitted by the assembly commission for the first reading established that the incorporation of the special pension regimes into the general pension would only be carried out when the new pension system was completely established. Besides, the value of the current pensions paid to the pensioners of the special regimes would be carried over into the new pension system. Despite the modifications made in the bill for the second reading, the compromise agreement regarding the special pension regimes came out in the bill prepared for the second reading without changes. As pointed out above, this bill received the approval of the national assembly on 6 December 2002.

3.2.3   Operationalization of the "Who" Question

The reconstruction of the power struggles over the social security system reform brought out: (1) the existence of a manifold entanglement of social actors involved in the struggles over the social security system reform, much more complex than the social actors presupposed by political class struggles approaches, and (2) the extraordinary importance of the government as social, economic, and political actor due to its prerogative over the oil sector.

Just as in the case of the "what" question, these two issues cannot be directly extrapolated into specific forms of power resources. However, the operationalization of the power resources mobilized by the contending actors cannot be carried out without clearly determining the contours of the actors at issue, for which the analysis of these issues must be necessarily undertaken.

As pointed out above, the actors involved in the power struggles over the reform divaricate from the actors presupposed by political class struggle approaches. In addition to the conventional class actors contemplated in political class struggles approaches (labor unions, employers' organizations and class political parties), the reconstruction of the power struggles showed up the existence of manifold entanglement of actors involved in the struggles over the reform. This multiple complexes of social actors commingled professional associations, expert groups, feminist organizations, lobby groups, nongovernmental organizations, bureaucratic groups, etc. Besides, the reconstruction brought out the centrality of the government as a contending actor in the struggles over the reform. This openly contravened the assumptions of political class struggle approaches in this regard as well.

Based on their scope, the contending actors can be categorized into two different types: macro and meso actors (Li 2012).

3.2.3.1   Macro Actors

The first type of actors comprises the macro actors. The macro actors commingle a nationwide organizational structure with the disposal of three or more types of power resources (structural, associational, institutional, mobilizational or communicational). Most of these actors are looked upon by political class struggle approaches: political parties, labor unions, and employers' organizations. The national government is comprised in this category as well. The relative power of macro actors can be approximated with relative ease in most cases.

Government

The government has always represented a constitutive factor of the Venezuelan society.[8] Nonetheless, since Chávez' assumption of power in 1999 the government maximized its participation in the social, economic and political affairs as never before (Córdova 2006; Cilano et al. 2009; Morales 2012).

As recounted above, the Chávez coming to power came about in the context of the crisis of the historic bloc initiated in 1958, which commingled the traditional political parties (the AD and the COPEI), the vested labor unions (CTV and CODESA) and the largest employers' organization (the FEDECAMARAS). For this reason, the political alliance which initially accompanied Chávez to the presidency in 1999 conglomerated a very heterogeneous amalgam of social, economic, and political actors excluded from the power bloc, including old and new political parties (such as the PCV, the MEP, the MAS, and the PPT), as well as old and new labor unions (such as the CUTV and the FBT). Even though this heterogeneous alliance represented a precarious political structure, Chávez successfully brought around the non-organized marginalized popular sectors making up the majority of the Venezuelan society.

As the social, economic, and political actors removed from power undertook an all-or-nothing offense against the elected government, the alliance between the marginalized popular sectors and the government was maximized and the marginalized popular sectors took over as the main support base of the Chávez' government, together with the military forces. Based on this alliance, the government successfully counterbalanced the coup and the oil strike carried out by the opposition between 2001 and 2002, and finally broke down the opposition in the presidential recall election held in 2004. In parallel, the government increasingly structuralized its political support base through the creation of grassroots organizations, which eventually brought about its remarking electoral successes, winning the presidential elections in 2006 and 2012, the assembly elections in 2005 and 2010, and the regional elections in 2004, 2008, and 2012.

The strengthening of the government since 2004 was not exclusively predicated on the definitive defeat of the opposition in the recall election of 2004 and the successful political organization of its support base. Along with this, the strengthening of the

---

[8]Even though the historical reasons of this centrality cannot be recapitulated here due to space constraints, the main finding of the researchers who broke down the relation between state and society in Latin America basically pointed out that the state brought about the society in the Latin American countries whereas the society brought about the state in the Northern industrialized countries (Oszlak 1979, 1981, 1982; Oszlak and O'Donnell 1981; Portantiero 1981, 1985, 1988; Aricó 1988).

government was correlated with the increase of the state economic resources and the expansion of the state apparatus (Cilano et al. 2009).

As analyzed above, the increase of the state economic resources was associated with the rise of the fiscal oil revenue, which was predicated on (1) the substantial increase of the international oil prices and (2) the reform of the oil sector carried out by the government which successfully canalized the extraordinary oil revenue to the public treasury.

The expansion of the state apparatus came about in two areas. First, the state maximized its participation in the economy through the nationalization, renationalization, and expropriation of private enterprises, as well as through the expansion of state credit (Cilano et al. 2009: 64). Second, the state massively broadened out its provision of social services, providing health care, subsidized food, education, job training, etc. To this end, a parallel state structure was established, what naturally brought about the expansion of the state apparatus (Cilano et al. 2009: 64–65). The expansion in both areas came about in conjunction with the amplification of the presence of the military forces in the state apparatus, as military members took over the control of the state enterprises and the social programs in most cases (Morales 2012). This amplification of the economic and political influence of the military forces, however, was not accompanied by the expansion of the military expenditure, which stabilized around 1.3% of the GDP since 1999.

In the matter of the social security system reform, the government has represented the driving force since its coming to power in 1999. Thereby, as soon as the government took over power in 1999, it immediately brought about the suspension of the neoliberal social security system reform initiated by the government of Caldera one year before. As pointed above, this reform purposed to establish an exclusively private pension system after the Chilean pension system imposed by the military government of Pinochet in 1980. However, the general agreement within Chávez' government regarding the suspension of the neoliberal reform in course came across the internal disagreement concerning the model of social security system which should be advocated. The main disagreement revolved around the pension system, about which the positions within the government divaricated between the creation of a state unified PAYG pension system and the creation of a mixed pension system with participation of the private sector. In the end, the radicalization of the hegemonic struggles between the government and the opposition brought about the defeat of the sector of the government in favor of the mixed pension system and the victory of the sector of the government supporting the creation of a unified PAYG state pension system.

Compared to other actors involved in the struggles over the social security system reform, the government falls back upon the widest assortment of power resources, comprising structural, associational, institutional, mobilizational, and communicational power resources.

Political Parties

Until the early 1990s, the Venezuelan party system corresponded to the Western European party systems, as the social democratic AD and the Christian democratic COPEI structuralized the left–right political spectrum. However, the crisis of the historic bloc initiated in 1958 brought about the decline of both the AD and the COPEI and the emergence of manifold new political parties, including the MVR led by Hugo Chávez. After Chávez coming to power in 1999 the foregoing left–right political axis (left social democratic, right democratic conservative) metamorphosed into pro-Chavist (left) and anti-Chavist (right). Accordingly, the pro-Chávez parties congregated in the electoral coalition known as the Polo Patriótico (English: Patriotic Pole) and the anti-Chávez parties congregated in the electoral coalition known as the "Coordinadora Democrática" (English: Democratic Coordinator) (CD) until its dissolution in 2004. In 2006 the opposition brought about a new electoral coalition initially known as the "Unidad Nacional" (English: National Unity) and later renamed into "Mesa de Unidad Democrática" (English: Democratic Unity Roundtable) (MUP).

The pro-Chávez political parties gathered in the PP comprised the Partido Comunista de Venezuela (English: Communist Party of Venezuela) (PCV), the Movimiento Electoral del Pueblo (English: Electoral Movement of the People's) (MEP), the Movimiento V República (English: Movement V Republic) (MVR), and the Patria para Todos (Fatherland for All) (PPT).

In turn, the anti-Chávez political parties gathered in the CD comprised the La Causa Radical (English: The Radical Cause) (LCR), the Movimiento al Socialismo (English: Movement toward Socialism) (MAS), the Un Nuevo Tiempo (English: A New Era) (UNT), the Primero Justicia (English: Justice First) (PJ), the Acción Democrática (English: Democratic Action) (AD), and the Comité de Organización Política Electoral Independiente (English: Committee of Political Electoral Independent Organization) (COPEI). Despite the clear ideological placement of the parties, their social bases do not necessarily correspond to the social bases of the ideologically analogous political parties of the Northern industrialized countries.

Founded in 1931, the Partido Comunista de Venezuela (English: Communist Party of Venezuela) (PCV), the PCV politically represents the revolutionary left. In 1998, the PCV participated in the electoral coalition of left-wing political parties which successfully advanced the candidacy of Hugo Chávez to the presidency. Since then, it has accompanied Chávez' government as the biggest allied party outside the MVR.

The PCV is politically associated with the Central Unitaria de Trabajadores de Venezuela (English: United Confederation of Workers of Venezuela) (CUTV), a historic labor confederation particularly strong in the metallurgical sector.

Regarding the social security system reform, the PCV has always advocated the universalization of social security and the establishment of a state unified PAYG pension system. As a matter of fact, the main advocates of the creation of a state universal and unified PAYG pension system within the government came down from the PCV.

The Movimiento Electoral del Pueblo (English: Electoral Movement of the People's) (MEP) conglomerated the national left until its dissolution in 2007. The MEP accompanied the presidential candidacy of Chávez in the presidential elections of 1998 and subsequently participated in the government coalition as a minor allied party. After the presidential elections held in 2006, Chávez undertook the creation of a unified political party in order to coalesce all pro-Chavist political parties into it, what finally determined the dissolution of the MEP and its integration into the PSUV.

With regard to the social security system reform, the MEP advocated the universalization of social security and the establishment of a state unified PAYG pension system.

Created in 1997, the Movimiento V República (English: Movement V Republic) (MVR) represented the political party of president Chávez till 2007 when it was coalesced into the Partido Socialista Unido de Venezuela (English: United Socialist Party of Venezuela) (PSUV). Until then, the MVR comprised the main political party within the PP, the pro-Chavist political coalition.

As government party, the MVR carried out political alliances with several preexisting labor unions affiliated to the Central de Trabajadores de Venezuela (English: Confederation of Workers of Venezuela) (CTV), the Confederación de Sindicatos Autónomos de Venezuela (English: Confederation of Autonomous Labor Unions of Venezuela) (CODESA) and the Confederación General de Trabajadores (English: General Confederation of Workers) (CGT), three historic labor confederations opposed to Chávez' government. These splinter labor unions commingled into a new labor confederation called Unión Nacional de Trabajadores (English: Nation Union of Workers) (UNT) which was politically associated with the government and the government party. Most importantly, the MVR successfully established a strong political relation with the unorganized urban popular classes, expanding its territorial power nationwide. In 2007 Chávez undertook the creation of a unified party in order to coalesce all pro-Chavist political parties into it, founding the Partido Socialista Unido de Venezuela (English: United Socialist Party of Venezuela) (PSUV), what eventually brought about the dissolution of the MVR into the PSUV.

As regards the social security system reform, the MVR was initially partitioned in two opposing fractions. The first fraction advocated the creation of a state universal and unified PAYG pension system, whereas the second fraction purposed the creation of a mixed pension system with participation of private pension administrators. As recounted above, the radicalization of the hegemonic struggles between government and opposition brought about the demise of the second fraction within the MVR.

The Patria para Todos (English: Fatherland for All) (PPT) was established in 1997 as a breakaway of the LCR. Just as the MVR, the PPT came out as a result of the crisis of the traditional political parties AD and COPEI during the 1990s, which generated the emergence of manifold new parties such as the MVR, the PPT, the IPCN, and the CONVERGENCIA (López Maya 2005; Bistoletti 2011). The PPT participated in the political coalition of left-wing political parties which advanced the candidacy of Chávez in 1998 but it broke away from the government in 2000 when it brought out its own candidates for the elections held after the sanction of the sanction of the new constitution. In 2002, the PPT reestablished its political alliance with the government, however, it did not coalesce into the PSUV in 2007 as demanded by Chávez.

The PPT is associated with the labor union Autonomía Sindical (English: Union Autonomy) which participated in the creation of the pro-Chavist labor confederation UNT.

Concerning the social security system reform, the PPT advocated the universalization of social security and the establishment of a state unified PAYG pension system.

Initially established in 1971, as a breakaway of the PCV, the La Causa Radical (English: The Radical Cause) (LCR) politically represents the moderate left. While founded in the 1970s, the LCR accomplished national recognition during the 1990s in the context of the aforementioned crisis of the traditional political parties. In 1997 the LCR determined not to accompany the presidential candidacy of Chávez, what brought about the split of its left wing and the aforesaid foundation of the PPT. After Chávez coming to power in 1999, the LCR advanced the creation of the CD which conglomerated the political parties opposed to the government. Since then, the LCR has repudiated Chávez' government and actively participated in the opposition.

Party leaders of the LCR participate in the national board of the CTV, the largest labor union opposed to the government.

Regarding the social security system reform, the LCR initially advocated the introduction of a universal system of social security and repudiated the creation of a mixed pension system. However, after the split of its left wing in 1997 and even more after the radicalization of the hegemonic struggles between government and opposition, the LCR has come around to the establishment of a mixed pension system with the participation of private pension administrators (López Maya 1997: 54–55)

The MAS coalesces the social democratic left. As the LCR, it came out as a breakaway of the PCV in the 1970s, but it just accomplished national recognition in the 1990s. The MAS participated in the coalition of left-wing political parties which successfully advocated the candidacy of Hugo Chávez to the presidency. However, it backed down from the government coalition in 2002 due to its alleged "authoritarianism" (Últimas Noticias 03/11/2013). Since then, the MAS has politically participated in the opposition to the government, both in the CD and later in the MUD.

Despite its social democratic ideology, the MAS advocated the creation of a mixed pension system since the 1990s.

The Un Nuevo Tiempo (English: A New Era) (UNT) came out as a regional breakaway of the AD in Zulia in 1999. Politically identified with the Third Way centrism, the UNT materialized as a national political party in 2006 when it brought forward the presidential candidacy of its founder Manuel Rosales who would eventually conglomerate the opposition vote against the government. Since its foundation, the UNT has repudiated Chávez' government, participating as one of the largest political parties within the MUD.

Due to its recent foundation, the UNT did not participate in the struggles over the social security system reform which eventually brought about the sanction of the LOSSSV in December 2002. However, the UNT openly advocated the introduction of a mixed system of social security with the participation of private administration funds in the pension system.

Founded in 2000 as a regional party, the Primero Justicia (English: Justice First) (PJ) represents the liberal-conservative right. The PJ came down from a nonprofit organization created by former law students of the private Catholic university Universidad Católica Andrés Bello (English: Catholic University Andrés Bello) in 1992. The PJ accomplished national recognition in 2003 when it participated in the recollection of signatures for the recall referendum. Since its foundation the PJ has repudiated Chávez' government, participating in the CD as one of the largest parties opposed to the government.

With regard to the social security system reform, the PJ repudiated the instauration of a state unified PAYG pension system, advocating the introduction of private pension administrators and the establishment of a mixed pension system.

The Acción Democrática (Democratic Action) (AD) was established in 1941 under military rule. In 1958, the AD participated in the political agreement known as Pacto de Punto Fijo (English: Agreement of Punto Fijo), which delineated the Venezuela political system between 1958 and 1998. During this period, the AD alternately took over the government five times in a two-party system in which it represented the left and the COPEI represented the right. During the 1990s, the social acceptance of the historic bloc initiated in 1958 rashly deteriorated and the political power of the AD precipitately decreased. The AD has openly repudiated Chávez' government from its beginning, participating in the CD and subsequently in the MUD as a minor political party.

The AD was politically associated with the CTV, the largest labor union in Venezuela before Chávez coming to power (Coppedge 1994).

Concerning the social security system reform, the AD purposed to establish a private pension system without the participation of the state during the late 1990s, reproducing the Chilean model of pension system imposed by Pinochet. To this aim, the AD actively participated in the neoliberal social security system reform initiated by Caldera and subsequently suspended by Chávez. Afterwards, the AD advocated the establishment of a mixed pension system with the participation of private pension administrators.

Founded in 1946, the Comité de Organización Política Electoral Independiente (English: Committee of Political Electoral Independent Organization) (COPEI) participated in the Pacto de Punto Fijo as well. Between 1958 and 1998, the COPEI alternately took over the government two times. During the 1990s the social acceptance of the historic bloc initiated in 1958 rashly deteriorated and the political power of the COPEI precipitately decreased. The COPEI has openly repudiated Chávez' government from its beginning, participating in the CD and subsequently in the MUD as minor political party.

The COPEI was politically associated with the CODESA, one of the historical labor unions of Venezuela affiliated to the Latin American Federation of Christian Trade Unionists.

Concerning the social security system reform, the COPEI actively participated in the neoliberal social security system reform initiated by Caldera which purposed the establishment of a completely private pension system. After Chávez' government determined its suspension, the COPEI advocated the creation of a mixed pension system with participation of the private sector.

By definition, the political parties fall back upon three forms of power resources: corporative associational, political associational, and mobilizational.

Labor Unions

Labor unions have historically represented a central part of the Venezuelan society. In fact, the unionization rate approximated 30.00% throughout the 1970s (Bonilla García 2011), resembling the unionization rate of the Western European countries at that time. However, the unionization rate steeply decreased during the 1990s due to the imposition of neoliberal policies of labor flexibilization. After Chávez coming to power in 1999, the labor unions started out a process of politicization which eventually brought about the strong decline of the traditional labor unions and the emergence of new labor unions subordinated to the government. Nonetheless, the unionization rate further deteriorated, falling from approximately 14.00% in 2001 (Lucena 2003) to 11.00% in 2008 (Díaz 2009) and 9.00% in 2013 (El Mundo 30/09/2013). In contrast, the number of labor unions was maximized, but the increase was actually predicated on the fragmentation of the previously existing unions (Díaz 2009).

Until 1999, the labor unions were structuralized into four traditional labor confederations: the Confedereación de Trabajadores de Venezuela (English: Confederation of Workers of Venezuela) (CTV), the Confederación de Sindicatos Autónomos (English: Confederation of Autonomous Unions) (CODESA), the Confederación General del Trabajo (English: General Confederation of Work) (CGT), and the Central Unitaria de Trabajadores de Venezuela (English: United Confederation of Workers of Venezuela) (CUTV). After Chávez coming to power in 1999, the hegemonic struggles between government and opposition came over the traditional labor confederations and their integrant labor unions, dividing them in pro-Chavist and anti-Chavist. In this context, the CTV, the CODESA, and eventually the CGT undertook a central role in the opposition, whereas the CUTV determined to accompany the government. In addition, numerous labor unions affiliated to the CTV, the CODESA, and the CGT abandoned them as they subscribed to the government. These labor unions established a pro-Chavist confederation called Unión de Nacional de Trabajadores (English: National Union of Workers) (UNTR) in 2003.

Created in 1947, the CTV represented the largest labor confederation by far until Chávez coming to power. It conglomerated labor unions from the public and private sectors, including the strategic oil sector. Politically, the CTV was associated with the AD, sharing numerous common leaders. The CTV openly repudiated Chávez' government since its assumption, because of which it actively participated in the coup of April 2002 and the oil strike held between December 2002 and February 2003. In the end, the central role assumed by the CTV in the opposition to Chávez' government brought about its steep decline when the government finally broke through as the winner of the conflict.

The CODESA was established in 1964 as a politically independent labor confederation opposed to the politicized CTV. While clearly smaller than the CTV, the CODESA conglomerated labor unions from the public and labor sectors, including the oil sector. Despite its claimed political independence, the CODESA was associated with the Frente de Trabajadores Copeyanos (English: Front of Copeyano Workers), the union branch of the COPEI which participated in the CTV following a union penetration strategy. The CODESA repudiated Chávez' government since its assumption, however, it did not take over a central role in the opposition as the CTV.

Founded in 1971, the CGT came out as a breakaway from the CODESA. Inspired by the liberation theology, the CGT repudiated the politicization of the CODESA and advocated a politically independent but still classist labor confederation. The CGT initially accompanied Chávez' government but it removed its support later.

The CUTV represents the labor confederation of the PCV. Officially created in 1963, the CUTV materialized from the breakaway of the union leaders of the CTV affiliated to the PCV, the MIR and the URD, who contravened the union leaders of the CTV affiliated to the AD and the COPEI. The CUTV is structuralized around the metallurgical labor unions. Unlike the rest of the traditional labor confederations, the CUTV has politically accompanied Chávez' government from its beginning, in parallel with the CTV.

After the radicalization of the hegemonic struggles between government and opposition, the labor unions which subscribed to the government massively abandoned the labor confederations opposed to Chávez' government, founding the UNTR in 2003. The UNTR conglomerated labor unions from the public and labor sectors, including the strategic oil sector. However, beyond their support to Chávez' government, the labor unions gathered in the UNTR profoundly divaricated with regard to the main objectives of the UNTR. Thus, the UNTR comprised four contending fractions since its creation: (1) the Corriente Clasista, Unitaria, Revolucionaria y Autónoma (English: Classist, United, Revolutionary and Autonomous Current) (CCURA), which accompanied Chávez' government but advocated the autonomy of the UNTR as a classist labor confederation, and (2) the Colectivo de Trabajadores en Revolución (English: Collective of Workers in Revolution) (CTR), which purposed an autonomous labor confederation but politically aligned to government, (3) the Trabajadores por la Patria (English: Workers for the Fatherland) (TPP), which came down from the PPT, and (4) the Fuerza Socialista Bolivariana de Trabajadores (English: Socialist Bolivarian Force of Workers) (FSBT), which was completely subordinated to the government and advocated the elimination of the UNTR and the creation of a unified pro-Chavist labor confederation following the model of the PSUV. The profound disagreements among these fractions brought about the breakaway of the FSBT in 2006 and the breakaway of the CCURA in 2007.

With regard to the social security system reform, the positions of the labor confederations completely divaricated. The CTV, the CODESA, and the CGT openly advocated the creation of a mixed social security system with the participation of private pension administrators (Interviews with Froilán Barrios and Manuel Cova).

As a matter of fact, the CTV, the CODESA, and the CGT had actively participated in the formulation of the neoliberal reform initiated by Caldera and suspended by Chávez. On the contrary, the CUTV and the UNT repudiated the introduction of the private profit-making sector into the pension system and purposed the establishment of a universal and unified system of social security (Interview with Orlando Chirino).

Finally, the Venezuelan labor unions fall back upon corporative associational power resources, mobilizational (even insurrectionary) power resources and structural power resources.

Employers' Organizations

Founded in 1944, the Federación de Cámaras y Asociaciones de Comercio y Producción de Venezuela (English: Federation of Chambers and Associations of Commerce and Production of Venezuela) (FEDECAMARAS) represents the largest and oldest employers' organization. The foundation of FEDECAMARAS materialized through the conflict between the state and the private sector regarding the participation of the state in the economy during the 1930s and 1940s (Hernández 2011). In this context, the FEDECAMARAS came out as a confederation of commerce and production chambers which repudiated the active intervention of the state in the economy promoted by the nationalist military governments (FEDECAMARAS 2014). This intervention purposed to advance from the existing agricultural economy to an industrialized capitalist economy. The oil policy initiated in 1941 by the nationalist military government of Isaías Mendina Angarita, which established the 50–50 distribution of the oil revenue between the state and the international oil companies, and the subsequent nationalization of the oil sector carried out during the 1970s maximized the rejection of FEDECAMARAS to the active participation of the state in the economy. In spite of this, the FEDECAMARAS increasingly maximized its political influence in the successive governments, actively participating in the neoliberal turn initiated in the 1980s and accentuated in the 1990s. Against this background, the FEDECAMARAS expectedly repudiated Chávez' government since its inception, becoming one of its most ferocious adversaries. In fact, the FEDECAMARAS participated in both, the coup of April 2002, which established a de facto government presided by Pedro Carmona, the president of FEDECAMARAS, until the restitution in power of Chávez three days later, and the oil strike, which stalemated the Venezuelan economy for three months. The open confrontation between the FEDECAMARAS and the government brought about its weakening, especially after 2004. In spite of this, the FEDECAMARAS still conglomerates the Consejo Nacional del Comercio y los Servicios (English: National Council of Commerce and Services) (CONSECOMERCIO), the Confederación Venezolana de Industriales (English: Venezuelan Confederation of Industrialists) (CONINDUSTRIA), the Federación Nacional de Ganaderos de Venezuela (English: National Federation of Stockbreeders of Venezuela) (FEDENAGA), and the Confederación de Asociaciones de Productores Agropecuarios (English: Confederation of Associations of Agricultural Producers) (FEDEAGRO), the four largest sectoral employers' organizations.

With regards to the social security system reform, the FEDECAMARAS consequently advocated the privatization of the social security services. In this context, it actively participated in the social security system reform initiated by Caldera, which promulgated the creation of a completely private pension system and the expansion of the private health services within the health system. Accordingly, the FEDECAMARAS repudiated the social security system reform aimed at the establishment of a state unified PAYG pension system which eventually received the sanction of the national assembly in December 2002. However, in recent years, a fraction of the FEDECAMARAS has advocated the implementation of the LOSSSV (Interview with Aurelio Concheso), probably because of its rejection to the Misiones Bolivarianas.

The government of Chávez undertook the foundation of a pro-Chavist employers' organization, promoting the creation of the Empresarios por Venezuela (English: Business for Venezuela) (EMPREVEN). However, the EMPREVEN did not accomplish its goals, practically disappearing in 2009 (El Universal 24/01/2010).

The employers' organizations fall back upon structural power resources through their relation with the upper managers of the oil sector, corporative associational power resources, mobilizational (even insurrectionary) power resources, and communicational power resources.

3.2.3.2   Meso Actors

The second type of actors encompasses the meso actors. Just as the macro actors, the meso actors represent organized groups. However, the meso actors do not accomplish the conditions of the macro actors (a national organizational structure and the disposal of three or more forms of power resources). Some meso actors fall back upon a nationwide organizational structure and sometimes even two forms of power resources (but not three), as in the cases of the peasant and indigenous organizations and the police and military forces. The meso actors comprise a complex of organizations with very diverse characteristics, such as peasant and indigenous groups, military, and police forces, professional associations, nongovernmental organizations, feminist groups, associations of social security beneficiaries, etc. The criterion used for the selection of the meso actors presented below is determined by their participation in the struggles over the reform which, in turn, is delineated in the reconstruction of the struggles effectuated before.

Professional Associations

The Federación de Asociaciones de Profesores Universitatios de Venezuela (English: Federation of Associations of University Professors of Venezuela) (FAPUV) conglomerates the associations of university professors of the public universities throughout Venezuela. Formally, the FAPUV does not represent a labor union but an "academic-trade" association which advocates the interests of the university professors. While formal, this differentiation corresponds with the strategy commonly used by the FAPUV to advance its interests, which capitalizes on its "academic" profile. Based on this strategy, the FAPUV has participated in practically all instances of the struggles over the social security system reform as a provider of expertise.

Above all, the FAPUV purposed the conservation of the special pension regimes, which provided pensions with very high replacement rates (between 80.00 and 100.00%) despite very low contributions (between 4.00 and 6.00%). For this reason, the FAPUV openly repudiated the establishment of a private or a mixed pension system, as the introduction of private pension administrators would necessarily bring about the deterioration of the pensions of its affiliates.

The FAPUV falls back upon corporative associational power resources in two ways. First, it can carry out labor strikes as any professional association. Second, it can participate in decision-making processes through its technical expertise.

Founded in 1941, the Colegio de Médicos del Distrito Metropolitano de Caracas (College of Physicians of the Metropolitan District of Caracas) (English: CMDMC) represents the professional association of the physicians domiciled in Caracas. As the FAPUV, the CMDMC has participated in the struggles over the social security system reform as a provider of expertise, advancing its own bill for the reform.

The CMDMC openly repudiated the establishment of a private or a mixed social security system, as the expansion of the private sector within the system would necessarily bring about the deterioration of both the social services and the labor conditions of its affiliates.

The CMDMC falls back upon corporative associational power resources due to its strike capability and its recognized expertise in health care.

Lobby Groups and Nongovernmental Organizations

The Asociación de Promotores de Administradoras de Fondos de Pensiones (English: Association of Promoters of Pension Funds Administrators) (APAFP) was established by the private financial institutions which purposed to participate in the pension system as private administrator funds. Accordingly, the APAFP advocated the establishment of a mixed pension system with the participation of the private sector. The lobbying of the APAFP revolved around the promotion of the advantages of the individual capitalization pension system and the denouncing of the drawbacks of the state PAYG pension system in the national printed and broadcasted media. Due to the relation between the private media and the private banks, often in the hands of the same owners, the message of the APAFP was copiously disseminated in the national media. The Coordinadora de Redes por una Seguridad Social Pública y Solidaria (English: Coordinator of Networks for Public and Solidary Social Security) (REDIUP) conglomerated the social organizations which repudiated the incorporation of the private administrator fund into the pension system. Even though the REDIUP did not accomplish the impact of the APAFP in the national media, it brought out analyses and commentaries on the draft bills and bills for the social security system reform formulated in the CPSS and in the CPDSI.

Founded in 1988, the Programa Venezolano de Educación-Acción en Derechos Humanos (English: Venezuelan Program for Education and Action in Human Rights) (PROVEA) represents the largest and oldest nongovernmental dedicated to the promotion and defense of human rights in Venezuela. Within the framework of the economic, social, and cultural rights, the PROVEA advocates the right to social security, constantly monitoring the current state of affairs in this regard. In this context, the PROVEA predicated its support for the establishment of a universal and unified social security system and its opposition against the introduction of private pension administrators into the pension system (PROVEA 2001a, b, 2002a, b, 2003).

3.2.4 Operationalization of the "How" Question

The reconstruction of the power struggles over the social security system reform brought out that (1) the struggles were not dissociated from the more general struggles for hegemony, which came about in manifold ways, (2) the struggles over the social security system reform were not exclusively determined by the corporative associational and political associational power resources of the actors involved, but they also comprised structural, mobilizational and communicational arenas in which the contending actors mobilized their power resources.

In the following, the corporative associational, the political associational, the mobilizational, and communicational power resources are broken down separately.

3.2.4.1 Corporative Associational Power Resources

As mentioned above, the assessment of the corporative associational power resources of the actors involved in the power struggles over the reform is carried out according to political class struggle approaches. The corporative associational resources are associated with the organizational capacity of the contending actors. For this reason, the assessment comprises indicators concerning the magnitude of the membership of the actors involved (government, political parties, labor unions, employers' organizations, etc.). However, in contrast to political class struggle approaches, the analysis of the corporative associational power resources effectuated below is not circumscribed to the corporative associational power resources of the labor unions, but it encompasses the corporative associational power resources of all the macro and meso actors involved in the struggles over the social security system reform. Therefore, the assessment of the organizational power resources additionally comprises the government, the political parties, the employers' organizations, and the professional associations as owners of organizational power resources next to the labor unions.

The incorporation of the government brings about complications regarding the "comparativity" of its corporative associational power resources, as the public officials and state workers who carry out duties within government institutions and state companies do not necessarily countenance the government in political terms. In order to counterbalance this, the assessment of the organizational power resources of the government brings forward a structural perspective, concentrating on the expansion of the government institutions and the state companies instead of focusing on the expansion of the government personnel. Table 3.10 tabularizes the structure of the government cabinet of the presidents Caldera and Chávez (Table 3.10)

Table 3.10 substantiates the expansion of the government cabinet since Chávez's coming to power (Table 3.10). The number of ministries branched out from 17 under the Caldera government in 1999 to 31 under the Chávez government in 2013. The expansion of the government cabinet was predicated on the partition of five previously existing ministries into 11 separate ministries and the creation of ten completely new ministries. In addition, the government cabinet commingled a council of ministers composed of the president, the vice president and five thematic vice presidents who carry out the coordination of the ministries assigned to their thematic areas. Since the thematic vice presidents preside over their own ministries, the council of ministers does not presuppose a duplicate ministerial structure. However, its creation brought out the necessity of a coordinating body due to the expansion of the ministries comprised in the government cabinet.

The government maximized its corporative associational power resources through the expansion of the companies in its possession as well. Since Chávez coming to power in 1999, the government has nationalized or renationalized numerous companies in key sectors of the economy, including the oil, telecommunications, electricity, cement, iron and steel, finance, ports and gas sectors (Cilano et al. 2009), as Table 3.11 corroborates (Table 3.11).

While not directly comparable with the organizational capabilities of the political parties, labor unions, social movements, etc., the expansion of the government institutions and the state companies definitely brought about an increase of the corporative associational power resources of the government.

The assessment of the corporative associational power resources of the political parties in Venezuela comes across the remarking unavailability of information concerning their membership. The Ley de Partidos Políticos, Reuniones Públicas y Manifestaciones (English: Law of Political Parties, Public Meetings and Demonstrations) (hereinafter LPPRPM) does not establish the obligatory report of information regarding the membership of the political parties. For this reason, the only available information concerning the membership of the political parties is provided by the parties on their own account. In consequence, this information cannot be corroborated. According to the public statement of its first vice president Alberto Müller Rojas, the PSUV comprised 5,595,938 members when its organization as the successor of the MVR commenced in 2007. Two years later, the secretary of organization Jorge Rodríguez asseverated that the number of members of the PSUV had advanced to 7,253,692 (Huérfano and Santolo 2013). However, only 2,539,852 members participated in the internal elections of the PSUV held on 2 May 2009. Unfortunately, no other pro-Chavist political party has publicly promulgated the number of their registered members. On the side of the anti-Chavist political parties, on the PJ has recently predicated the number of their registered volunteers (not members), which allegedly approximates 1,000,000 volunteers (Correo del Orinoco 29/10/2015). The

Table 3.10 Structure of the government cabinet

Government of Rafael Caldera (February 1999)	Government of Hugo Chávez (March 2013)
Council of Ministers	
	Primer Vicepresidente del Consejo de Ministros del Gobierno Bolivariano
	Segunda Vicepresidenta del Consejo de Ministros del Gobierno Bolivariano para el Área Social
	Tercer Vicepresidente del Consejo de Ministros del Gobierno Bolivariano para el Área Económico Financiera
	Cuarto Vicepresidente del Consejo de Ministros del Gobierno Bolivariano para el Área Económico Productiva
	Quinto Vicepresidente del Consejo de Ministros del Gobierno Bolivariano para el Área de Desarrollo Territorial
	Sexto Vicepresidente del Consejo de Ministros del Gobierno Bolivariano para el Área Política
	Secretario Permanente del Consejo de Ministros del Gobierno Bolivariano
Ministries	
Minsterio del Despacho	Ministerio del Poder Popular del Despacho de la Presidencia
Ministerio de Sanidad y Asistencia Social	Ministerio del Poder Popular para la Salud
	Ministerio del Poder Popular para las Comunas y Protección Social
Ministerio de la Familia	Ministerio del Poder Popular para la Mujer y la Igualdad de Género
	Ministerio del Poder Popular para la Juventud
	Ministerio del Poder Popular para los Pueblos Indígenas
Ministerio de Educación	Ministerio del Poder Popular para la Educación
	Ministerio del Poder Popular para la Educación Universitaria
	Ministerio del Poder Popular para la Cultura
	Ministerio del Poder Popular para el Deportes
	Ministerio del Poder Popular para Ciencia y Tecnología

(continued)

Table 3.10 (continued)

Government of Rafael Caldera (February 1999)	Government of Hugo Chávez (March 2013)
Ministerio de Energía y Minas	Ministerio del Poder Popular de Petróleo y Minería
	Ministerio del Poder Popular para la Energía Eléctrica
Ministerio de Desarrollo Urbano	Ministerio del Poder Popular para Vivienda y Hábitat
Ministerio de Ambiente	Ministerio del Poder Popular para el Ambiente
Ministerio de Fomento	Ministerio del Poder Popular para el Turismo
	Ministerio del Poder Popular de Planificación y Finanzas
Ministerio de Hacienda	
	Ministerio de Estado para la Banca Pública
Ministerio de Relaciones Interiores	Ministerio del Poder Popular para Relaciones Interiores y Justicia
Ministerio de Justicia	
	Ministerio del Poder Popular para el Servicio Penitenciario
Ministerio de Defensa	Ministerio del Poder Popular para la Defensa
Ministerio de Relaciones Exteriores	Ministerio del Poder Popular para Relaciones Exteriores
Ministerio de Industria y Comercio	Ministerio de Poder Popular para el Comercio
	Ministerio del Poder Popular de Industrias
Ministerio de Agricultura y Cría	Ministerio del Poder Popular para la Agricultura y Tierras
	Ministerio del Poder Popular para la Alimentación
Ministerio de Trabajo	Ministerio del Poder Popular para el Trabajo y Seguridad Social
Ministerio de Transporte y Comunicaciones	Ministerio del Poder Popular para el Transporte Terrestre
	Ministerio del Poder Popular para el Transporte Aéreo y Acuático
	Ministerio del Poder Popular para la Comunicación y la Información

(continued)

Table 3.10 (continued)

Government of Rafael Caldera (February 1999)	Government of Hugo Chávez (March 2013)
	Ministerio de Estado para la Transformación Revolucionaria de la Gran Caracas

Source Prepared by the author

Table 3.11 Nationalized and renationalized companies

Economic sector	Company
Oil	– 13 oil companies in the Orinoco Belt – 60 complementary oil companies in the Lake Maracaibo – 9 fuel transport companies
Telecommunications	– Compañía Anónima Nacional Teléfonos de Venezuela (CANTV)
Electricity	– Electricidad de Caracas (EDC) – Sistema Eléctrico del Estado Nueva Esparta (SENECA)
Cement	– Cementos Mexicanos (CEMEX) – Lafarge – Holcim
Iron and steel	– Siderúrgica del Orinoco (SIDOR)
Finance	– Banco de Venezuela
Ports	– Puerto de Maracaibo, – Puerto Cabello
Gas	– Planta Compresora de Gas PIGAP II

Source Prepared by the author

AD has not annunciated the number of its members since 1985, probably because of the increasing decline of its membership since then. According to its latest claim, the AD comprised 2,253,887 registered members in 1985 (Coppedge 1994: 29). The number of the registered members of the COPEI approximated 800,000 by that time (Ramos Jiménez 199: 6). Unfortunately, the rest of the anti-Chavist political parties have not promulgated the number of their registered members.

In the absence of information regarding the membership of the political parties, their electoral results in the legislative elections bring forward an outlook of their corporative associational power resources for two reasons. First, the legislative elections are dissociated from the presidential elections, in which charismatic candidates (such as Chávez) may captivate the voters who are not associated to the political parties.

Table 3.12 Legislative electoral results

	2000	2005	2010
PCV	15,997	94,033	5,451,382
MEP	3738	38,690	
MVR/PSUV	1,977,992	2,041,293	
PPT	101,246	197,459	354,677
LCR	196,787		5,334,305
MAS	224,170		
UNT	78,109		
PJ	109,900		
AD	718,148		
COPEI	227,349		

Source Prepared by the author

Second, in the presidentialist systems of government, the legislative elections are characterized by a much higher voter turnout than the presidential elections, as the power of the legislative branch does not correspond with the power of the executive branch. For these reasons, the electoral results of the legislative elections are mostly associated with the capacity of the political parties to mobilize their active members and sympathizers. Table 3.12 tabularizes the results of the legislative elections since 1999.

The legislative electoral results substantiate that the government party (initially the MVR and subsequently the PSUV) accumulated an enormous amount of associational power resources between 2000 and 2010. No other political party fell back upon comparable corporative power resources during this period. Even combining their corporative associational power resources, the opposition parties could barely counterbalance the amount of power resources of the government party.

The corporative associational power resources represent the power resources *par excellence* of the labor unions. Venezuelan labor unions accomplished their maximum expansion during the 1970s. The neoliberal policies initiated in the 1980s and intensified in the 1990s brought about the generalized weakening of the labor unions, affecting the four traditional labor confederations (CTV, CODESA; CGT and CUTV) alike. However, with the only exception of the CUTV the CTV, the CODESA and the CGT actively participated in the promotion and implementation of the neoliberal policies, including the privatization of the pension system. After Chávez coming to power in 1999, the CTV, the CODESA, and the CGT fiercely repudiated the government, actively participating (especially the CTV) in the hegemonic struggles between government and oppositions. In this context, the labor unions undertook a process of reconfiguration which brought about the decline of the traditional labor confederations and the emergence of new pro-Chavist labor confederation (UNT).

Tables 3.13 and 3.14 bring out the profound restructuring of the labor confederations occurred between 2001 and 2004 (Tables 3.13 and 3.14). In 2001, 46 out of 60 national labor federations and 45 out of 75 national unions were associated with

Table 3.13 Labor confederations in 2001

Confederations		CTV	CGT	CODESA	Not confederated	Total
Federations	National	44	2	–	14	60
	Regional	1	1	–	1	3
	Provincial	23	6	5	3	37
Unions	National	42	2	1	29	75
	Regional	86	7	5	47	145
	Provincial	1.090	23	20	327	1.460
	Local	758	8	3	423	1.192
Total		1.976	40	29	826	2.871

Source Díaz (2006)

Table 3.14 Union members under collective bargaining in 2004

Confederation	Workers	Share (%)
UNTR	1,160,311	76.50
CTV	305,965	20.17
CUTV	12,517	0.80
CODESA	5001	0.33
Not confederated	32,917	2.10

Source Díaz (2006)

the CTV, the CGT and the CODESA in 2001 (Table 3.13). The executive secretary of the CTV Froilán Barrios asseverated in an interview that the CTV conglomerated 1,000,000 out of 1,300,000 unionized workers in 2002 (Hernández Ledezma 2009). However, only 20.50% of the workers under collective bargaining were associated with the CTV, the CGT, and CODESA in 2004 (Table 3.14). By that time, the recently created UNTR had taken over the representation of 76.50% of the workers under collective bargaining, comprising 1,160,311 unionized workers.

As pointed out above, the sudden restructuring of the labor confederations was predicated on from the withdrawals of the labor unions associated with the CTV, the CGT, and the CODESA which accompanied the government and their incorporation into the UNTR (Díaz 2006; Schütt 2008). Nevertheless, the meteoric expansion of the UNTR soon came across the internal differences among its leaders regarding the relation of the UNTR with the government. As mentioned before, the profound disagreements among the internal fractions of the UNTR in this regard precipitated the breakaway of the fraction promoting the subordination of the UNTR to the government in 2006 and the breakaway of the fraction advocating the autonomy of the UNTR from the government in 2007. Since then, the aggressive cooptation policy of the government towards the pro-Chavist labor unions has further deteriorated the UNTR (Díaz 2006; Bonilla García 2011; López Sánchez 2012).

The available figures regarding union density (i.e., the rate of unionized workers with respect to the labor force) corroborate this. Despite the discrepancies among the

Table 3.15 Union density

	Bonilla (2011) (%)	Lucena (2003) (%)	Díaz (2009) (%)	El Mundo (2013) (%)
1970s	ca. 30.0			
2001		14.0		
2008			11.0	
2013				9.0

Source Lucena (2003), Díaz (2009), Bonilla (2011) and El Mundo 30/09/2013

figures depending on their sources, all of them substantiate the continuous decrease of the unionized workers within the labor force (Table 3.15).

The decrease of the union density substantiates that in general terms the corporative associational power resources of the labor unions have clearly decreased since Chávez coming to power in 1999. Naturally, this process of deterioration has knocked down the anti-Chavist labor unions with much more intensity than the pro-Chavist labor unions, however, the corporative associational power resources of the pro-Chavist labor unions have deteriorated as well.

The assessment of the corporative associational power resources of the employers' organizations divaricates from the assessment of the corporative associational power resources of the labor unions. This is associated with the fact that, unlike the labor unions, the corporative associational power resources of the employers' organizations are not determined by the amount of their individual members but rather by the amount of their organizational members. In this regard, the FEDECAMARAS conglomerates 400 employers' chambers and associations and 5000 employers' organization leaders throughout Venezuela. This comprises the four largest sector employers' organizations: (1) CONSECOMERCIO (tertiary sector), (2) CONINDUSTRIA (secondary sector), (3) FEDENAGA (stockbreeding sector), and (4) FEDEAGRO (agricultural sector). Additionally, the FEDECAMARAS branches out in 18 regional branches and 24 binational chambers. The electoral defeat of the opposition in the recall election held in 2004, which determined the end of the cycle of hegemonic struggles initiated in 2001, brought about the weakening of the FEDECAMRAS. However, this relative weakening did not break it down as the corporative organization par excellence of the employers in Venezuela, since the government could not successfully establish an alternative employers' organization through the promotion of the EMPREVEN.

3.2.4.2 Political Associational Power Resources

As pointed out above, the assessment of the political associational power resources of the actors involved in the power struggles over the reform is carried out according to political class struggle approaches. The political associational power resources are associated with the control of the democratic institutions (i.e., the institutions composed by democratically elected members). For this reason, the political asso-ciational power resources encompass indicators concerning the composition of the national assembly and the composition of the government cabinet.

However, the assessment of the political associational power resources carried out below brings out one fundamental difference with regard to political class struggle approaches, for it comprises the government as a possessor of political democratic power resources next to the political parties. The reason for this is partially associated with the aforementioned centrality of the governments in the Latin American societies (Venezuela specially included), in which the governments clearly take over among all social actors. In addition to this, the inclusion of the government is associated with the fact that the amount of political democratic power resources of the government does not always correspond with the amount of political democratic power resources of the government party, due to the making and remaking of political alliances in support of the government on the one side, and the internal conflicts between the government and the government party, on the other side.

Following political class struggle approaches, the analysis of the political associational power resources revolves around the composition of the legislative power, on the one side, and the composition of executive power, on the other side. As pointed out above, political class struggle approaches break down the composition of the executive power because they presuppose parliamentary systems of government in which the configuration of the government cabinets is associated with the strength of the political parties participating in them. Due to the (hyper-) presidentialist system of government of Venezuela, the assessment of its government cabinet cannot be undeviatingly correlated with the assessment of the government cabinets of the parliamentary countries considered by political class struggle approaches. Nevertheless, the analysis of the changes occurred within the government cabinet since Chávez coming to power may bring out interesting findings.

Table 3.16 delineates the composition of the legislative power since 2000, including the seats and the share corresponding to the government and the political parties (Table 3.16).

Table 3.16 substantiates that the government has preponderated in the legislative power since 2000, holding an absolute majority throughout the three latest legislative periods (Table 3.16). This preponderance accomplished its peak during the 2006–2011 legislative period, in which the electoral withdrawal of the opposition brought about the total control of the national assembly by the government. Interestingly, the sanction of the LOSSSV and the four specific laws connected to it (the LRPVH, the LOPCYMAT, the LSSV and the LRPE) came about during the 2000–2006 legislative period. The political parties allied to the government (the PCV, the MEP, the PPT and initially the MAS) fell back upon limited political associational power resources of their own, even during the 2006–2011 in which the absence of the opposition maximized their legislative representation. In fact, when some of these political parties purposed to advance their own candidates to the national assembly, either as independent parties as in the case of the PPT in 2000, or as opposition parties as in the case of the MAS since 2006, they accomplished meager electoral results. For this reason, most political parties allied to the government coalesced into the PSUV

Table 3.16 Composition of the legislative power

	Const. Assembly 1999		National Assembly 2000 - 2006		National Assembly 2006 - 2011		National Assembly 2011 - 2016	
	Seats	Share (%)	Seats	Share (%)	Seats	Share (%)	Seats	Share (%)
Government								
National Government	122 (+3)	95.42	92 (+11)	62.42	114 (+53)	100.00	95 (+5)	60.61
Political Parties								
PCV					8	4.79	1	0.61
MEP					1	0.60		
MVR / PSUV	122	93.13	92	55.76	114	68.26	95	57.58
PPT			1	0.61	11	6.59	2	1.21
MAS			6	3.64				
LCR			3	1.82			3	1.82
UNT			3	1.82			16	9.70
PJ	6	4.58	5	3.03			6	3.64
AD			33	20.00			14	8.48
COPEI			6	3.64			10	6.06
Others	3	2.29	16	9.70	33	19.76	18	10.91
Total	131		165		167		165	

Source Prepared by the author

in 2007, as in the case of the MEP and other minor parties (the UPV, the IPCN, the LS, etc.). The political parties opposed to the government accumulated considerable political associational power resources in the assembly during the 2000–2006 and the 2011–2016 legislative periods, controlling approximately one-third of the assembly seats. However, these power resources were disseminated among numerous political parties, what naturally decreased its potency.

Table 3.17 delineates the composition of the first (in 1999) and the last (in 2013) government cabinets of president Chávez (Table 3.17).

The previous table brings out two significant things.

First, from the outset, the government cabinet congregated a large majority of members of the government party, as nine out of fourteen ministers were associated with the MVR. Nevertheless, the first cabinet comprised five ministers who did not participate in the government party, including three independent ministers, one minister from the indigenous movement and one minister affiliated with to the MAS, which accompanied the government by then. On the contrary, only one out of thirty-one ministers was not associated with the PSUV in the last government cabinet, what

Table 3.17 Composition of the government cabinet

Council of Ministers		
Primer Vicepresidente	Nicolás Maduro Moros	MVR / PSUV
Segunda Vicepresidenta para el Área Social	Marlene Yadira Córdova	MVR / PSUV
Tercer Vicepresidente para el Área Económico Financiera	Jorge Giordani	MVR / PSUV
Cuarto Vicepresidente para el Área Económico Productiva	Ricardo Menéndez	MVR / PSUV
Quinto Vicepresidente para el Área de Desarrollo Territorial	Rafael Ramírez Carreño	MVR / PSUV
Sexto Vicepresidente para el Área Política	Elías Jaua Milano	MVR / PSUV
Secretario Permanente	Carlos Granadillo Sierra	MVR / PSUV
Ministries		
Ministerio del Poder Popular del Despacho de la Presidencia	Alfredo Peña	(Ex) MVR / PSUV
	Carmen Meléndez	MVR / PSUV (M)
Ministerio del Poder Popular para la Salud	Gilberto Rodríguez Ochoa	MVR / PSUV
	María Eugenia Sader	MVR / PSUV
Ministerio del Poder Popular para las Comunas y Protección Social	Gilberto Rodríguez Ochoa	MVR / PSUV
	Isis Ochoa	MVR / PSUV
Ministerio del Poder Popular para la Mujer y la Igualdad de Género	Gilberto Rodríguez Ochoa	MVR / PSUV
	Nancy Pérez	MVR / PSUV
Ministerio del Poder Popular para la Juventud	Gilberto Rodríguez Ochoa	MVR / PSUV
	Mary Pili Hernández	MVR / PSUV
Ministerio del Poder Popular para los Pueblos Indígenas	Gilberto Rodríguez Ochoa	MVR / PSUV
	Aloha Núñez	Indigenous movement
Ministerio del Poder Popular para la Educación	Héctor Navarro	(Ex) MVR / PSUV
	Maryann Hanson	MVR / PSUV

(continued)

Table 3.17 (continued)

Ministerio del Poder Popular para la Educación Universitaria	Héctor Navarro	(Ex) MVR / PSUV
	Marlene Yadira Córdova	MVR / PSUV
Ministerio del Poder Popular para la Cultura	Héctor Navarro	(Ex) MVR / PSUV
	Pedro Calzadilla	MVR / PSUV
Ministerio del Poder Popular para el Deporte	Héctor Navarro	(Ex) MVR / PSUV
	Héctor Rodríguez	MVR / PSUV
Ministerio del Poder Popular para Ciencia y Tecnología	Héctor Navarro	(Ex) MVR / PSUV
	Jorge Arreaza	MVR / PSUV
Ministerio del Poder Popular de Petróleo y Minería	Alí Rodríguez Araque	MVR / PSUV
	Rafael Ramírez Carreño	MVR / PSUV
Ministerio del Poder Popular para la Energía Eléctrica	Alí Rodríguez Araque	MVR / PSUV
	Héctor Navarro	(Ex) MVR / PSUV
Ministerio del Poder Popular para Vivienda y Hábitat	Luis Reyes Reyes	MVR / PSUV (M)
	Ricardo Molina	MVR / PSUV
Ministerio del Poder Popular para el Ambiente	Atala Uriana	Indigenous movement
	Francisco Ortíz	MVR / PSUV
Ministerio del Poder Popular de Planificación y Finanzas	Jorge Giordani	MVR / PSUV
	Jorge Giordani	MVR / PSUV
Ministerio de Estado para la Banca Pública	Maritza Izaguirre	Independent
	Rodolfo Marco Torres	MVR / PSUV (M)
Ministerio del Poder Popular para el Turismo	Jorge Giordani	MVR / PSUV
	Alejandro Fleming	MVR / PSUV
Ministerio del Poder Popular para Relaciones Interiores y Justicia	Luis Miquilena	(Ex) MVR / PSUV
	Néstor Luis Reverol	MVR / PSUV (M)
Ministerio del Poder Popular para el Servicio Penitenciario	Luis Miquilena	(Ex) MVR / PSUV
	Iris Varela	MVR / PSUV

(continued)

Table 3.17 (continued)

Ministerio del Poder Popular para la Defensa	Raúl Salazar	(Ex) MVR / PSUV (M)
	Diego Alfredo Molero	MVR / PSUV (M)
Ministerio del Poder Popular para Relaciones Exteriores	José Vicente Rangel	MVR / PSUV
	Elías Jaua Milano	MVR / PSUV
Ministerio de Poder Popular para el Comercio	Gustavo Márquez	MVR / PSUV
	Edmée Betancourt	MVR / PSUV
Ministerio del Poder Popular de Industrias	Gustavo Márquez	MVR / PSUV
	Ricardo Menéndez	MVR / PSUV
Ministerio del Poder Popular para la Agricultura y Tierras	Alejandro Riera	Independent
	Juan Carlos Loyo	MVR / PSUV
Ministerio del Poder Popular para la Alimentación	Alejandro Riera	Independent
	Carlos Osorio Zambrano	MVR / PSUV (M)
Ministerio del Poder Popular para el Trabajo y Seguridad Social	Leopoldo Puchi	MAS
	María Cristina Iglesias	MVR / PSUV
Ministerio del Poder Popular para el Transporte Terrestre	Luis Reyes Reyes	MVR / PSUV (M)
	Juan García Toussaintt	MVR / PSUV (M)
Ministerio del Poder Popular para el Transporte Aéreo y Acuático	Luis Reyes Reyes	MVR / PSUV (M)
	Elsa Gutiérrez	MVR / PSUV
Ministerio del Poder Popular para la Comunicación y la Información	Luis Reyes Reyes	MVR / PSUV (M)
	Ernesto Villegas	MVR / PSUV
Ministerio de Estado para la Transformación Revolucionaria de la Gran Caracas	-	
	Francisco Sesto Novas	MVR / PSUV

        : First cabinet 1999

        : Last cabinet 2013

           (M): Military

Source Prepared by the author

clearly substantiates the increasing concentration of power in the government. No member of the MEP, the PCV, and the PPT have ever participated in the cabinet since Chávez coming to power, with the only exception of the former minister of education Aristóbulo Istúriz, who was associated with the PPT but transmigrated to the PSUV in 2007.

Second, the first government cabinet comprised two ministers who came out from the military forces, the ministry of defense Raúl Salazar and the minister of transport and communications Luis Reyes Reyes. In contrast, the last government cabinet congregated five military ministers appointed in the key ministries of the presidential office, interior and justice, defense, state banks, food, and ground transport. Since the military ministers were presupposed as unconditionally loyal to the president, the expansion of the military members in the cabinet can be conceptualized as an indicator of the concentration of power around president Chávez.

In a nutshell, the analysis of the composition of the legislative and executive powers brings out that the government has maximized its political associational power resources since its assumption 1999, predominating in the national assembly and univocally controlling the government cabinet. On the contrary, the political associational power resources of the parties allied to the government have barely advanced since then. The political parties opposed to the government accumulated considerable political associational power resources in the national assembly during this period but always falling behind the government.

3.2.4.3 Mobilizational Power Resources

The assessment of the mobilizational power resources of the actors involved in the struggles over the social security system reform in Venezuela represents a fundamental part of the analysis because of two reasons. The first reason is predicated on the increasing use of mobilizational power resources made by the contending actors since 2001. As pointed out above, the struggles over the social security system reform were increasingly associated with the hegemonic struggles between government and opposition since 2001. In this context, the actions of the contending actors increasingly comprised the use of mobilizational power resources. The second reason is associated with the reverse of this situation. Insofar as, a context of no-holds-barred struggles for hegemony, the more the use of mobilizational power resources advanced, the more the use of "conventional" corporative associational and political associational power resources decreased. As explained before, the correlation between the sharpening of hegemonic struggles and the increasing utilization of mobilizational power resources is predicated on the particular characteristics of the mobilizational power resources, which represent a much more direct (less channeled) manifestation of power than the associational power resources.

In order to delineate a context for the assessment of the mobilizational power resources, Table 3.18 brings out the progression of public protests from 1993 to 2012 (Table 3.18).

Table 3.18 Progression of public protests

	Total protests	Non violent protests	Violent protests
1993	1047	1047	
1994	1099	1099	
1995	581	581	
1996	534	534	
1997	550	550	
1998	385	385	
1999	855	805	50
2000	1414	1263	151
2001	1312	1169	143
2002	1262	1141	121
2003	1543	1243	300
2004	1255	1037	218
2005	1534	1417	117
2006	1383	1280	103
2007	1576	1521	55
2008	1763	1680	83
2009	2893	2822	71
2010	3312	3266	46
2011	4534	4472	62
2012	3986	3925	61

Source Prepared by the author based on PROVEA annual reports

Table 3.18 brings out that the number of protests has continuously branched out since 1999 when the confrontation between pro-Chavist government and the anti-Chavist opposition commenced (Table 3.18). However, the radicalization of the hegemonic struggles between government and opposition came about between 2001 and 2004, as the sudden increase in the number of violent protests substantiates. Due to the enormous significance of these years, in which government and opposition undertook a no-holds-barred battle which eventually brought about the total defeat of the opposition in 2004, the analysis of the mobilizational power resources of the actors involved in the struggles over the social security system reform is circumscribed to this period. Besides, the most significant struggles over the formulation and sanction of the LOSSSV came about during these years, increasingly connected with the hegemonic struggles between government and opposition.

The assessment of mobilizational power resources presupposes manifold difficulties compared with the associational power resources. These difficulties percolate both the quantification and the qualification of the mobilizational power resources. In order to circumvent these difficulties, the assessment of the power resources of the contending actors is circumscribed to the public mobilizations of national scope.

The definition used for the assessment comes down from two theoretical approaches to the subject: (1) the perspective of the British Marxist historiography

(Hobsbawm 1959; Thompson 1963) and (2) the perspective contribution of the sociology of contentious politics (Tilly 1978; Tarrow 1994). Adapting their theoretical definitions to the requirements of the assessment, mobilizations are conceptualized as collective demonstrative actions effectuated by social groups aimed at publicly disclosing their positions regarding something. The reference to the public character of the mobilizations points out that they are carried out in the public space. This way, a workers' strike confined to their working place is not categorized as a public mobilization, whereas a worker's strike demonstrating on the streets falls under public mobilization indeed. For practical reasons, the cyberspace is precluded from the public space for the assessment of the mobilizational power resources. Unlike the protests analyzed above, which comprise all protest actions, the national scope of the mobilizations is associated with their territorial extension. Thus, mobilizations are categorized as of national scope either when they come about in several locations throughout the national territory, including the most populated areas (Caracas, Maracaibo, Valencia, etc.), or when they are carried out in the national capital (Caracas) with the concurrence of participators coming from several locations throughout the national territory.

Table 3.19 tabularizes the public mobilizations of national scope between December 2001 and August 2003 (Table 3.19). During this period, the opposition purposed to take over the control of the streets, which had been practically monopolized by the pro-Chavist forces since 1999, in order to bring down the government. In response, the government countervailed the massive mobilizations with massive counter-mobilizations, what rapidly brought about the radicalization of the hegemonic struggles between government and opposition into an all-or-nothing confrontation which would eventually bring about the total defeat of the opposition with the recall election won by the government in 2004. For this reason, Table 3.19 breaks down the dates, the organizers the motives and (if available) the slogans of the mobilizations effectuated by the opposition, as well as the counter-mobilizations organized by the government (Table 3.19). For the sake of the analysis, the public mobilizations carried out in the context of electoral campaign for the recall election are precluded from the table.

Table 3.19 brings out that the period between December 2001 and February 2002 was characterized by an outbreak in the mobilization of the contending actors (Table 3.19). As a matter of fact, no general strikes and no general lockouts had been carried out by the labor confederations and the employers' organizations opposed to the government since 1999. In contrast, the aforementioned period comprised four general strikes (including the two-months-long oil strike), numerous political mobilizations, even several military mutinies and even one failed coup. The contradicting reports regarding the massiveness of the mobilizations, which divaricate depending on the political position of the media reporting, circumscribe the assessment of the exact number of people who participated in them. However, all of them conglomerated countless people, including estimations in the hundreds of thousands and even millions of demonstrators. In any case, the fact that all mobilizations were reciprocated by counter-mobilizations substantiates that the hegemonic struggles between government and opposition brought about a situation of "catastrophic equilibrium"

Table 3.19 Public mobilizations of national scope

Date	Organizer	Mobilization	Counter-mobilization
19/12/2001	FEDECAMARAS	First civic strike against the government	Countermarch in support of the government
23/01/2002	CTV. Supported by AD, COPEI, PJ and Union	March "Marcha unitaria por la libertad y la democracia" commemorating the destitution of the military dictator Carlos Pérez Jiménez in 1958	Countermarch commemorating the destitution of the military dictator Carlos Pérez Jiménez in 1958
04/02/2002	NGOs	March repudiating the failed coup lead by Chávez in February 1992	March celebrating the failed coup lead by Chávez in February 1992
21/02/2002	Students and professors of the UCV	March "Marcha de las antorchas" against the government	Counteraction in support of the government
08/03/2002	NGOs	March "Marcha de las cacerolas" against the government	Countermarch in support of the government
09/04/2002–10/04/2002	CTV and FEDECAMARAS	Second civic strike against the government	Countermarches in support of the government
11/04/2002	CTV and FEDECAMARAS	March "Ni un paso atrás" against the government demanding the destitution of the president	Conglomeration around the seat of government in defense of the government
01/05/2002	CTV	March "La libertad sindical y el régimen de libertades" against the government"	Countermarch in support of the government
11/05/2002	NGOs. Supported by AD, COPEI, PJ, MAS, ABP	Marcha "No olvidar" commemorating the victims killed on 11 April	Countermarch commemorating the victims killed on 11 April
13/05/2002			Conglomeration "No a la impunidad" with Hebe de Bonafini commemorating the victims killed on 11 April

(continued)

Table 3.19 (continued)

Date	Organizer	Mobilization	Counter-mobilization
11/07/2002	CD	March against the government demanding the destitution of the president	Conglomeration around the seat of government in defense of the government
11/09/2002	Independent groups. Supported by CTV	March "El trancazo" against the government	Conglomeration "El terrorismo y el golpismo es lo mismo" commemorating the victims killed on 11 April
10/10/2002	CD, CTV and FEDECAMARAS	March "Toma de Caracas" against the government demanding the convocation of a recall election	
13/10/2002			Countermarch in support of the government
22/10/2002	CD, CTV and FEDECAMARAS	Third civic strike against the government	
04/11/2002	CD	March against the government demanding the convocation of a recall election	Countermarch in support of the government repudiating the convocation of a recall election
02/12/2002	CD, CTV, FEDECAMARAS	Fourth civic strike against the government	
04/12/2002	CD, CTV and FEDECAMARAS	March against the government (Chuao)	Countermarch in support of the government (Plaza O'Leary)
05/12/2002	CD, CTV and FEDECAMARAS	March against the government (Chuao)	Countermarch in support of the government (La Campina).

(continued)

Table 3.19 (continued)

Date	Organizer	Mobilization	Counter-mobilization
14/12/2002	CD, CTV and FEDECAMARAS	March against the government demanding the destitution of the president	
17/12/2002	CD, CTV and FEDECAMARAS	March against the government commemorating the death of Simón Bolívar	Conglomeration in support of the government commemorating the death of Simón Bolívar
20/12/2002	CD, CTV and FEDECAMARAS	March "Megamarcha de Caracas" against the government	Countermarcha "PDVSA es del pueblo" in support of the government
29/12/2002	CD and CTV	March "Marcha de la Victoria" against the government	
31/12/2002	CD, CTV and FEDECAMARAS	Conglomeration against of the government celebrating the new year	
03/01/2003	CD, CTV and FEDECAMARAS	March "La gran batalla" against the government demanding the destitution of the president	Conglomeration in support of the government
23/01/2003			"Marcha por la paz y la constitución" in support of the government
25/01/2003–26/01/2003	CD, CTV and FEDECAMARAS	Conglomeration against the government demanding the convocation of a recall election	
31/01/2003	CD, CTV and FEDECAMARAS	March "Con mis medios no te metas" against the government repudiating the censorship the of the private media	

(continued)

Table 3.19 (continued)

Date	Organizer	Mobilization	Counter-mobilization
02/02/2003	CD, CTV and FEDECAMARAS	Collection "El firmazo" against the government collecting signatures for the convocation of a recall election	
08/02/2003	CD	March "Marcha en Solidaridad con Pdvsa "against the government demanding the restitution of the workers and managers of PDVSA fired	
21/08/2003	CD	March against the government presenting the collected signatures for the recall election	

Source Prepared by the author

during this period (García Linera 2008), in which the unified opposition (the CTV, the FEDECAMARAS and the CD) counterbalanced the mobilizational power resources of the government but could not bring the government down, leading to an unsustainable indefinite prolongation of the confrontation. This situation eventually brought about the weakening of the opposition, whose capacity to mobilize clearly deteriorated after the oil strike, as the appeasement of the massive mobilizations during 2003 corroborates (Table 3.19). Finally, the electoral defeat of the opposition in the recall election held in 2004 brought about the collapse of the opposition and the end of the non-holds-barred hegemonic struggles, with the subsequent decrease of the violent protests registered since then (Table 3.19).

3.2.4.4 Communicational Power Resources

As explained in Chap. 2, communicational power resources are predicated on the control of the mass media. Unfortunately, the assessment of the communicational power resources of the actors involved in the struggles over the social security system reform in Venezuela represents a very difficult task due to the scarcity of empirical data concerning mass media. Practically no information comes out regarding TV and radio ratings, or newspapers and magazines circulation. Information concerning the control of the media usually comprises contradictions. Despite these difficulties, Table 3.20 tabularizes the available information regarding national TV networks (Table 3.20).

Table 3.20 National TV networks

	Foundation	Closure	Type	Owner
Venevisión	1961		Private	Organización Cisneros
Radio Caracas Televisión (RCTV)	1953	2007	Private	Empresas 1BC
Televen	1988		Private	Corporación Televen
Puma TV	1995	2007	Private	José Luis Rodríguez
Canal I	2007		Private	Canal I Television
Meridiano TV	1997		Private	Bloque de Armas
Globovisión	1994		Private	Globovisión C.A.
Canal Metropolitano Televisión (CMT)	1993	2007	Private	Umberto Petricca Zugaro
Venezolana de Televisión (VTV)	1964		Public	
Visión Venezuela Televisión (ViVe)	2003		Public	
Asamblea Nacional Televisión (ANTV)	2005		Public	
TeleSUR	2005		Public	
Fundación Televisora Venezolana Social (Tves)	2007		Public	
Televisora Colombeia	2012		Public	

Source Prepared by the author

Table 3.20 brings out the predominance of private TV networks in national television until the mid-2000s (Table 3.20). In 2002, national television comprised seven private TV networks and only one public TV network (Venezolana de Televisión).

Four private economic groups (Grupo Cisneros, Empresas 1BC, Corporación Televen, and Globovisión) owned by four families (Cisneros, Granier-Phelps, Camero Zamora, and Zuloaga) practically monopolized mass media, including newspapers, magazines, radio networks, and four national TV networks (Venevisión, Radio Caracas Television, Televen y Globovisión).

The private media fiercely repudiated Chávez' government since its coming to power, contravening its policies with no exception. In line with this, the private media deprecated the social security system reform proposed by the government and advocated the introduction of private pension funds, as prescribed by the suspended LOSSSI. During the formulation of the LOSSSV, the private media regularly publicized in newspapers, magazines, radio and TV networks the positions of the actors opposed to the universalization and unification of the social security system.

Over time, private national TV networks took over the vanguard of the opposition to the government and even undertook insurrectionary actions, as in April 2002. For this reason, Venevisión, Radio Caracas Television, Televen y Globovisión were ironically characterized as "the four horsemen of the apocalypse" by Chávez.

However, Chávez' government increasingly accentuated its position in the mass media system after the end of the fourth civic strike in February 2003. Thus, the government established the second public TV Network (Visión Venezuela Televisión "ViVe") in November 2003, the third one (Asamblea Nacional TV "ANTV") in March 2005, and the fourth one (TeleSUR) in July 2005. In 2007, TeleSUR carried out the purchase of Canal Metropolitano Televisión (CMT), taking over its broadcast frequency. In addition, the government determined not to reestablish the broadcasting license of Radio Caracas Televisión (RCTV) due to its active participation in the coup of April 2002. This way, Radio Caracas Televisión (RCTV) was taken out of the air and its broadcast frequency was handed over to the fifth public TV network (Fundación Televisora Venezolana Social "Tves"), created in 2007. Besides, the ownership of Puma TV was carried over to a private group which did not advocate an anti-government position. Finally, the government established the sixth public TV network (Televisora Colombeia) in 2012.

All in all, mass media was practically monopolized by a reduced conglomerate of private groups until the mid-2000s. After that, Chávez' government increasingly branched out the public media structure, considerably advancing its communicational power resources.

3.3 Summary

Following the complementary approach to social policy proposed above, the contextualization of the power struggles over the social security system reform in Venezuela was carried out on the basis of the Poulantzian approach to social policy. As pointed out before, the Poulantzian approach conceptualizes social policy within the context of the construction of hegemony, therefore, associating social policy with the historical, social economic, and political conditions in which it materializes. Accordingly, the contextualization carried out a detailed reconstruction of the power struggles over the social security system reform in Venezuela which delineated the social, economic, and political conditions in which they came about. With regard to the four "questions" proposed as analytical guidelines for the contextualization of the struggles over the reform (where, what, who, and how), the reconstruction determined the following.

Concerning the "where" question, the reconstruction brought out that the struggles over the social security system reform materialized in a structural context defined by (1) a largely rent-based economic structure, in which the oil revenues represented a central factor for the economy and the state, (2) a highly informal labor market, which contravened the development of a "conventional" social security system based on generalized (formal) wage relations.

Against this framework, the social security system reform aimed at the universalization of social security was brought forward by the government with a view toward the incorporation of the population excluded from the existing system of social security. To this aim, a universal state public social security system financed through oil revenue was to be established. For this reason, the struggles over the social security system reform were associated with the struggles over the control of the oil resources in a context of extraordinary oil revenue due to the increase of the international oil prices.

Regarding the "what" question, the reconstruction of the power struggles over the reform determined that the sticking points among the contending actors revolved around (1) the introduction of individual capitalization pension funds managed by private administrators and (2) the continuity of the existing collective capitalization pension funds known as "special pension regimes".

The introduction of individual capitalization pension funds managed by private administrators, commonly referred to as the privatization of the pension system, had been undertaken by the previous government of President Rafael Caldera. However, the implementation of the privatization reform broke down when President Hugo Chávez took over power in 1999. In spite of this, the government and the government party initially came under conflicting internal positions in this regard between those who advocated a state public pension system and those who advocated a mixed pension system. The sanction of the LOSSSV in December 2002 finally advantaged the first position.

The continuity of the special collective capitalization pension funds contravened the unification of the existing social security regimes into a universal social security system, as intended by a sector of the government. In the end, the sector of the government promoting the unification and the beneficiaries of the existing special pension regimes came around with a tacit compromise according to which the special regimes would only be coalesced into the general pension regime when the new pension system was fully established. After that, the amount of the pensions of the beneficiaries of the special regimes would additionally be preserved.

However, the radicalization of the struggles for hegemony between government and opposition generated a turnaround in the struggles over the social security system reform. Initially, this turnaround determined the end of the conflicting positions within the government concerning the reform and brought about the sanction of the LOSSSV. Yet in the end, the total defeat of the opposition completely restructuralized the core of the struggles over the social security system reform, which thereupon revolved around the implementation of the sanctioned LOSSSV or the development of a parallel system of social policy based on the ad hoc programs known as Misiones Bolivarianas and Grandes Misiones.

With respect to the "who" question", the reconstruction of the power struggles over the reform brought out (1) the existence of a manifold entanglement of social, economic, and political actors involved in the struggles over the reform, whose stances regarding the reform did not necessarily correspond with their positions in the productive process, as presupposed by political class struggle approaches, and (2) the extraordinary importance of the government as social, economic and political actor due to its prerogative over the oil sector.

The entanglement of social actors coalesced the government, the political parties, the labor unions, the employers' organizations, the professional associations, the lobby groups, and the nongovernmental organizations. The positions assumed by the aforementioned actors with regard to the social security system reform initially commingled their corporative interests and their positioning in the general hegemonic struggles between government and opposition. However, the radicalization of the struggles for hegemony eventually brought about the complete subordination of the struggles over the social security system reform to the hegemonic struggles between government and opposition, in which the dualistic logic "for" or "against" the government predetermined the positions of the actors in all regards. Thereupon, the political parties, labor unions and social organizations allied to the government advocated the reform whereas the political parties, labor unions and employers' organizations opposed to the government repudiated it. Against this polarized context, the conflicting positions within the government were brushed aside and the LOSSSV was finally promulgated. However, in the context of a full-scale hegemonic confrontation between government and opposition the struggles over the social security system reform were subordinated to a secondary position, as several interviewees corroborated (Interview with Óscar Figuera). As a result, despite their support of the LOSSSV, the political parties, labor unions, and social movements allied to the government did not mobilize to bring about its implementation, which was eventually held back by the development of the structure of the Misiones Bolivarianas.

Table 3.21 delineates the contending actors included in the preceding reconstruction and their positions regarding the social security system reform prescribed by the LOSSSV) (Table 3.21).

The extraordinary importance of the government as a social, economic and political actor was brought about by the combination of structural and conjunctural factors. The structural factors were associated with the aforementioned characteristics of the Venezuelan economy concerning its dependency on the oil revenue and its elevated level of labor informality. Because of this, the government has historically taken over a structuring role in the economy and the society, both as the main economic driver and as the exclusive interlocutor of the socially and economically excluded groups. In addition, the government has maximized its participation in the social, economic, and political realms since Chávez's coming to power in 1999. This expansion materialized in the increase of the state participation within the economy and in the enlargement of the state apparatus (Córdova 2006; Alonso 2009, 2010; Morales 2012). Both brought about the recentralization of the public administration and the development of a parallel ad hoc state structure, which not only handed out health

Table 3.21 Position of the contending actors regarding the social security system reform prescribed by the LOSSSV

	Before	After		Before	After
Government			Military and Police Forces		
Government	For	For	FANB		
Political Parties			Police Forces		
MVR / PSUV	For	For	Professional Associations		
PCV	For	For	FAPUV	For	For
PPT	For	For	FMV	For	For
AD	Against	Against	CMDMC	For	For
COPEI	Against	Against	Lobby Groups		
MAS	For	Against	APAFP	Against	Against
UNT	For	Against	REDIUP	For	For
PJ	For	Against	Non-Governmental Organizations		
Labor Unions			PROVEA	For	For
CTV	Against	Against			
CODESA	Against	Against			
CGT	For	For			
CUTV	For	For			
FBT	For	For			
Employer's Organizations					
FEDECAMARAS	Against	Against			
CONSECOMERCIO	Against	Against			
CONINDUSTRIA	Against	Against			
FEDENAGA	Against	Against			
FEDEAGRO	Against	Against			

        : For   : Against   : Neutral

Source Prepared by the author

care but also education, employment, pensions, food, housing, and even security services (Córdova 2006: 505).

Regarding the "how" question, the reconstruction established that (1) the struggles over the social security system reform were not dissociated from the general struggles for hegemony, which came out through manifold ways of expression, and (2) the struggles over the social security system reform were not exclusively determined by the corporative associational and political associational power resources of the contending actors, as reckoned by the class center approach, but they additionally concatenated structural, mobilizational, and communicational arenas in which the participating actors mobilized their power resources.

The relation between the power struggles over the social security system reform and the general struggles for hegemony concatenated three subsequent phases. In the first phase, the struggles over the social security system reform came about in parallel with the general struggles for hegemony between government and opposition. These hegemonic struggles principally revolved around the control of the oil and agriculture sectors. In this phase, the contending actors commingled their corporative interests and their positions in the hegemonic struggles. In the second phase, however, the radicalization of the hegemonic struggles completely subordinated the struggles over the social security system reform to the struggles for hegemony. Against this background of total confrontation, the hegemonic struggles finally revolved around the continuity or the overthrow of the government of President Hugo Chávez. In this phase, the actors involved in the struggles over the social security system reform had to accommodate their corporative interests to their positions in the struggles for hegemony between government and opposition. The situation of FEDECAMARAS represented a perfect example in this regard. Barely one month after commanding a failed coup against the government, FEDECAMARAS participated in the consultations for the formulation of the LOSSSV in the legislative commission of the national assembly, convocated by the assembly members of the government party. In this commission, the representatives of FEDECAMARAS actively advocated the introduction of private pension funds, as they represented a billion-worth business opportunity for the banking sector. However, with the beginning of the oil strike the possibility of dissociating its fierce opposition to the government from its participation in the sectoral bargaining over the formulation of LOSSSV simply dematerialized. In turn, the sectors within the government in favor of a mixed pension system were brought down by the radicalization of the struggles for hegemony between government and opposition. In the third phase, the government party took over absolute control of the assembly due to the electoral withdrawal of the opposition parties in the legislative elections held on 2005. Besides, the government accumulated remarkable structural, associational, and mobilizational power resources. In spite of this, the government party did not bring about the specific laws concerning the health and pension systems, which represented the core of the LOSSSV. For this reason, the implementation of the social security system reform prescribed by the LOSSSV was not carried out. Instead, the government accelerated the establishment of a parallel structure of social policy based on the social programs known as Misiones Bolivarianas and Grandes Misiones.

The struggles over the social security system reform were not circumscribed to the institutionalized political arena associated with the "conventional" power resources (corporative associational and political associational), but they comprised manifold interrelated arenas in which diverse types of power resources (structural, mobilizational and communicational, etc.) were mobilized by the contending actors. As the radicalization of the hegemonic struggles advanced, the actors increasingly mobilized their mobilizational (sometimes even insurrectional) and communicational power resources at the expense of their corporative associational and political associational power resources.

Following the complementary approach to social policy explained above, the operationalization of the power struggles over the post-neoliberal social security system reform in Venezuela was carried out on the basis of the concept of power resources, initially devised by political class struggle approaches to social policy.

However, this concept was not simply reduplicated in its original form but it was completely transubstantiated in order to circumvent its shortcomings when dealing with the social policy of the Global South.

Accordingly, the operationalization of the power struggles over the reform correlated the four analytical dimensions ("where", "what", "who", and how") included in the contextualization of the Venezuelan case. As pointed out above, these four dimensions revolve around (1) the structural underpinnings underlying the struggles over social security system reform, (2) the concrete points of conflict over the reform, (3) the real actors involved in the struggles over the reform, and (4) the channels through which the struggles were canalized.

Regarding the "where" question, the operationalization established that (1) the government maximized its oil resources since the oil reform sanctioned 2001, and (2) the moderate decrease of the labor informality since 2004 did not bring about the increase of the corporative associational or the political associational power resources of the labor unions and the labor political parties.

The maximization of the oil resources of the government was partially associated with the steep increase in the international oil prices initiated in 2001. However, it was mainly predicated on the reform of the oil sector promulgated by the government itself in 2001. This reform brought about a remarkable increase of the oil resources in possession of the government and a significant decrease of the oil resources in possession of the private oil companies. The reform of the oil sector not only successfully maximized the oil resources in possession of the government, but it also brought about the increase of the oil resources in control of the government due to the expansion of the participation of the state oil companies in the extraction, refining, transportation, and distribution of oil. In contrast, the control of oil resources exercised by the private oil companies clearly diminished. In addition, the government threw out the oil workers and managers of the state oil company who contravened the reform of the oil sector, debilitating the control of oil resources exercised by the labor unions and employers' organizations opposed to the government.

The substantial expansion of the economy experienced since 2004 brought about a steep decrease in unemployment and underemployment, and a sheer increase in minimum and average salaries. However, labor informality decreased only moderately, for which labor unions and labor political parties barely capitalized on it in terms of their corporative associational and political associational power resources. Likewise, the moderate decrease in labor informality registered since 2004 did not bring about the substantial expansion of the tax revenues collected by the government, which was actually predicated on other causes.

With regard to the "what" question, the operationalization brought out the specific forms of power resources which the contending actors mobilized in the struggles over the two sticking points concerning the social security system reform: (1) the introduction of individual capitalization pension funds managed by private administrators and (2) the maintenance or elimination of the existing special pension regimes.

The struggles over the introduction of individual capitalization pension funds managed by private administrators concatenated three subsequent phases: (1) the struggles in the constituent assembly over the constitutional articles regarding social security, (2) the struggles within the government over the formulation of the draft bill for the social security system reform before its introduction in the national assembly, (3) the struggles in the national assembly over the bill for the social security system reform at first and second reading. Throughout the first and second phases, the contending actors mobilized their corporative associational, their political associational and marginally their communicational power resources. In the third phase, the struggles over the introduction of the private administrators increasingly dovetailed with the struggles between government and opposition for hegemony. Against this background, the actors increasingly mobilized their communicational and mobilizational power resources, including insurrectionary actions.

In the case of struggles over the maintenance or elimination of the existing special pension regimes, the contending actors mobilized their corporative associational and their political associational power resources. Since the actors accomplished a compromise solution before the escalation of the hegemonic struggles between government and opposition, the struggles over the maintenance or elimination of the existing special regimes did not coalesce with them. In consequence, the actors involved in the struggles over the special regimes did not mobilize their communicational and mobilizational power resources in this regard.

Concerning the "who" question, the operationalization delineated the main characteristics of the actors involved in the struggles over the reform and pointed out what forms of power resources they could eventually mobilize.

The aforementioned centrality of the government was corroborated by the wide range of power resources at its disposal: structural, corporative associational, political associational, mobilizational, and communicational. The political parties fell back upon corporative associational, political associational and, in the context of the Coordinadora Democrática, mobilizational power resources; the labor unions comprised structural, corporative associational, and mobilizational power resources; and the employers' organizations comprised structural, corporative associational, mobilizational and communicational power resources. Among the meso actors, the professional associations fell back upon corporative associational power resources in two ways due to their strike capability and their recognized expertise regarding social security. The lobby groups and the nongovernmental organizations comprised corporative associational and communicational power resources.

With regard to the "how" question, the operationalization broke down the corporative associational, the political associational, the mobilizational, and the communicational power resources of the actors involved in the struggles over the social security system reform.

Concerning the corporative associational power resources, the operationalization brought out that the bloc of the government and the MVR/PSUV (the government party) accumulated extraordinary corporative associational power resources in terms of their membership as much as in terms of their control of the government institutions and the state companies. The rest of the macro and meso actors (political parties, labor unions, employers' organizations, etc.) clearly fell behind them.

With respect to the political associational power resources, the operationalization brought out that the government clearly outdistanced its opponents since its coming to power in 1999. Thus, the government party took over the absolute majority of the constituent assembly and the national assembly between 1999 and 2016, reaching its peak during the 2006–2011 legislative period in which the electoral withdrawal of the opposition brought about the total control of the national assembly by the MVR/PSUV. Besides, the political parties allied to the government barely participated in the government cabinet, which almost exclusively comprised members of the government party. The political parties opposed to the government accumulated considerable political associational power resources in the assembly during the 2000–2006 and the 2011–2016 legislative periods, controlling approximately one-third of the assembly seats. However, these power resources were disseminated among numerous political parties, what naturally decreased its potency.

Regarding the mobilizational power resources of the actors involved in the struggles over the social security system reform, the operationalization brought out that the contending actors massively mobilized their mobilizational power resources in the context of the non-holds-barred struggles for hegemony between government and opposition between December 2001 and February 2002. During this period the hegemonic struggles were characterized by a situation of "catastrophic equilibrium", in which the unified opposition, led by the CTV, the FEDECAMARAS and the CD, counterbalanced the mobilizational power resources of the government but it could not bring the government down. This situation eventually brought about the weakening of the opposition, whose capacity to mobilize clearly deteriorated after the oil strike and even more after its electoral defeat in the recall election held in August 2004. Following this, the government not only reestablished its mobilizational supremacy but it maximized it.

With regard to the communicational power resources, the operationalization brought out that mass media was practically monopolized by a reduced conglomerate of private groups until the mid-2000s. Since these groups fiercely repudiated Chávez government, the private media actively publicized the in newspapers, magazines, radio, and TV networks the positions of the actors opposed to the social security system reform proposed by the government. However, since the mid-2000s, the government increasingly branched out the public media structure, advancing its communicational power resources more and more.

References

Alonso O (2009) Crisis global, integración regional y desempleo en Venezuela. Instituto Latinoamericano de Investigaciones Sociales, Caracas

Alonso O (2010) Los trabajadores ante la nueva estructura económica. Instituto Latinoamericano de Investigaciones Socialesx, Caracas

Alvarado Chacín N (2003) La atención a la pobreza en Venezuela del Gran Viraje a la V República, 1989–2002. In: Revista Venezolana de Análisis de Coyuntura, vol 9, no 2. Universidad Central de Venezuela, Caracas

Alviárez JC (2013) Regímenes especiales de jubilaciones y pensiones de los funcionarios públicos. Superintendencia de Seguridad Social, Caracas

Aricó J (1988) La cola del diablo. Itinerario de Gramsci en América Latina. Puntosur Editores, Buenos Aires

Arrieta JI (2003) Ley orgánica de seguridad social: un cascarón costoso. In: Revista SIC, no 656. Centro Gumilla, Caracas

Barrios L, Camejo A (2006) El proceso de reforma de la seguridad social en Venezuela: una visión desde el movimiento sindical venezolano (CTV). In: Nómadas. Revista Crítica de Ciencias Sociales y Jurídicas, vol 14, no 2. Universidad Complutense de Madrid, Madrid

Bistoletti EL (2011) Estudio sobre los orígenes del chavismo. El ascenso político del movimiento encabezado por Hugo Chávez en perspectiva sociopolítica. Editorial Académica Española, Saarbrücken

Boffi S (2015) Sistemas de protección social mixtos: pisos de protección social e interacciones con el mercado de trabajo. Estudio del caso de la asignación universal por hijo en Argentina. Facultad Latinoamericana de Ciencias Sociales, Buenos Aires

Bonilla García J (2011) El movimiento sindical venezolano frente a la situación socio-laboral: desafíos y propuestas. Instituto Latinoamericano de Investigaciones Sociales, Caracas

Chávez H (1998) La propuesta de Hugo Chávez… para transformar a Venezuela: una revolución democrática. Caracas

Chávez H (2007) [1996] Agenda alternativa bolivariana: una propuesta patriótica para salir del laberinto. Ministerio del Poder Popular para la Comunicación e Información, Caracas

Chen MA (2005) Rethinking the informal Economy: linkages with the formal economy. United Nations University, Helsinki

Cilano J, Córdova E, Chaguaceda A (2009) Participación ciudadana y reforma del estado en Venezuela: entender la política a través del ciudadano. In: OSAL, no 26. Consejo Latinoamericano de Ciencias Sociales, Buenos Aires

COORDIPLAN (Oficina Central de Coordinación y Planificación) (1990) El gran viraje": lineamientos generales del VIII plan de la nación. Mimeo, Caracas

Coppedge M (1994) Strong parties and lame ducks: presidential partyarchy and factionalism in Venezuela. Stanford University Press, Stanford

Córdova É (2006) Administración pública en Venezuela: aproximaciones a los cambios y transformaciones. In: Revista de Ciencias Sociales, vol 12, no 3. Universidad del Zulia, Maracaibo

CPDSI (Comisión Permanente de Desarrollo Social Intergral de la Asamblea Nacional de la República Bolivariana de Venezuela) (2002) Informe para su segunda discusión. Mimeo, Caracas

CPSS (Comisión Presidencial para la Elaboración del Proyecto de ley Orgánica de Seguridad Social) (2001) Propuesta. Mimeo, Caracas

D'Elía Y (2002) Cambiando la orientación de las políticas públicas hacia el impacto en la calidad de vida desde una perspectiva de derechos y equidad. In: Venezuela informe social, no 7. Instituto Latinoamericano de Investigaciones Sociales, Fundación Friedrich Ebert, Caracas

Díaz R (2006) Panorama sindical de Venezuela. Friedrich Ebert Stiftung, Bonn

Díaz R (2009) Los sindicatos en Venezuela: de la negociación a la confrontación. In: Revista sobre Relaciones Industriales y Laborales, no 45. Universidad Católica Andrés Bello, Caracas

España LP (1997) El programa de enfrentamiento a la pobreza 1989–1993: recomendaciones para su reforma. Fundación Escuela de Gerencia Social, Ministerio de la Familia, Caracas

FEDECAMARAS (Federación de Cámaras y Asociaciones de Comercio y Producción de Venezuela) (2014) Actualidad Empresarial, vol 3, no 3. Federación de Cámaras y Asociaciones de Comercio y Producción de Venezuela, Caracas

Fernández ME (2002) La reforma de la seguridad social en Venezuela. In: Cuadernos del CENDES, vol 51, no 51. Centro de Estudios del Desarrollo, Caracas

Fernández A (2007) La seguridad social en Venezuela: 1958–1998. Universidad Central de Venezuela, Caracas

Fernández ME (2012) La protección social frente a la vejez en Venezuela. In: Anuario de derecho, vol 29, no 29. Universidad de los Andes, Mérida

Filgueira F (1998) El nuevo modelo de prestaciones sociales en América Latina eficiencia, residualismo y ciudadanía estratificada. In: Roberts B (ed) Ciudadanía y política social latinoamericana. Facultad Latinoamericana de Ciencias Sociales, San José

Filgueira F (2007) Cohesión, riesgo y arquitectura de protección social en América Latina. Comisión Económica para América Latina y el Caribe, Santiago de Chile

García Guadilla MP (2007) Social movements in a polarized setting: myths of venezuelan civil society. In: Ellner S, Tinker Salas M (eds) Venezuela: Hugo Chávez and the decline of an "exceptional democracy". Rowman & Littlefield Publishers, Lanham

García Linera Á (2008) Empate catastrófico y punto de bifurcación. In: Crítica y Emancipación. Revista Latinoamericana de Ciencias Sociales, vol 1, no 1. Consejo Latinoamericano de Ciencias Sociales, Buenos Aires

Gutiérrez Briceño T (2008) Actores e ideas de política social en Venezuela (1989–2007). In: Revista Orbis, no 11. Fundación Unamuno, Maracaibo

Hernández Ledezma S (2009) Los procesos de cabildeo político entre la CTV, FEDECAMARAS y los gobiernos nacionales 1994–2004. Universidad Simón Bolívar, Caracas

Hobsbawm E (1959) Primitive rebels: studies in archaic forms of social movements in the 19th and 20th centuries. The University Press, Manchester

Huber E, Stephens J (2005) Successful social policy regimes? Political economy and the structure of social policy in Argentina, Chile, Uruguay, and Costa Rica. University of Notre Dame, Notre Dame

Huérfano J, Santolo D (2013) La conflictividad: escenarios post-electorales luego del 14 de abril de 2013. In: Revista Memoria Política, no 2. Universidad de Carabobo, Centro de Estudios Políticos y Administrativos, Valencia

ILO (International Labour Organization) (2011) Statistical update on employment in the informal economy. International Labour Organization, Geneva

Lander LE (2004) La insurrección de los gerentes: PDVSA y el gobierno de Chávez. In: Revista Venezolana de Economía y Ciencias Sociales, vol 10, no 2. Universidad Central de Venezuela, Caracas

Li B (2012) From a micro–macro framework to a micro–meso–macro framework. In: Christensen S, Mitcham C, Li B (eds) Engineering, development and philosophy. Springer Publishing, New York

López Maya M (1997) Los nuevos partidos de vocación popular en Venezuela: tras una alternativa política en la transición. In: Revista Venezolana de Economía y Ciencias Sociales, vol 3, no 4. Universidad Central de Venezuela, Caracas

López Maya M (2005) Del viernes negro al referendo revocatorio. Alfadil, Caracas

Lucena H (2003) Situación político-laboral en Venezuela: la estabilidad perdida. In: Papers. Revista de Sociología, no 71. Universitat Autònoma de Barcelona, Bellaterra

Méndez Cegarra A (1998) Reforma del sistema de pensiones en Venezuela. In: Revista Venezolana de Análisis de Coyuntura, vol 4, no 2. Universidad Central de Venezuela, Caracas

Méndez Cegarra A (2001) Comentarios generales al proyecto de ley orgánica del sistema de seguridad social. Universidad Central de Venezuela, Caracas

Méndez Cegarra A (2005) El derecho a la seguridad social en la Constitución de la República Bolivariana de Venezuela. Editorial vLex, Barcelona

Méndez Cegarra A (2006) Tres momentos en el proceso de reforma de la seguridad social en Venezuela. In: Salcedo González AM (ed) Consideraciones sobre la reforma de la seguridad social en Venezuela. Comisión de Estudios de Postgrado, Facultad de Ciencias Económicas y Sociales, Universidad Central de Venezuela, Fondo Editorial Tropykos, Caracas

Morales L (2012) La Administración Pública en Venezuela: ¿evolución o involución? In: Economía y Políticas Públicas. http://economiaypoliticavenezuela.blogspot.de/2012/11/la-administracion-publica-en-venezuela.html

O'Donnell G (1975) Reflexiones sobre las tendencias generales de cambio del estado burocrático-autoritario. In: Documento CEDES, núm. 1. Centro de Estudios de Estado y Sociedad, Buenos Aires

O'Donnell G (1977) Estado y alianzas en la Argentina, 1956–1976. In: Desarrollo Económico, vol 16, núm. 64. Instituto de Desarrollo Económico y Social, Buenos Aires

Oszlak O (1979) Notas criticas para una teoría de la burocracia estatal. In: Desarrollo Económico, vol 19, no 74. Instituto de Desarrollo Económico y Social, Buenos Aires

Oszlak O (1981) The historical formation of the state in Latin America: some theoretical and methodological guidelines for its study. In: Latin American research review, vol 16, no 2. Instituto de Desarrollo Económico y Social, Pittsburgh

Oszlak O (1982) Reflexiones sobre la formación del estado y la construcción de la sociedad argentina. In: Desarrollo Económico, vol 21, no 84. Instituto de Desarrollo Económico y Social, Buenos Aires

Oszlak O, O'Donnell G (1981) Estado y políticas estatales en América Latina: hacia una estrategia de investigación. In: Documento CEDES/CLACSO, no 4. Centro de Estudios de Estado y Sociedad, Buenos Aires

Portantiero JC (1973) Clases dominantes y crisis política en la Argentina. In: Braun O (ed) El capitalismo argentino en crisis. Siglo XXI Editores, Buenos Aires

Portantiero JC (1977) Economía y política en la crisis argentina: 1958–1973. In: Revista Mexicana de Sociología, vol 39, no 2. Universidad Nacional Autónoma de México, México

Portantiero JC (1981) Los usos de Gramsci. Folios Ediciones, México

Portantiero JC (1985) Notas sobre crisis y producción de acción hegemónica. In: Labastida J, Del Campo M (eds) Hegemonía y alternativas políticas en América Latina (Seminario de Morelia). Siglo XXI Editores, México

Portantiero JC (1988) La producción de un orden. Ensayos sobre la democracia entre el estado y la sociedad. Ediciones Nueva Visión, Buenos Aires

PROVEA (Programa Venezolano de Educación-Acción en Derechos Humanos) (2001a) Situación de los derechos humanos en Venezuela: informe anual 2001. Programa Venezolano de Educación-Acción en Derechos Humanos (PROVEA), Caracas

PROVEA (Programa Venezolano de Educación-Acción en Derechos Humanos) (2001b) Boletín derechos humanos y coyuntura, no 73. Programa Venezolano de Educación—Acción en Derechos Humanos (PROVEA), Caracas

PROVEA (Programa Venezolano de Educación-Acción en Derechos Humanos) (2002a) Situación de los derechos humanos en Venezuela: informe anual 2002. Programa Venezolano de Educación—Acción en Derechos Humanos (PROVEA), Caracas

PROVEA (Programa Venezolano de Educación-Acción en Derechos Humanos) (2002b) Boletín derechos humanos y coyuntura, no 108. Programa Venezolano de Educación - Acción en Derechos Humanos (PROVEA), Caracas

PROVEA (Programa Venezolano de Educación-Acción en Derechos Humanos) (2008) Situación de los derechos humanos en Venezuela: informe anual 2008. Programa Venezolano de Educación—Acción en Derechos Humanos (PROVEA), Caracas

REDIUP (Coordinadora de Redes Por Una Seguridad Social Pública y Solidaria) (2002) Comentarios a la "propuesta del proyecto de ley orgánica del sistema de seguridad social" elaborada por el equipo técnico asesor de la asamblea nacional

Salcedo González AM (2006) Consideraciones sobre la reforma de la seguridad social en Venezuela. Comisión de Estudios de Postgrado, Facultad de Ciencias Económicas y Sociales, Universidad Central de Venezuela, Fondo Editorial Tropykos, Caracas

Schütt KP (2008) La situación de los sindicatos en Venezuela. In: Kurzberichte aus der internationalen Entwicklungszusammenarbeit. Friedrich Ebert Stiftung, Bonn

Tarrow S (1994) Power in movement: social movements and contentious politics. Cambridge University Press, Cambridge

Thompson EP (1963) The making of the English working class. Victor Gollancz, London

Tilly C (1978) From mobilization to revolution. McGraw-Hill, New York

Vifañe ML (1991) La seguridad social en Venezuela: 1958–1998. Caracas, Fundación Escuela de Gerencia Social, Ministerio de Planificación y Desarrollo

Zambrano Gutiérrez OC (2004) Reforma de las pensiones de vejez en Venezuela en el marco de las reformas estructurales en América Latina: antecedentes, crisis y perspectivas. Freie Universität Berlin, Berlin

Constitutions, Laws, Decrees and Regulations

Constitución de la República de Venezuela (1961)
Constitución de la República Bolivariana de Venezuela (1999)
Decreto 2744, G.O. 36557, 09/10/1998
Decreto con Rango y Fuerza de Ley 2944, G.O. 36568, 27/10/1998
Decreto con Rango y Fuerza de Ley 2963, G.O. 36575, 05/11/1998
Decreto con Rango y Fuerza de Ley 2992, G.O. 36575, 05/11/1998
Decreto con Rango y Fuerza de Ley 2993, G.O. 36575, 05/11/1998
Decreto con Rango y Fuerza de Ley Orgánica de Reforma de la Ley Orgánica de la Administración
   Central, Decreto Ley 369, G.O. 36775, 30/08/1999
Decreto con Rango y Fuerza de Ley de Reforma Parcial de la Ley Orgánica del Sistema de Seguridad
   Social Integral, Decreto Ley 424, G.O.E. 5398, 25/10/1999
Decreto con rango y fuerza de Ley de Reforma Parcial del Decreto 2944 de fecha 14 de Octubre de
   1998, Decreto Ley 425, G.O.E. 5398, 25/10/1999
Decreto con rango y fuerza de Ley de Reforma Parcial del Decreto 2993 de fecha 4 de noviembre
   de 1998, Decreto Ley 426, G.O.E. 5398, 25/10/1999
Estatuto Orgánico del Seguro Social Obligatorio, G.O.E. 310, 05/10/1951
Hernández R (2011) FEDECÁMARAS: expresión del cambio institucional en Venezuela (1944).
   Economía 36(31) (Universidad de los Andes, Mérida)
Ley del Trabajo, G.O. 19640, 16/07/1936
Ley del Seguro Social Obligatorio, 24/06/1940
Ley del Seguro Social, G.O.E. 1023, 11/07/1966
Ley Orgánica del Sistema de Seguridad Social Integral, G.O.E. 5199, 30/12/1997
Ley Orgánica del Sistema de Seguridad Social, G.O 37600, 30/12/2002
Ley del Régimen Prestacional de Vivienda y Hábitat, G.O. 38182, 09/05/2005
Ley Orgánica de Prevención, Condiciones y Medio Ambiente de Trabajo, G.O. 38236, 26/07/2005)
Ley de Servicios Sociales, G.O. 38270, 12/09/2005
Ley del Régimen Prestacional de Empleo, G.O. 38281, 27/09/2005
Ley de Reforma Parcial de la Ley Orgánica del Sistema de Seguridad Social, G.O.E 5867,
   28/12/2007
López Maya M (2003) Venezuela en la encrucijada. In: OSAL, no 9. Consejo Latinoamericano de
   Ciencias Sociales, Buenos Aires
López Sánchez R (2012) El movimiento de trabajadores en la Venezuela bolivariana. Configuración
   de tendencias: autonomistas contra leninistas. In: Espacio Abierto, vol 21, no 1. Universidad del
   Zulia, Maracaibo
Pribble J (2006) Women and welfare: the politics of coping with new social risks in Chile and
   Uruguay. Latin American Studies Association, Pittsburgh
Segura-Ubiergo A (2007) The political economy of the welfare state in Latin America: globalization,
   democracy, and development. Cambridge University Press, Cambridge
Transparencia Venezuela (2013) Análisis de riesgos de corrupción e integridad en Gran Misión
   Vivienda Venezuela. Transparencia Venezuela, Caracas

Statistical Databases

INEV (Instituto Nacional de Estadística de Venezuela) (2015). www.ine.gov.ve
BCV (Banco Central de Venezuela) (2015). http://www.bcv.org.ve/
CEPALSTAT (2015). http://estadisticas.cepal.org/cepalstat/WEB_CEPALSTAT/Portada.asp?idio
   ma=e
MPPEF (Ministerio del Poder Popular de Economía y Finanzas) (2015). http://www.mppef.gob.v
   e/

Chapter 4
Analysis of the Power Struggles over the Post-neoliberal Social Security System Reform in Ecuador

This chapter breaks down the power struggles over the post-neoliberal social security system reform in Ecuador. The analysis is carried out following the complementary approach brought forward in Chap. 2, which commingles the conceptual framework of the Poulantzian approach and the operational framework of the political class struggle approaches. The chapter is structuralized into three parts.

The first part contextualizes the power struggles over the reform, for which it carries through a detailed reconstruction of the reform process and its social, economic, and political context.

The second part operationalizes the power struggles over the reform resorting to the concept of power resources, which is transubstantiated for the analysis of the reform in Ecuador. Both, the contextualization and the operationalization are predicated on the four analytical dimensions explained in Chap. 2, symbolized by the questions "where", "what", "who", and "how".

Finally, the third part recapitulates the findings of the analysis.

4.1 Contextualization of the Power Struggles over the Post-neoliberal Social Security System Reform

As explained above, the contextualization of the power struggles over the post-neoliberal social security system reform in Ecuador is carried out on the basis of the Poulantzian approach to social policy. The use of the Poulantzian approach for the contextualization is predicated on its overall theoretical perspective, which conceptualizes social policy within the context of the construction of hegemony. By doing so, the Poulantzian approach inherently associates social policy with the historical, social, economic, and political conditions in which social policy materializes. Following this perspective, the subsequent contextualization carries out a detailed reconstruction of the power struggles over the social security system reform in Ecuador

© Springer Nature Switzerland AG 2019
E. L. Bistoletti, *The Power Struggles over the Post-neoliberal Social Security System Reforms in Venezuela and Ecuador*, The Latin American Studies Book Series, https://doi.org/10.1007/978-3-319-98168-0_4

which delineates the social, economic, and political conditions in which they came about.

The reconstruction undertakes to puzzle out the four "questions" proposed in the first chapter as analytical guidelines for the contextualization: (1) "where", (2) "what", (3) "who", and (4) "how". As pointed out, these questions correlate four analytical dimensions: (1) the structural underpinnings underlying social policy, (2) the concrete points of conflict over social policy, (3) the real actors involved in the struggles over social policy, and (4) the channels through which the struggles are canalized. In order to carry out an intelligible recount of the power struggles over the reform, the reconstruction is chronologically structuralized. However, the four aforementioned questions can be easily acknowledged throughout the reconstruction. In addition, the answers to the "where", "what", "who", and "how" questions are broken down in the summary of the contextualization.

4.1.1 The History of Social Security in Ecuador

The first social insurance in Ecuador was established in 1923, when the congress determined the creation of the pension fund for teachers. Before that only the military and their families were ensured against old age, invalidity and death. Inspired by the pension fund for teachers, President Ysidro Ayora promulgated the Ley de Jubilación, Montepío Civil, Ahorro y Cooperativa (English: Law of Old-Age Pension, Civil Widows' Pension, Saving and Cooperative) (R.O. 591, 13/03/1928) in 1928 which established the Caja de Pensiones (English: Pension Fund). Since its very inception the Caja de Pensiones accomplished a formidable expansion, rapidly congregating over 20,000 affiliates. However, the complete absence of actuarial projections soon brought about a financial imbalance, which precipitated the first reform of the social insurances system in 1935 with the passing of the Ley de Seguro Social Obligatorio (English: Law of Obligatory Social Insurance) (Decreto Supremo 12, 02/10/1935) by decree. Among other things, this law established the Instituto Nacional de Previsión as the lead institution for the social insurances system, subordinating the Caja de Pensiones to it. Besides, this law authorized the Caja de Pensiones to purchase land and manufacture homes for the affiliates, what factually represented the beginning of the activities of the social insurances system in the housing sector. In February 1937, the Ley del Seguro Social Obligatorio underwent a modification in order to incorporate the health insurance for the affiliates. One month later the Caja del Seguro Social (English: Social Insurance Fund) was established as well.

Nevertheless, the actuarial problems of the (continuously expanding) social insurances system perseverated. For this reason, the second reform was carried out in 1942 (Decreto 1179, 14/07/1942) and the third reform in 1958 (Ley de Emergencia 27, 16/07/1958). In 1963, the Caja de Pensiones and the Caja del Seguro Social were commingled into a unified fund called the Caja Nacional del Seguro Social (English: National Social Insurance Fund) (Decreto Supremo 517, 19/12/1963) and a year later, in 1964, the occupational hazards insurance, the craftsman insurance, the professional insurance, and the domestic workers insurance were undertaken. In 1968, the Seguro Social Campesino (Peasant Social Insurace) (hereinafter SSC) commenced as a pilot program aimed at the incorporation of peasants, the largest population group at the time, into to the social security system. Even though the SSC only handed over health care in the beginning, it would soon represent a central part of the Ecuadorian social security system.

The unification of both funds actually purposed to resolve the persistent financial problems of the social insurances system. However, this goal was not consistently accomplished, because of which de facto President José María Velasco Ibarra determined the elimination of the Instituto Nacional de Previsión on 23 June 1970. One month later, Velasco Ibarra promulgated the creation of the Instituto Ecuatoriano de Seguridad Social (English: Ecuadorian Institute of Social Security) (hereinafter IESS) by decree in replacement of the extinguished Instituto Nacional de Previsión (Decreto 40, 25/07/1970).

During the 1970s, the IESS carried out its duties with positive results, expanding both its services and its coverage (Lo Vuolo and Mesa-Lago 1998: 313). Moreover, the IESS straightened out its financial situation throughout these years. However, the budgetary position of the IESS deteriorated during the 1980s, as several contemporary assessments pointed out (Mesa-Lago 1984, 1989, 1992; Thullen 1987). The severe financial problems experienced by the Ecuadorian social security system since the 1980s did not represent an exception within the Latin American context. As a matter of fact, the social security systems of the Latin American pioneering countries (Argentina, Brazil, Chile, and Uruguay) came under increasing financial difficulties since the early 1980s as well. However, the financial problems of these latter systems were associated to a "systemic" crisis, as they were to hand down universal coverage despite a continuously decreasing ratio between their active and passive members (Lo Vuolo and Mesa-Lago 1998: 324). On the contrary, the increasing financial deterioration of the Ecuadorian system of social since the early 1980s was predicated on the following internal and external causes.

Regarding the internal causes, the aforementioned assessments remarked (1) the poor results of the investments made by the IESS with its surplus capital and eventually the complete immobilization of its surplus capital in a context of high inflation, which contributed to the liquefaction of its value; (2) the exploding increase of incompetent personnel at the IESS, (3) the massive concession of credits to a subsidized rate by the IESS, which denaturalized its function, converting the IESS in a quasi-financial institution, and (4) the persistence of a curative (and more expensive) approach to health care which precluded the transition to a preventive (and less expensive) approach (Paéz Zumárraga 2001: 39–49).

With regard to the external causes the aforementioned assessments pointed out (1) the recurrent nonpayment of the private employers' contributions to the IESS, which generated a remarkable debt of the private employers with the IESS, (2) the recurrent nonpayment of the state employers' contributions to the IESS, which brought about a considerable debt of the state with the IESS, (3), the recurrent nonpayment of the state additional contribution to the IESS, which represented 40% of the old-age pensions paid by the IESS according to the Ley del Seguro Social Obligatorio,

(4) the utilization of the surplus capital of the IESS for the financing of the state deficit, which constrained the IESS to compulsory purchase state debt bonds (Paéz Zumárraga 2001: 39–49).

Despite these serious problems, the IESS could gradually maximize its population coverage during the 1980s, especially in rural areas. This expansion derived for the most part from the continuous extension of the SSC, which incorporated the provision of old-age pension for peasants in November 1981, when the Ley de Extensión del Seguro Social Campesino (English: Law of Extension of the Peasant Social Insurance) (R.O. 124, 20/11/1981) was promulgated. Besides, the IESS represented the only state institution with operational surplus (revenue higher than expenditure) at the beginning of the 1980s (Mesa-Lago 1984). Precisely for this reason, the funds of the IESS were increasingly misappropriated by the consecutive governments in power since the early 1980s to resolve their fiscal problems. As a result, the financial situation of the IESS drastically deteriorated during the 1980s, what eventually brought about the first privatization attempt in the early 1990s.

4.1.2   The Privatization of the Social Security System

The first step was accomplished in February 1993, when the social insurances of the military forces were dissociated from the IEES and relocated in an exclusive institution of social security for the military forces called Instituto de Seguridad Social de las Fuerzas Armadas (English: Institute of Social Security of the Armed Forces) (hereinafter ISSFA), in compliance with the Ley de Seguridad Social de las Fuerzas Armadas (English: Law o Social Security of the Armed Forces) approved 6 months earlier, in August 1992 (R.O.S. 995, 07/08/1992). This way the military forces were precluded from the forthcoming privatization of the IESS, as they held over their special regime of social security guaranteed by the state (Lo Vuolo and Mesa-Lago 1998: 322).

Shortly after, in June 1993, President Sixto Durán Ballén brought out the document "Agenda para el Desarrollo" (English: Agenda for Development) which delineated his plan of government for the rest of his presidential term (CND 1996). This document predicated the problems of the Ecuadorian social security system on the lack of private competition, for which it advocated the creation of private enterprises for the administration of the old and health insurances (CND 1996: 11–13). In order to carry out the "modernization" of the state proposed in the Agenda para el Desarrollo, the Comisión Nacional de Modernización del Estado (English: National Council for State Modernization) (hereinafter CONAM) was established in December 1993. A few months later, in May 1993 President Durán Ballén commissioned the CONAM to devise the social security system reform. As a first step in this direction, the CONAM immediately publicized a document containing the guidelines for the reform of the pension system called "Lineamientos para la Reforma al Sistem de Pensiones del Ecuador" (English: Guidelines for the Reform of the Ecuadorian Pension System) (Lo Vuolo and Mesa-Lago 1998: 323). This document brought forward the introduction of private pension funds into the pension system but it did not determine under what model, for the members of the CONAM still deliberated at this point between a mixed model with one public and one private pillars as in Argentina and Uruguay, and a completely private model with only one private pillar as in Chile. Finally, the CONAM brought out its reform proposal in January 1995, which branched out in two independent reforms: a reform of the health system and a reform of the pension system (CONAM 1995).

The proposed reform of the health system established a mixed system consisting of two pillars: (1) a state public non-contributory regime for those without contributory capacity, and (2) a private contributory regime managed by private insurance companies called Organización Promotora de Salud (English: Health Promoting Organization) (hereinafter OPS). The reform prescribed that the OPS selected by the workers received their obligatory contributions previously paid to the IESS, while the IESS itself became one OPS.

After the aforementioned deliberations within the CONAM regarding the model of the pension system, the proposed reform finally established a completely private model managed by private funds denominated Administradora de Fondos de Jubilación y Pensión (English: Retirement and Pension Fund Administrator) (hereienfater AFJP) as in Chile. Actually, the proposed model closely corresponded with the Chilean model, except for the fact that the former established a minimum pension financed through an obligatory contribution paid by all members of 0.5% and administered by the AFJPs, whereas the latter did not. In addition, the reform proposal increased the rate and the base of the contributions, and held over the retirement age from 55 to 65 years. On top of this, the proposed reform determined the elimination of the IESS and the suppression of the pension insurance of the SSC, which only carried over as a health insurance.

A few months after the presentation of the reform proposal of the CONAM, in June 1995, the government promulgated the Ley de Seguridad Social de la Policía Nacional (English: Law of Social Security of the National Police) (R.O. 707, 01/06/1995), which dissociated the social insurances of the police forces from the IESS and established an exclusive institute of social security for the police forces called Instituto de Seguridad Social de la Policía Nacional (English Institute of Social Security of the National Police) (hereinafter ISSPOL) (Durán Valverde 2008: 130). This measure purposed to remove the opposition of both military and police forces to the forthcoming privatization of the IESS by preserving their special social security regimes guaranteed by the state.

The reform proposal of the CONAM was repudiated by the National Assembly, where the political opposition had taken over. In this context, President Durán Ballén determined to carry out a referendum in order to bring about 11 drastic reforms (including the social security system reform) without the consent of the assembly. The referendum was carried through on 26 November 1995 with considerable voter turnout (58.65% of the electoral register). The voters massively repudiated all reforms, including the social security system reform, with an average rejection of 58.46%. After this, the privatization attempt of the social security system was deactivated for a few years.

During this privatization impasse, the situation of the IESS further deteriorated. Its aforementioned problems not only carried over but also were maximized due to the continuous decline of the Ecuadorian economy. On top of that, the IESS was dreadfully supervised by its consecutive directive boards, probably with the ulterior aim of undermining the public opinion on the IESS in order to advocate its privatization (Páez Zumárraga 2001; Cañizares and Sánchez 2005).

The drive for the privatization of the social security system recommenced in 1998, when a new constitution was promulgated during the interim government of Fabián Alarcón. This constitution established that social security was carried out by the public and private sectors (Constitución Política de la República del Ecuador 1998: Article 55)

Additionally, the constitution countenanced the creation of administrators of old-age and health insurances, bringing about the possibility of private pension funds and private medical insurances (Constitución Política de la República del Ecuador 1998: Article 58).

Finally, the constitution established that the next government would undertake a thoroughgoing social security system reform, including the IESS. In this context, neoliberal President Jamil Mahuad determined the intervention of the IESS immediately after taking over the presidency in August 1998. To this aim, Mahuad established a controller commission for the IESS (called Comisión Interventora) composed of three business-related members: Alfredo Mancero Samán, Enrique Arosemena Baquerizo, and Gladys Palán Tamayo (Nieto Puente 2013: 28). This commission took over the control of the IESS and undertook its reform. In accordance with the constitutional mandate, the controller commission handed over its reform proposal to the National Assembly in February 1999. The reform proposal commingled two drafts: (1) Ley de Bases del Seguro General Obligatorio (English: Law on Bases of the Obligatory Social Insurance) containing 129 articles, and (2) Ley Reformatoria del Sistema de Pensiones (English: Reform Law of the Pension System) containing 147 articles (Hoy 24/02/1999). All in all, the reform proposal of the controller commission brought forward a mixed model à la Uruguay for the pension system and a mixed system à la Colombia for the health system (Páez Zumárraga 2001: 265).

The pension system contrived in the reform proposal established a mixed pension system based on three pillars: (1) an obligatory PAYG regime administered by the state encompassing the workers' remunerations up to 60 USD, (2) an obligatory individual capitalization regime administered by private pension funds encompassing the workers' remunerations from 60 USD up to 150 USD, and (3) a voluntary individual capitalization regime administered by private pension funds encompassing the affiliates' remunerations over 150 USD.

The National Congress commingled both bills into a single bill without substantial modifications, as most congress members countenanced the introduction of private pension funds into the pension system (Páez Zumárraga 2001: 266). Despite this generalized consensus, discussions on the bill carried over for more than 2 years in the congress. Finally, the congress accommodated the preestablished limits for the three pillars in order to maximize the scope of the PAYG regime before passing the bill on July 2001 (Hoy 12/07/2001). Even though the core of the reform proposal of the controller commission of the IESS came through unchanged, President Gustavo Noboa did not promulgate the bill and brought out a partial veto against it adducing the unconstitutionality of several articles of the bill approved by the congress. For this reason, the Tribunal Constitucional (English: Constitutional Court) was commissioned to determine the constitutionality of the articles at stake in August 2001. Two months later the Tribunal Constitucional determined that some of the articles vetoed by the president in effect contravened the constitution, for which it commissioned the Congress to straighten them out (R.O.S. 438, 23/10/2001). The congress restructuralized the contested articles and the bill was finally promulgated under the title Ley de Seguridad Social (English: Law of Social Security) (hereinafter LSSE) on 30 November 2001 (R.O. 465, 30/11/2001) (Sasso 2011). However, the subsequent modifications suffered by the bill during more than 3 years of discussions convoluted it so much that in the end the approved bill carried over manifold contradictions and inconsistencies.

During the prolonged discussion process, the economy of Ecuador deteriorated with severe financial consequences for the IESS. In 1999, the Ecuadorian GDP decreased 4.7% and the Ecuadorian national currency (called sucre) dramatically depreciated against the U.S. dollar, losing 67% of its value. For this reason, President Jamil Mahuad annunciated on January 2000 the adoption of the U.S. dollar as national currency. Since the dollarization was carried out at a very high conversion rate due to the aforementioned process of the depreciation of the sucre, it immediately generated a precipitous fall of labor remunerations (including their contributions to social security) and old-age pensions. In addition to this, the dollarization brought about a tremendous reduction of the funds accumulated by the IESS and the debt of the state with the IESS, as both were established in sucres (Interview with Luis Alfredo Muñoz Neira).

After its tortuous approval in November 2001, the LSSE came across further obstacles which eventually struck down its implementation. In May 2002, the Tribunal Constitucional determined for the second time the unconstitutionality of several key passages of the LSSE concerning the introduction of private pension funds. However, this sentence could not be carried out because its official publication was staved off by a writ of protection which eventually carried over its enforcement until February 2005 (Torres 2008: 2). This brought about a legal void, as the mixed pension system prescribed by the LSSE could not be established and this, in turn, precluded the implementation of the remaining articles of the law (Viteri Llanga 2008: 62). This "legal limbo" remained unsolved until the Tribunal Constitucional definitively determined the unconstitutionality of the passages of the law at stake in a second sentence in February 2005 (R.O.S. 525, 16/02/2005) (Corral 2008: 127). After this, a commission was established for the formulation of the required reforms of the LSSE in 2005. Under the name Comisión Interinstitucional para la Reforma de la Ley de Seguridad Social (English: Interinstitutional Commission for the Reform of the Law of Social Security) (hereinafter CIRLSS), this commission commingled congress members, members of the IESS, and members of the Superintendencia de Bancos (English: Superintendence of Banks), and even members of the United Nations Development

Program (Sojo 2009: 215). The CIRLSS finally handed over its reform proposal to the congress in August 2006 (CIRLSS 2006), but it was never deliberated by the congress due the political turbulences which convulsed Ecuador during the time.

The 3-year period of legal void between the suspension of the LSSE in May 2002 and the final sentence of the Tribunal Constitucional in February 2005 generated a controversial situation with regard to the collected pension funds during this time. As pointed out above, the sentence of the Tribunal Constitucional declaring the unconstitutionality of several passages of the LSSE in May 2002 precluded the creation of the private pension funds prescribed by the law. Nonetheless, the employees' contributions were still accumulated in personal accounts at the IESS in accordance with the LSSE, what eventually generated the collection of individual pension funds for 615 million US dollars' fund. Against this background, the congress determined the voluntary devolution of the accumulated funds to the affiliates in early July 2005.

Due to the foreseeable financial consequences of this decision, Economy Minister Rafael Correa repudiated the decision, anticipating that the devolution of the funds would drastically deteriorate the actuarial situation of the IESS. Because of this, Correa advocated the use of the accumulated funds for the provision of unsecured credits to the IESS members (Hoy 03/06/2005). Finally, President Alfredo Palacio brought out a partial veto to the law, which repudiated the devolution of all funds at once but established the devolution of the funds in parts (Hoy 23/07/2005). The congress countenanced the presidential veto and the devolution of the accumulated funds in parts was promulgated at last in August 2005 (R.O. 73, 02/08/2005).

The disagreement between Economy Minister Rafael Correa, who had been recently commissioned to this post, and President Alfredo Palacio, undermined the (already precarious) position of Correa. A few weeks later Minister Correa was publicly discredited by President Palacio again because of Correa's critical position against the neoliberal economic guidelines imposed to Ecuador by the IMF. After this, Correa was naturally constrained to renounce. However, during his three and a half months as Economy Minister, Correa became very popular for his heterodox economic measures. Based on this, he determined to participate in the forthcoming presidential election to be celebrated in November 2006. To this aim, Correa and a reduced group of intellectuals and academics congregated manifold preexisting leftist political organizations in a political movement called Alianza PAIS (English: Alliance PAIS) (hereinafter AP) (Hernández and Buendía 2011: 132)

4.1.3 The Subject of Social Security in the Electoral Campaign of Rafael Correa for the Presidential Election of 2006

Throughout the electoral campaign none of the main presidential candidates (Álvaro Noboa, Rafael Correa, Gilmar Gutiérrez and León Roldós) predominantly concentrated on the subject of social security, as one of the members of the directive board of the IESS publicly pointed out in an interview with a national newspaper (El Universo 04/11/2006). However, the subject of social security did represent a factor of differentiation among the candidates, since their positions on social security extremely divaricated.

Correa openly repudiated the incorporation of private pension funds into the pension system and the expansion of private medical insurances. Instead, he subscribed the modernization and expansion of the existing PAYG regime and the unification of the health system. Even though his electoral campaign revolved around the proposal of a constituent assembly, the subject of social security was addressed in his political program.

Correa's political program was recapitulated in a document entitled "Plan de Gobierno del Movimiento PAIS 2007–2011" (English: Government Plan of the Movement PAIS 2007–2011) (hereinafter PGMP). The PGMP repudiated the neoliberal policies implemented in Ecuador since the early 1990s and advocated a "revolución ciudadana" (English: citizens' revolution) in order to undertake a radical change in Ecuador's history (AP 2006: 4, 12). Accoding to the PGMP, this radical change revolved around five lines of actions: (1) revolución constitucional y democrática (English: constitutional and democratic revolution), (2) revolución ética: combate frontal a la corrupción (English: ethical revolution: frontal combat of corruption), (3) revolución económica y productiva (English: economic and productive revolution), (4) revolución educativa y de la salud (English: educational and health revolution), and (5) revolución por la dignidad, la soberanía y la integración latinoamericana (English: revolution for dignity, sovereignty, and Latin American integration).

The PGMP broke down these five lines of action thoroughly. As pointed out above, the congregation of a constituent assembly for the formulation of a new constitution represented the nucleus of Correa's political plan. For this reason, the proposal of a constituent assembly was brought forward as the first line of action of the citizen's revolution.

The subject of social security was interestingly broken down in the context of the third line of action (economic and productive revolution), correlating social security with labor. Thus, the subject of social security was associated with labor-related subjects, such as employment generation, wage policy, labor stability, employment protection, dignification of labor, popular economy, and economic empowerment of women (AP 2006: 27–32). Moreover, the PGMP advanced beyond this point and conceptualized social security in the context of the democratization of the economy, predicating the public propriety of social security, oil, electricity, and communications (AP 2006: 44).

Concerning the IESS, the PGMP advocated its modernization but repudiated its privatization very emphatically. In line with this, the document came out for the full payment of the state's debt to the IESS (AP 2006: 30). Besides, the PGMP brought forward the incorporation of representatives of the affiliates into the directive board of the IESS and the improvement of the pension in real terms, which had drastically deteriorated with the dollarization in 2001 (AP 2006: 30).

With regard to the LSSE passed in 2001, the PGMP brought forward a thoroughgoing reform aimed at the efficient control of the contributions made to the social security system, the supervision of the use of the collected funds and the aforementioned payment of the state's debt with the IESS. Additionally, the document advocated the coverage of the elder not covered by the existing social security system (AP 2006: 30).

In order to accomplish this goal, the PGMP brought forward the expansion and strengthening of the SSC. Notwithstanding, the document pointed out that different sectors of activity would come under differential treatment, what actually represented a gesture of compromise to the sectors of activity with special social security regimes (AP 2006: 30).

Finally, the PGMP advocated the incorporation of female domestic workers to social security and, for the first time pointed out the subject of the universalization of social security (AP 2006: 31).

Noboa's posture regarding social security and the IESS completely divaricated from Correa's position (Hoy 20/10/2006). Noboa openly advocated the incorporation of private pension funds into the pension system and the expansion of private medical insurances in the health system, in line with the bill under discussion in the congress. Moreover, he repeatedly asseverated that he would carry out the neoliberal policies of former US President Ronald Reagan (El Universo 03/11/2006). Beyond this, Noboa circumvented pronouncements on "programmatic issues" during his electoral campaign (Quintero López 2005: 138–139), including the subject of social security, and did not publicize a political program or anything like it.

The Ecuadorian electoral regime established a two-round system for the election of the president since the sanction of the constitution of 1998. In the first election held on 15 October 2006, no candidate accomplished the required absolute majority since the electorate was partitioned in five blocks. Noboa and Correa accumulated the most votes (26.83 and 22.84%, respectively), therefore accessing to the second (and definitive) election. Finally, in the second election held on 26 November 2006 Correa countervailed the results of the first election, attaining the absolute majority with 56.65% of the votes against Noboa, who accumulated 43.33% of the votes.

4.1.4   The Struggles over the Formulation and Passing of the Constitutional Articles Concerning Social Security

In his presidential assumption, on 15 January 2007, Correa promulgated two decrees. In the first one, he officially took over as president of Ecuador. In the second one he convocated a plebiscite concerning the call for a constituent assembly, as promised during his electoral campaign. Three months later, the Tribunal Supremo Electoral (English: Supreme Electoral Tribunal) countenanced the plebiscite and annunciated its execution for 15 April 2007.

However, the opposition was determined to strike down the plebiscite at all costs (Ortiz 2008). Using its majority in the congress, the opposition determined to bring down the president of the Tribunal Supremo Electoral in order to contravene the ruling of the tribunal. In response, the Tribunal Supremo promulgated the displacement of the congress members who had countenanced the removal its president 1 day later. The removed congress members reciprocated this through a legal injunction but the competent judge finally repudiated it.

In the end, the referendum was carried out as planned on 15 March 2007. With a 71.58% of electoral participation, the Ecuadorian electorate countenanced the call of a constituent assembly for the formulation of a new constitution. After this, a national election was carried through in order to constitute the national assembly on 30 September 2007. In these elections AP, the political movement of the President Correa, received 69.47% of the votes, obtaining the absolute majority of the seats at the assembly. Finally, the constituent assembly commenced its work 2 months later, on 30 November 2007. The elected constituent Alberto Acosta, who represented AP, was commissioned as the president of the assembly.

In alliance with other left-wing parties represented at the constituent assembly, such as the Movimiento Popular Democrático (English: Democratic People's Movement) (hereinafter MPD), the Movimiento de Unidad Plurinacional Pachakutik (English: Pachakutik Plurinational Unity Movement) (hereinafter MUPP) and the Red Ética y Democracia (English: Ethics and Democracy Network) (hereinafter RED), AP could advance a very progressive program which encompassed manifold civil, political economic, social, and cultural rights, the unprecedented rights of nature, and the paradigm of buen vivir (English: good living) as an alternative world view in which humans and nature correlate in harmony (Ramírez 2010). Naturally, the subject of social security came out during the work of the constituent assembly as well.

The work of the constituent assembly was partitioned in 9 thematic working groups called "mesas constituyentes" (English: constituent tables), each of them containing 13 constituents. These working groups comprised: (1) Derechos fundamentales y garantías constitucionales (English: Fundamental rights and constitutional guarantees), (2) Organización, participación social y ciudadana, y sistemas de representación (English: Organization, social and civil participation, and systems of representation), (3) Estructura e instituciones del Estado (English: State structure and institutions), (4) Ordenamiento territorial y asignación de competencias (English: Territorial organization and designation of powers), (5) Recursos naturales y biodiversidad (English: Natural resources and biodiversity), (6) Trabajo, producción e inclusión social (English: Labor, production, and social inclusión), (7) Régimen de desarrollo (English: Model of development), (8) Justicia y lucha contra la corrupción (English: justice and fight against corruption), and (9) Legislación y fiscalización (Englih: Legislation and Auditing).

Interestingly, the subject of social security was mainly addressed in the working group 7, which was dedicated to the discussion of the model of development, instead of being deliberated in the working group 6, devoted to labor, production, and social inclusion. The inclusion of the subject of social security in the working group 7 was predicated on the approach given to social security, which conceptualized it in the context of the paradigm of buen vivir, and therefore concatenated the right to social security with all the social, economic, and cultural rights prescribed by the constitution, including the rights to education, health, environment, housing, culture, sport, leisure, information, communication, migration, transportation, and public security. This comprehensive approach was transposed to an institutional arrangement made up of specialized systems of institutions, such as the national system of education, the national system of health, the national system of social security, the national system of culture, and so on. Altogether these systems constituted the Sistema Nacional de Inclusion y Equidad Social (English: National System of Social Inclusion and Equity).

The working group 1, committed to the discussion of fundamental rights and constitutional guarantees undertook the subject of social security as well, what eventually brought about a dispute with the working group 7. Finally, the assembly determined this dispute in favor of the working group 7 and the working group 1 collaborated with the group 7 under the terms of this latter.

The presidency of the working group 7 was commissioned to Pedro Morales, an indigenous leader of MUPP, politically allied to AP. Besides, the group congregated a vast majority of constituents of AP, including the president of the assembly Alberto Acosta. All in all, the working group 7 in charge of the subject of social security comprised the following constituents: Pedro Morales (MUPP), Ricardo Zambrano (AP), Norman Wray (AP), Germánico Pinto (AP), Galo Borja (AP), Jaime Ruiz (AP), Bety Tola (AP), María Isabel Segovia (AP), Alberto Acosta (AP), Martha Roldós (RED), Gilmar Gutiérrez (Sociedad Patriótica) (English: Patriotic Society), Pablo Lucio Paredes (Movimiento Futuro Ya) (English: Movement Future Now), and Julián García (Partido Renovador Institucional Acción Nacional) (English: Institutional Renewal Party of National Action).

During its work sessions, the group received the visits of several groups, including expert groups from the Secretaría Nacional de Planificación y Desarrollo (English: National Secretariat of Planning and Development) (hereinafter SENPLADES) and the Banco de Fomento (Bank of the Development), indigenous and peasant organizations such as the Federación Nacional de Trabajadores Agroindustriales, Campesinos e Indígenas Libres del Ecuador (English: National Federation of Agroindustrial Workers, Free Peasants and Indigenous of Ecuador) (hereinafter FENACLE), the Confederación de Nacionalidades Indígenas del Ecuador (English: Confederation of Indigenous Nationalities of Ecuador) (hereinafter COANIE), and the Unión de Organizaciones Campesinas del Ecuador (English: Union of Peasant Organizations of Ecuador) (hereinafter UCAE), organizations of members of the SSC such as the Federación Única Nacional de Afiliados al Seguro Social Campesino (National Federation of Members of the Peasant Social Insurance), women organizations such as the Movimiento Mujeres del Ecuador (English: Movement Women of Ecuador), and microcredit and cooperative associations such as the Movimiento Nacional Cooperativo de Ahorro y Crédito (English: National Cooperative Movement of Savings and Loans) and the Unión de Cooperativas de Ahorro y Crédito del Sur (English: Union of Savings and Loans Cooperatives of the South). Interestingly, no employers' organization participated in the discussions of the working group 7.

Following the legislative procedure of the constituent assembly, the working group 7 brought forward a first proposal for discussion in the plenary assembly. Unlike the proposals submitted by other working groups, the proposal of the working 7 was not countenanced by all its members but only by the members allied to the government.

In general terms, the first proposal of the working group corresponded with the guidelines previously prescribed by the PGMP. Thus, the proposal established the right of the population to social security and explicitly repudiated its privatization. Besides, in line with the PGMP, the first proposal of the working group advocated the expansion of the coverage of the SSC, the incorporation of the family members of the insured into the social insurances, and the inclusion of domestic and care workers into the social security system (ACE 02/07/2008: 22, 25–26).

However, the proposal outdistanced the PGMP in terms of universalization, as it established the creation of a comprehensive system of social security called "Sistema de Seguridad Social" (English: System of Social Security) aimed at the universalization of social security and, even more important, the inception of a universal social insurance called "Seguro Universal Obligatorio" (English: Universal Obligatory Insurance) managed by the IESS (ACE 02/07/2008: 22, 25–26).

Additionally, the proposal brought forward two very important transitory dispositions concerning the creation of the state agency in charge of the financial management of the pension funds collected by the IESS, and the provision of non-contributory pension funds to those without universal protection (ACE 02/07/2008: 26).

The universalization of social security prescribed by the proposal of the working group 7 corresponded with the comprehensive paradigm of buen vivir which, as pointed out above, correlated the economic, social, and cultural rights. In line with this, the universalization of social security postulated by the proposal promulgated the unification of the existing fragmented social security system. This unification necessarily presupposed two forms of unification: (1) the unification of the existing pension regimes, (2) the unification of the health system.

The unification of the pension regimes, which would bring about the combination of the four existing pension regimes (the general regime administered by the IESS, the military regime administered by the ISSFA, the police regime administered by the ISSPOL, and the SSC regime), was to be accomplished through the institution of the aforementioned Sistema de Seguridad Social and, moreover, through the implementation of a universal social insurance.

The unification of the health system contemplated the combination of the fragmented parts of the existing health system, including the state public non-contributory sector administered by the ministry of health, the state public contributory sector administered by the IESS, the ISSFAA, and the ISSPOL, and the private sector. According to the proposal, these three sectors of the existing health system were to coalesce into a unified system of universal access called Sistema Nacional de Salud (English: National System of Health). The justification of the proposal on health pointed out that the unification of the health system predicated on the necessity of overcoming the existing fragmentation, which would be accomplished through the instauration of a universal and unified health system based on a multidimensional approach to human health.

On this basis, the proposal of the working group 7 brought forward seven constitutional articles on health. These articles delineated a unified health system including both public and private health sectors, established the universal and free provision of healthcare by the public health sector, determined the obligation of the private health sector of handing out health care in emergency cases, and acknowledged the obligation of the state in the provision of health care (ACE 02/07/2008: 23–25). Thus, the Sistema Nacional de Salud (English: National System of Health) prescribed by the proposal did not repudiate the existence of private providers of health services, but it clearly subordinated them to the control of the state.

In the first plenary discussion, the proposal came under manifold criticisms from the constituents opposed to the government. Since the proposal submitted by the working group dovetailed the subject of social security with the paradigm of buen vivir, some of the criticisms concerning social security denunciated the paradigm of buen vivir rather than the social security proposal. These criticisms usually revolved around the socialist character of the proposal, which would bring about class warfare in the otherwise harmonious Ecuadorian society, and the excessive state social assistance proposed by the proposal, which would bring about the encouragement of laziness. Constituent Roberto Ponce Noboa, who represented the political party Partido Renovador Institucional de Acción Nacional (English: Institutional Renewal Party of National Action) (hereinafter PRIAN), a conservative party opposed to the government, pointed out these arguments in his speech (ACE 10/04/2008: 29–33).

In line with this but from a more liberal perspective constitutent Mae Montaño, who represented the political party Una Nueva Opción (English: A New Option), a liberal party averse to the government, denounced the gigantic state structure prescribed by the proposal. According to Montaño, this enormous structure of social assistance would not advantage people but, instead, it would eventually represent a burden to them (ACE 02/07/2008: 43–46).

Criticisms specifically concerning social security revolved around two issues: (1) the categorical prohibition of the private sector within the pension system, and (2) the unification of the health and social systems prescribed by the proposal.

As recounted above, the participation of private pension funds within the pension system had been established by the LSSE in 2001 but then definitively repudiated by the TC in 2005. However, the possibility of privatization carried over in the political arena and some constituents still requisitioned the incorporation of private pension funds into the pension system, either as a complement to the existing state public PAYG regime or directly replacing it. In this context, several constituents openly advocated the inclusion of the private sector into the social security system in their speeches. The arguments used for this usually pointed out the benefits resulting from economic competition or the natural inefficiency of the state for management, as in the case of the constituent Gissel Rosado of PRIAN (ACE 02/07/2008: 95–96).

Constituent César Rohón, who represented the political party Partido Social Cristiano (English: Social Christian Party) (hereinafter PSC), requisitioned the incorporation of the private sector into the social security system too. His arguments corresponded with those of Rosado, however, in his speech Rohón acknowledged the existence of lobby groups involved in the discussions on the subject, as the Consejo Nacional de Enseñanza Superior (English: National Council for Higher Education) (hereinafter CONESUP). According to Rohón, CONESUP, a state autonomous agency devoted to the regulation of universities, had handed over a constitutional draft subscribing the participation of the private sector within the social security system (ACE 02/07/2008: 107–108).

The constitutional draft of CONESUP did not represent the only proposal submitted by lobby organizations in favor of the participation of the private sector within the social security system. The Asociación Nacional de Clínicas y Hospitales Privados del Ecuador (English: National Association of Private Clinics and Hospitals of Ecuador) (hereinafter ACHPE) handed over its own proposal to the assembly, which naturally established the private provision of health services and the incorporation of the private sector into the social security system (ACHPE 2008)

Both the denunciations of the socialist and statist character of the social security system prescribed by the proposal and the objections against the proscription of the private sector from the pension system included in the proposal were exclusively brought forward by constituents opposed to the government. On the contrary, the unification of the social security system aimed at the universalization of social security brought about an intense debate in which some constituents allied to the government brought out their discontent with the proposal. As explained above, the unification postulated in the proposal presupposed two types of unification: (1) the unification of the existing social insurances, (2) the unification of the health system.

With regard to the first type of unification, the unification of the existing social insurances, the objections revolved around the elimination of the special social security regimes of the military and police forces. As recounted above, these special social security regimes were established in the early 1990s in order to preclude the opposition of the military and police forces to the forthcoming privatization of the pension system. As explained before, the attempted privatization was never accomplished due to the ruling of the TC, which determined its unconstitutionality. In spite of this, the military and police forces held out their own social security regimes, which brought about considerable advantages compared to the general regime of social security administered by the IESS. These advantages presupposed a much higher rate of return on pensions, with a minimum 70% rate of return of the last salary received (but usually approximating 100%), a much higher rate of employers' contribution (26.00% for the ISSFA, 25.75 for the ISSPOL, and 9.15 for the IESS), and a higher state contribution to the pension system, which represented 60% of the pensions paid by the ISSFA and the ISSPOL against 40% of the pensions paid by the IESS.

Unlike the SSC, the ISSFA and the ISSPOL were not specifically acknowledged in the constitutional articles proposed by the working group 7. Instead, the proposal encompassed a transitory disposition which postulated that the ISSFA and the ISSPOL represented a component of the System of Social Security which provided social security services in compliance with their constitutive laws.

For several constituents, the inclusion of ISSFA and ISSPOL in the transitory dispositions instead of in the articles on social security presupposed the intention of the government and its political allies to take down the special social security regimes of both military and police forces. Constituent Gilmar Gutiérrez, a retired military officer who had participated in the military coup lead by his brother Lucio Gutiérrez against president Jamil Mahuad in January 2000, pointed out this in his speech during the plenary discussion (ACE 02/07/2008: 120–121). For this reason, Gutiérrez requisitioned the incorporation of the transitory disposition on the ISSFA and the ISSPOL into the articles of the proposal. Suggestively Gutiérrez, who as a retired officer held out connected to active officers of the military and police forces, materialized this request in the name of the military and police forces themselves (ACE 02/07/2008: 121).

As expected, other right-wing constituents opposed to the government advocated this request too, including the aforementioned constituent Roberto Ponce Noboa of PRIAN (ACE 02/07/2008: 122). However, the incorporation of the transitory disposition concerning the ISSFA and the ISSPOL into the articles of the proposal was also requisitioned by some left-wing constituents allied to the government, as constituent Luis Hernández of RED (ACE 02/07/2008: 160). This situation brought out the existence of disagreements regarding the future of ISSFA AND ISSPOL within the constituents allied to the government and the overarching political influence of the military and police forces.

The disagreement regarding the incorporation of the ISSFA and the ISSPOL into Sistema de Seguridad Social not only percolated into the constituents allied to the government. In fact, no one advocated the dissolution of the ISSFA and the ISSPOL into a universal and unified social security system as openly as constituent Juan Pablo Aguilar, who actually represented the right-wing political movement Movimiento Futuro Ya (Movement Future Now) (ACE 02/07/2008: 69–70).

With regard to the second type of unification, the unification of the health system, the criticisms made against the proposal revolved around two issues: (1) the subordination of the private health sector to the Sistema Nacional de Salud controlled by the state, and (2) the provision of health services by the public institutions of social security (IESS, ISSFA, and ISSPOL) to non-insured.

Concerning the first issue, the constituents who advocated a wider participation of the private sector in the health system simply repudiated the idea of a unified health. Constituent Leonarno Viteri of the PSC predicated this position on the existence of countless health providers in Ecuador (ACE 02/07/2008: 48).

Regarding the second issue, the provision of health services by the public institutions of social security (IESS, ISSFA and ISSPOL) to non-insured, the criticisms against the proposal pointed out that the access of the non-insured to the health services of the IESS would bring about the deterioration of the health services provided to the affiliates. Interestingly, this position was not represented by constituents opposed to the government but, on the contrary, it was advocated by constituents allied to the government, such as constituent Martha Roldós of RED (ACE 02/07/2008: 139–141).

The differences among the constituents allied to the government with regard to this subject came out in full view during the plenary debate. In fact, several constituents celebrated the universalization of social security prescribed by the proposal and openly advocated the expansion of the health services of the IESS to the entire population within the context of the Sistema Nacional de Salud. In line with this constituent Lenín Hurtado of MPD additionally requisitioned that the SSC was held over within the institutional structure of the IESS instead of being repositioned into the Sistema de Seguridad Social as prescribed in the proposal.

Based on the debate in the plenary discussion the working group 7 carried out modifications in its proposal before finally handing it over to the plenary assembly for vote. These modifications can be broken down into three groups.

The first group of modifications brought about numerous changes in the wording, some of which presupposed meaningful semantic changes such as the substitution of "Sistema Nacional de Salud" with "red pública integral de salud" (ACE 02/07/2008: 51–54).

The second group of modifications was associated with an issue which had not been deliberated in the plenary assembly at all, such as the voluntary affiliation of Ecuadorians living abroad to the seguro universal obligatorio of the IESS.

The third and most important group of modifications brought about changes in the aforementioned bone of contention. Thus, the proposal submitted to the plenary assembly carried over the prohibition against the participation of the private sector in the social security system, but it countenanced the changes requested during the plenary discussion concerning the special social security regimes. In this regard, the modified proposal brought out three substantial changes.

On the first place, it carried over the SSC within the IESS instead of repositioning it within the more general Sistema de Seguridad Social, as constituent Lenín Moreno of MPD had openly requisitioned during the plenary discussion. This request originally had initially been brought forward by the organizations of members of the SSC and the indigenous and peasant organizations participating as visitors in the reunions of the working group 7, as mentioned above.

On the second place, it countenanced the changes requested by several constituents who had requisitioned the inclusion of the temporary disposition concerning the maintenance of the special social security regimes of the military and police forces into the articles of the proposal. Unlike the aforementioned request concerning the SSC, which was directly brought forward by representative organizations of the SSC members, the request regarding the special regimes of the military and police forces was never openly requisitioned by any representative organization of the ISSFA and ISSPOL members, and even less by any member of the military and police forces. However, the incorporation of the transitory disposition into the articles of the proposal represented a fundamental issue for all of them, as the interviews conducted with high authorities of the ISSFA and ISSPOL corroborated (Interviews with Alejandro Vela Loza and Juan Javier Silva). Precisely, for this reason constituent Gilmar Gutiérrez of SP, a retired officer known for his close relation to the military and police forces, brought forward this request as "a necessity, a request, a clamor of the military forces and the national police" and openly repudiated the alleged government's attempt to take down the ISSFA and ISSPOL. In the end, the modified proposal repositioned the temporary disposition regarding the ISSFA and ISSPOL within the constitutional articles on social security as requested. However, the text was also demarcated by an introductory sentence which established that the military and police forces "could" be associated to a special regime of social security, but it did not predicate that they necessarily had to be associated to it. This way, the possibility of a unified and universal social security system was not completely taken down.

On the third place, the modified proposal established that the Sistema de Seguridad Social would hand out social security services through the universal social insurance and the special social security regimes.

Finally, the modified proposal was countenanced by the absolute majority of the constituents on 17 July 2008. Despite the modifications introduced into the proposal, the articles concerning the IESS, ISSFA, and ISSPOL were still repudiated by some constituents who, after their approval by the plenary assembly, officially requisitioned their reconsideration without success. The fact that these (unsuccessful) reconsideration requests were brought forward by one constituent opposed to the government (María Cristina Kronfle of PSC) and two constituents allied to the government (León Roldós and Luis Hernández of RED) (ACE 17/07/2008: 18, 19) bore out the aforementioned disagreements regarding the social security system reform within the political alliance supporting Correa's government once again. On the night of 24 July the plenary assembly lastly countenanced the definitive text for the new constitution (ACE 24/07/2008), which was handed over to the Tribunal Supremo Electoral on the next day. As agreed, the Tribunal Supremo Electoral called out a final plebiscite so that the Ecuadorian people conclusively determined the approval or rejection of the constitution formulated by the constituent assembly. In this conclusive plebiscite held on 28 September 2008, in which 75.72% of the electorate participated, the constitution was countenanced by 63.93% of the voters.

The sanction of the new constitution represented a major milestone in the history of the Ecuadorian social security system. All in all, the new constitution comprised eight thoroughgoing articles exclusively dedicated to the subject of social security along with numerous articles directly or indirectly related to it. The new constitution not only promulgated unprecedented rights and duties concerning social security, but also preestablished the outlines of the social security system.

Besides, the discussions on social security held within the constituent assembly brought out the key points of contention regarding the social security system reform intended by Correa' government, the contending actors involved in the struggles over the reform and the positions assumed by these actors. As pointed out above, these struggles revolved around (1) the participation of the profit-making private sector in the social security system and especially in the pension system, and (2) the future of the existing special social security regimes in the context of the intended universalization of social security. The sanction of the new constitution definitively determined the end of the struggles over the participation of the private sector in the social security system, for it unequivocally stamped out the privatization of social security (Constitución de la República del Ecuador 2008). However, it did not determine the struggles over the future of the existing special regimes, which would soon bring about a new confrontation between the government and the supporters of the social security regimes administered by the ISSFA and ISSPOL.

Over and above the subject of social security, the new constitution brought about fundamental changes for the social, economic, and political life of Ecuador. In line with this, the new constitution prescribed the holding of elections for all elective offices (including president and vice president of the country, prefects and vice prefects of the provinces, mayors and vice mayors of the councils, and the members of the new national assembly), in order to relegitimize their powers.

Without doubt, the constitutional articles concerning the oil and mining sectors represented one of the most significant elements contained in the new constitution, for they brought about the beginning of a profound process of restructuring in these two fundamental sectors of the Ecuadorian economy. This process of restructuring was subsequently rounded out with the sanction of the Ley de Minería (English Law of Mining) (R.O. 517, 29/01/2009) for the mining sector and the Ley Reformatoria a la Ley de Hidrocarburos y a la Ley de Régimen Tributario Interno (English: Reform Law of the Law of Hydrocarbons and the Law of Internal Tax Regime) (R.O. 244, 27/07/2010) for the oil sector. Basically, the reform of the oil and mining sectors carried out by the government brought about two main consequences. First, it repositioned the state at the center of these sectors, subordinating the private oil and mining companies to the state companies and the state control. Second, it based on the foregoing it generated the conditions for the state to capitalize the extraordinary increase of the commodity prices (in particular of oil and minerals) worldwide.

While seemingly unrelated, the social security system reform and the reform of the oil and mining sector devised in the new constitution were inextricably associated. For the reform of the oil and mining sectors initiated with the sanction of the new constitution represented an essential financial condition for the universalization of social security prescribed in the constitution. Without it, any discussion on the universalization of social security would have come about as a mere theoretical matter.

Unlike the comparable cases of Bolivia and Venezuela, the reform of the oil and mining sectors accomplished by Correa's government in Ecuador did not precipitate insurrectionary attempts. Interestingly, the insurrectionary attempt occurred in Ecuador in September 2010 was rather associated with the resisted reform of the military and policy forces pushed by the government. The following section brings out to what extent the struggles over the future of the special social security regimes of the military and police forces represented a fundamental part of this failed insurrection.

4.1.5   The Struggles over the Formulation and Passing
of the LRLSS 2009 and the LRLSS 2010

A few months after the sanction of the new constitution the struggles over the social security system reform came out again when the government handed over a bill for the partial reform of LSSE to the Congresillo (English: small congress). The Congresillo had been established as the temporary legislative power until the inception of the national assembly prescribed by the new constitution.

In truth, the government hankered after the sanction of a completely new LSSE based on the guidelines established by the new constitution. However, during the course of the constituent assembly the government had made out that its intended social security system reform was repudiated by very powerful social actors, whom it could not easily overpower under the current relation of forces. Besides, the government had not yet delineated a bill for the intended reform beyond the position papers formulated by the SENPLADES during the constituent assembly. For these reasons, the government determined to bring out a bill for the partial reform of the LSSE as soon as possible while it carried out the formulation of a completely new LSSE.

The government's rush for the passing of this bill before the inception of the national assembly was associated with the fact that its members had taken over the absolute majority of the seats in the Congresillo, whereas no one could anticipate that AP would carry over its absolute majority after the legislative elections for the national assembly. The bill brought forward by the government concatenated three main points. First, it determined the pegging of the minimum pensions to the (continuously increasing) minimum salary. Second, it established the automatic annual indexation of the pensions based on the annual inflation rate. Third, it determined that the pensioners who recommenced working would not receive the state contribution to their pensions (40% to the IESS and 60% to the ISSFA and ISSPOL pensioners) until being completely retired again.

Even though the first two main points brought about clear benefits for all pensioners, the third main point was perceived as an infringement to the constitutional right of the elders to old-age pensions. For this reason, the Confederación de Jubilados del Ecuador (English: Confederation of Pensioners of Ecuador) (hereinafter CJE), which represented the pensioners belonging to the IESS, the Club de Clases y Policías (English: Club of Classes and Police Officers), which conglomerated the pensioners of the ISSPOL, and the Asociación de Militares en Servicio Pasivo (English: Association of Militaries in Passive Service), and ISSFA, which represented the pensioners of the ISSFA, jointly annunciated mobilizations in Quito and Guayaquil against the passing of the government's bill (El Universo 18/02/2009; La Hora 08/03/2009). Basically, the pensioners' organizations advocated a 40 USD increase in all pensions and the full payment of the pensions (including the state contribution) for the pensioners, who had taken over paid jobs after their retirement.

The demand concerning the 40 USD increase soon came out as meaningless, because the pegging of the minimum pensions to the minimum salary proposed by the bill would bring about a 30 USD increase due to the recent raise of the minimum salary. Besides, the automatic annual indexation included in the bill would additionally generate an increase of 10 USD based on the annual estimated. Nevertheless, the demand regarding the full payment of pensions to the working pensioners was not reciprocated. The leaders of the mobilized pensioner's organizations predicated that pensioners with low pensions took over paid jobs against their will because of their meager economic situation. In response to this, the government asseverated that the bill actually undertook to strike down the abuses of pensioners who capitalized on both high salaries and high pensions (El Universo 17/02/2009).

Finally, the bill was accommodated and the suppression of the state contribution to the pensions of the working pensioners (40% in the case of IESS pensioners and 60% in the case of ISSFA and ISSPOL pensioners) was circumscribed to the portion of the pensions of the salaried working pensioners exceeding the basic market basket. After this revision, the bill received the approval of the Congresillo on 9 March 2009 and it was promulgated on 30 March 2009 under the name of Ley Reformatoria a la Ley de Seguridad Social, a la Ley de Seguridad Social de las Fuerzas Armadas y a la Ley de Seguridad Social de la Policía Nacional (English: Reform Law of the Law of Social Security, the Law of Social Security of the Armed Forces and the Law of Social Security of the National Policy) (hereinafter LRLSS 2009) (R.O. 559, 30/03/2009).

The struggles over the sanction of the LRLSS 2009 brought out the aforementioned conflicts over the social security system reform again. Just as in the constituent assembly, the struggles over the LRLSS 2009 revolved around the future of the special social security regimes in the context of the universalization of social security purposed by the government. However, in the case of the LRLSS 2009, the struggles brought out two differences compared to the contentions within the constituent assembly.

First, the dispute over the future existence of the ISSFA and ISSPOL disappeared as such from the table after the passage regarding them was transposed from the temporary dispositions to the constitutional text finally approved by the constituent assembly. Against this background, the government partially renounced to its original plan of unifying the social security system in order to accomplish universal access and concentrated on the incorporation of the non-insured into the existing social security regimes. Because of this, the reorientation of the state contribution to the insured became the main objective of the government in its attempt to provide social security to the non-insured. In the case of the LRLSS 2009, the suppression of the state contribution to the existing social security regimes was circumscribed to the working pensioners, however, the government was actually determined to reorientate the entire state contribution (Interview with Luis Alfredo Muñoz Neira). This intention was even pointed out in the introduction to the LRLSS 2009 (LRLSS 2009: 9).

Second, the struggles over the LRLSS 2009 were not exclusively associated with the special social security regimes of the military and armed forces as in the constituent assembly but, for the first time, they also comprised the general regime of social security administered by the IESS. For this reason, the opposition to the bill pushed by the government was not constrained to lobby actions and concealed pressure exercised by the military and police forces as during the constituent assembly, but it also encompassed mobilizations on the streets led by the associations of pensioners of the IESS.

In retrospect, the sanction of the LRLSS 2009 brought about clear benefits to the pensioners by indexing all pensions to the annual inflation and pegging minimum pensions to the minimum salary. Besides, the LRLSS 2009 was promulgated in a general context of substantial real increases in both salaries and pensions in Ecuador. Nevertheless, the suppression of the state contribution to the pension of the working pensioners generated resentment against the government among the members of the IESS, and even more among the members of the ISSFA and ISSPOL. This was probably associated with the fact that the suppression of the state contribution to the pensions of the working pensioners particularly came down on pensioners of the ISSFA and ISSPOL, who undertook jobs in the security branch after retiring. The resentment of the military and police forces against the government sparked by the sanction of the LRLSS 2009 would be soon capitalized on by insurrectionary sectors during the failed assassination attempt of September 2010.

A few weeks after approving the LRLSS 2009, the Congresillo undertook the consideration of another bill submitted by the government concerning the creation of the Banco del Instituto Ecuatoriano de Seguridad Social (English: Bank of the Ecuadorian Institute of Social Security) (hereinafter BIESS) (El Universo 02/03/2009). The creation of a public bank for the administration of the funds of the IESS was prescribed by the new constitution and purposed to maximize the return on the pension funds of the IESS, which until then simply remained immobilized in the central bank. Again, the CJE repudiated the government's bill and annunciated mobilizations against it. Basically, the conflict revolved around the nature of the future bank (La Hora 03/08/2009). Whereas the bill established a "second-tier" bank working as both, investment and development bank, the opponents to the bill advocated a "first-tier" bank exclusively working as investment bank (El Comercio 08/03/2010). Unlike in the case of the LRLSS 2009, the government successfully brought around its opponents (El Universo 30/03/2009). Finally, the Ley del Banco del Instituto Ecuatoriano de Seguridad Social (English: Law of the Bank of the Ecuadorian Intitute of Social Security) was countenanced by the Congresillo on 6 April 2009 and it was promulgated on 11 May 2009 (R.O.S. 587, 11/05/2009).

On 26 April 2009, the presidential election prescribed by the new constitution was carried out. Correa accomplished a notable victory in the first round obtaining 51.99% of the votes. The second most voted candidate, former president Lucio Gutiérrez was outdistanced by over 24%, receiving only 28.24% of the votes. However, the government party could not take over the absolute majority of the national assembly, where it received 59 out of 124 seats.

Over and above his personal charisma, Correa's major electoral victory was predicated on the economic prosperity experienced by Ecuador since his coming to power in January 2007. In part, this prosperity was associated to the unprecedented increase of Ecuador's oil income resulting from the steep rise of the international oil prices, as Acosta pointed out (Acosta 2012: 330). However, this simplified evaluation brushes aside four key points concerning the economic upturn under Correa's government.

Table 4.1 Fiscal revenue

	Oil revenue (USD millions)	Non-oil revenue (USD millions)
2002–2006	10,618.4	30,965.3
2007–2011	37,984.5	64,851.9
Variation	27,366.1	33,886.6

Source BCE (2015)

First, the increase of international oil prices and the resulting increase of Ecuador's oil revenue did not break out in 2007, when Correa took over the presidency, but in 2004 during Gutiérrez' administration.[1] However, the period between 2004 and 2007 was characterized by mediocre economic and social results in terms of employment, wages, poverty, and inequality (CEPALSTAT 2015; INECE 2015) and by extreme political instability. On the contrary, Ecuador accomplished substantial economic and social achievements in terms of employment, wages, poverty, and inequality during Correa's first mandate in a general context of political stability (CEPALSTAT 2015; INECE 2015).

Second, Ecuador came across the highest oil revenue in history under Correa's government, as Mejía Rivadeneira and Acosta sharply pointed out (Mejía Rivadeneira 2012a, b; Acosta 2012). Nonetheless, both Mejía Rivadeneira and Acosta also acknowledged that the non-oil revenue branched out even more during the same period (Mejía Rivadeneira 2012a, b, c; Acosta 2012), what naturally relativized the hypothesis according to which the social and economic upturn since Correa's coming to power was exclusively predicated on the international oil prices boom (Table 4.1).

Third, the positive effects of the increase of the international oil prices on Ecuador's economy during Correa's government would not have come about if the government had not restructuralized the oil sector. As explained above, the reform of the oil sector initiated in the constituent assembly and continued afterward capacitated the state to canalize the extraordinary oil revenue to strategic sectors of the economy. Without this restructuring the substantial economic and social improvements would have never materialized.

Fourth, based on this "recovery" of the state's power, Correa's government maximized public expenditure while holding down fiscal discipline. This extraordinary increase of public expenditure not only accelerated the economy through massive investments in infrastructure and increased aggregate demand, but also brought about unprecedented investments in education, health, and social policy (Acosta 2012: 331) (Table 4.2). According to Mejía Rivadeneira, these policies generated substantial improvements in terms of poverty and inequality, what naturally substantiated Correa's electoral success (Mejía Rivadeneira 2012a: 176–178) (Table 4.3).

In this general context of economic prosperity, several pensioners' organizations advocated another increase of the pensions during the first months of 2010.

---

[1] Sect. 4.2.1.1 brings forward figures on international oil prices.

Table 4.2 Central government expenditure

	Transportation and communication (USD millions)	Urban development and housing (USD millions)	Education and culture (USD millions)	Health and communal development (USD millions)	Social welfare and labor (USD millions)	Total (USD millions)
2006	360.5	83.2	1088.5	504.5	274.9	7010.8
2007	426.2	172.1	1383.6	606.4	434.9	8627.3
2008	568.8	457.6	1836.5	873.2	695.7	14,388.9
2009	1119.9	183.7	2038.1	879.5	840.8	14,217.9
2010	1103.8	213.7	2162.8	1130.6	1087.6	15,641.4
2011	1110.4	208.1	2696.6	1288.7	1243.7	18,434.6
2012	1362.5	448.6	2986.3	1658.5	1266.2	21,239.7
2013	1809.8	800.6	3688.8	1951.2	1494.5	25,861.3
2014						26,793.8

Source BCE (2015)

Table 4.3 Poverty and inequality

	National poverty by income (%)	National extreme poverty by income (%)	Gini coefficient	Theil coefficient
2006	37.60	16.89	0.540	
2007	36.74	16.45	0.551	0.630
2008	35.09	15.69	0.515	0.562
2009	36.03	15.37	0.504	0.491
2010	32.76	13.09	0.505	0.512
2011	28.64	11.61	0.473	0.461
2012	27.31	11.18	0.477	0.455
2013	25.55	8.61	0.485	0.460
2014	22.49	7.65	0.467	0.428

Source INECE (2015)

Only this time, the demanded increase was initially established at 50 USD (El Universo 20/01/2010). The demand of the pensioner's organizations was taken over by the opposition assembly members of the Comisión de los Derechos de los Trabajadores y Seguridad Social (Commission of Labor Rights and Social Security) (hereinafter CDTSS) of the national assembly, who brought forward three bills for the partial reform of the LSSE proposing an increase of 57 USD (Ecuadorinmediato 16/07/2010). Besides, these bills established the automatic annual actualization of all pensions based not only on the inflation but also on the return of the investments obtained by the IESS. In response Ramiro González, the president of the IESS, brought out another bill for the partial reform of the LSSE which established an increase of no less than 30 USD.

The bills were handed over to the plenary assembly, which deliberated on them for the first time on 5 August 2010. During this first debate, three different positions came out (El Universo 06/08/2010). First, the position of the president of the IESS, who participated in the debate, subscribed to an increase of no less than 30 dollars. Second, the position of the opposition assembly members of the CDTSS, who advocated a 57 USD increase and the automatic actualization beyond the annual inflation. Third, the position of the AP assembly members, who postulated an intermediate increase of 40 USD and the discussion of the method for the automatic actualization of pensions. Since no agreement could be accomplished under these circumstances, a second debate was annunciated for September after the forthcoming legislative recess (El Universo 16/08/2010).

Meanwhile, the government advanced the formulation of an organic law of social security in order to substitute the existing LSSE, as Jeannette Sánchez, the Coordinadora de Desarrollo Social (English: Coordinator of Social Development), publicly asseverated in an interview with a national newspaper (El Universo 04/08/2010). According to Sánchez the draft bill, which the government would bring out during 2011, established the redirection of the state's contribution of 40% to the IESS pensioners and 60% of the ISSFA and ISSPOL pensioners to the non-contributory pillar of a unified social security system of social composed by the ministry of health, the IESS, and the local governments. The reason of this reform was predicated on the regressive character of the Ecuadorian social security system, which canalized the state contribution to the pensioner belonging to the highest quintiles of income (El Universo 04/08/2010).

After the legislative recess, the national assembly recommenced its activities in September. The second debate on the bills for the partial reform of the LSSE could not be carried out during this month, because the assembly was exclusively consecrated to the legislative treatment of the partial veto of the president to the Ley Orgánica del Servicio Público (English: Organic Law of Public Service) (hereinafter LOSP). The partial veto of the president dictated the rejection of 80 articles of the bill approved by the assembly, including the exceptions provided for the military and police forces. Due to internal differences, the assembly could not contravene the veto concerning these exceptions, for which the LOSP was finally promulgated on 29 September 2010 (R.O 294, 06/10/2010). In the end, the LOSP prescribed the suppression of the economic bonuses for decorations and promotions for all public servants, including the military and police forces. This was repudiated by military members and police officers alike, for it diminished their income. In response, the government asseverated that the LOSP overcompensated this income loss with the full payment of extra hours.

On the morning of the next day, about 1000 police officers took over Quito's police main station and annunciated an immediate nationwide police strike. Soon after, the police guard of the national assembly accompanied the revolt blocking the entrance to the assembly. Even though the police forces did not take over other public buildings, they massively walked out in support of the protest, what quickly brought about riots in Quito and other places. Unlike the police forces, the military forces did not massively participate in the revolt, except for a reduced number of military members temporarily blockading Quito's airport and the ministry of defense. These blockades were deactivated by the personal intervention of the minister of defense in a few hours (Ospina 2011a: 20).

President Correa miscalculated the situation and purposed to resolve it with his personal charisma. In front of the about 1000 insubordinate police officers seizing the police main station, Correa delivered a fiery speech demanding the end of the insurrection, what exacerbated the insubordinates even more. The situation dramatically escalated and Correa, who was physically diminished due to a recent operation on his knee, had to abandon the place hobbling under the attack of the insubordinate police officers, who fell upon him and his escort with strikes and tear gas. The president and his escort safeguarded themselves in the police hospital located right next to the seized police station, and the insubordinate police officers blockaded the building, virtually hijacking him. After this, the insubordinate police officers publicly annunciated a list of nine demands. Not surprisingly, one of these demands advocated the continuity of the regime of social security administered by the ISSPOL in its current form. Finally, after more than 10 h in captivity, president Correa was released by a combined squad of military and police elite members in a cinematographic escape under a hail of bullets. Altogether, the revolt brought about the death of five people, including one of the police elite members who participated in Correa's rescue.

The police revolt came about on 30 September 2010 (hereinafter 30S) became a wake-up call for the government regarding the formidable power of the social actors opposed to its thoroughgoing reform plans, including the intended universalistic social security system reform (Ospina 2011a: 26). A few days after the 30S, the government promulgated a wage increase for both police and military forces but it repudiated that it was associated with the police revolt occurred a couple of days before (El Universo 05/10/2010).

The assembly recommenced the treatment of the second partial reform of the LSSE during October 2010. This time, both the president of the IESS and the AP assembly members came out with a more conciliatory position. Rapidly, all the parties at stake (the president of the IESS, the assembly members of the government, and the assembly members of the opposition) countenanced a compromise bill which brought forward retroactive annual increases ranging between 40 USD and 60 USD depending on the value of the pensions (El Universo 22/10/2010a). Besides, the compromise bill established a more generous method for the automatic annual actualization of the pensions than the inflation rate and maximized the coverage of the health insurance of the children of the insured until they became 18 years old.

Before the second debate in the assembly, President Correa publicly annunciated that he would not bring about his veto to the compromise bill once passed (El Universo 22/10/2010b). At last, the second debate was carried out on 21 October 2010 and the bill received the approval of most assembly members. Less than a month later, the bill was officially promulgated under the name of Ley Reformatoria a la Ley de Seguridad Social (English: Reform Law of the Law of Social Security) (hereinafter LRLSS 2010) (R.O. 323, 18/11/2010).

4.1.6 The Struggles over the Formulation of the LOSSSE and the Sanction of the LRLSS 2014 and the LOJL

After the 30S, the government determined to advance the formulation of the draft bill for the social security system reform with extreme discretion. For this reason, the government did not bring forward any bill for the modification of the existing LSSE during 2011. Instead, the government undertook the realization of a referendum for the modification of a couple of constitutional articles and the formulation of a couple of laws (Larrea 2011: 39). One of these laws, however, was to establish harder sanctions for the employers who did not register their employees in the social security system (Larrea 2011: 42). Government consultants in charge of the formulation of the draft bill carried out nonpublic meetings with the directors of the IESS, ISSFA, and ISSPOL during 2012, as the interviews conducted with several members of the aforementioned institutions corroborated (Interviews with Alejandro Vela Loza and Juan Javier Silva). The government did not come out with a statement about these approachments.

Nevertheless, in February 2013, a draft bill entitled Ley Orgánica del Sistema de Seguridad Social (English: Organic Law of the Social Security System) (LOSSS) supposedly formulated by the government leaked out (El Telégrafo 08/02/2013). The leak came out just a few weeks before the presidential election, in which an overwhelming victory of Correa was anticipated. In this context, the revelation clearly purposed to browbeat the government before its reelection. The leaked draft bill was circulated by email among military and police members. With inflammatory rhetoric, the emails denounced that the social government was going to bring down the ISSFA and ISSPOL.

Faced with the possibility of a new revolt, the government immediately reciprocated with a joint statement by the minister of defense, María Fernanda Espinosa, the minister of the internal, José Serrano, the minister of social development, Richard Espinosa, and the military and police high commands, broadcasted on national television (Diario Opinión 09/02/2013). In this statement, the government repudiated the whispering campaign and ruled out any relation with the leaked draft bill (Youtube 08/02/2013).

In the presidential election held on 17 February 2013, Correa accumulated 57.17% of the votes, assuring himself the presidential reelection in the first round. Besides, the government finally took over the control of the national assembly by winning the absolute majority of its seats.

In the past, the government would have certainly capitalized on this majority in order to undertake its intended social security system reform as soon as possible. However, after the 30S, the government had acknowledged the formidable power of the social actors opposed to any modification of the existing social security system. For this reason, the government determined to advance the reform with extreme precaution.

Two months after the election, Correa brought out the leaked draft bill during his Saturday television program (YouTube 06/04/2013). Holding the draft bill in his hands, Correa acknowledged that it had been delineated by experts on request of the government as a starting point for discussion. However, Correa also pointed out that the draft bill had not been handed over to him before it was surreptitiously brought out 2 months ago. After this, he repudiated that the leaked draft bill would bring about the elimination or the unification of the ISSFA and ISSPOL, as maliciously claimed, and publicly brought forward the specific articles of the draft bill which established the further existence of both the ISSFA and ISSPOL. Finally, Correa asseverated that the draft bill in question was still being ameliorated by the government.

The analysis of a copy of the leaked draft bill obtained for this research corroborated that, as a matter of fact, it did not determine the elimination of the ISSFA and ISSPOL. On the contrary, it established a public universal social security system called Sistema de Seguridad Social (English: System of Social Security) (hereinafter SSS) which, predicated on the principles of the National System of Social Inclusion and Equity prescribed by the constitution, brought about a basic floor of social security for all people (Draft Bill LOSSS Ecuador: 15).

The SSS was comprised by two subsystems: (1) the Subsistema Contributivo (English: Contributory Subsystem), and (2) the Subsistema No Contributivo (English: Non Contributory Subsystem) (Draft Bill LOSSS Ecuador: 15).

The Contributory Subsystem was circumscribed to the population with income over the poverty line and was carried out by the IESS, ISSFA, and ISSPOL. This subsystem comprised six different regimes: (1) the Régimen de Trabajadores Subordinados (English: Regime of Employees, (2) the Régimen de Trabajadores No Subordinados y del Seguro Social Campesino (English: Regime of Self-Employed Workers and Workers of the Peasant Social Insurance), (3) Régimen de Trabajadores No Remunerados del Hogar (English: Regime of the Unpaid Homemakers), (4) Régimen de Ecuatorianos Domiciliados en el Exterior (English: Regime of the Ecuatorians Domiciled Abroad), (5) the Régimen de Seguridad Social de las Fuerzas Armadas (English: Regime of Social Security of the Military Forces), and (6) the Régimen de Seguridad Social de la Policía Nacional (English: Regime of Social Security of the National Police) (Draft Bill LOSSS Ecuador: 15–16).

The Non Contributory Subsystem was circumscribed to the population with income below the poverty line and was carried out by the Instituto Nacional de Protección Social (English: National Institute of Social Protection). This subsystem comprised the Régimen de Población que Accede a los Programas de Protección Social (English: Regime of Population Who Benefit from the Programs of Social Protection), aimed at the population who received social assistance from the state (Draft Bill LOSSS Ecuador: 16).

Both the Contributory Subsystem and the Non Contributory Subsystem were to carry out the Seguro Universal Obligatorio (English: Universal Social Insurance) (hereinafter SUO) prescribed by the constitution to everyone, regardless of his or her employment status. The SUO brought about social security services in case of sickness, maternity, paternity, labor risks, unemployment, old age, disability, and death (Draft Bill LOSSS Ecuador:7, 14–15).

Interestingly, the draft bill did not regulate the provision of health care included in the SUO, but it only established that the health services were to be handed out by the

Red Pública Integral de Salud (English: Integral Public Health Network) prescribed by the constitution, including first, second, and third level of medical assistance (Draft Bill LOSSS Ecuador: 17).

Instead, the draft bill revolved around the economic benefits included in the SUO, which divaricated depending on the aforementioned regimes. For the population covered by the Regime of Population Who Benefit from the Programs of Social Protection the economic benefits were circumscribed to old-age, disability and death (funeral) benefits. The same benefits corresponded to the population covered by the Regime of the Self-Employed Workers and Workers of the Peasant Social Insurance, the Regime of the Unpaid Homemakers and the Regime of the Ecuadorians Domiciled Abroad, all belonging to the Contributory Subsystem. For the population covered by the Regime of Employees of the Contributory Subsystem, the economic benefits were associated with old-age, disability, death (funeral, widows' and orphans'), maternal, paternal, occupational risks, and unemployment benefits. The same economic benefits corresponded to the population covered by the Regime of Social Security of the Military Forces and the Regime of Social Security of the National Police, both belonging to the Contributory Subsystem, with the addition of supplementary death (allowance) benefits.

According to the leaked draft bill, the amount of the economic benefits was to be established in the regulation of the law. Expectedly, this document did not accompany the leaked draft bill. Nevertheless, the draft bill delineated the amount of the obligatory contributions to the social security system, which noticeably divaricated from the current structure of contributions (Table 4.4).

In a nutshell, the draft bill brought about an increase of the total contributions for the Regime of Employees (RE) of the IESS, but this increase was actually disbursed by the employers, as the employees' contributions diminished. In contrast, the total contributions for the Regime of Social Security of the Military Forces (RSSMF) of the ISSFA and the Regime of Social Security of the National Police (RSSNP) of the ISSPOL decreased despite the increase of the obligatory contributions imposed to the military and police members, as the contribution made by their employer (the state) clearly diminished. This abrupt decrease (from 22.52 to 3.5%) was probably counterbalanced with the introduction of a maximum pension limit of 80% of the taxable wage, which brought down the current maximum pension limit of 100% in 20%.

Even more important than this, the draft bill completely struck down the state contribution of 40% to the pensions paid by the IESS to the employees and the state contribution of 60% to the pensions paid by the ISSFA and ISSPOL to the military and police members. Instead, these state resources were canalized to the pensions of the population covered by the Regime of Population Who Benefit from the Programs of Social Protection (RPWBPSP), the Regime of Self-Employed Workers and Workers of the Peasant Social Insurance (RSEWWPSI), the Regime of the Unpaid Homemakers (RUH), and the Regime of the Ecuadorians Domiciled Abroad (REDA). In turn, the draft law took out the current compulsory contribution of 0.35% of the members of the general regime of social security of the IEES to the SSC.

Table 4.4 Contributions to the RE, RSSMF, and RSSNPF

	RE (IESS)				RSSMF (ISSFA)				RSSNPF (ISSPOL)			
	LSSE		LOSSS		LSSE		LOSSS		LSSE		LOSSS	
	EPE (%)	EPR (%)	EPE (%)	EPR (%)	EPE (%)	EPR (%)	EPE (%)	EPR (%)	EPE (%)	EPR (%)	EPR (%)	EPE (%)
1. Old age, disability, and death	8.64	1.10	6.64	6.51	12.40	13.15	12.77	3.10	12.77	10.50	12.77	3.10
2. Supplementary death	0.00	0.00	0.00	0.00	0.20	0.20	TBD	TBD	0.13	0.25	TBD	TBD
3. Sickness, maternity, and paternity	0.00	5.71	TBD	TBD	3.35	5.85	TBD	TBD	2.50	3.00	TBD	TBD
4. Occupational risks	0.00	0.55	0.00	1.55	0.15	0.15	0.75	0.00	0.26	0.75	0.75	0.00
5. Unemployment	2.00	1.00	2.00	1.00	6.25	6.25	8.50	0.00	7.00	8.50	8.50	0.00
6. Professional indemnity	0.00	0.00	0.00	0.00	0.00	0.00	0.00	0.00	0.04	0.10	0.00	0.00
7. Contingency funds	0.00	0.00	0.00	0.00	0.00	0.00	0.00	0.00	0.00	0.50	0.50	0.00
8. Housing funds	0.00	0.00	TBD	TBD	0.65	0.40	TBD	TBD	0.40	2.00	TBD	TBD

(continued)

Table 4.4 (continued)

	RE (IESS)				RSSMF (ISSFA)				RSSNPF (ISSPOL)			
	LSSE		LOSSS		LSSE		LOSSS		LSSE		LOSSS	
	EPE (%)	EPR (%)	EPE (%)	EPR (%)	EPE (%)	EPR (%)	EPE (%)	EPR (%)	EPE (%)	EPR (%)	EPR (%)	EPE (%)
9. Peasant social insurance	0.35	0.35	0.00	0.00	0.00	0.00	0.00	0.00	0.00	0.00	0.00	0.00
10. Administration costs	0.36	0.44	0.00	0.00	0.00	0.00	0.00	0.00	0.00	0.00	0.00	0.00
Subtotal (excluding 2, 3, 8)	11.35	3.44	8.64	9.06	18.80	19.55	22.52	3.10	20.07	20.35	22.52	3.10
Total contribution (excluding 2,3,8)	14.79		17.70		38.35		25.62		40.42		25.62	
State contribution to 1	40.00		0.00		60.00		0.00		60.00		0.00	

RE Regime of Employees, *RSSMF* Regime of Social Security of the Military Forces, *RSSNPF* Regime of Social Security of the National Police, *LSSE* Ley de Seguridad Social (2001), *LOSSS* Ley Orgánica del Sistema de Seguridad Social, *EPE* Employee, *EPR* Employer

Source Prepared by the author

Table 4.5 Contributions to the NCS, RSEWWPSI, RUH, and REDA

	RPWBPSP (INPS)		RSEWWPSI (IESS)		RUH (IESS)		REDA (IESS)	
	IND (%)	STATE (%)	IND (%)	STATE (%)	IND (%)	STATE (%)	IND (%)	STATE (%)
Old age, disability, and death	2.86[a]	10.29	6.64	6.51	6.64	6.51	13.19[b]	0.00
Subtotal	2.86	10.29	6.64	6.51	6.64	6.51	13.19	0.00
Total contribution	13.15		13.15		13.15		13.19	

[a] 2.86% of the Human Development Voucher
[b] 13.19% of two minimum salaries
Source Prepared by the author

Basically, the draft bill brought forward a universal social security system in which the existing contributory pillar was financially dissociated from the state so that the state resources could be canalized to the coverage of the population excluded from the current system. Besides, the incorporation of the non-insured population was conceptualized with a non-assistentialist approach, as everyone (self-employed workers, peasants, homemakers, and even beneficiaries of social assistance) was to carry out a payment to the system according to his or her income (Table 4.5). This way, self-employed workers, peasants, and unpaid homemakers were to reciprocate the state contribution to their regime of social security with their own contribution of 6.64% of their income (or eventually their partners' income). The draft law established that even the beneficiaries of the social assistance programs without any income had to carry out a payment of 2.86% of their social assistance benefits.

RPWBPSP: Regime of Population Who Benefit from the Programs of Social Protection. RSEWWPSI: Regime of Self-Employed Workers and Workers of the Peasant Social Insurance. RUH: Regime of Unpaid Homemakers. REDA: Regime of the Ecuadorians Domiciled Abroad.

As it could be anticipated, the leaders of the pensioners' organizations of the IESS, ISSFA, and ISSPOL openly repudiated the elimination of the state contribution to their pensions. This could be corroborated in the interviews conducted with the leaders of the CJE for this research (Interviews with Osvaldo Santana and Wilson Oswaldo Rivadeneira Ruiz). Interviews conducted with the authorities of the ISSFA and ISSPOL brought out that the ISSFA and ISSPOL clearly contravened the elimination of the state contribution as well (Interviews with Alejandro Vela Loza and Juan Javier Silva). Finally, the elimination of the state contribution postulated in the leaked draft law also came across the opposition of the Sindicato Nacional Único de Obreros del Instituto Ecuatoriano de Seguridad Social (English: Single National Union of Workers of the Ecuadorian Institute of Social Security) (hereinafter SIN-

DUOIESS), which conglomerated the workers of the IESS (Interview with Rosa Argudo Coronel). Probably because of this, the government did not bring its draft bill forward during the rest of 2013. Instead, it canalized its efforts toward the sanction of the Ley Orgánica de Comunicación (English: Organic Law of Communication) (hereinafter LOC), which purposed to take down the oligopolistic structure of the mass media, which openly repudiated Correa's government. Among other things, the LOC restructuralized the distribution of radio and television frequencies, assigning for the private sector, the public sector, and the cooperative sector one-third of the frequency spectrum, respectively.

The sanction of the LOSSS was anticipated for the second half of 2014, as Betty Carrillo, president of the CDTSS of the national assembly publicly annunciated during the first legislative week of 2014 (El Universo 13/01/2014). As a matter of fact, no relevant bill was to be deliberated before the provincial elections coming in February 2014. In these elections, the government party accomplished modest results at the provincial level, winning 10 out of 23 prefectures (only 1 prefecture more than in the previous elections). However, the government party clearly lost out at the cantonal level, winning 68 out of 221 mayoralties (4 mayoralties less than in the previous elections). Most importantly, the political opposition preserved the government of Guayaquil, Ecuador's largest city, and took over the government of Quito, Ecuador's capital. Above all, the cantonal elections were characterized by the electoral success of Avanza (English: Advance), a new political party allied to the government which took over 34 mayoralties in its first provincial elections (Ibarra et al. 2014).

After this, the government determined to hold off the sanction of the LOSSS for the rest of 2014. Instead, the government persevered in its strategy of partially restructuring the social security system without the sanction of the LOSSS. Based on this strategy, the government had successfully circumscribed the state contribution to the pensions of the pensioners who recommenced working, revise the method for the annual actualization of the pensions, establish the BIESS, and maximize the coverage of the health insurance of the children of the insured. Only this time, the partial reforms would bring about structural changes, following the main guidelines proposed in the leaked draft bill of the government.

In this context, the government brought forward a bill to the national assembly proposing the modification of the article 220 of the LSSE. The bill prescribed that the complementary closed pension funds which had received economic contributions from the state were to be directly supervised by the BIESS. The holders of the funds, however, were carried over without changes.

Among the 68 existing pension funds of this kind, the Fondo de Cesantía del Magisterio (English: Retirement Fund of the Magisterium) (hereinafter FCME) administered by the Unión Nacional de Educadores (English: National Union of Educators) (hereinafter UNE) represented the largest one, amounting to 90% of all complementary closed pension funds. (El Universo 15/05/2015). Against this background, the government purposed three main goals with this bill. First, it endeavored to coalesce the pension system aiming at its unification. Second, it purposed to financially advance the BIESS through the injection of the complementary closed pension funds. Third, it endeavored to diminish the power of the UNE, the largest teachers' union which repudiated Correa's government and politically accompanied the MPD (Ecuadorinmediato 09/05/2015).

Despite the fierce opposition of the UNE, which barricaded the offices of the FCME around the country (La República 14/05/2015), the bill received the sanction of the national assembly in September 2014 and it was finally promulgated on 20 November 2014 under the name of Ley Reformatoria a la Ley De Seguridad Social y a la Ley del Banco del Instituto Ecuatoriano de Seguridad Social para la Administración de los Fondos Complementarios Previsionales Cerrados (English: Reform Law of the Law of Social Security and the Law of the Bank of the Ecuadorian Institute of Social Security for the Administration of the Complementary Closed Pension Funds) (hereinafter LRLSS 2014) (R.O. 379, 20/11/2014). Six months later, the BIESS effectively took over the administration of the FCME.

During the first months of 2015, the government finally determined to carry out the intended reorientation of the state contribution to the pension system. At the inauguration of the Ambato–Guaranda highway Correa publicly annunciated that the state would no longer disburse 40% of the old-age pensions paid by the IESS as dictated by the LSSE, since the IESS carried over a budgetary surplus and could take over its old-age pensions on its own account (El Universo 26/03/2015). Correa also asseverated that the state obligation of financing 40% of the pensions of the IESS imposed by the LSSE represented an absurdity, for the state was to canalize funds to the IESS with which the IESS subsequently carried out the purchase of state bonds, bringing about an unnecessary debt of the state with the IESS (El Universo 26/03/2015).

After this, the government brought forward a bill which took out the state's obligation to subsidize 40% of the pensions administered by the IESS and simultaneously established a pension regime for the unpaid homemakers called "Régimen de Pensiones del Trabajo No Remunerado del Hogar" (English: Pension Regime of the Unpaid Homemaking), which resembled the one proposed in the draft bill revealed 2 years ago (El Telégrafo 10/04/2015). This pension regime comprised old-age, disability, widows', and orphans' pensions, as well as funeral benefits. Besides, the bill predicated an obligatory economic contribution for the homemakers, depending on their household income. In turn, the state was to carry out the payments required for financing the pensions of the homemakers. Finally, the bill established that the state was to subsidize the pensions administered by the IESS if the IESS eventually came out as incapable of paying out them on its own account.

The bill was strategically brought forward by the government, as it correlated the elimination of the state contribution to the pensions of the general regime administered by the IESS, which was naturally repudiated by the members of the IESS, with the incorporation of the homemakers to the social security system, which was advocated by the homemakers. According to the government, the sanction of the bill would bring about the incorporation of one and a half million homemakers to the social security system (El Universo 14/04/2015). Besides, the bill did not strike down the state contribution of 60% of the pensions administered by the ISSFA and

ISSPOL, brushing aside the possibility of a conflict with the military and police forces.

During the first weeks of April, pensioners' organizations carried out demonstrations against elimination of the state contribution to the IESS in Quito and Guayaquil (Ecuavisa 13/04/2015). However, they could not counterbalance the position of the government. In the end, the bill received the sanction of the national assembly on 14 April 2015 under the name of Ley Orgánica para la Justicia Laboral y Reconocimiento del Trabajo en el Hogar (English: Organic Law for the Labor Justice and Recognition of the Homemaking) (hereinafter LOJL) despite the abstention of the five assembly members of Avanza, who usually subscribed to the government's initiatives (El Universo 14/05/2015). The LOJL was promulgated on 20 April 2015 (R.O. 483, 20/04/2015).

Even though the sanction of the LOJL did not bring about the thoroughgoing reform of the Ecuadorian social security system delineated in the leaked draft bill, it certainly represented a major advance (and probably not the last one) toward the universalization of social security intended by the government.

4.2 Operationalization of the Power Struggles over the Post-neoliberal Social Security System Reform

As explained above, the operationalization of the power struggles over the post-neoliberal social security system reform in Ecuador is carried out on the basis of the concept of power resources devised by political class struggle approaches to social policy. However, this concept is not simply reduplicated in its original form, but it is completely transubstantiated in order to overcome its shortcomings when dealing with social policy in the Global South.

The operationalization of the power struggles in Ecuador correlates the four analytical dimensions ("where", "what", "who", and "how") included in the previous contextualization of the Ecuadorian case. As pointed out, these four dimensions encompass (1) the structural underpinnings underlying social policy, (2) the concrete points of conflict over social policy, (3) the real actors involved in the struggles over social policy, and (4) the channels through which the struggles are canalized.

As noticed before, the incorporation of these multiple analytical dimensions to the study of power struggles brings about as a natural consequence the increase of both the actors involved in the struggles and the power resources used by the actors. Unlike the associational power resources used by political class struggle approaches, which can be usually correlated with all (or almost all) the actors in conflict, many of the power resources examined below do not correspond with all the involved actors, and sometimes they even correlate with only one of them. For this reason, the operationalization of the different types of powers resources presented in the following sections initially breaks down the particular characteristics of the specific

type of power resources under examination in order to bring out how they advantage
the actors controlling them and disadvantage the actors deprived of them.

4.2.1 Operationalization of the "Where" Question

The reconstruction of the power struggles over the post-neoliberal social security
system reform in Ecuador brought out the centrality of two structural factors which
predetermined the clashes on the intended reform: (1) the oil resources and (2) the
labor informality. According to the definition given above, both oil resources and
labor informality represent power resources, for they advantage their possessors over
their nonpossessors by providing them with the capability to determine outcomes
according to their preference, even over the preferences of others.

4.2.1.1 Oil Resources as Power Resources

As power resources, oil resources resemble "conventional" power resources (economic, associational, etc.), for their possession brings about a relational power which
advantages their possessor(s) over their nonpossessor(s). Following this logic, the
bigger the possession of oil resources, the bigger the relational power of its possessor
and vice versa. Considered as power resources, oil resources are usually associated
with the government. However, private oil companies may capitalize on oil resources
as well if they take over their control.

The availability of oil resources as power resources commingles two interrelated
dimensions: (1) the ownership of oil resources per se, and (2) the control of oil
resources. The ownership of oil resources presupposes the ownership of the oil revenue derived from them. In turn, the control of oil resources brings about the free
availability of the oil resources and, consequently, the free availability of the oil
revenue for its owner. For the government, the control of oil resources is usually
associated with the possible limitations to its discretionary use. These limitations
comprise coercive restrictions, such as the stoppages to the oil exploitation imposed
by labor unions and employers' organizations, as well as legal restrictions, such as
the mandatory accountability of the oil resources and the prescribed distribution of
the oil revenue among the national, provincial, and municipal governments.

Oil resources represent a crucial factor for the Ecuadorian economy, state, and
government, as Table 4.6 brings out (Table 4.6). As a matter of fact, the sudden
emergence of the subject of the universalization of social security in the Ecuadorian
political agenda was undoubtedly associated with the extraordinary availability of
oil revenue derived from the oil boom.

Before the reform of the oil sector undertaken by Correa's government in 2007,
private oil companies had taken over de facto the control of oil resources, even
though the state held over de jure the ownership of oil resources. The control over
the oil resources exercised by international oil companies until 2007 maximized

Table 4.6 Exports of goods and services

	Total exports (millions of USD FOB)	Oil exports (millions of USD FOB)	Oil exports share of total exports (%)	Non-oil exports (millions of USD FOB)
2000	4907	2418	49.28	2489
2001	5479	1900	34.68	3579
2002	5036	2055	40.80	2981
2003	6223	2607	41.89	3616
2004	7753	4234	54.61	3519
2005	10,100	5870	58.12	4230
2006	12,728	7545	59.27	5184
2007	14,321	8329	58.16	5993
2008	18,818	11,721	62.28	7098
2009	13,863	6965	50.24	6898
2010	17,490	9673	55.31	7817
2011	22,345	12,913	57.79	9432
2012	23,765	13,792	58.04	9973
2013	24,848	14,108	56.78	10,740
2014	25,732	13,303	51.70	12,430

Source BCE (2015)

their profits, however, it did not bring about the strengthening of the Ecuadorian employers' organizations for two reasons. First, the employers' organizations in Ecuador were characterized by a quite undeveloped organizational structure and second, the international oil companies never really undertook to accentuate their relations with the Ecuadorian employers' organizations, as they rather represented their corporative interests on their own. For this reason, from the power resources perspective the oil resources are mainly associated with the government in Ecuador.

The following sections break down the ownership and control of oil resources.

Ownership of Oil Resources

In order to contextualize the development of Ecuador's oil revenue since 2000, Table 4.7 delineates an outline of the evolution of the Ecuadorian oil production and the international oil prices since then (Table 4.7).

Table 4.7 brings out two things (Table 4.7). First, the crude oil production remained practically unchanged during the first 7 years of Correa's government (2007–2013), barely expanding 2.99% during this period. This exiguous increase presupposed a massive slowdown compared to the 33.73% increase registered during the 7 years before Correa's coming to power (2000–2006). The increase of 6.93% in the production of oil derivatives between 2007 and 2013 corresponded to the increase of 6.72%

Table 4.7 Oil production and oil prices

	Crude oil (thousands of barrels)	Oil derivatives (thousands of barrels)	Oil price WTI (USD per barrel)	Oil price brent (USD per barrel)
1997	141,708	46,120	20.61	19.11
1998	137,079	50,220	14.42	12.76
1999	136,291	47,285	19.34	17.9
2000	146,209	58,940	30.38	28.66
2001	148,746	56,809	25.98	24.46
2002	143,759	55,467	26.18	24.99
2003	153,518	52,696	31.08	28.85
2004	192,315	59,678	41.51	38.26
2005	194,172	61,620	56.64	54.57
2006	195,523	62,902	66.05	65.16
2007	186,547	65,139	72.34	72.44
2008	184,727	67,553	99.67	96.94
2009	177,414	68,545	61.95	61.74
2010	177,422	61,886	79.48	79.61
2011	182,357	69,808	94.88	111.26
2012	184,323	71,566	94.05	111.63
2013	192,119	69,654	97.98	108.56
2014	203,142	65,986	93.26	99.02
Variation 2000–2006	33.73	6.72	117.41	127.36
Variation 2007–2013	2.99	6.93	35.44	49.86

Source BCE (2015) and US EIA

between 2000 and 2006. Second, the extraordinary increase of the oil prices did not commence under Correa's government but it preceded it. As a matter of fact, the increase of 127.37% in the WTI oil price registered between 2000 and 2006 clearly outnumbers the increase of 35.44% registered during 2007 and 2013.

Despite this, Correa's government successfully appropriated a significantly higher oil revenue than the previous governments, both in absolute and relative terms. Table 4.8 conclusively substantiates this assertion (Table 4.8).

Based on the above, the unprecedented increase in the fiscal oil revenue since Correa's coming to power could only be predicated on the reform of the oil sector effectuated by Correa's government. The reform of the oil sector thoroughly restructuralized the oil contracts between the state and the private oil companies, substituting the existing participation model based on profit-sharing agreements for the service delivery model based on flat-free service contracts (Guaranda 2010; Acosta 2011). Since then, the private oil companies received a fixed sum per produced barrel,

Table 4.8 Fiscal oil revenue

	Total (millions of USD)	Variation (%)
2000	1460	
2001	1352	−7.42
2002	1393	3.03
2003	1664	19.45
2004	2115	27.15
2005	2212	4.55
2006	3235	46.27
2007	3318	2.57
2008	8675	161.46
2009	5212	−39.93
2010	7845	50.53
2011	12,935	64.88
2012	12,220	−5.53
2013	11,433	−6.43
2014	10,906	−4.61
Acummulated 2000–2006	13,430	121.57
Acummulated 2007–2013	61,638	244.58

Source BCE (2015)

what precluded them from appropriating the extraordinary rent caused by the steep increase of the oil prices. On the contrary, the Ecuadorian state suddenly became the main beneficiary of the extraordinary oil rent. As recounted before, the reform of the oil sector was initially brought forward in the new constitution sanctioned in 2008 and later fully carried out by the Reform Law of the Law of Hydrocarbons and the Law of Internal Tax Regime sanctioned in 2010 (Table 4.9).

As shown above, the increase in the fiscal oil revenue was accompanied by an even higher increase in the fiscal non-oil revenue. Based on this combined expansion of the fiscal revenue the government could finally pay off the accumulated state debt with the IESS and regularly disburse the state contribution to the pension system (40% of the pensions administered by the IESS and 60% of the pensions administered by the ISSPOL and the ISSFA) established by law. However, the government could not disburse the obligatory state contribution to the pension system and simultaneously undertake the financial cost of the intended social security system reform. For this reason, the struggles over the reform revolved around the reorientation of the state resources from the existing pension system to the universal social security system purposed by the government.

In a nutshell, the steer increase of the international oil prices and the reform of the oil sector conjointly brought about a remarkable increase of the oil resources owned by the central government. On the contrary, the oil resources owned by the private oil companies clearly diminished, but this situation did not necessarily bring about the

Table 4.9 Oil legislation

	Standing legislation	Contractual model
1971–2007	– Ley de Hidrocarburos (R.O. 322, 01/10/1971) – Decreto Supremo 2967 (R.O. 711, 06/11/1978) – Ley de Reforma a la Ley de Hidrocarburos (R.O. 326, 28/11/1993) – Constitución Política de la República del Ecuador (R.O. 1, 11/08/1998) – Ley para la Transformación Económica del Ecuador (R.O. 34, 13/032000) – Ley para la Promoción de la Inversión y la Participación Ciudadana (R.O. 144, 18/08/2000) – Decreto Ejecutivo 1215 (R.O. 265, 13/02/2001) – Acuerdo Ministerial 389, (R.O. 671, 26/09/2002) – Ley Reformatoria a la Ley de Hidrocarburos (R.O. 257, 25/04/2006) – Decreto Ejecutivo 1672 (11/07/2006) – Ley Orgánica Reformatoria de la Ley Orgánica de la Contraloría General del Estado, la Ley de Hidrocarburos y la Ley de la Honorable Junta de Defensa Nacional, (R.O. 267, 10/05/2006)	Participation model (profit-sharing agreements)
2007–2015	– Ley Reformatoria a la Ley de Hidrocarburos y al Código Penal (R.O. 170, 14/09/2007) – Decreto 662 (R.O 312, 18/10/2007) – Constitución de la República del Ecuador (R.O. 449, 20/10/2008) – Ley Reformatoria a la Ley de Hidrocarburos y a la Ley de Régimen Tributario Interno (R.O. 244, 27/07/2010 – Decreto Ejecutivo 546 (R.O. 330, 29/11/2010) – Ley de Fomento Ambiental y Optimización de los Ingresos del Estado, (R.O. 583, 24/11/2011) – Resolución 1 (R.O. 662, 15/03/2012)	Service delivery (flat-free service)

Source Prepared by the author

Table 4.10 Public and prívate oil production share

	Crude oil (thousands of barrels)	Public companies (thousands of barrels)	Private companies (thousands of barrels)	Public share (%)	Private share (%)
2000	146,209	85,047	61,162	58.17	41.83
2001	148,746	82,929	65,817	55.75	44.25
2002	143,759	80,775	62,984	56.19	43.81
2003	153,518	74,514	79,004	48.54	51.46
2004	192,315	71,948	120,368	37.41	62.59
2005	194,172	70,972	123,200	36.55	63.45
2006	195,523	90,438	105,085	46.25	53.75
2007	186,547	94,334	92,213	50.57	49.43
2008	184,727	97,571	87,157	52.82	47.18
2009	177,414	102,768	74,647	57.93	42.07
2010	177,422	109,944	67,478	61.97	38.03
2011	182,357	130,528	51,829	71.58	28.42
2012	184,323	133,656	50,667	72.51	27.49
2013	192,119	144,921	47,198	75.43	24.57
2014	203,142	157,976	45,166	77.77	22.23

Source BCE (2015)

weakening of the Ecuadorian employers' organizations since they were not really coalesced.

Control of Oil Resources

With regard to the control over the oil resources, the reform of the oil sector initiated in 2007 did not restructuralize the relation between the national, provincial, and municipal governments respecting the oil exploitation and taxing, which was exclusively associated with the national government. However, two changes regarding the practical control of oil resources must be pointed out. First, the reform established that the state was to carry out the exploitation of the oil resources through public oil companies or, eventually, though mixed oil companies with the state as the majority holder. For this reason, the share of the public oil companies (mainly Petroecuador and Petroamazonas) in the oil sector was maximized, as Table 4.10 corroborates (Table 4.10). Between 2000 and 2014, the public share of the oil production branched out from 58.17 to 77.77%, which naturally brought about an increased control over the oil resources by the national government.

Nevertheless, the reform additionally determined that the private oil companies could carry out the exploitation of the oil resources in exceptional cases. This exception, however, became accustomed as several private oil companies received oil wells in concession for their exploitation (Guaranda 2010; Acosta 2011).

In short, since the reform of the oil sector the central government substantially advanced in the control of oil resources as a result of the expansion of the share of the public oil companies in the oil sector. Undoubtedly, this presupposed the extension of the power resources of the government. However, the public oil companies did not undertake the complete control of the oil sector as prescribed by the new constitution, for the exceptional concessions to the private oil contemplated in the constitutional text became accustomed.

4.2.1.2   Labor Informality as Power Resource

As power resource, labor informality is characterized by extraordinary features compared to the "conventional" power resources. First, it is not correlated with its possession, for labor informality does not represent something "possessable". On the contrary, labor informality predetermines the possibilities of social, economic, and political actors to accumulate other power resources (associational, institutional, mobilizational, etc.). For this reason, labor informality is usually conceptualized as a contextual factor which determines the development of the power resources of the contending actors instead of a power resource itself (Filgueira 1998, 2007; Huber and Stephens 2005; Pribble 2006; Segura-Ubiergo 2007). However, this approach presupposes that labor informality represents a structurally given condition to which labor-related actors are inevitably subordinated. This assumption may correspond with the situation of the labor unions, around which political class struggles approaches revolve. However, as soon as the analytical scope is maximized in order to comprise the remaining actors involved in the conflict (most specially the government and the employers' organizations), labor informality materializes as the result of the very conscious actions of the social, economic, and political actors who manipulate labor informality as a recourse in order to accomplish their goals. In this sense, though not "possessable" as conventional power resources, labor informality clearly represents a type of power resource available to some of the contending actors. Second, labor informality brings about dissimilar effects depending on the social, economic and political actors in question. No doubt, high labor informality decreases the potential power of labor unions and working-class political parties in terms of their associational, institutional, and mobilizational power resources and vice versa (Boffi 2015). However, high labor informality maximizes the potential power resources of non-labor-related social organizations and non-labor-related political parties and vice versa. Employers' organizations definitively capitalize on the relative weakening of labor unions and working-class political parties, but high labor informality does not necessarily advance their own power resources. The effect of labor informality on the power resources of the government divaricates depending on several factors. In principle, informal workers do not come under taxation (Chen 2005: 6), which generates a decrease of the tax revenue collected by the government. Additionally, informal workers do not carry out payments for social security and are associated with the

Table 4.11 Labor force

	Total population	Working-age population	Economically active population	Labor participation (%)	Female labor participation (%)
2000	12,566,623			65.2	48.4
2001	12,812,800			72.6	59.8
2002	13,060,229			...	...
2003	13,308,060			–	–
2004	13,555,444			69.4	56.0
2005	13,801,532			69.0	54.8
2006	14,045,504			70.0	55.8
2007	13,682,302	9,309,490	6,336,029	68.1	53.7
2008	13,878,704	9,648,996	6,385,421	66.2	51.8
2009	14,081,060	10,032,716	6,548,937	65.3	51.3
2010	14,279,685	10,291,500	6,436,257	62.5	48.0
2011	14,478,129	10,533,003	6,581,621	62.5	47.8
2012	14,682,556	10,864,147	6,701,014	61.7	47.4
2013	15,872,755	11,200,371	6,952,986	62.1	47.7
2014	16,148,648	11,159,255	7,194,521	64.5	50.2
2015	16,279,252	11,201,636	7,374,083	65.8	52.4

Source INECE (2015) and CEPALSTAT (2015)

social services of the non-contributory pillar of the social security system. In this regard, labor informality rather diminishes the potential economic power resources of the government. Nevertheless, precisely for these reasons informal labor brings about the context for the clientelistic use of social policy by the government, in which case the beneficiaries of the social services provided by the government must reciprocate them with their political support. Under these circumstances, the increase of labor informality can eventually generate the potential increase of the government's associational, electoral, and mobilizational power. However, this situation cannot be presupposed in advance, since it is determined by the way in which the government and the popular sectors typically associated to the informal labor correlate with one another.

As pointed out above, the economy of Ecuador is characterized by a high level of labor informality (ILO 2011), defined as unregistered and unprotected labor, including both self-employed and waged employed workers (Chen 2005). In fact, the subject of the universalization of social security in Ecuador is inextricably associated with the high level of labor informality, which precludes the majority of the population from social security.

In order to contextualize the labor situation in Ecuador since 2000, Tables 4.11 and 4.12 delineate a compendium of fundamental labor indicators (Tables 4.11 and 4.12).

Table 4.12 Labor situation

	General Unemployment rate (%)	Female unemployment rate (%)	General underemployment rate (%)s	Female underemployment rate (%)	Minimum salary (USD)	Minimum salary variation (%)
2000	8.98				57	
2001	10.93				86	50.88
2002	9.24				105	22.09
2003	11.55				122	16.19
2004	9.67				136	11.48
2005	8.49				150	10.29
2006	8.07				160	6.67
2007	5.00	6.71	18.24	18.63	170	6.25
2008	5.95	8.31	15.00	15.82	200	17.65
2009	6.47	8.39	16.36	16.45	218	9.00
2010	5.02	6.44	13.82	13.37	240	10.09
2011	4.21	5.57	10.73	10.65	264	10.00
2012	4.12	4.81	9.01	9.54	292	10.61
2013	4.15	5.37	11.64	11.65	318	8.90
2014	3.80	4.87	12.87	12.98	340	6.92
2015	3.84	5.67	13.37	12.60	354	4.12

Source INECE (2015) and CEPALSTAT (2015)

Tables 4.11 and 4.12 substantiate that the labor situation in Ecuador clearly ame-liorated since Correa's coming to power in 2007 (Tables 4.11 and 4.12). The unem-ployment came down from 8.07 in 2006 to 3.80% in 2014, a situation of virtual full employment. The underemployment, a chronic deficiency of the Ecuadorian labor market, diminished as well, nonetheless remaining relatively high (12.87% in 2014). While presenting a slightly worse situation, female unemployment and female underemployment also came down since 2007, respectively, amounting to 4.87 and 12.98% in 2014. In line with this, the minimum salary accumulated a 57.1% real increase between 2007 and 2015 (INECE 2015).

The labor participation rate was held over since 2000, revolving around 65% (65.2% in 2000 and 64.5% in 2014). The female labor participation rate delineated a similar fluctuation but on a much lower level. Both the general and female labor participation rates fall behind the labor participation rates of the Northern industri-alized countries, but they actually correspond with the average participation rates of Latin America (CEPAL 2014a).

In this context, informal labor accompanied the positive development of the labor situation, diminishing between three and six percentage points since 2007, depending on the source of the statistics (Table 4.13). According to CEPAL, the informal labor rate (including domestic labor) came down from 56.9% in 2006 to 53.5% in 2013, and the female informal labor rate diminished from 62.7% in 2006 to 58.8% in 2013

Table 4.13 Informal labor

	Informal labor rate 1 (%)	Female informal labor rate 1 (%)	Formal labor rate 2 (%)	Informal labor rate 2 (%)	Domestic labor rate 2 (%)	Non-classified labor rate 2 (%)
2000	55.7	60.3				
2001	56.0	61.9				
2002	55.6	62.8				
2003	–	–				
2004	57.5	63.7				
2005	57.3	63.3				
2006	56.9	62.7				
2007	56.7	63.8	41.0	45.1	3.3	10.6
2008	56.9	63.2	43.9	43.5	3.5	9.2
2009	56.4	62.5	43.7	43.8	3.4	9.1
2010	54.9	59.2	47.2	42.8	2.9	7.1
2011	55.0	60.2	46.5	42.7	2.3	8.4
2012	54.0	58.0	48.7	40.8	2.4	8.0
2013	53.5	58.8	49.4	40.1	3.1	7.5
2014	56.4	62.6	50.9	39.7	3.2	6.2
2015			51.3	39.3	2.7	6.8

Source INECE (2015) and CEPALSTAT (2015)

(CEPAL 2014b). According to INECE, informal labor (excluding domestic labor) came down from 45.1% in 2007 to 39.3% in 2015, while domestic labor diminished from 3.3 to 2.7% during these years (INECE 2015).

While certainly important, the reduction of informal labor registered since 2007 does not fully correspond with the steep decrease of unemployment and underemployment registered since then. This corroborates the structural character of informal labor in Ecuadorian (ILO 2011) and reciprocates the difficulties experienced by all Latin American countries in reducing labor informality below a predetermined threshold (CEPAL 2010, 2011, 2012, 2013, 2014a).

For this reason, the moderate reduction of labor informality did not bring about a relevant increase of the associational, institutional, and mobilizational power resources of the labor unions and the working-class political parties. Likewise, it did not presuppose a substantial increase of the tax revenue collected by the government. However, the moderate decrease of the labor informality registered since 2007 effectively diminished the potential use of social policy by the government, as the universe of its potential beneficiaries came down.

4.2.2   Operationalization of the "What" Question

The reconstruction of the power struggles over the post-neoliberal social security system reform in Ecuador brought out that the conflicts revolved around (1) the continuity of the special social security regimes of the police and military forces, and (2) the orientation of the sate contribution to the pension system.

In the case of Ecuador, the struggles over the privatization of the pension system anteceded the post-neoliberal social security system reform undertaken by Correa's government since 2007. As recounted above, the struggles over the privatization of the pension system commenced in the early 1990s and settled down in the mid- 2000s, when the ruling of the Tribunal Constitucional declaring the unconstitutionality of the private pension funds prescribed by the LSSE was finally carried out.

The power struggles over the special social security regimes and the sate contribution to the pension system cannot be directly extrapolated into specific forms of power resources. However, due to their specific characteristics these struggles were associated with particular forms of power resources (structural, associational, mobilizational, etc.). The following sections break down both struggles, particularizing what types of power resources were mobilized in them.

4.2.2.1   The Struggles over the Continuity of the Special Social Security Regimes of the Military and Police Forces

The struggles over the continuity of the special social security regimes of the military and police forces started out in the constituent assembly. As explained above, the proposal for the constitutional articles on social security formulated by the working group 7 established a unified social security system and only acknowledged the autonomy of the special social security regimes of the military and police forces in a transitory disposition. This was fiercely repudiated by the military and police forces, which purposed to preserve their special (and much better) social security regimes. In this context, the military and police forces initially mobilized their lobbying capacity in order to advance their position within the working group 7. Unlike other social actors such as the CONAIE, the Unión de Organizaciones Campesinas del Ecuador (English: Union of Peasant Organizations of Ecuador), the Federación Única Nacional de Afiliados al Seguro Social Campesino (National Federation of Members of the Peasant Social Insurance), and the Movimiento Mujeres del Ecuador (English: Movement Women of Ecuador), which publicly participated in the discussions of the working group 7 regarding the constitutional articles on social security, the lobbying of the military and police forces was carried out in secrecy (Interview with Alejandro Vela Loza) and, therefore, not documented. Nevertheless, the lobbying within the working group fell through and the military and police forces had to mobilize their associational power resources in order to accomplish their objective.

The military and police forces are not politically represented by military or police political parties as labor political parties represent the working class. However, the

Ecuadorian military and police forces are politically associated with the Sociedad Patriótica (English: Patriotic Society), the right-wing political party founded by the retired military officer Lucio Gutiérrez. Lucio Gutiérrez became publicly known as the leader of the military and indigenous movement which removed constitutional President Jamil Mahuad from power in January 2000. After receiving the amnesty of the national congress for this, Gutiérrez established Sociedad Patriótica in 2002 in order to participate in the presidential elections held that year. From the beginning, the national board of Sociedad Patriótica comprised retired military officers who had participated in the coup of January 2000, such as Gilmar Gutiérrez (Lucio Guitiérrez' brother), Renán Borbúa, Patricio Ortiz, Patricio Acosta, Eddy Sánchez, Francisco Fierro, and others (El Universo 31/12/2002). Since then, Sociedad Patriótica purposed to maximize its social and political basis, forging alliances with other political parties such as the indigenous party Pachakutik. However, the strong political connection between Socidead Patriótica and the military and police forces never really dematerialized (Pérez Enríquez 2004; Nesbet Montecinos 2010).

For this reason, when constituent Gilmar Gutiérrez denounced that the proposal of the working group 7 ultimately purposed to take down the ISSPOL and the ISSFA during the plenary discussion of the constituent assembly, he clearly pointed out that he was representing the military and police forces' clamor.

The struggles over the continuity of the special social security regimes of the police and military forces carried through with the contention over the LRLSS 2009. As explained before, the LRLSS 2009 proposed by the government established that the pensioners who recommenced working would not receive the state contribution to their pensions (40% to the IESS and 60% to the ISSPOL and the ISSFA pensioners) until being completely retired again. This particularly disadvantaged the retired police and military members, who carried out labor activities as security guards. As in the case of the struggles over the constitutional articles on social security, the contention over the LRLSS 2009 brought about the mobilization of the corporative associational and political associational power resources of the police and military forces. In parallel, the conflict became increasingly communicational, as the demands of the police and military forces received a notable impact in the printed, broadcasted, and online press (La Hora 08/03/2009, El Universo 18/02/2009), most especially in the media opposed to the government.

The police and military forces mobilized their mobilizational power resources during the revolt initiated on 30 September 2010, when about 1000 police officers took over the police main station and undertook a national police strike against the changes in their economic bonuses imposed by the government. The revolt, which eventually brought about a failed assassination attempt, was not exclusively predicated on the conflict over the special regimes of the police and military forces. Nevertheless, it was undoubtedly associated with it, as the demands of the insurgent police officers corroborated. During the 30S, the police and military forces mobilized their mobilizational (and even insurrectionary) power resources to the utmost in detriment of their associational power resources.

The increasing importance of the communicational power resources became absolutely clear during the electoral campaign for the presidential election held on February 2013, when the draft bill of the LOSSS prepared by experts on request of the government was leaked out. As recounted before, the leak maliciously disseminated the rumor that the special social security regimes of the military and police forces would be taken down if president Correa accomplished the reelection. The entire affair concerning the leak of the draft bill not only brought out the central role of the mass media in the conflict over the continuity of the special regimes, but it also brought out how the contending actors mobilized their communicational power resources in order to carry through their goals.

In a nutshell, the struggles over the continuity of the special social security regimes of the military and police forces comprised two phases: (1) the struggles over the constitutional articles on social security and (2) the struggles over formulation and passing of the LRLSS 2009 and the LRLSS 2010. In the first phase, the police and military forces mobilized their corporative associational, political associational, and, to some extent, communicational power resources. Since they could not accomplish their goals, in the second phase they mobilized their corporative associational, political associational, mobilizational (including insurrectionary actions), and fully fledged communicational power resources.

4.2.2.2   The Struggles over the Orientation of the State Contribution to the Pension System

The struggles over the orientation of the state contribution to the pension system were associated with the struggles over the continuity of the special social security regimes of the police and military forces. For this reason, the power resources mobilized by the contending actors in the context of the former resembled the power resources mobilized in the context of the latter.

Nevertheless, the struggles over the orientation of the state contribution to the pension system presupposed the availability of the state economic resources required for the contended contribution. As explained above, these economic resources derived to a great extent (yet not exclusively) from the extraordinary oil revenue captured by the state since the reform of the oil sector carried out by the government. In this regard, the struggles over the orientation of the state contribution to the pension system represented an indirect struggle over the control of oil resources between the government and the beneficiaries of the preexisting social security regimes. In this struggle, the government wanted to canalize its economic resources to the incorporation of the non-insured into the social security system, whereas the beneficiaries of the preexisting social security regimes wanted those economic resources for themselves. All in all, the struggles over the orientation of the state contribution to the pension system revolved around the mobilization of the state oil resources.

In this context, the contention over the LRLSS 2009 represented the "first round" of the struggles over the state contribution to the pension system between the government and the beneficiaries of the social security regimes administered by the IESS, the ISSPOL and the ISSFA. As pointed out above, in this case the contending actors mobilized their electoral power resources and, to a lesser extent, their mobilization power resources.

The dispute over the creation of the BIESS brought about the "second round" of the conflict, displaying very similar characteristics with regard to the power resources mobilized by the actors. However, the contention over the creation of the BIESS divaricated from the contention over the LRLSS 2009, inasmuch as the beneficiaries of the special regimes of the military and police forces did not participate in the conflict because they did not come under the government's measure. This naturally diminished the potential power resources which the opponents of the creation of the BIESS could mobilize against the government, especially in terms of mobilizational power resources.

The "third round" of the struggles over the state contribution of the pension system commenced with the contention over the LRLSS 2014. With regard to the mobilized power resources, the contention over the LRLSS 2014 resembled the contention over the creation of the BIESS. However, this time the potential power resources which could be mobilized against the government decreased even more, as the contention was circumscribed to the members of the UNE. For this reason, the mobilization of both the electoral and mobilizational power resources of the UNE could not preclude that the BIESS took over the administration of the complementary pension funds of the teachers.

The dispute over the LOJL represented the "final round" of the struggles over the state contribution of the pension system, as the government finally struck down the state obligation to subsidize 40% of the pensions administered by the IESS and simultaneously established a pension regime for the unpaid homemakers which resembled the one proposed in its leaked draft bill. Since the LOJL did not remove the state contribution of 60% to the social security regimes of the military and policy forces, the potential mobilizational power resources which could be mobilized against the government diminished significantly. Besides, the simultaneous introduction of the pension regime for the unpaid homemakers maximized the potential mobilizational power resources which could be mobilized in favor of the government. As in the previous struggles, the opponents of the LOJL mobilized both their electoral and mobilizational power resources. The contention over the LOJL, however, brought out an additional dimension, for it was also accompanied by a fierce communicational struggle in which the contending actors actively mobilized their communicational power resources.

4.2.3   Operationalization of the "Who" Question

The reconstruction of the power struggles over the social security system reform brought out: (1) the existence of a manifold entanglement of social actors involved in the struggles over the social security system reform, much more complex than the social actors presupposed by political class struggle approaches, and (2) the extraordinary importance of the government as social, economic, and political actor due to its prerogative over the oil sector.

Just as in the case of the "what" question, these two issues cannot be directly extrapolated into specific forms of power resources. However, the operationalization of the power resources mobilized by the contending actors cannot be carried out without clearly determining the contours of the actors at issue, for which the analysis of these issues must be necessarily undertaken.

As pointed out above, the actors involved in the power struggles over the reform divaricate from the actors presupposed by political class struggle approaches. In addition to the conventional class actors contemplated by political class struggle approaches (labor unions, employers' organizations, and class political parties), the reconstruction of the power struggles brought out the existence of manifold entanglement of actors involved in the struggles over the reform. This multiple complex of social actors comprised professional associations, expert groups, military and policy forces, feminist organizations, lobby groups, nongovernmental organizations, bureaucratic groups, indigenous and peasant organizations, etc. Besides, the reconstruction brought out the centrality of the government as a contending actor in the struggles over the reform. This openly contravened the assumptions of political class struggle approaches as well.

Based on their scope, the contending actors can be categorized in three different types: macro, meso, and micro actors (Li 2012).

4.2.3.1 Macro Actors

The first type of actors comprises the macro actors. The macro actors commingle a nationwide organizational structure with the disposal of three or more types of power resources (structural, associational, institutional, mobilizational, or communicational). Most of these actors are comprised by political class struggle approaches: political parties, labor unions, and employers' organizations. The national government is comprised in this category as well. The relative power of macro actors can be approximated with relative ease in most cases.

Government

Historically, the government has always represented a constitutive factor of the Ecuadorian society.[2] Notwithstanding, since Correa's coming to power in 2007, the government maximized its participation in the social, economic, and political affairs as never before (Ospina 2013; Unda 2013).

---

[2]Even though the historical reasons of this centrality cannot be recapitulated here due to space constraints, the main finding of the researchers who broke down the relation between state and society in Latin America basically pointed out that in Latin American countries the state brought about the society, whereas in Northern industrialized countries the society brought about the state (Oszlak 1979, 1981, 1982; Oszlak and O'Donnell 1981; Portantiero 1981, 1985, 1988; Aricó 1988).

As recounted, the political alliance which initially advocated Correa's presidential candidacy conglomerated the entire spectrum of leftist political forces, from the revolutionary left represented by the MPD to the moderate left represented by the RED, including also the indigenous movement organized in the CONAIE and politically represented by the MUPP. However, the constituent assembly held between 2007 and 2008 brought out the existence of tensions within the government alliance, drifting apart the government and the AP from the MPD, the CONAIE, and MUPP. Since then, the relation between the government and the MPD, the CONAIE and the MUPP deteriorated rashly, leading to the public breakup of the MPD, the CONAIE, and the MUPP from the government alliance in 2010. After that, the distance between the government and the AP on the one hand, and the MPD, the CONAIE, and the MUPP on the other hand, divaricated irreconciliably.

In spite of this, the government maximized its political basis through the consolidation of the government party. Based on this, the government became reelected in 2009 and 2013 and the government party took over the absolute majority of the national assembly in 2013.

The strengthening of the government since 2007 was not exclusively predicated on the consolidation of its political basis in electoral terms. Along with this, the strengthening of the government was correlated with the increase of the state economic resources and the expansion of the state apparatus (Polga-Hecimovich 2013).

As analyzed above, the increase of the state economic resources was associated with the rise of the fiscal oil revenue and the rise of the fiscal non-oil revenue. The rise of the fiscal oil revenue was predicated on (1) the substantial increase of the international oil prices and (2) the reform of the oil sector carried out by the government, which successfully canalized the extraordinary oil revenue to the public treasury. The rise of the fiscal non-oil revenue was predicated on the tax reform accomplished by the government in a general context of economic upswing.

The expansion of the state apparatus concatenated two consecutive phases. The first phase revolved around the "decorporatization" of the state, which determined the expulsion of corporative groups from the state apparatus, such as the financial sector ingrained within the financial administration, but also brought about the exclusion of indigenous organizations from the local management of public affairs, such as the removal of the CONAIE from the direction of the bilingual education, the health services in rural areas, and the drinking water provision (Ospina 2009). The second phase comprised the enlargement of the state apparatus, including both the administrative and productive state sectors. In this regard, the amount of ministries increased from 17 in 2007 to 28 (22 ministries and 6 coordinating ministries) in 2015 and the participation of the state enterprises in the economy clearly advanced as well, in particular in the hydrocarbon, telecommunications, electricity, and security sectors (SENPLADES 2013).

In the matter of the social security system reform, the government has represented the driving force since its coming to power in 2007. Accordingly, the government has carried out two main actions in this regard. First, it has discursively advocated the reform in order to accomplish the universalization of social security. Second, it has brought forward the reform bills required for the progression of the social security system reform. Since no other actor involved in the struggles over the reform has brought out its own reform proposal (neither as a thorough reform bill nor as a policy document), the government could determine the agenda of the struggles over the reform (yet not its outcome). In this context, the government clearly materialized as the main actor involved in the struggles as all other actors merely reciprocated its actions, either supporting or repudiating them

Compared to other actors involved in the struggles over the social security system reform, the government falls back upon the widest assortment of power resources, comprising structural, associational, institutional, mobilizational, and communicational power resources.

Political Parties

Ecuadorian political parties are clearly structuralized along the conventional left—right axis based on their political ideologies. In this manner, the left and centre-left spectrum of national political parties comprises the Movimiento Popular Democratico[3] (English: Democratic People's Movement) (MPD), the Movimiento de Unidad Plurinacional Pachakutik (English: Pachakutik Plurinational Unity Movement) (MUPP), the Alianza País (English: PAIS Alliance) (AP), the Avanza (English: Advance) (hereinafter AV), and the Red Ética y Democracia (English: Ethics and Democracy Network) (RED). The right and centre-right spectrum of national political parties comprises the Una Nueva Opción (English: A New Option) (hereinafter UNO), Partido Social Crisitiano (English: Social Christian Party) (PSC), the Partido Renovador Institucional Acción Nacional(PRIAN), and the Partido Sociedad Patriótica (English: Patriotic Society Party) (hereinafter PSP). Despite the clear ideological placement of the parties, their social bases do not necessarily correspond to the social bases of the ideologically analogous political parties of the Northern industrialized countries.

Derived from the Partido Comunista Marxista Leninista del Ecuador (English: Marxist Leninist Communist Party of Ecuador), the MPD conglomerates the revolutionary left. The MPD initially participated in the alliance of left-wing political parties which advanced the presidential candidacy of Correa in 2006, but it abandoned it in 2010 and became opposed to the government (Ramírez Gallego 2011). In 2015 the MPD was restructuralized into the Unidad Popular after the CNE stroke down its legal identity.

The MPD is politically associated with the Frente Unitario de Trabajadores (English: United Worker's Front) (FUT), an umbrella labor confederation opposed to the government, and the Unión Nacional de Educadores (English: National Educators Union) (UNE), the largest single labor union.

Regarding the social security system reform, the MPD advocated the universalization of social security during the constituent assembly, but it repudiated the LRLSS 2014, which transposed the administration of the complementary pension funds of

---

[3]Recently converted to the Unidad Popular (English: Popular Unity).

the teachers from the UNE to the BIESS, as well as the LOJL, which removed the state contribution of 40% to the pensions paid by the IESS and established a pension regime for the unpaid homemakers.

The MUPP represents the indigenous left. Just as the MPD, the MUPP initially participated in the alliance of left-wing political parties which advanced the presidential candidacy of Correa in 2006, but it abandoned it in 2010 and became opposed to the government (Ramírez Gallego 2011).

The MUPP is politically associated with the CONAIE, the largest indigenous organization, the UCAE, a peasant organization opposed to the government, and the Federación Única Nacional de Afiliados al Seguro Social Campesino (English: Unified Federation of Members of the Peasant Social Insurance) (FEUNASSC), an organization of members of the SSC opposed to the government as well. In general terms, the MUPP is organically dissociated from the labor unions.

With regard to the social security system reform, the MUPP advocated the universalization of social security during the constituent assembly, but it repudiated the LOJL, which removed the state contribution of 40% to the pensions paid by the IESS and established a pension regime for the unpaid homemakers.

The AP represents the political party of president Correa. As government party, the AP carried out political alliances with several preexisting labor unions affiliated to the Central de Trabajadores del Ecuador (Workers Confederation of Ecuador) (CTE) and the Central Ecuatoriana de Organizaciones Clasistas (English: Ecuadorian Confederation of Class Organizations) (CEDOC CLAT). Likewise, the AP materialized political alliances with the Confederación Nacional de Organizaciones Campesinas, Indígenas y Negras (English: National Confederation of Peasant, Indigenous and Black Organizations) (FENOCIN) and the Federación Nacional de Trabajadores Agroindustrialies, Campesinos e Indígenas Libres del Ecuador (National Federation of Agroindustrial Workers, Free Peasants and Indigenous of Ecuador) (FENACLE), indigenous and peasant organizations not affiliated to the CONAIE. Most importantly, the AP successfully established a strong political relation with the unorganized urban popular classes, even though this relation might be deteriorating lately (Ortiz Crespo 2015; Ospina 2015).

Being the government party, the AP naturally advocates the social security system reform intended by the government.

Founded in 2012 by Ramiro González, former prefect of Pichincha and president of the IESS, the AV predominantly represents the middle classes, being dissociated from the labor unions, the peasant organizations, and the indigenous organizations. Ideologically rooted in social democracy, the AV was associated with the government until April 2015.

Due to its political alliance with the government, the AV initially advocated the social security system reform. However, when the government advanced the LOJL, which removed the state contribution of 40% to the pensions paid by the IESS, the AV took back its support and abandoned the government alliance in April 2015.

The RED politically came down from the social democratic Partido Socialista—Frente Amplio (English: Socialist Party—Broad Front). The RED initially participated in the alliance of left-wing political parties which advanced the presidential candidacy of Correa in 2006, but it abandoned it in 2010 and became opposed to the government (Ramírez Gallego 2011). Since 2013, the RED is coalesced in the Alianza Plurinacional de las Izquierdas (English: Plurinational Alliance of the Left).

The RED predominantly represents the middle classes, being dissociated from the labor unions, the peasant organizations, and the indigenous organizations. Founded in 2006, the UNO represents the liberal right. The UNO is associated with the employers' organizations, especially with the Cámara de Comercio de Guayaquil (English: Commerce Chamber from Guayaquil), the largest and oldest employer's organization in Ecuador. Since 2012, the UNO is coalesced with the liberal Creando Oportunidades (English: Creating Opportunites) (CREO), founded by the banker Guillermo Lasso in 2012.

Regarding the social security system reform purposed by the government, the UNO openly repudiates it, advertising the incorporation of private pension funds into the pension system instead.

The PSC conglomerates the Christian democratic right. It is politically associated with the conservative Movimiento Cívico Madera de Guerrero (English: Civic Movement Warrior's Spirit) (MCMG), founded by the mayor of Guayaquil Jaime Nebot. Unlike the Christian democratic parties of the Northern industrialized countries, the PSC is organically dissociated from the employers' organizations.

PRIAN MISSING

The PSP represents the nationalistic right. Founded by the retired officer Lucio Gutiérrez, it is organically associated with the military and police forces.

The PSP openly repudiates the social security system reform proposed by the government. Instead, it advocates the suppression of the employers' contributions to the IESS and the elimination of the state contribution to the pension system. However, it harshly contravenes the elimination of the special social security regimes of the military and police forces.

Political parties comprise three forms of power resources: corporative associational, political associational, and mobilizational.

Labor Unions

Labor unions come under an extremely complex situation in Ecuador. According to the ministry of labor, the amount of labor unions approximates the 4000 (El Telégrafo 01/05/2014). However, 80% of these labor unions are associated with the public sector and only 20% from the private sector, what brings out the importance of public employment in Ecuador.

Despite the large amount of labor unions, the power of the labor movement in Ecuador does not correspond with the power of the labor movements in other Andean countries such as Bolivia or Venezuela, where the labor confederations carry over considerable strength despite the effects of neoliberalism (CSA 2010). Without doubt, the relative weakness of the Ecuadorian labor unions is partially associated with the labor relations model, which is predicated on enterprise and skill-based labor unions or, brushing aside the constitution of branch labor unions (Harari 2010).

In addition, since the coming to power of president Correa the labor unions undertook a process of fragmentation which broke down the four labor confederations associated within one umbrella confederation into nine labor confederations associated within three (or even four) umbrella confederations (El Mercurio 16/03/2015). Thus, the Frente Unitario de Trabajadores (English: Unitary Front of Workers) (FUT) which conglomerated the Confederación de Trabajadores del Ecuador (English: Confederation of Workers of Ecuador) (CTE), the Confederación Ecuatoriana de Organizaciones Sindicales Libres (English: Ecuadorian Confederation of Free Labor Organizations) (CEOSL), the Central Ecuatoriana de Organizaciones Clasistas Unitarias de Trabajadores (English: Ecuadorian Confederation of Unitary Class Labor Organizations) (CEDOCUT), and the Unión General de Trabajadores (English: General Union of Workers) (UGT) before Correa's coming to power, dissociated into three (or even four) umbrella labor confederations since then: (1) the Parlamento Laboral Ecuatoriano (English: Ecuadorian Labor Parliament) (PLE) made up by the Confederación Sindical del Ecuador (English: Labor Confederation of Ecuador) (CSE), the Central Ecuatoriana de Organizaciones Clasistas (Ecuadorian Confederation of Class Organizations) (CEDOC-CLAT) and the Confederación de Trabajadores del Sector Público del Ecuador (Confederation of Public Workers of Ecuador) (CTSPE), (2) the Central Unitaria de Trabajadores (English: Unitary Confederation of Workers) (CUT), and (3) the Frente Unitario de Trabajadores (English: Unitary Front of Workers) (FUT) composed by fractions of the CTE, the CEDOCUT, the CEOSL, and the UGT. Addittionally, a fourth umbrella labor organization also called Central Unitaria de Trabajadores (English: Unitary Confedaration of Workers) was being constituted by fractions of the CEOSL and the CTE by the end of 2014.

Created in 2013, the Parlamento Laboral Ecuatoriano conglomerates labor confederations from both the public and private sectors. While not completely aligned with the government, the PLE usually subscribes to its labor policies. Besides, the three labor confederations comprised in the PLE (CSE, CEDOC-CLAT and CTSPE) participate in the Consejo Nacional de Salarios (CONADES), where representatives of labor, capital, and the state carry out wage bargaining on initiative of the government every year. However, the PLE repudiated the suppression of the state contribution of 40% to the pension system resolved by the government in April 2015.

The Central Unitaria de Trabajadores was established on initiative of Carlos Marx Carrasco, the minister of labor, in 2014. The founding of the CUT purposed to commingle the existing labor unions in a unified pro-government umbrella labor confederation. On this basis, the CUT is politically associated with the government and openly advocates its policies. The labor unions subsumed in the CTU comprise the Confederación Unitaria de Trabajadoras y Trabajadores Autónomos del Ecuador (English: Unitary Confederation of Autonomous Worlers of Ecuador) (CUTTAE), the Federación Trabajadores Petroleros del Ecuador (Federation of Oil Workers of Ecuador) (FETRAPEC), the Red de Maestros (English: Teachers Network) (RM), and the Federación de Empleados y Trabajadores de la Salud y Anexos (English:

Federation of Health and Annexed Employees and Workers), all of which participate in the CONADES.

Founded in 1979, the Frente Unitario de Trabajadores conglomerated the three largest labor confederations at the time. During the 1980s, the FTU actively participated in the political and economic life of Ecuador, including the struggles over the nationalization of oil and foreign trade (Borja Nuñéz 2011). However, due to the imposition of neoliberal policies, the FUT gradually disappeared from the center of social struggles during the 1990s (El Telégrafo 27/05/2013). After the revolutionary left abandoned the government's coalition in 2010, the FUT recaptured strength as the umbrella labor confederation opposed to the government. The FUT is politically associated with the MPD. Notwithstanding the labor unions included in it (the CTE, the CEDOCUT, the CEOSL, and the UGT) participate in the CONADES promoted by the government.

In November 2014 a fraction of the FUT established the Central Unitaria de Trabajadores in order to counterbalance the umbrella labor confederation of the same name created on initiative of the government. The anti-government CUT conglomerates the Federación de Trabajadores de Consejos Provinciales (English: Confederation of Workers of Provincial Councils), the Federación de Trabajadores del Sector Público (English: Confederation of Workers of the Public Sector), and the Central Única de Trabajadores Azucareros del Ecuador (English: Unified Confederation of Sugar Workers of Ecuador) (CUTAE).

Beyond internal union struggles, the fragmentation of the Ecuadorian labor unions since Correa's coming to power is mainly associated with the division between pro-government and anti-government labor unions. This division does not represent an exclusive characteristic of the labor unions whatsoever, for it characterizes all social and political organizations in Ecuador since 2007. However, in the case of the labor unions the division between pro-government and anti-government unions clearly debilitated the labor movement as a whole and maximized the power of the government (Vallejo 2015). In consequence, neither the pro-government nor the anti-government labor unions can successfully bring forward their own labor agenda. Moreover, their actions are basically circumscribed to supporting or repudiating the government's labor initiatives.

The causes why the pro-government labor unions coalesced with the government do not divaricate from the causes of all other social and political organizations allied to the government. These causes commingle the attainment of substantial social gains, such as the remarkable increase of minimum and average salaries in real terms, the steep decrease of unemployment and restoration of collective bargain since 2007, with the cooptation of their leaders, who received positions both in the government and in the government party (Vallejo 2015: 81).

In this context, the position of the labor unions regarding the social security system reform, regardless of their political adherences, was circumscribed to taking up a stance on the reform proposed by the government, either supporting it or rejecting it. However, neither the pro-government labor unions nor the anti-government labor unions brought forward their own proposals on social security, as the reconstruction of the struggles over the reform brought out. In this regard, the official discourse of both pro- and anti-government labor unions, which unfailingly asseverates that social security represents an excruciating priority for them, flagrantly contravenes their inactivity in the subject.

The Ecuadorian labor unions fall back upon corporative associational power resources, mobilizational power resources, and eventually structural power resources.

Employers' Organizations

Employers' organizations scarcely participate in Ecuador's public life. The marginal role of the Ecuadorian employers' organizations is associated with two factors. First, the underdevelopment of the industry holds back the crystallization of strong employers' organizations beyond the commercial sector (Schuldt and Acosta 2006). Second, for the most part international companies, including oil and mining companies, carry out their businesses without local partners, because of which they are not predisposed to advance the corporative representation of local employers (Schuldt and Acosta 2006).

In this context, regional commerce chambers represent the most significant employers' organizations, including the Cámara de Comercio de Guayaquil (English: Guayaquil Chamber of Commerce) and the Cámara de Comercio de Quito (English: Quito Chamber of Commerce).

Regarding the social security system reform proposed by Correa's government, the employers' organizations did not promulgate their position on it, completely brushing aside the subject. In line with this, they did not participate in the reform process at all, as the reconstruction of the power struggles over the social security system reform brought out.

4.2.3.2   Meso Actors

The second type of actors encompasses the meso actors. Just as the macro actors, the meso actors represent organized groups. However, the meso actors do not accomplish the conditions of the macro actors (a national organizational structure and the disposal of three or more forms of power resources). Some meso actors fall back upon a nationwide organizational structure and sometimes even two forms of power resources (but not three), as in the cases of the indigenous and peasant organizations and the police and military forces. The meso actors comprise a complex of organizations with very diverse characteristics, such as indigenous and peasant groups, military and police forces, professional associations, nongovernmental organizations, feminist groups, associations of social security beneficiaries, etc. The criterion used for the selection of the meso actors presented below is determined by their participation in the struggles over the reform which, in turn, is delineated in the reconstruction of the struggles effectuated before.

Indigenous and Peasant Organizations

The indigenous and peasant organizations represent a fundamental part of Ecuador's public life. The importance of the indigenous organizations is predicated on the ethnic composition of the Ecuadorian society, which coalesces 7.0% of people self-identified as indigenous, 7.4% of people self-identified as montubio, and 71.9% self-identified as mestizo, according to the population and housing census carried out in 2010 (INECE 2012). However, the indigenous organizations asseverate that the indigenous population represents 30, 45, and even 70% of the total population (Chisaguano 2006)

The organizations of the indigenous movement materialize in a pyramidal structure composed of three levels: communal, regional, and national (Bretón 2003). However, this pyramidal structure does not connote authority hierarchies, for the local and regional organizations autonomously determine their actions, positions, and even their political adhesions (Botero 1998).

The Federación Ecuatoriana de Indios (English: Ecuadorian Confederation of Indians) (FEI) represents the first national indigenous organization of Ecuador. Founded as the indigenous branch of the CTE in 1944, the FEI is politically associated to the Partido Comunista del Ecuador(English Communist Party of Ecuador) (PCE). Accordingly, the FEI commingles the indigenous and the class perspectives (Altmann 2013a). During the 1950s, the FEI actively participated in the peasant struggles, however, its influence diminished since the 1960s. Nonetheless, the FEI still partakes in protests and manifestations together with the CTE and other indigenous organizations. As the PCE, the FEI accompanies the government since its coming to power in 2007.

Created in 1980, the Consejo Ecuatoriano de Pueblos y Organizaciones Indígenas Evangélicos (FEINE) conglomerates the evangelical indigenous movement. The FEINE commenced as a confessional organization ingrained in the rural areas on the basis of the existing structure of evangelical churches (Barrera 2005). The FEINE was consecrated to its organizational consolidation during the 1980s and it only broke out in the indigenous movement during the early 1990s. In opposition to the MUPP of the CONAIE, the FEINE established the Amauta Jatari, later renamed to Amauta Yuyay, as its own political party in 1996 (Altmann 2013a). Because of its reluctance to the CONAIE; the FEINE is deprecated as an illegitimate representation of the indigenous and denounced for disuniting the indigenous movement (Barrera 2005).

Since its inception, the FEINE commingles class, ethnic, and political demands. While not completely subordinated, the FEINE is politically associated with the government of president Correa since its coming to power (León 2010).

Despite its active participation in public life, the indigenous movement has barely participated in the struggles over the social security system reform. This notorious absence is probably predicated on the political agenda of the indigenous movement, which revolves around the recognition of the plurinationality of the state, the administrative autonomy of the territories occupied by the indigenous, the community economics, the autonomous management of water provision, the elimination of large-scale mining, and the abolition of the neo-extractivist model.

The Confederación Nacional de Organizaciones Campesinas, Indígenas y Negras (English: National Confederation of Peasant, Indigenous and Black Organizations) (FENOCIN) comes down from the peasant movement. For this reason, its history started out with the foundation of the Federación de Trabajadores Agropecuarios (English: Confederation of Rural Workers) (FETAP) in 1950 as the farming branch of the Confederación Ecuatoriana de Obreros Católicos (English: Ecuadorian Confederation of Christian Workers) (CEDOC). In the heat of the peasant struggles over land reform in which it actively participated during the 1960s, the FETAP restructuralized into the Federación Nacional de Organizaciones Campesinas (English: National Confederation of Peasant Organizations) (FENOC) in 1968. In the 1980s, the FENOC decisively participated in the social protests during the 1980s as the largest peasant organization. Due to the increasing participation of indigenous organizations in it, the FENOC metamorphosed into the Federación Nacional de Organizaciones Campesinas-Indígenas (National Confederation of Indigenous and peasant Organizations) (FENOC-I) in 1988. During the 1990s, the FENOC-I undertook a profound process of reform which acknowledged its multi-ethnic and intercultural character. This brought about the renaming of the FENOC-I into the aforementioned Confederación Nacional de Organizaciones Campesinas, Indígenas y Negras (FENOCIN) in 1999. Since then, the FENOCIN repudiates the CONAIE, which asseverates to represent the only legitimate indigenous organization (FENOCIN 2004). Unlike the CONAIE, the FENOCIN participates in the government alliance up to the present (Altmann 2013a).

The Confederación de Nacionalidades Indígenas del Ecuador (English: National Confederation of Indigenous Nationalities of Ecuador) (CONAIE) represents the largest national indigenous organization by far. Officially founded in 1986, the CONAIE comes down from the alliance of the Ecuador Runacunapak Rikcharimui (English: Movement of the indigenous people of Ecuador) (ECUARUNARI), a regional indigenous organization from the Sierra region, and the Confederación de Nacionalidades Indígenas de la Amazonía Ecuatoriana (English: Confederation of Indigenous Naitonalities of the Ecuadorian Amazonia) (CONFENAIE), a regional indigenous organization of the Oriente region. Together, the ECUARUNARI and the CONFENAIE established the Consejo Nacional de Coordinación de Nacionalidades Indígenas del Ecuador (CONACNIE) in 1980, which would eventually bring about the constitution of the CONAIE in 1986.

Since its foundation the CONAIE has commingled ethnic and class demands. However, in contrast to the FEI and the FENOCIN the ethnic perspective has always predominated over the class perspective within the CONAIE. During the 1990s, the CONAIE actively participated in the indigenous uprisings for the redistribution of land and the provision of water, and against the neoliberal economic reforms and the privatizations pushed by the president Sixto Durán Ballén (Santillana y Herrera 2009). In 1996, the CONAIE established the Movimiento de Unidad Plurinacional Pachakutik (MUPP) in order to partake in party politics. Since then, the ethnic perspective clearly advanced at the expense of the class perspective within the CONAIE (Altmann 2013a), what did not preclude the CONAIE from participating in the uprisings which brought down the neoliberal government of Abdalá Bucaram in 1997 and the neoliberal government of Jamil Mahuad in 2000. The CONAIE and the MUPP advocated the presidential candidacy of Lucio Gutiérrez in 2002 but then abandoned the government alliance in 2003. After this the CONAIE maximized its ethnic perspective, concentrating on the demand of a plurinational state. Since then, the CONAIE has postulated the exclusive representation of the indigenous interests and repudiated the representation of the FEI, the FENOCIN and the FEINE, regarding them as conspirers against the unity of the indigenous movement (Altmann 2013a).

The CONAIE participated in the political alliance, which successfully advanced the candidacy of Rafael Correa in the presidential election of 2006. However, the CONAIE abandoned the government alliance in 2010 and became bitterly opposed to the government.

The indigenous and peasant organizations fall back upon two forms of power resources: corporative associational and mobilizational.

Police and Military Forces

Even though the police and military forces cannot legally participate in politics, the actively partake in Ecuadorian politics, even in recent times. Whereas in most Latin American countries the transition from the military dictatorships imposed in the 1970s to the democratic governments instituted in the 1980s brought about the withdrawal of the military and police forces from politics (O'Donnell and Schmitter 1986; O'Donnell et al. 1986), in the case of Ecuador they did not completely renounce national politics. In fact, after the culmination of the latest military dictatorship in 1979, the police and national forces actively participated in four attempted coups, two of them occurred in the 2000s.

In an attempt to democratically canalize the participation of the police and military forces in politics, the new constitution sanctioned in 2008 established the right to vote for the members of the police and military forces. Ideologically, the police and military members are predisposed to the PSP, the nationalistic right party founded by the retired officer Lucio Gutiérrrez. In spite of this, the police and military forces are characterized by a multifarious position in terms of political adhesions.

With regard to organization, the Ecuadorian police and military forces comprise the Policía Nacional del Ecuador (National Police of Ecuador) (PNE) and the Fuerzas Armadas del Ecuador (Armed Foreces of Ecuador) (FAE). The PNE materializes in a centralized structure which is directly subordinated to the national government (more concretely to the Ministerio del Interior). Cantonal (municipal) police forces only represent a very small minority of the police forces. The FAE is conventionally structuralized into three forces: the Ejército Ecuatoriano (English: Ecuadorian Army), the Armada del Ecuador (English: Navy of Ecuador), and the Fuerza Aérea Ecuatoriana (English: Ecuadorian Air Force).

The police and military forces actively partook in the struggles over the social security system reform since they commenced in 2007. In a nutshell, the police and military forces repudiated the incorporation of their special social security regimes into a unified universal social security system. Their participation in the struggles over the reform was initially circumscribed to lobbying, as in the case of the formulation and passing of the constitutional articles on social security during the constituent assembly. However, a group of police and military members even desecrated the rule of law when they carried out an armed revolt demanding the continuance of their bonuses and the preservation of their special social security regimes in 2010.

The police and military forces fall back upon corporative associational power resources and, despite its insurrectionary character, mobilizational power resources.

4.2.4   Operationalization of the "How" Question

The reconstruction of the power struggles over the social security system reform brought out that (1) the struggles were not dissociated from the more general struggles for hegemony, which came about in manifold ways, (2) the struggles over the social security system reform were not exclusively determined by the corporative associational and political associational power resources of the actors involved, but they also comprised structural, mobilizational, and communicational arenas in which the contending actors mobilized their power resources.

In the following, the corporative associational, the political associational, the mobilizational, and communicational power resources are broken down separately.

4.2.4.1   Corporative Associational Power Resources

As mentioned above, the assessment of the corporative associational power resources of the actors involved in the power struggles over the reform is carried out resorting to the operational framework of political class struggle approaches. The corporative associational resources are associated with the organizational capacity of the contending actors. For this reason, the assessment of corporative associational power resources looks upon indicators concerning the magnitude of the membership of the actors involved (government, political parties, labor unions, social movements, etc.). However, unlike political class struggle approaches, the analysis of the corporative associational power resources effectuated below is not circumscribed to the corporative associational power resources of the labor unions, but it encompasses the corporative associational power resources of all the macro and meso actors involved in the struggles over the social security system reform. Therefore, the assessment of the organizational power resources additionally comprises the government, the political parties, the social movements, and the police and military forces as possessors of organizational power resources next to the labor unions.

The incorporation of the government brings about complications regarding the "comparativity" of its corporative associational power resources, as the public officials who carry out duties within government institutions do not necessarily subscribe to the government in political terms. In order to countervail this, the assessment of the organizational power resources of the government brings forward a structural

Table 4.14 Structure of the government cabinet

Government of Alfredo Palacio	Government of Rafael Correa
Ministerios de Coordinación	
	Ministerio Coordinador de Desarrollo Social
	Ministerio Coordinador de Sectores Estratégicos
	Ministerio Coordinador de Seguridad
	Ministerio Coordinador de Política Económica
	Ministerio Coordinador de Producción, Empleo y Competitividad
	Ministerio Coordinador de Conocimiento y Talento Humano
	Ministerios del Sector Social del Ecuador
Ministerio de Bienestar Social	Ministerio de Inclusión Económica y Social
Ministerio de Desarrollo Urbano y Vivienda	Ministerio de Desarrollo Urbano y Vivienda
Ministerio de Salud Pública	Ministerio de Salud Pública
Ministerio del Deporte	
	Ministerios de los Sectores Estratégicos
Ministerio de Energía	Ministerio de Hidrocarburos
	Ministerio de Minería
	Ministerio de Electricidad y Energía Renovable
	Ministerio de Telecomunicaciones y Sociedad de la Información
Ministerio de Ambiente	Ministerio del Ambiente
	Ministerios del Sector Económico
Ministerio de Economía	Ministerio de Finanzas
	Ministerios del Sector Seguridad
Ministerio de Defensa	Ministerio de Defensa
Ministerio de Relaciones Exteriores	Ministerio de Relaciones Exteriores y Movilidad Humana
Ministerio de Gobierno	Ministerio del Interior
	Ministerio de Justicia, Derechos Humanos y Cultos
	Ministerios del Sector Productivo
Ministerio de Industrias y Comercio Exterior	Ministerio de Industrias y Productividad

(continued)

perspective, concentrating on the expansion of the government apparatus instead of focusing on the expansion of the government personnel. Table 4.14 tabularizes the structure of the government cabinet of presidents Palacio and Correa (Table 4.14)

Table 4.14 brings out the expansion of the government cabinet since Correa's coming to power (Table 4.14). The number of ministries was maximized from 15 under the Palacio government in 2006 to 27 under the Correa government in 2015.

Table 4.14 (continued)

Government of Alfredo Palacio	Government of Rafael Correa
	Ministerio de Comercio Exterior
Ministerio de Agricultura y Ganadería	Ministerio de Agricultura, Ganadería, Acuacultura y Pesca
Ministerio de Trabajo	Ministerio de Relaciones Laborales
Ministerio de Obras Públicas	Ministerio de Transporte y Obras Públicas
Ministerio de Turismo	Ministerio de Turismo
	Ministerios del Sector del Conocimiento y Talento Humano
Ministerio de Educación	Ministerio de Educación
	Ministerio de Cultura y Patrimonio

Source Prepared by the author

The expansion of the government cabinet is predicated on the creation of six coordinating ministries (the Ministerio Coordinador de Desarrollo Social, the Ministerio Coordinador de Sectores Estratégicos, the Ministerio Coordinador de Seguridad, the Ministerio Coordinador de Política Económica, the Ministerio Coordinador de Producción, Empleo y Competitividad, and the Ministerio Coordinador de Conocimiento y Talento Humano), the promotion of four preexisting secretaries into four ministries (the Ministerio del Deporte, the Ministerio de Telecomunicaciones y Sociedad de la Información, the Ministerio de Justicia, Derechos Humanos y Cultos, and the Ministerio de Cultura y Patrimonio), and the division of two preexisting ministries (the Ministerio de Energía and the Ministerio de Industrias y Comercio Exterior) into five ministries (the Ministerio de Hidrocarburos, the Ministerio de Minería and the Ministerio de Electricidad y Energía Renovable, and the Ministerio de Industrias y Productividad and the Ministerio de Comercio Exterior). The number of national secretaries was maximized as well, increasing from 6 to 11.

While not directly comparable with the organizational capabilities of the political parties, labor unions, social movements, etc., the expansion of the government apparatus definitively brought about an increase of the organizational power resources of the government.

The assessment of the organizational political parties in Ecuador comes across the remarking unavailability of information concerning their membership. The Ley Orgánica Eleectoral (English: Organic Electoral Law) (hereinafter LOE) establishes that the political parties must carry out a register of their members, however, this information, if really existent, is not promulgated neither by the political parties nor by the Consejo Nacional Electoral (English: Naitonal Electoral Council), the highest electoral authority. Only the AP and the UP (ex MPD) have lately annunciated the number of their active members: 161,913 and 34,792, respectively (El Comercio 01/09/2014; El Universo 05/10/2015). Since this information was promulgated on the own initiative of the AP and the UP it was not corroborated by the CNE or any other external entity.

Table 4.15 Endorsements and active members of the national political parties

	Endorsements		Active members
	2012	2015	
MPD/UP	134,773	193,597	34,792[a]
MUPP	145,145		
AP	826,812		161,913[b]
AV	162,385		
RED	–		
UNO/CREO	163,765		
PSC/MSMG	161,090		
PSP	161,691		

[a]El Comercio 01/09/2014
[b]El Universo 05/10/2015
Source Prepared by the author

The LOE additionally establishes that the political parties must bring about the signed endorsements of 1.5% of the electorate in order to participate in elections, what in the case of the presidential election held in 2013 amounted to 157,943 endorsements. Unlike the figures regarding the active members of the parties, the figures concerning the signed endorsements of the parties are publicized by the CNE. Even though the endorsements do not necessarily presuppose the active participation in the parties, they somehow represent an indicator of certain party engagement, even more so considering that the endorsements can only subscribe to one single political party. Besides, the CNE authenticates the endorsements submitted by the political parties in order to close out fraudulent registrations. Table 4.15 brings forward the endorsements of the national political parties validated by the CNE in 2012 and 2015, as well as the number of active members declared by the political parties themselves (Table 4.15).

Table 4.15 brings out that the AP clearly outdistances the other political parties in terms of organizational power resources (Table 4.15). Meanwhile, the MPD/UP, the MUPP, the AV, the UNO/CREO, the PSC/MCMG, and the PSP accumulate a comparable amount of organizational resources. Since the number of active members of the AP and the MPD/UP represents about 20% of their endorsements, it could be made out that the MUPP, the AV, the UNO/CREO, the PSC/MCMG, and the PSP separately approximate 35,000 active members.

The organizational power resources represent the power resources *par excellence* of the labor unions. Unfortunately, the Ecuadorian labor unions do not bring out information regarding their membership, and even if they eventually brought it out, it would not straighten out the difficulties for the assessment of their power resources. As pointed out above, after three decades of neoliberal policies which extremely deteriorated the labor movement, the labor unions undertook a process of reconfiguration since Correa's coming to power in 2007. This process brought about the disappearance of numerous old labor unions, on the one side, and the appearance of numerous

Table 4.16 Union density

	Lora and Pagés (1997)	Johnson (2004)	SENPLADES (2011)	CSA (2010)
1981–1985	15.0			
1986–1990	14.3			
1991–1995	13.5			
1995		11.0		
1998		9.0		
2008			3.0	
2010				2.0

Source Prepared by the author

new labor unions, on the other side. In any case, the current existence of 4000 recognized labor unions does not presuppose the strengthening of the labor movement but rather the contrary. Despite the extraordinarily favorable economic context experienced over the recent years, the labor movement has increasingly deteriorated, becoming more and more dependent on the state (Harari 2010).

The available figures regarding union density (i.e., the rate of unionized workers with respect to the labor force) substantiate this. Despite the discrepancies among the figures depending on their sources, all of them bring out the continuous decrease of the unionized workers within the labor force (Table 4.16).

The decline of the UNE, the largest single labor union in Ecuador represents a paradigmatic example of the weakening of the labor unions since 2007. The UNE conglomerated 120,000 affiliated members by default who monthly disbursed the union dues of 1.5% of their salaries in 2007. Since the new constitution established the voluntary character of the union membership in 2008, the number of affiliated members currently approximates to 100,000 but only 400,000 of them disburse the union dues (Interview with Emma Rosana Palacios; El Comercio 17/02/2015). In addition to this, the government took away the management of the complementary closed pension funds of the teachers from the UNE and advanced the creation of the Red de Maestros (English: Network of Teachers), another teacher's labor union opposed to the UNE.

The assessment of the corporative associational power resources of the indigenous and peasant organizations brings about difficulties as well. In this case, the difficulties are associated with the fact that the national indigenous organizations conglomerate communal and regional organizations, but these represent autonomous entities in front of those (Altmann 2013a). For these reasons, the leadership of the national indigenous organizations cannot simply determine the actions and positions of the communal and regional organizations, as regarding their participation in protests or their positioning toward the government. This distinction represents a fundamental factor to deliberate the current situation of the CONAIE, in which the fierce opposition to the government of its national leaders does not necessarily correlate the position of its social bases, at least in electoral terms (Ospina 2011).

Table 4.17 Members and regional organizations of the national indigenous organizations

	Members	Regional organizations
FEI	5655	2
FEINE	26,384	18
FENOCIN	109,278	52
CONAIE	804,801	141

Source CODENPE (2007), Chisaguano (2006), Altmann (2013a, b)

Table 4.18 Members of the police and military forces

	2005	2008	2012	2014
Police forces	32,654	21,399		44,904
Military forces	46,500	37,448	38,264	40,242
Army	37,000	24,135	23,704	24,726
Navy	5500	7258	8357	9127
Air force	4000	6055	6203	6389

Source IISS (2005), RESDAL (2012, 2014), Olaya y Pontón (2006), Pontón (2009), PNE (2015)

This said, Table 4.17 tabularizes the latest available figures regarding the membership and the organizational structure of the national indigenous organizations (Table 4.17).

Table 4.17 corroborates that the CONAIE represents the largest national indigenous organization and probably the largest social organization of Ecuador (Ospina 2011) (Table 4.17). In turn, the FENOCIN conglomerates 109,278 members in 52 regional organizations, constituting the second largest national indigenous organization and providing considerable support for the government.

The corporative associational power resources of the police and armed forces can be easily measured in quantitative terms through the mensuration of their membership. However, as explained above the corporative associational power resources of the police and military forces do not directly correlate their effective power because of two reasons. First, even though the members of the police and military forces can individually participate in elections as voters since the sanction of the new constitution in 2008, it is naturally not countenanced that the military and police forces partake in politics as organizations since they are provided with the monopoly of violence. Second, despite the "natural" political proximity of the police and military members to the PSP, the nationalistic right party founded by the retired officer Lucio Gutiérrrez, the police and military forces are characterized by a multifarious position in terms of political adhesions.

Table 4.18 tabularizes the latest available figures regarding the membership of the police and armed forces during the last 10 years (Table 4.18).

Table 4.18 substantiates that the number of military members has increasingly decreased during the last 10 years, falling 13% between 2005 and 2015, whereas the number of police members has tendentiously advanced during the last 10 years, increasing 38% between 2005 and 2015 (Table 4.18). This tendency does not necessarily presuppose the weakening of the military forces; however, it certainly brings out the strengthening of the police forces throughout this period.

4.2.4.2   Political Associational Power Resources

As pointed out above, the assessment of the political associational power resources of the actors involved in the power struggles over the reform is carried out resorting to the operational framework of political class struggle approaches. The political associational power resources are associated with the control of the democratic institutions (i.e., the institutions composed by democratically elected members). For this reason, the assessment of political associational power resources looks upon indicators concerning the composition of the national assembly and the composition of the government cabinet.

However, the assessment of the political associational power resources carried out below presupposes one fundamental difference with regard to political class struggle approaches, for it contemplates the government as a possessor of political democratic power resources next to the political parties. The reason for this is associated with the aforementioned centrality of the governments in the Latin American societies (Ecuador specially included), in which the governments clearly preponderate over all social actors. In addition, the inclusion of the government is associated with the fact that the amount of political democratic power resources of the government does not always correspond with the amount of political democratic power resources of the government party, due to the making and remaking of political alliances in support of the government on the one side, and the internal conflicts between the government and the government party, on the other side.

Table 4.19 delineates the composition of the legislative power since 2007, including the seats and the share corresponding to the government and the political parties (Table 4.19).

Table 4.19 brings out that the government preponderated in the legislative power since 2007 but it only accomplished an absolute majority during the constituent assembly and the "Congresillo" (between November 2007 and July 2009) and during the second legislative period of the national assembly (between May 2013 and May 2017) (Table 4.19). In order to puzzle out this problem, the government carried out an alliance with seven opposition assembly members during the first legislative period. However, the resulting alliance did not provide an assured absolute majority to the government because it was circumscribed to specific legislative subjects. Besides, it presupposed concessions and compromises on the side of the government. For this reason, the most significant legislation regarding the social security system reform introduced by the government came about during the constituent assembly, when the majority bloc of the AP, the MPD, the MUPP, and the RED advanced the constitutional articles on social security, and during the second legislative period, when the majority bloc of the AP advocated the LRLSS 20014 and the LOJL.

Table 4.19 Composition of the legislative power

	Constituent Assembly		"Congresillo"		National assembly 2009–2013		National assembly 2013–2017	
	Seats	Share (%)	Seats	Share (%)	Seats	Share (%)	Seats	Share (%)
Government								
National government	80 (+13)	71.54	46 (+7)	69.74	59 (+7)	53.23	100 (+5)	76.64
Political parties								
AP	80	61.54	46	60.53	59	47.58	100	72.99
AV	–	–	–	–	–	–	5	3.65
RED	3	2.31	2	2.63	0	0,00	5	3.65
MPD	4	3.08	2	2.63	5	4.03		0.00
MUPP	4	3.08	3	3.95	4	3.23		0.00
UNO/CREO	2	1.54	1	1.32	–	–	11	8.03
PSC/MCMG	5	3.85	3	3.95	11	8.87	6	4.38
PRIAN	8	6.15	4	5.26	7	5.65	0	0.00
PSP	19	14.62	10	13.16	19	15.32	5	3.65
Others	5	3.85	5	6.58	19	15.32	5	3.65
Total	130		76		124		137	

Source Prepared by the author

Tables 4.20 and 4.21 particularize the results of the voting on the legislation regarding the social security system reform and the positions assumed by the political parties in the voting (Tables 4.20 and 4.21).

Tables 4.20 and 4.21 substantiate that the most significant legislation regarding the reform introduced by the government came about during the constituent assembly and during the second legislative period (Tables 4.20 and 4.21). The LRLSS 2010 represented the only bill approved during the first legislative period, and the fact that it was only countenanced on the basis of a toilsome political agreement among all political parties, even though the LRLSS basically established a substantial increase of all pensions, corroborates the argument.

However, the assessment of the political associational power resources of the contending actors in the legislative power brings about a fundamental question, as the government did not capitalize on its absolute majority in the national assembly since 2013 in order to bring forward its draft bill for the thoroughgoing social security system reform entitled LOSSS. As explained above, this question cannot be puzzled out through the analysis of the associational power resources proposed by political class struggle approaches, but it should be broken down from a wider analytical perspective in order to acknowledge all relevant power resources.

Table 4.22 delineates the composition of the most significant part of the government cabinet since 2007 (Table 4.22).

Table 4.20 Results of the voting on the legislation regarding the social security system reform

Constituent assembly		"Congresillo"		National assembly 2009–2013		National assembly 2013–2017	
CA 8		LRLSS 2009		LRLSS 2010		LRLSS 2014	
Yes	87	Yes	43	Yes	109	Yes	87
No	3	No	15	No	0	No	26
Abstention	12	Abstention	2	Abstention	0	Abstention	1
Blank	1	Blank	0	Blank	0	Blank	0
Absent	27	Absent	16	Absent	15	Absent	23
CA 9						LOJL	
Yes	82					Yes	91
No	8					No	29
Abstention	12					Abstention	0
Blank	1					Blank	0
Absent	27					Absent	1
CA 10							
Yes	88						
No	4						
Abstention	16						
Blank	0						
Absent	22						
CA 31							
Yes	90						
No	18						
Abstention	0						
Blank	6						
Absent	16						
CA 32							
Yes	88						
No	17						
Abstention	6						
Blank	2						
Absent	17						
CA 33							
Yes	87						
No	5						
Abstention	17						
Blank	4						
Absent	17						
CA 34							
Yes	90						

(continued)

Table 4.20 (continued)

Constituent assembly		"Congresillo"		National assembly 2009–2013		National assembly 2013–2017	
No	4						
Abstention	18						
Blank	1						
Absent	17						
CA 35							
Yes	98						
No	1						
Abstention	11						
Blank	2						
Absent	18						
CA 36							
Yes	97						
No	1						
Abstention	11						
Blank	3						
Absent	18						
CA 37							
Yes	93						
No	1						
Abstention	19						
Blank	0						
Absent	17						
CA 38							
Yes	95						
No	3						
Abstention	15						
Blank	1						
Absent	16						
TD 23							
Yes	95						
No	3						
Abstention	13						
Blank	3						
Absent	16						

CA Constitutional Article, *TD* Transitory Disposition
Source Prepared by the author

Table 4.21 Position of the political parties in the voting on the legislation regarding the social security system reform

	Constitutent assembly	"Congresillo"	National assembly 2009–2013	National assembly 2013–2017	
	CA	LRLSS 2009	LRLSS 2010	LSRSS 2014	LOJL
AP					
AV	–	–	–		
RED			–		
MPD					
MUPP					
UNO/CREO			–		
PSC/MCMG					
PRIAN				–	–
PSP					
Others					

Source Prepared by the author

Table 4.22 brings out two remarkable circumstances.

First, from the outset the government cabinet exclusively conglomerated members of the AP, even though Correa's government alliance initially coalesced the AP, the RED, the MUPP, and the MPD. The ministers of health, who were characterized by a nonparty and technical profile, and the second coordinating minister of economic policy Diego Borja, who was associated with the allied Movimiento Poder Ciudadano (English: Movement Citizen Power) (MPC), represented the only exceptions to this.

Although the exclusive presence of members of the AP in the government cabinet could come across as a sign of the power of the government party, it actually represents the opposite, since the AP does not participate in the selection of the ministers whatsoever. On the contrary, the selection of the ministers is exclusively carried out by the president, who clearly preponderates over the government party in this regard. For this reason, the ministers who renounced their positions due to fundamental disagreements with president Correa (most notably Alberto Acosta and Gustavo Larrea) were to abandon the AP as well.

Second, the composition of the most significant part of the government cabinet brings out recurrent replacements and constant rotations of the ministers. Three ministries (the Ministerio Coordinador de Producción, Empleo y Competitividad, the Ministerio de Defensa and the Ministerio de Transporte y Obras Públicas) came up to seven different ministers since Correa's coming to power in 2007, approximating a ratio of one new minister every fifteen and a half months. Many other ministries came under six or five different ministers during the same period. In parallel, many ministers were relocated in the government cabinet in several occasions. For instance,

Table 4.22 Composition of the government cabinet

Minsterios de Coordinación			Ministerios del Sector Social		
Ministerio Coordinador de Desarrollo Social	Nathalie Cely	AP	Ministerio de Inclusión Económica y Social	Jeannette Sánchez	AP
	Jeannette Sánchez	AP		Maria Duarte	AP
	Doris Soliz	AP		Ximena Ponce	AP
	Richard Espinoza	AP		Doris Soliz	AP
	Cecilia Vaca	AP		Betty Tola	AP
Ministerio Coordinador de Sectores Estratégicos	Derlis Palacios	AP	Ministerio de Salud Pública	Caroline Chang	Tec Act
	Galo Borja Pérez	AP		David Chiriboga	Tec Act
	Jorge Glas	AP		Carina Vance	Tec Act
	Rafael Poveda	AP	Ministerios del Sector Seguridad		
Ministerio Coordinador de Política Económica	Pedro Páez	AP	Minsterio del Interior	Gustavo Larrea	(Ex) AP
	Diego Borja	MPC		Fernando Bustamante	AP
	Katiuska King	(Ex) AP		Alfredo Vera	AP
	Jeannette Sánchez	AP		Gustavo Jalkh	AP
	Patricio Rivera	AP		José Serrano	AP
Ministerios del Sector Económico			Ministerio de Defensa	Guadalupe Larriva	AP
Ministerio de Finanzas	Ricardo Patiño	AP		Lorena Escudero	AP

(continued)

the current executive secretary of the AP, Doris Solís, circumambulated the following cabinet positions since 2007: coordinating minister of the Ministerio Coordinador de Desarrollo Social, coordinating minister of the (eliminated) Ministerio Coordinador de Patrimonio Natural y Cultural, coordinating minister of the (eliminated) Ministerio de Coordinación de la Política y Gobiernos Autónomos Descentralizados (two times), minister of the Ministerio de Inclusión Económica y Social, secretary of the Secretaría Nacional de Gestión Política, and secretary of the (eliminated) Secretaría De Pueblos, Movimientos Sociales y Participación Ciudadana.

Table 4.22 (continued)

Minsterios de Coordinación			Ministerios del Sector Social		
	Fausto Ortiz	(Ex) AP		Wellington Sandoval	AP
	Wilma Salgado	(Ex) AP		Javier Ponce	AP
	María Elsa Viteri	AP		Miguel Carvajal	AP
	Patricio Rivera	AP		Fernanda Espinoza	AP
	Fausto Herrera	AP		Fernando Cordero	AP
Ministerios de los Sectores Estratégicos			Ministerio de Relaciones Exteriores y Movilidad	Fernanda Espinoza	AP
Ministerio de Hidrocarburos	Alberto Acosta	(Ex) AP		Isabel Salvador	AP
	Galo Chiriboga	AP		Fander Falconí	AP
	Derlis Palacios	AP		Ricardo Patiño	AP
	Germánico Pinto	AP			
	Wilson Pástor	AP			
	Pedro Merizalde	AP			
Ministerio de Minería	Javier Córdova	AP			
Ministerio de Telecomunicaciones	Jorge Glas	AP			
	Jaime Guerrero	AP			
	Augusto Espín	AP			

Tec Act Technician and activist
Source Prepared by the author

Even though the recurrent replacements and the constant rotations within the government cabinet were partially predicated on the general scarcity of politically and technically competent personnel, they also bring out the power of the president and his absolute preponderance over the government party.

4.2.4.3 Mobilizational Power Resources

The assessment of the mobilizational power resources of the actors involved in the struggles over the social security system reform in Ecuador represents a fundamental part of the analysis because of two reasons. The first reason is predicated on the generalized utilization of mobilizational power resources by the actors involved in the struggles. This generalized use of mobilizational power resources comes about in a context of intense political mobilization in which the actions of the social actors are not exclusively circumscribed to the use of corporative associational and the political associational power resources, as presupposed by political class struggle approaches. The second reason is associated with the previously explained fact that the power struggles over the social security system reform materialize in the context of the more general struggles for hegemony, in which the centrality of the "conventional" corporative associational and political associational power resources diminishes as the mobilizational power resources are maximized. As explained above, the correlation between the sharpening of hegemonic struggles and the increasing utilization of mobilizational power resources is predicated on the particular characteristics of the mobilizational power resources, which represent a much more direct (less channeled) manifestation of power than associational power resources.

The assessment of mobilizational power resources presupposes manifold difficulties compared with the associational power resources. These difficulties pervade both the quantification and the qualification of the mobilizational power resources. In order to circumvent these difficulties, the assessment of the power resources of the contending actors is circumscribed to the public mobilizations of national scope.

The definition used for the assessment comes down from two theoretical approaches to the subject: (1) the perspective of the British Marxist historiography (Hobsbawm 1959; Thompson 1963) and (2) the perspective contribution of the sociology of contentious politics (Tilly 1978; Tarrow 1994). Adapting their theoretical definitions to the requirements of the assessment, mobilizations are conceptualized as collective demonstrative actions effectuated by social groups aimed at publicly disclosing their positions regarding something. The reference to the public character of the mobilizations points out that they are carried out in the public space. This way, a workers' strike confined to their working place is not categorized as a public mobilization, whereas a worker's strike demonstrating on the streets falls under public mobilization indeed. For practical reasons, the cyberspace is precluded from the public space for the assessment of the mobilizational power resources. Finally, the national scope of the mobilizations is associated with their territorial extension. Thus, mobilizations are categorized as of national scope either when they come about in several locations throughout the national territory, including the most populated areas (Quito, Guayaquil, Cuenca, etc.), or when they are carried out in the national capital (Quito) with the concurrence of participators coming from several locations throughout the national territory.

Table 4.23 tabularizes the public mobilizations of national scope since Correa's coming to power in 2007 (Table 4.23). The table breaks down the dates, the main organizers, and the demands of the mobilizations. Additionally, it points out the existence of inexistence of countermobilizations. For the sake of the analysis, the public mobilizations carried out in the context of electoral campaigns or celebrations of the international workers' day are precluded from the table.

Table 4.23 brings out that the frequency of the public mobilizations clearly accelerated since 2014 (Table 4.23). Whereas only four public mobilizations of national scope were carried out between 2007 and 2013, seven public mobilizations of national scope were carried through between 2014 and September 2015. Unfortunately, the unsystematic and contradictory available information regarding the massiveness of the mobilizations circumscribes their quantitative comparison. However, the increase of the frequency of the mobilizations since 2014 was undoubtedly reciprocated by the increase of their massiveness (Ospina 2014, 2015; Daza and Santillana 2015).

The government and its allies carried out countermobilizations of analogous massiveness even since 2014, what brings out the persistence of its considerable mobilizational capacity. Nonetheless, the increase of the frequency and the massiveness of the public mobilizations organized by the actors opposed to the government reactivated the dispute over the "control" of the streets after years of undisputed supremacy by the government. Besides, the increase of the mobilizations brought about the reactivation of the FUT and the CONAIE, which had clearly backed down since the 1980s and the 1990s, respectively (Ospina 2011; Vallejo 2015).

The mobilization organized by the mayor of Guayaquil Jaime Nebot against the government in June 2015 represented the only public mobilization of national scope effectuated by an opposition party outside the electoral campaign period since 2007. In this regard, the intensification of the mobilizations since 2014 revitalized the actors opposed to the government but it did not bring about the consolidation of the opposition in political terms. The electoral results of the latest elections, held in February 2014, substantiated this assertion. As mentioned above, the latest provincial and cantonal elections certainly represented a setback for the government party in relative terms, for the two most populated cities (Guayaquil and Quito) were taken over by opposition parties. However, the government still came out as the winner in general terms, taking over the government of the most populated provinces (Guayas, Pichincha, and Manabí) and 68 cantons. Moreover, the electoral performance of the political parties associated with the FUT and the CONAIE, the MPD, and the MUPP actually deteriorated compared to the previous provincial and cantonal elections. In any case, this does not contravene the actual fact that the intensification of the public mobilizations since 2014 maximized the mobilizational power resources of the FUT and the CONAIE, bringing about a dispute over the "control" of the streets after years of undisputed supremacy by the government.

Notwithstanding the aforesaid, a quick glance at the demands triggering the mobilizations immediately brings out that none of them were associated with the social security system reform, with the only exception of the police revolt occurred in September 2010. In this case, one of the nine demands requested by the insubordinate police members during the revolt advocated the continuity of the special social security regimes of the police and military forces administered by the ISSFA and the ISSPOL, as recounted above. Even though the number of police members directly or indirectly participating in it did not closely correspond to the number of demonstra-

Table 4.23 Public mobilizations of national scope

Date	Organizer	Reason/slogan	Counter-mobilization
29/09/2009	CONAIE	"Movilización por la dignidad, la vida y la plurinacionalidad"	No
30/09/2010	PNE	Against the Ley Orgánica de Servicio Público	Yes
05/10/2011	UNE	Against the Ley Orgánica de Educación Intercultural	No
08/03/2012–22/03/2012	CONAIE	"Marcha por el agua, la vida y la dignidad"	Yes
17/09/2014	FUT	Against the sanction of the Código Orgánico de Trabajo	Yes
19/11/2014	FUT	Against the reform of the Código de Trabajo and the reform of the constitution	No
19/03/2015	FUT	Against the reform of the Código de Trabajo and the reform of the constitution	No
08/06/2015–15/06/2015	Spontaneous	Against the sanction of the Ley Orgánica para la Redistribución de la Riqueza and the Ley Orgánica Reformatoria al Código Orgánico de Organización Territorial, Autonomía y Descentralización	Yes
25/06/2015	MCMG	Against the government	No
14/08/2015	FUT	Against the reform of the Código de Trabajo and the reform of the constitution	Yes
16/09/2015	CONAIE	Against the reform of the constitution	No

Source Prepared by the author

Table 4.24 National TV networks

	Foundation	Closure	Type	Owner
Ecuavisa	1967		Private	Grupo Alvarado Roca
Teleamazonas	1974		Private	Grupo Egas
Red Telesistema	1960		Private	Grupo González
			Private	
Telerama	1993		Private	Grupo Eljuri
Canal Uno	1992		Private	Grupo Rivas
Televicentro	2016		Private	Grupo González
TC Televisión	1968	2008	Private	Grupo Isaías
	2008		Public	
Gama TV	1977	2008	Private	Grupo Isaías
	2008		Public	
Ecuador TV	2007		Public	

Source Prepared by the author

tors participating in the mobilizations organized by the FUT and the CONAIE since 2014, the police revolt brought about a tremendous disruptive effect for it represented an immediate threat to the survival of the government —and naturally to the survival of President Correa as well. In this regard, the disruptive effect of the police revolt of 2010 certainly outdistanced the disruptive effect of the mobilizations organized by the FUT and the CONAIE since 2014, which successfully counterbalanced the mobilizational power resources of the government.

4.2.4.4 Communicational Power Resources

As explained in Chap. 2, communicational power resources are predicated on the control of the mass media. Unfortunately, the assessment of the communicational power resources of the actors involved in the struggles over the social security system reform in Ecuador represents a very difficult task due to the scarcity of empirical data concerning mass media. Practically no information comes out regarding TV and radio ratings, or newspapers and magazines circulation. Information concerning the control of the media usually comprises contradictions. Despite these difficulties, Tables 4.24 and 4.25 tabularize the available information regarding national TV networks and national newspapers (Tables 4.24 and 4.25).

Table 4.24 brings out the predominance of private TV networks in national television before Correa's coming to power (Table 4.24). In 2006, national television comprised seven private TV networks and no public TV network. Similarly, Table 4.25 brings out the highly concentrated ownership of national newspapers (Table 4.25).

Table 4.25 National newspapers

	Foundation	Closure	Type	Owner
El Universo	1921		Private	Grupo Pérez
Diario Súper	2005		Private	Grupo Pérez
Diario hoy	1982	2014	Private	Grupo Mantilla
El Comercio	1906	2015	Private	Grupo Mantilla
	2015		Private	Grupo González
Últimas Noticias	1938	2015	Private	Grupo Mantilla
	2015		Private	Grupo González
Diario Extra	1974		Private	Grupo Martínez Merchán
Diario Expreso	1973		Private	Grupo Martínez Merchán
El Telégrafo	1884	2008	Private	Grupo Aspiazu
	2008		Public	
PP El Verdadero	2010		Public	

Source Prepared by the author

Seven private economic groups (Grupo Alvarado Roca, Grupo Egas, Grupo Eljuri, Grupo Isaías, Grupo Pérez, Grupo Mantilla, and Grupo Martínez Marchán) practically monopolized mass media, including newspapers, (El Universo, Diario Súper, Diario Hoy, El Comercio, Últimas Noticias, Diario Extra, and Diario Expreso), magazines, radio networks, and four national TV networks (Ecuavisa, Teleamazonas, Telerama, TC Televisión, and Gama TV).

The private media fiercely repudiated Correa's government since its coming to power, contravening its policies with no exception. In line with this, the private media strongly deprecated the social security system reform proposed by the government and regularly publicized in newspapers, magazines, radio, and TV networks the positions of the actors opposed to the reform. In addition, since the inception of the constituent assembly in 2007 the private media disseminated the information that the government purposed to take down the special social security regimes, in order to predispose the police and military forces against the reform.

However, Correa's government increasingly accentuated its position in the mass media system since coming to power. Thus, the government established the first public TV network (Ecuador TV) in 2007 in order to televise the sessions of the constituent assembly. In 2008, the government took over the private TV networks of the bankrupt Grupo Isaías (TC Televisión and Gama TV) and the newspaper of the bankrupt Grupo Aspiazu (El Telégrafo). Finally, the government brought out the second public newspaper (PP El Verdadero) in 2010. In parallel, the government advanced the acquisition of private TV networks (Red Telesistema) and newspapers (El Comercoio and Últimas Noticias) by the Grupo González, an international media group which does not advocate an anti-government position.

All in all, mass media was practically monopolized by a reduced conglomerate of private groups until 2007. After that, Correa's government increasingly branched out the public media structure, considerably advancing its communicational power resources.

4.3 Summary

Following the complementary approach to social policy proposed above, the contextualization of the power struggles over the social security system reform in Ecuador was carried out on the basis of the Poulantzian approach to social policy. As pointed out before, the Poulantzian approach conceptualizes social policy within the context of the construction of hegemony, and therefore, associating social policy with the historical, social, economic, and political conditions in which it materializes. Accordingly, the contextualization carried out a detailed reconstruction of the power struggles over the social security system reform in Ecuador which delineated the social, economic and political conditions in which they came about. With regard to the four "questions" proposed as analytical guidelines for the contextualization of the struggles over the reform (where, what, who, and how), the reconstruction brought out the following.

Concerning the "where" question, the reconstruction brought out that the struggles over the social security system reform materialized in a structural context signed by (1) a largely (though not exclusively) rent-based economic structure, in which the oil revenue represented a central factor for the economy and the state, (2) a highly informal labor market which contravened the development of a "conventional" social security system based on generalized (formal) wage relations.

Against this framework, the social security system reform aimed at the universalization of social security was brought forward by the government with a view toward the incorporation of the population excluded from the existing system of social security. To this aim, a universal state public social security system financed through oil revenue was to be established. For this reason, the struggles over the social security system reform were associated with the struggles over the control of oil resources in a context of extraordinary oil revenue due to the increase of the international oil prices.

Regarding the "what" question, the reconstruction of the power struggles over the reform determined that the points of contention among the contending actors revolved around (1) the continuity of the existing special social security regimes of the military and police forces, and (2) the orientation of the sate contribution to the pension system.

The continuity of the special (and privileged) social security regimes of the military and police forces came across the unification of the existing social security regimes into a universal social security system, as initially proposed by the government. Among other causes, the contention between the government and the military and police forces over this point eventually escalated into an armed police revolt, which flabbergasted Ecuadorian society and compromised the rule of law. In the end, the government forcedly countenanced the continuity of the special regimes of the military and police forces despite holding the absolute majority of the seats in the national assembly.

The orientation of the state contribution to the pension system brought about the confrontation between the members of the general regime of social security administered by the IESS and the government, which purposed to reorientate the state contribution of 40% to the contributory pensions paid by the IESS to the non contributory pensions included in the universal pension system. In spite of the protests organized by the members of the IESS and their political allies, the government could finally canalize the state contribution to pensions of the general regime to the newly created regime of social security for the homemakers.

With respect to the "who" question, the reconstruction of the power struggles over the reform brought out (1) the existence of a manifold entanglement of social, economic, and political actors involved in the struggles over the reforms, whose stances regarding the reforms did not necessarily correspond with their positions in the productive process, as presupposed by political class struggle approaches, and (2) the extraordinary importance of the government as social, economic, and political actor due to its prerogative over the oil sector.

The entanglement of social, economic, and political actors coalesced the government, the political parties, the labor unions, the military and police forces, the indigenous and peasant organizations, and the associations of social security beneficiaries. The positions assumed by the aforementioned actors with regard to the social security system reform commingled their corporative interests and their positioning in the general hegemonic struggles in which the struggles over the reform came about. In some cases, the positions assumed by the actors regarding the reform were principally associated with the defense of their corporative interests. The opposition of the military and police forces to the incorporation of their special social security regimes into a universal social security system, and the opposition of the members of the general regime of social security to the suspension of the state contribution of 40% to their pensions represented paradigmatic examples in this regard. However, in most cases the positions assumed by the contending actors correlated their positioning in the general hegemonic struggles, in which the dualistic logic "for" or "against" the government predetermined their stances. This way, the political parties, labor unions, and indigenous organizations allied to the government advocated the reform whereas the political parties, labor unions, and indigenous organizations opposed to the government repudiated it. Accordingly, the position regarding the social security system reform assumed by the political parties and indigenous organizations, which initially participated in the government alliance but later abandoned it, accompanied this realignment, supporting the reform earlier and rejecting it later. Table 4.26 points out the contending actors included in the preceding reconstruction and their positions regarding the social security system reform proposed by the government (Table 4.26).

The extraordinary importance of the government as a social, economic, and political actor was brought about by the combination of structural and conjunctural factors.

Table 4.26 Position of the contending actors regarding the social security system reform proposed by the government

	Before	After		Before	After
Government			Military and Police Forces		
Government			FAE		2010
Political Parties			PNE		2010
MPD / UP		2010	Indigenous and Peasant Organizations		
MUPP		2010	CONAIE		2010
AP			FEI		
AV		2015	FENOCIN		
RED		-	FEINE		
UNO / CREO			Associations of Social Security Beneficiaries		
PSC / MCMG			CJE		
PRIAN			CCP		2010
PSP			AMSP		2010
Labor Unions			FEUNASSC		2010
FUT		2010	CONFEUNASSC		
PLE	-				
CUT	-				
Employer's Organizations					
CCG					
CGQ					
AMCHAM					
CCAP					
CEE					

: For   : Against   : Neutral   -   : Inexistent

Source Prepared by the author

The structural factors were associated with the aforementioned characteristics of the Ecuadorian economy concerning its dependency on the oil revenue and its elevated level of labor informality. Because of this, the government has historically taken over a structuring role in the economy and the society, both as the main economic driver, and as the exclusive interlocutor of the socially and economically excluded groups. In addition, the government has maximized its participation in the social, economic, and political realms since Correa's coming to power in 2007 (Ospina 2013; Unda 2013). This expansion materialized in the increase of the state economic resources and the enlargement of the state apparatus (Polga-Hecimovich 2013).

Regarding the "how" question, the reconstruction established that (1) the struggles over the social security system reform were not dissociated from the general struggles for hegemony, which came about in manifold ways, and (2) the struggles over the social security system reform were not exclusively determined by the corporative associational and political associational power resources of the contending actors, as reckoned by political class struggle approaches, but they additionally concatenated structural, mobilizational, and communicational arenas in which the participating actors mobilized their power resources.

The relation between the power struggles over the social security system reform and the general struggles for hegemony materialized in two complementary ways. First, it associated the struggles over the social security system reform with the struggles over the reform of the oil and mining sectors, the struggles over the reform of the tax regime and the struggles over the reform of the communications sector. Second, it correlated the positions of the actors involved in the struggles over the social security system reform with their positioning in the general hegemonic struggles, which as mentioned above revolved around the dualistic logic of "for" or "against" the government. For this reason, changes in the positioning of the actors toward the hegemonic project driven by the government brought about changes in the positions of the actors involved in the struggles over the reform, as in the cases of the CONAIE and the MPD. Naturally, the positions of the contending actors regarding the reform did not exclusively predicate on their positioning within the hegemonic struggles, but they commingled their corporative interests as well.

The struggles over the social security system reform were not circumscribed to the institutionalized political arena associated with the "conventional" power resources (corporative associational and political associational), but they concatenated manifold interrelated arenas in which diverse types of power resources (structural, mobilizational, and communicational, etc.) were mobilized by the contending actors. Thereby, the institutional political struggles over the reform, encompassing the struggles over the constitutional articles concerning social security in the constituent assembly, the struggles over the LRLSS 2009 in the Congresillo, and the struggles over the LRLSS 2010, the LRLSS 2014, and the LOJL in the national assembly, came about in connection with the public national mobilizations against the reform of the labor code, the police revolt against the suppression of the bonuses for decorations and promotions, the communicational campaigns for and against the leaked draft bill of the government, and so on.

Following the complementary approach to social policy explained above, the operationalization of the power struggles over the post-neoliberal social security system reform in Ecuador was carried out on the basis of the concept of power resources, initially devised by political class struggle approaches to social policy. However, this concept was not simply reduplicated in its original form but it was completely transubstantiated in order to circumvent its shortcomings when dealing with social policy in the Global South.

Accordingly, the operationalization of the power struggles over the reform correlated the four analytical dimensions ("where", "what", "who", and "how") included in the contextualization of the Ecuadorian case. As pointed out, these four dimensions revolve around (1) the structural underpinnings underlying the struggles over social security system reform, (2) the concrete points of conflict over the reform, (3) the real actors involved in the struggles over the reform, and (4) the channels through which the struggles were canalized.

Regarding the "where" question, the operationalization brought out that (1) the government maximized its oil resources since 2007, and (2) the modcrate decrease of the labor informality since 2007 did not bring about the increase of the corporative associational or the political associational power resources of the labor unions and the labor political parties.

The maximization of the oil resources of the government was partially associated with the steep increase of the international oil prices initiated in 2001. However, it was mainly predicated on the reform of the oil sector promulgated by the government itself between 2007 and 2010. This reform brought about a remarkable increase of the oil resources in possession of the government and a significant decrease of the oil resources in possession of the private oil companies. In spite of this, the Ecuadorian employers' organizations were not really debilitated by the reform for they were not truly commingled with the international oil companies. The reform of the oil sector not only undertook to maximize the oil resources in possession of the government, but it also brought about the expansion of the oil resources in control of the government due to the increase of the oil production carried out by public oil companies. The control over the oil resources exercised by the oil workers and the oil managers did not come under significant changes, remaining very scarce.

The substantial expansion of the economy experienced since 2007 brought about a steep decrease of unemployment and underemployment, and a sheer increase of minimum and average salaries. However, labor informality decreased only moderately, for which labor unions and labor political parties barely capitalized on it in terms of their corporative associational and political associational power resources. Likewise, the moderate decrease of labor informality registered since 2007 did not bring about to the substantial expansion of the tax revenue collected by the government, which was actually predicated on other causes

With regard to the "what" question, the operationalization brought out the specific forms of power resources which the contending actors mobilized in the struggles over the two points of contention concerning the social security system reform: (1) the continuity of the special social security regimes of the police and military forces, administered by the ISSPOL and the ISSFA, and (2) the orientation of the sate contribution to the pension system.

In the case of the struggles over the continuity of the special social security regimes administered by the ISSPOL and the ISSFA, the police and military forces completely repudiated the incorporation of their special regimes into an unified and universal social security system, as intended by the government. Therefore, the police and military forces initially undertook a two-pronged strategy. On the one side, they mobilized their lobbying capacity in secrecy; on the other side, they politically canalized their opposition to the elimination of the special regimes administered by the ISSPOL and the ISSFA through the PSP. However, the apparent failure of this strategy precipitated that a fraction of the police and military forces fell back upon their mobilizational power resources in September 2010,[4] when they carried through

---

[4]Due to the obvious fact that the police and military forces carry out the state monopoly of violence, their mobilizational power resources could be reasonably categorized as "insurrectional" power

a strike which subsequently brought about an open insurrectionary revolt against the rule of law. In addition to this, the police revolt of September 2010 brought out that the struggles over the social security system reform likewise came about in a communicational arena in which the contending actors increasingly mobilized their communicational power resources.

In the case of the orientation of the state contribution to the pension system, the struggles concatenated four consecutive "rounds": (1) the contention over the LRLSS 2009, (2) the dispute over the creation of the BIESS, (3) the contention over the LRLSS 2014, and (4) the contention over the LOJL. The power resources mobilized by the contending actors in these four rounds corresponded to the power resources mobilized in the struggles over the continuity of the special social security regimes of the military and police forces. In fact, as the struggles over the orientation of the state contribution precipitated, the contending actors increasingly mobilized their mobilizational power resources alongside their corporative associational and political associational power resources, just as in the case of the struggles over the continuity of the special regimes. However, since the government successfully dissociated the struggles over the orientation of the state contribution to the pension system from the struggles over the continuity of the special regimes of the police and military forces, the PNE and the FAE did not participate in the struggles over the orientation of the state contribution to the pension system, what naturally diminished the potential power resources which could be mobilized against the reform proposed by the government, especially in terms of ("insurrectionary") mobilizational power resources.

Additionally, the struggles over the orientation of the state contribution of 40% to all pensions paid by the IESS came about in a structural arena, in which the government undertook to canalize the state economic resources to the provision of social security services to the non-insured, whereas the beneficiaries of the existing general regime of social security repudiated the reorientation of the state contribution to the existing pension system and advocated its continuity.

Concerning the "who" question, the operationalization delineated the main characteristics of the actors involved in the struggles over the reform and pointed out what forms of power resources they could eventually mobilize.

The aforementioned centrality of the government was substantiated by the wide range of power resources at its disposal: structural, corporative associational, political associational, mobilizational, and communicational. The political parties concatenated corporative associational, political associational, and, to a lesser extent, mobilizational power resources; the labor unions fell back upon corporative associational, increasingly mobilizational and eventually structural power resources; and the employers' organizations did not participate in the struggles over the social security system reform at all. Among the meso actors, the indigenous and peasant organiza-

---

resources. The illegal character of police and military mobilizations in Ecuador would certainly substantiate this approach. However, for the sake of analytical comparison the "insurrectional" power resources of the police and military forces are conceptually correlated with the mobilizational power resources of the rest of the contending actors throughout this research.

tions commingled corporative associational and mobilizational power resources; the police and military forces fell back upon corporative associational and (despite its insurrectionary character) mobilizational power resources; the associations of social security beneficiaries congregated corporative associational power resources; and the feminist organizations accumulated associational power resources as well.

With regard to the "how" question, the operationalization broke down the corporative associational, political associational, mobilizational, and communicational power resources of the contending actors.

Concerning the corporative associational power resources, the operationalization established that the bloc of the government and the AP (the government party), and the CONAIE fell back upon remarkable corporative associational power resources, whereas the rest of the macro and meso actors were clearly outdistanced by them.

With respect to the political associational power resources the operationalization brought out that the government represented the strongest actor in this regard even though it did not accomplish an absolute majority of its own until 2013, when the AP took over 100 out of 137 seat in the national assembly. Before that, the government could only bring about its bills with the support of its political allies (the MPD, the MUPP, and the RED), which abandoned the government alliance in 2010. Apart from the AP, no political party separately accomplished a comparable level of political associational power resources.

Regarding the mobilizational power resources of the actors involved in the struggles over the social security system reform, the operationalization determined that the actors increasingly mobilized their mobilizational power resources since 2014. In this context, the labor unions and the indigenous and peasant organizations opposed to the government maximized their mobilizational capacity, challenging the "control" of the streets held by the government after years of undisputed supremacy. However, the quantitative and qualitative increase of the public mobilizations carried out by the actors opposed to the government since 2014 was not associated with the social security system reform. In fact, the only public mobilization of national scope related to the social security system reform was carried through by a fraction of the police forces which perpetrated an insurrectionary revolt in September 2010. Even though this mobilization did not conglomerate more than 1000 police members at its peak, it brought about a tremendous disruptive effect due its insurrectional and armed character.

With regard to the communicational power resources, the operationalization brought out that mass media was practically monopolized by a reduced conglomerate of private groups until 2007. Since these groups fiercely repudiated Correa's government, the private media actively publicized in newspapers, magazines, radio, and TV networks the positions of the actors opposed to the social security system reform proposed by the government. However, since the mid 2000s, the government could increasingly branch out the public media structure, advancing its communicational power resources more and more.

References

Acosta A (2011) La reforma a la ley de hidrocarburos y la renegociación de los contratos petroleros. In: La Tendencia, no 11. Friedrich Ebert Stiftung, Centro Andino para la Formación de Líderes Sociales, Quito

Acosta A (2012) Breve historia económica del Ecuador. Corporación Editora Nacional, Quito

Altmann P (2013a) Una breve historia de las organizaciones del movimiento indígena del Ecuador. In: Cuadernos de Investigación, no 12. Pontificia Universidad Católica del Ecuador, Quito

Altmann P (2013b) El movimiento indígena ecuatoriano como movimiento social. In: Revista Andina de Estudios Políticos, vol 3, no 2. Instituto de Estudios Políticos Andinos, Lima

Aricó J (1988) La cola del diablo. Itinerario de Gramsci en América Latina. Puntosur Editores, Buenos Aires

Barrera A (2005) Ecuador: el movimiento indígena entre lo social y lo político. In: Duterme B, Borón A (eds) Movimientos y Poderes de Izquierda en América Latina. Editorial Popular, Madrid

Boffi S (2015) Sistemas de protección social mixtos: pisos de protección social e interacciones con el mercado de trabajo. Estudio del caso de la asignación universal por hijo en Argentina. Facultad Latinoamericana de Ciencias Sociales, Buenos Aires

Borja Nuñez R (2011) Los movimientos sociales en los 80 y 90: La incidencia de las ONG, la iglesia y la izquierda. Centro de Investigaciones CIUDAD, Quito

Botero LF (1998) Estado, cuestión agraria y movilización india en Ecuador. In: Nueva Sociedad, no 153. Friedrich Ebert Stiftung, Buenos Aires

Bretón V (2003) Desarrollo rural y etnicidad en las tierras de Ecuador. In: Bretón V, García F (eds) Estado, etnicidad y movimientos sociales en América Latina. Ecuador en crisis, Barcelona, Icaria

CEPAL (Comisión Económica Para América Latina y el Caribe) (2010) Social panorama of Latin America. Comisión Económica para América Latina y el Caribe, Santiago de Chile

CEPAL (Comisión Económica Para América Latina y el Caribe) (2011) Social panorama of Latin America. Comisión Económica para América Latina y el Caribe, Santiago de Chile

CEPAL (Comisión Económica Para América Latina y el Caribe) (2012) Social panorama of Latin America. Comisión Económica para América Latina y el Caribe, Santiago de Chile

CEPAL (Comisión Económica Para América Latina y el Caribe) (2013) Social panorama of Latin America. Comisión Económica para América Latina y el Caribe, Santiago de Chile

CEPAL (Comisión Económica Para América Latina y el Caribe) (2014a) Social panorama of Latin America. Comisión Económica para América Latina y el Caribe, Santiago de Chile

CEPAL (Comisión Económica Para América Latina y el Caribe) (2014b) Pactos para la igualdad: hacia un futuro sostenible. Comisión Económica para América Latina y el Caribe, Santiago de Chile

Chen MA (2005) Rethinking the informal economy: linkages with the formal economy. United Nations University, Helsinki

Chisaguano S (2006) La población indígena del Ecuador: análisis de estadísticas sociodemográficas. Instituto Nacional de Estadística y Censos, Quito

CIRLSS (Comisión Interinstitucional Para la Reforma a la Ley de Seguridad Social) (2006) Proyecto de ley de reforma de la seguridad social del ecuador. Mimeo, Quito

CONAM (Consejo Nacional de Modernización del Estado) (1995) Propuesta de reforma a la seguridad social. Consejo Nacional de Modernización del Estado, Quito

Constitución Política de la República del Ecuador (1998)

Corral C (2008) Situación del sistema de pensiones en el Ecuador, la perspectiva de la Superintendencia de Bancos y Seguros. In: Espinosa B (ed) Mundos del trabajo: pluralidad y transformaciones contemporáneas. Facultad Latinoamericana de Ciencias Sociales—Sede Ecuador, Quito

CSA (Confederación Sindical de Trabajadores y Trabajadoras de las Américas) (2010) Sindicalización y densidad sindical en las Américas. Confederación Sindical de Trabajadores y Trabajadoras de las Américas, Sao Paulo

Daza E, Santillana A (2015) Movilizaciones en Ecuador: cambio de ciclo y perspectivas críticas. In: La Línea de Fuego. Pensamiento Crítico. http://lalineadefuego.info

Durán Valverde F (2008) Diagnóstico del sistema de seguridad social del Ecuador. Organización Internacional del Trabajo—Oficina Subregional para los Países Andinos, Lima

FENOCIN (Confederación Nacional de Organizaciones Campesinas, Indígenas y Negras) (2004) Noveno Congreso Nacional: Ambato, 20–22 de mayo de 2004. Confederación Nacional de Organizaciones Campesinas, Indígenas y Negras, Quito

Filgueira F (1998) El nuevo modelo de prestaciones sociales en América Latina eficiencia, residualismo y ciudadanía estratificada. In: Roberts B (ed) Ciudadanía y política social latinoamericana. Facultad Latinoamericana de Ciencias Sociales, San José

Filgueira F (2007) Cohesión, riesgo y arquitectura de protección social en América Latina. Comisión Económica para América Latina y el Caribe, Santiago de Chile

Guaranda W (2010) La necesidad imperiosa de reformar una Ley Caduca. Análisis sobre las reformas a la Ley de Hidrocarburos. In: Boletines INREDH. Fundación Regional de Asesoría en Derechos Humanos, Quito. http://inredh.org/index.php?option=com_content&view=article&id=363:analisis-sobre-las-reformas-a-la-ley-de-hidrocarburos&catid=88:boletines-ambientales&Itemid=126

Harari R (2010) Modelo productivo y modelo sindical en Ecuador. In: Ecuador Debate, no 81. Centro Andino de Acción Popular, Quito

Hernández V, Buendía F (2011) Ecuador: avances y desafíos de Alianza PAIS. In: Nueva Sociedad, no 234. Friedrich Ebert Stiftung, Buenos Aires

Hobsbawm E (1959) Primitive rebels: studies in archaic forms of social movements in the 19th and 20th centuries. The University Press, Manchester

Huber E, Stephens J (2005) Successful social policy regimes? Political economy and the structure of social policy in Argentina, Chile, Uruguay, and Costa Rica. University of Notre Dame, Notre Dame

Ibarra H, Ospina P, Ortiz S, León J (2014) Diálogo sobre la Coyuntura: El significado de las elecciones locales del 23 de febrero de 2014. In: Ecuador Debate, no 91. Centro Andino de Acción Popular, Quito

IISS (International Institute for Strategic Studies) (2005) The military balance. International Institute for Strategic Studies, London

ILO (International Labour Organization) (2011) Statistical update on employment in the informal economy. International Labour Organization, Geneva

Johnson S (2004) An empirical examination of union density in six countries: Canada, Ecuador, Mexico, Nicaragua, the United States and Venezuela. Inter-American Development Bank, Washington

Larrea G (2011) Del 30-S a la inflexión del gobierno de Correa. In: La Tendencia, no 11. Friedrich Ebert Stiftung, Centro Andino para la Formación de Líderes Sociales, Quito

León J (2010) Las organizaciones indígenas y el gobierno de Rafael Correa. In: Íconos, no 37. Facultad Latinoamericana de Ciencias Sociales—Sede Ecuador, Quito

Li B (2012) From a micro–macro framework to a micro–meso–macro framework. In: Christensen S, Mitcham C, Li B (eds) Engineering, development and philosophy. Springer Publishing, New York

Lo Vuolo R, Mesa-Lago C (1998) Social security in Ecuador: mixed or substitutive reform? In: Cruz Saco MA, Mesa-Lago C (eds) Do options exist? The reform of pension and health care systems in Latin America. University of Pittsburgh, Pittsburgh

Lora E, Pagés C (1997) La legislación laboral y el proceso de reformas estructurales de América Latina y el Caribe. In: Cárdenas M (ed) Empleo y distribución del ingreso en América Latina: ¿hemos avanzado? TM Editores, Bogotá

Mejía Rivadeneira S (2012a) Rafael Correa: ¿por qué es popular? In: Mantilla S, Mejía Rivadeneira S (eds) Rafael Correa: balance de la revolución ciudadana. Centro Latinoamericano de Estudios Políticos, Editorial Planeta del Ecuador, Quito

Mejía Rivadeneira S (2012b) Rafael Correa: un presidente popular. Causas de los altos índices de aceptación. Facultad Latinoamericana de Ciencias Sociales—Sede Ecuador, Quito

Mejía Rivadeneira S (2012c) Revolución ciudadana: presencia del estado, ingresos y temas pendientes. In: Tribuna Democrática, no 40. Ediciones Legales, Quito

Mesa-Lago C (1984) Social security in Ecuador: final report to the world bank public investment mission. World Bank, Washington

Mesa-Lago C (1989) Financial and economic evaluation of social insurance (IESS) in Ecuador. World Bank, Washington

Mesa-Lago C (1992) The Ecuadorian Social Security Institute (IESS): economic evaluation and options for reform. Health Financing and Sustainability, Quito

Nesbet Montecinos F (2010) Políticos de verde olivo: apuntes sobre el militarismo latinoamericano y su influencia política en las últimas décadas. In: Revista Austral de Ciencias Sociales, no 18. Universidad Austral de Chile, Valdivia

Nieto Puente ZN (2013) Cooperación internacional en materia de seguridad social en el Ecuador. Un análisis de los convenios bilaterales suscritos por el Ecuador durante el período 2008–2012 con aplicabilidad del Instituto Ecuatoriano de Seguridad Social. Universidad Internacional del Ecuador, Quito

Olaya H, Pontón D (2006) Elementos para una reforma policial en el Ecuador. In: Ciudad Segura, no 4. Facultad Latinoamericana de Ciencias Sociales—Sede Ecuador, Quito

Ortiz Crespo P (2015) Ecuador: las protestas y el fracaso de la 'Ley de herencias. In: Nueva Sociedad. Democracia y Política en América Latina. http://nuso.org/documento/ecuador-las-protestas-y-el-fracaso-de-la-ley-de-herencias/

Ospina P (2009) Corporativismo, estado y revolución ciudadana. El Ecuador de Rafael Correa. In: IEE (Instituto de Estudios Ecuatorianos) Estado, movimientos sociales y gobiernos progresistas. Instituto de Estudios Ecuatorianos, Quito

Ospina P (2011a) Ecuador: ¿intento de golpe o motín policial? In: Nueva Sociedad, no 231. Friedrich Ebert Stiftung, Buenos Aires

Ospina P (2013) Estamos haciendo mejor las cosas con el mismo modelo antes que cambiarlo. La revolución ciudadana en Ecuador (2007–2012). In: Arze C, Gómez J, Ospina P, Álvarez V (eds) Promesas en su laberinto: Cambios y continuidades en los gobiernos progresistas de América Latina. Instituto de Estudios Ecuatorianos, Centro de Estudios para el Desarrollo Laboral y Agrario, Centro Internacional Miranda, La Paz

Ospina P (2014) Movilización y organización social en la revolución ciudadana: informe de coyuntura, diciembre de 2014. In: La Línea de Fuego, Pensamiento Crítico. http://lalineadefuego.info

Ospina P (2015) Protesta social, crisis económica y escenario político: Ecuador, junio y julio de 2015. In: La Línea de Fuego, Pensamiento Crítico. http://lalineadefuego.info

Oszlak O (1979) Notas críticas para una teoría de la burocracia estatal. In: Desarrollo Económico, vol 19, no 74. Instituto de Desarrollo Económico y Social, Buenos Aires

Oszlak O (1981) The historical formation of the state in Latin America: some theoretical and methodological guidelines for its study. In: Latin American Research Review, vol 16, no 2. Instituto de Desarrollo Económico y Social, Pittsburgh

Oszlak O (1982) Reflexiones sobre la formación del estado y la construcción de la sociedad argentina. In: Desarrollo Económico, vol 21, no 84. Instituto de Desarrollo Económico y Social, Buenos Aires

Oszlak O, O'Donnell G (1981) Estado y políticas estatales en América Latina: hacia una estrategia de investigación. In: Documento CEDES/CLACSO, no 4. Centro de Estudios de Estado y Sociedad, Buenos Aires

Páez Zumárraga R (2001) Historia de un atraco: de la seguridad social a la inseguridad total. Casa de la Cultura Ecuatoriana "Benjamín Carrión", Quito

Pérez Enríquez DF (2004) Los liderazgos militares-civiles: los casos de Ecuador y Venezuela. Universidad Andina Simón Bolívar, Quito

PNE (Policía Nacional del Ecuador) (2015) Polinoticias, vol 4, no 35. Policía Nacional del Ecuador, Quito

Polga-Hecimovich J (2013) Ecuador: estabilidad institucional y la consolidación de poder de Rafael Correa. In: Revista de Ciencia Política, vol 33, no 1. Centro de Estudios de Estado y Sociedad, Santiago de Chile

Pontón D (2009) Policía comunitaria y cambio institucional en el Ecuador. Facultad Latinoamericana de Ciencias Sociales - Sede Ecuador, Quito

Portantiero JC (1981) Los usos de Gramsci. Folios Ediciones, México

Portantiero JC (1985) Notas sobre crisis y producción de acción hegemónica. In: Labastida J, Del Campo M (eds) Hegemonía y alternativas políticas en América Latina (Seminario de Morelia). Siglo XXI Editores, México

Portantiero JC (1988) La producción de un orden. Ensayos sobre la democracia entre el estado y la sociedad. Ediciones Nueva Visión, Buenos Aires

Quintero López R (2005) Electores contra partidos en un sistema político de mandos. Ediciones Abya-Yala, Quito

Ramírez R (2010) La transición ecuatoriana hacia el buen vivir. In: León I (ed) Sumak kawsay/buen vivir y cambios civilizatorios. Fundación de Estudios, Acción y Participación Social, Quito

Ramírez Gallego F (2011) Fragmentación, reflujo y desconcierto. Movimientos sociales y cambio político en el Ecuador (2000–2010). In: Modonesi M, Rebón J (eds) Una década en movimiento. Luchas populares en América Latina en el amanecer del siglo XXI. Consejo Latinoamericano de Ciencias Sociales, Buenos Aires

RESDAL (Red de Seguridad y Defensa de América Latina) (2012) Atlas comparatico de la defensa en América Latina y el Caribe. Red de Seguridad y Defensa de América Latina, Buenos Aires

RESDAL (Red de Seguridad y Defensa de América Latina) (2014) Atlas comparatico de la defensa en América Latina y el Caribe. Red de Seguridad y Defensa de América Latina, Buenos Aires

Sasso J (2011) La seguridad social en el Ecuador, historia y cifras. In: Actuar en Mundos Plurales, no 6. Facultad Latinoamericana de Ciencias Sociales - Sede Ecuador, Quito

Schuldt J, Acosta A (2006) Petróleo, rentismo y subdesarrollo: ¿una maldición sin solución? In: Nueva Sociedad, no 204. Friedrich Ebert Stiftung, Buenos Aires

SENPLADES (Secretaría Nacional de Planificación y Desarrollo) (2011) Tendencias de la participación ciudadana en el Ecuador. Secretaría Nacional de Planificación y Desarrollo, Quito

SENPLADES (Secretaría Nacional de Planificación y Desarrollo) (2013) Empresas públicas y planificación: Su rol en la transformación social y productiva. Secretaría Nacional de Planificación y Desarrollo, Quito

Sojo A (ed) (2009) Hacia la universalidad, con solidaridad y eficiencia: el financiamiento de la protección social en países pobres y desiguales. Naciones Unidas, Santiago de Chile

Tarrow S (1994) Power in movement: social movements and contentious politics. Cambridge University Press, Cambridge

Thompson EP (1963) The making of the English working class. Victor Gollancz, London

Thullen P (1987) Informe sobre aspectos escogidos del seguro social ecuatoriano, Quito

Tilly C (1978) From mobilization to revolution. McGraw-Hill, New York

Torres LF (2008) Seguridad social y derechos sociales: los avances en la Asamblea Constituyente del Ecuador. In: Debate Constitucional, no 5. Fundación Hanss Seidel, Quito

Unda M (2013) Modernización del capitalismo y reforma del Estado. In: Cuvi J, Machado D, Oviedo A, Sierra N (eds) El correísmo al desnudo. Montecristi Vive, Quito

Vallejo G (2015) Los trabajadores agrupados en el F.U.T., proceso de lucha y perspectivas. In: La Tendencia, no 14. Cooperativa Riobamba, Quito

Viteri Llanga J (2008) La seguridad social ecuatoriana y su reforma. In: Revista Seguridad Social, no 256. Conferencia Interamericana de Seguridad Social, México

Constitutions, Laws, Decrees and Regulations

Constitución de la República del Ecuador (2008)
Ley de Jubilación, Montepío Civil, Ahorro y Cooperativa, Registro Oficial 591, 13/03/1928
Ley de Seguro Social Obligatorio, Decreto Supremo 12, 02/10/1935
Ley de Extensión del Seguro Social Campesino, Registro Oficial 124, 20/11/1981
Ley de Seguridad Social de las Fuerzas Armadas Registro Oficial Suplementario 995, 07/08/1992
Ley de Seguridad Social de la Policía Nacional Registro Oficial, 707, 01/06/1995
Ley de Seguridad social, Registro Oficial 465, 30/11/2001
Ley de Minería, Registro Oficial 517 29/01/2009
Ley Reformatoria a la Ley de Hidrocarburos y a la Ley de Régimen Tributario Interno, Registro
   Oficial 244, 27/07/2010)
Ley Reformatoria a la Ley de Seguridad Social, a la Ley de Seguridad Social de las Fuerzas Armadas
   y a la Ley de Seguridad Social de la Policía Nacional, Registro Oficial 559, 30/03/2009)
Ley del Banco del Instituto Ecuatoriano de Seguridad Social, Registro Oficial Complementario 587,
   11/05/2009)
Ley Orgánica del Servicio Público, Registro Oficial 294, 06/10/2010
Ley Reformatoria a la Ley de Seguridad Social, Registro Oficial 323 18/11/2010
Ley Reformatoria a la Ley De Seguridad Social y a la Ley del Banco del Instituto Ecuatoriano de
   Seguridad Social para la Administración de los Fondos Complementarios Previsionales Cerrados,
   Registro Oficial 379, 20/11/2014
Ley Orgánica para la Justicia Laboral y Reconocimiento del Trabajo en el Hogar, Registro Oficial
   483 20/04/2015

Statistical Databases

BCE (Banco Central del Ecuador) (2015). https://www.bce.fin.ec/
CEPALSTAT (2015). http://estadisticas.cepal.org/cepalstat/WEB_CEPALSTAT/Portada.asp?idio
   ma=e
CODENPE (Consejo Nacional de Desarrollo de las Nacionalidades Indígenas del Ecuador) (2007).
   www.codenpe.gov.ec
INECE (Instituto Nacional de Estadística y Censos del Ecuador) (2015). http://www.ecuadorencif
   ras.gob.ec/

Chapter 5
Comparative Analysis of the Power Struggles over the Post-neoliberal Social Security System Reforms in Venezuela and Ecuador

Based on the preceding analyses of both research cases, this chapter carries out a comparative analysis between them. Following the method of comparative case studies known as "structured, focused comparison" as defined by George and Bennett (George and Bennet 2005: 67), the comparative analysis is structuralized into the four analytical questions utilized above ("where," "what," "who," and "how"). Thus, the comparative analysis correlates the answers to the "where," "what," "who," and "how" questions obtained for both research cases in order to determine the similarities and dissimilarities between them.

5.1 Comparative Analysis Regarding the "Where" Question

With regard to the where question, the contextualization brought out that the struggles over the social security system reforms in Venezuela and Ecuador materialized in a structural context characterized by (1) a largely rent-based economic structure, in which the oil revenue represented a central factor for the economy and for the state and (2) a highly informal labor market, which precluded the development of a "conventional" social security system based on generalized (formal) wage relations.

Beyond the rent-based character of both economies, Venezuela was characterized by a higher level of oil dependency than Ecuador. Besides, the oil dependency of Venezuela was maximized even more since Chávez' coming to power in 1999, whereas the oil dependency of Ecuador diminished since Correa's coming to power in 2007, in part because of the aforementioned tax reform carried out by Correa's government. Still, the performance of the Ecuadorian economy is strongly associated with the vicissitudes of the oil revenue up to the present, as substantiated above. The high level of informality characterized the labor market of both countries, without distinctions.

© Springer Nature Switzerland AG 2019
E. L. Bistoletti, *The Power Struggles over the Post-neoliberal Social Security System Reforms in Venezuela and Ecuador*, The Latin American Studies Book Series, https://doi.org/10.1007/978-3-319-98168-0_5

Regarding the "where" question, the operationalization of the struggles over the social security system reforms in Venezuela and Ecuador brought out that (1) the Venezuelan and the Ecuadorian governments maximized their oil resources since they carried out their respective oil reforms in 2001 and 2007 and (2) the moderate decrease of the labor informality in Venezuela since 2001 and in Ecuador since 2007 did not bring about the expansion of the corporative associational and the political associational power resources of the labor unions and the working class political parties.

The oil reforms effectuated by the governments of Chávez and Correa maximized their oil resources in terms of possession and control of the oil resources. Based on their reforms of the oil sector, the Venezuelan and the Ecuadorian governments could capitalize on the steep increase of the international oil prices occurring between 2002 and 2014. The labor situation notably ameliorated in terms of unemployment and minimal wages since 2004 in Venezuela and since 2007 in Ecuador. In the case of Ecuador, since Correa's coming to power the average wages came under a remarkable improvement as well. Besides, the dollarization of the Ecuadorian economy circumvented the rise of inflation, whereas the nominal wage increases achieved in Venezuela were partially depreciated by elevated inflation. Beyond these differences, the labor informality did not substantially come down in either country. In fact, this common situation represented the basis for the post-neoliberal social security system reforms in Venezuela and Ecuador, as they undertook to establish a universal social security system in which the access to social security was not circumscribed to the registered workers.

All in all, with regard to the "where" question the analysis of the power struggles over the post-neoliberal social security system reforms in Venezuela and Ecuador brought out substantial resemblances concerning their economic structures, and labor markets, and the changes occurring in them since the left-wing governments of Chávez and Correa took over power.

5.2 Comparative Analysis Regarding the "What" Question

Regarding the "what" question, the reconstruction of the power struggles over the social security system reforms in Venezuela and Ecuador determined that in the case of Venezuela the points of contention were associated with (1) the introduction of individual capitalization pension funds managed by private administrators and (2) the continuity of the existing collective capitalization pension funds known as "special pension regimes", while in the case of Ecuador, the points of contention revolved around (1) the continuity of the existing special social security regimes of the military and police forces and (2) the orientation of the state contribution to the pension system.

Even though the points of contention over the reforms in Venezuela and Ecuador may come across as dissimilar, they actually presuppose considerable similarities.

   The fact that the introduction of individual capitalization pension funds admin-istered by private administrators represented the bone of contention in the struggles over the social security system reform in Venezuela was predicated on the historical context in which the struggles over the reform came about. As recounted above, the struggles over the post-neoliberal reform promoted by Chávez' government already started out in 1999 as a response to the ongoing neoliberal social security system reform initiated by the government of Caldera. In this early context, the hegemony of the Washington consensus still carried over among the Latin American governments, advancing the focalization of the noncontributory social assistance and the privati-zation of the contributory social insurances. For this reason, the reform proposed by Chávez' government aimed at the universalization of social security directly contra-vened the ongoing reform aimed at its privatization. Just as in the case of Venezuela, the struggles over the privatization of social security in Ecuador came about during the late 1990s and the early 2000s. However, these struggles were not associated with the introduction of a post-neoliberal social security system reform aimed at universal-ization, but they revolved around the defense of the existing social security regimes. As explained above, the privatization of the social insurances in Ecuador was con-clusively knocked down in 2005, when the Tribunal Constitucional finally struck it down. For this reason, when the struggles over the post-neoliberal reform promoted by Correa's government broke out in 2007, the contention over the privatization of social security had already been determined.

   The struggles over the continuity of the existing collective capitalization pen-sion funds known as "special pension regimes" in Venezuela and the struggles over the continuity of the existing special social security regimes of the military and police forces in Ecuador presupposed a common kernel, as in both cases the strug-gles revolved around the continuity of the extraordinary social security regimes of particular social groups. These regimes provided substantially better social security services and allowances than the general regime with state funding. Only the scope of the extraordinary regimes and the social groups affiliated to them divaricated between both countries. In the case of Venezuela, in the absence of a unified pension system, the special pension regimes proliferated since the 1950s, approximating 400 at the present. In the case of Ecuador, only the military and police forces were advantaged with extraordinary social security regimes, which were established in the early 1990s in order to preclude the military and police forces from the forthcoming privatization of the social security system. Before that, the Ecuadorian military and police forces were comprised in the general social security regime just as the rest of the registered workers. In contrast, the social security regime of the Venezuelan military forces had always been dissociated from the general social security regime, even before the introduction of the special social security regimes in the 1950s. Despite these differ-ences, both the struggles over the continuity of the existing "special pension regimes" in Venezuela and the struggles over the continuity of the existing special social secu-rity regimes of the military and police forces in Ecuador likewise revolved around the defense of the existing prerogatives of particular social groups, which contravened the establishment of a universal and unified social security system as proposed by the governments of Chávez and Correa.

The struggles over the orientation of the state contribution to the pension system in Ecuador were correlated with the defense of the prerogatives of particular social groups as well. Even though, in this case, the social groups opposed to the reform were not associated with extraordinary social security regimes, they basically repudiated the reorientation of the 40% state contribution to the general pension regime towards the provision of social security services and allowances for the people excluded from social security.

With regard to the "what" question, the operationalization of the power struggles over the social security system reforms in Venezuela and Ecuador determined what power resources the contending actors mobilized in the struggles over the aforementioned points of contention.

In this respect, the operationalization brought out that the contending actors carried out analogous strategies for the mobilization of their power resources in both countries, regardless of the points of contention at issue. Put briefly; the actors initially mobilized their corporative associational, their political associational and, to some extent, their communicational power resources. If they did not accomplish satisfactory results this way, they subsequently mobilized their structural, their mobilizational, and their fully-fledged communicational power resources. In this case, the contending actors could even undertake insurrectionary actions, depending on how confrontations came along.

In a nutshell, with regard to the "what" question the analysis of the power struggles over the post-neoliberal social security system reforms in Venezuela and Ecuador established considerable resemblances concerning the points of contention around which the struggles revolved and the power resources mobilized by the involved contending actors.

5.3 Comparative Analysis Regarding the "Who" Question

Concerning the "who" question, the contextualization of the power struggles over the social security system reforms in Venezuela and Ecuador brought out two findings: (1) the existence of manifold and interrelated social, economic and political actors involved in the struggles over the reforms, whose stances on the reforms did not necessarily correspond with their positions in the productive process, as presupposed by the political class struggle approach and (2) the extraordinary importance of the government as a social, economic, and political actor due to its prerogative over the oil sector.

The ascertainment of the complex arrays of actors involved in the struggles over the reforms in both countries corroborated the criticism expounded above regarding the restricted analytical focus of the political class struggle approach. In addition, it substantiated the capacity of the theoretical approach of this research to acknowledge the multiplicity of social, economic and political actors involved in the struggles over social policy.

Next to the labor unions and the class political parties presupposed by the political class struggle approach, the entanglement of actors involved in the struggles over the reforms additionally comprised the government, nonclass political parties, employers' organizations, military and police forces, peasant and indigenous organizations, professional associations, lobby groups, nongovernmental organizations, and associations of social security beneficiaries.

In the context of the struggles over the reforms, the defining characteristics of the contending actors were not determined by their position in the productive process, as presupposed by the political class struggle approach but, instead, they were associated with their positions in relation to the existing social security systems. In this sense, the actors who capitalized on state-subsidized social security regimes, which provided comparatively superior social security services, could be categorized in general terms as opponents of the post-neoliberal social security system reforms. This group comprised diverse actors such as the affiliates of Venezuela's special social security regimes associated with the public sector, who repudiated both the neoliberal privatization and the post-neoliberal incorporation of their special regimes into a universal social security system, or the affiliates of Ecuador's special police and military social security regimes, who contravened the incorporation of their special regimes into a universal social security system, or even the affiliates of Ecuador's general social security regime, who repudiated the reallocation of the state contribution of 40% to their pension regime into the pension regime of homemakers and informal workers. In contrast, the actors who were precluded from the existing social security systems could be categorized in general terms as supporters of the post-neoliberal social security system reforms. This group also comprised diverse actors such as peasants, urban informal workers, domestic workers, homemakers, etc., who were not necessarily represented by corporative organizations but politically accompanied the left-wing governments.

Naturally, the relative importance of each of these actors in the struggles over the social security system reforms in both countries brought out particularities depending on the case. In Venezuela, the employers' organizations represented a primary actor in the struggles over the reform from the very beginning, whereas in Ecuador, they barely participated in them. Similarly, in Venezuela, the professional associations, lobby groups, and nongovernmental organizations carried out a much more significant role than in Ecuador. In contrast, in Ecuador, the military and police forces actively participated in the struggles over the reform, whereas in Venezuela, they were precluded from them. Likewise, in Ecuador, the indigenous organizations represented a primary actor in the struggles over the reform, whereas in Venezuela, they did not participate in them at all.

In principle, the positions assumed by the social, economic, and political actors with regard to the social security system reforms commingled their corporative interests and their general political positions. However, the contextualization determined that the escalation of the hegemonic struggles between government and opposition increasingly brought about the subordination of the actors' corporative interests regarding the reforms to their positioning in the hegemonic struggles, in which the dualistic logic "for" or "against" the government predetermined their positions in all regards. In this context and against the assumptions of political class struggle approaches, the largest Venezuelan and Ecuadorian labor unions and parties repudiated the social security system reforms because they contravened the governments of Chávez and Correa.

The extraordinary importance of the governments as social, economic, and political actors in Venezuela and Ecuador was predicated on the combination of structural and conjunctural factors. The structural factors were associated with the aforementioned rent-based character of the Venezuelan and Ecuadorian economies, which maximized the economic and political power of the governments due to their prerogative over the oil sector. Because of this, in both countries, the governments have historically taken over a structuring role in economy and society, both as the main economic drivers, and as the exclusive interlocutors of the socially and economically excluded groups. In addition, the Venezuelan and Ecuadorian governments have maximized their participation in the social, economic, and political realms since the assumptions of Chávez and Correa in 1999 and 2007, respectively. This expansion comprised the increase of the state participation in the economy and the enlargement of the state apparatus

With respect to the "who" question, the operationalization of the power struggles over the reforms in Venezuela and Ecuador delineated the main characteristics of the contending actors and pointed out what types of power resources they could eventually mobilize.

With few exceptions, the power resources at the disposal of the Venezuelan social, economic, and political actors corresponded to the power resources of the Ecuadorian social, economic, and political actors and vice versa. The aforementioned centrality of the governments in both countries was corroborated by the wide range of power resources at their disposal: structural, corporative associational, political associational, mobilizational, and communicational. Both the Venezuelan and Ecuadorian political parties comprised corporative associational, political associational and to a lesser extent, mobilizational power resources. The labor unions fell back upon corporative associational and mobilizational power resources in both cases, but the Venezuelan labor unions additionally comprised structural power resources. The employers' organizations fell back upon corporative associational, mobilizational, communicational, and structural power resources in Venezuela, however, the employers' organizations barely participated in the power struggles over the social security system reform in Ecuador. Among the meso actors, the Ecuadorian peasant and indigenous organizations comprised corporative associational and mobilizational power resources in Ecuador, whereas the Venezuelan peasant and indigenous organizations did not predicate their positions regarding the social security system reform proposed by Chávez' government. Similarly, the Ecuadorian police and military forces mobilized their corporative associational and mobilizational (insurrectionary) power resources in connection with the reform proposed by Correa's government. In contrast, the Venezuelan military forces did not participate in the struggles over the reform as they were precluded from it from the beginning.

All in all, with regard to the "who" question the analysis of the power struggles over the post-neoliberal social security system reforms in Venezuela and Ecuador established considerable resemblances regarding the social, economic, and political actors involved in the struggles over the reforms, their positions concerning the reforms, the power resources at their disposal and the extraordinary importance of the government as social, economic, and political actor due to its prerogative over the oil sector.

5.4 Comparative Analysis Regarding the "How" Question

Regarding the "how" question, the reconstruction of the power struggles over the social security system reforms in Venezuela and Ecuador brought out that (1) the struggles over the social security system reform were not dissociated from the general struggles for hegemony, which came about in manifold ways and (2) the struggles over the social security system reform were not exclusively determined by the corporative associational and political associational power resources of the contending actors, as reckoned by the class center approach, but they additionally comprised structural, mobilizational, and communicational arenas in which the participating actors mobilized their power resources.

The contextualization of the power struggles over the reforms in Venezuela and Ecuador brought out that they were associated with the power struggles for hegemony between government and opposition. This parallelism actually determined the dissimilar outcome of the social security system reforms in both countries, as the hegemonic struggles in Venezuela and Ecuador came about differently.

In the case of Venezuela, the radicalization of the hegemonic struggles triggered by the reform of the oil and agriculture sectors initially brought down the obstacles to the sanction of the reform proposed by Chávez government, because it took down the internal opposition to the reform from within the government and the government party, as well as the opposition from the social, economic, and political actors antagonistic to the government. However, the hegemonic struggles between government and opposition subsequently brought about the establishment of a parallel structure of social policy, including social security, which eventually contravened the implementation of the system of social security prescribed by the LOSSS sanctioned in December 2002. In consequence, after more than 10 years since its sanction, the implementation of the social security system reform has not been carried out.

Contrarily, in the case of Ecuador, the reform of the oil and mining sectors accomplished by Correa's government did not precipitate a radical escalation of the hegemonic struggles between government and opposition which eventually brought about the final defeat of the opposition, as it came about in Venezuela. In fact, despite the strengthening of Correa's government in economic and political terms since 2007, the insurrectionary police revolt perpetrated in September 2010 brought out the potential insurrectionary power of some sectors of the opposition which repudiated the social security system reform intended by the government. For this reason, the government determined to carry out a stepwise strategy, even though it could have autonomously brought out its initially intended law for the social security system reform after taking over the absolute majority of the national assembly in 2013. In consequence, it countenanced the demanded continuity of the special social security regimes of the police and military forces, superseded its originally intended thoroughgoing reform with subsequent partial reforms of the existing social security system, and correlated the creation of a special social security regime for homemakers with the reorientation of the state contribution of 40% to the pensions of the existing general pension regime, thereby counterbalancing the opposition of the affiliates of the general pension regime with the support of the homemakers. Based on this stepwise strategy, Correa's government successfully brought about a substantial part of its originally intended reform.

Both in Venezuela and Ecuador, the struggles over the social security system reforms came out through manifold ways of expression, which materialized in several interconnected arenas of confrontation. These comprised the institutionalized political arena as well as structural, mobilizational, and communicational arenas. For this reason, the struggles over the social security system reform were not exclusively associated with the mobilization of corporative associational and political associational power resources, as reckoned by political class struggle approaches, but they were increasingly determined by the mobilization of structural, mobilizational, and communicational power resources by the contending actors.

With regard to the "how" question, the operationalization of the power struggles over the reforms in Venezuela and Ecuador broke down the corporative associational, political associational, mobilizational, and communicational power resources of the contending actors.

In both countries, the left-wing governments and their government parties accumulated extraordinary structural, corporative associational, political associational, mobilizational, and communicational power resources since coming to power. In the case of Venezuela, the government and the government party accomplished an even higher amount of power resources than in the case of Ecuador, especially regarding their massive mobilizational capacity.

The political parties allied to the governments of Chávez and Correa either carried over their limited power resources or diminished them, as they could not successfully materialize as autonomous alternatives of power. The case of the AV in Ecuador probably represented the only exception to this. The political parties which initially accompanied the left-wing governments but later abandoned them did not advance their power resources either. The labor unions allied to the government diminished their power resources as well, in line with the general weakening of all labor unions in Venezuela and Ecuador.

The social, economic, and political actors opposed to the left-wing governments in Venezuela and Ecuador conglomerated substantial power resources, including remarkable mobilizational power resources. However, in the case of Venezuela, the power resources of the political parties, labor unions, and employers' organizations opposed to the government drastically decreased after their total defeat in 2004, which culminated the all or nothing struggles for hegemony initiated in December 2001 between government and opposition. On the contrary, in the case of Ecuador, the power resources of the political parties, labor unions, and peasant and indigenous organizations have increasingly advanced since 2014.

In a nutshell, with regard to the "how" question, the analysis of the power struggles over the post-neoliberal social security system reforms in Venezuela and Ecuador brought out substantial differences concerning the effects of the struggles for hegemony between government and opposition in both countries.

The fact that the implementation of the social security system reform was not carried out in Venezuela, where Chávez' government accumulated extraordinary power resources and the opposition backed down after 2004, brought out that the government backed down with the social security system reform as originally intended. Instead, the government advanced the establishment of a parallel structure of social policy based on the social programs known as Misiones Bolivarianas and Grandes Misiones. This changeover was associated with the development of the struggles for hegemony between government and opposition which, after 2004, brought about the extension of the missions as a substantial part of the political project of Chávez' government.

In contrast, the social security system reform has been increasingly carried through in Ecuador, where the power resources controlled by Correa's government did not correspond to those controlled by Chávez' government, and the opposition did not back down after a total defeat as in Venezuela. This divergent development was predicated on the fact that the struggles for hegemony between government and opposition in Ecuador did not precipitate the establishment of a parallel structure of social policy at the expense of the originally intended social security system reform, as it came about in Venezuela. On the contrary, the hegemonic struggles in Ecuador brought out the potential insurrectionary power of some sectors of the opposition opposed to the reform. Against this background, the government had to restructuralize its strategy in this regard, undertaking a stepwise approach. Based on this tactic, Correa's government successfully brought about a substantial part of its originally intended social security system reform.

5.5 Conclusions

The comparative analysis of the power struggles over the social security system reforms in Venezuela and Ecuador accomplished remarkable results. Table 5.1 recapitulates these results following the aforementioned "where," "what," "who," and "how" questions (Table 5.1).

Regarding the "where," "what," and "who" questions, the contextualization and the operationalization of the struggles in both countries established extensive resemblances. However, with regard to the "how" question, the contextualization and the operationalization of the struggles in both countries brought out substantial divergences.

In the case of the "where" question, the comparative analysis of the power struggles over the post-neoliberal social security system reforms in Venezuela and Ecuador

Table 5.1 Comparative analysis results

	Venezuela	Ecuador
"Where" question	*Contextualization*	*Contextualization*
	(1) The structural context is characterized by a largely rent-based economic structure, in which the oil revenue represented a central factor for the economy and for the state	(1) The structural context is characterized by a largely rent-based economic structure, in which the oil revenue represented a central factor for the economy and for the state
	(2) In addition, the structural context is characterized by a highly informal labor market, which precluded the development of a "conventional" social security system based on generalized (formal) wage relations	(2) In addition, the structural context is characterized by a highly informal labor market, which precluded the development of a "conventional" social security system based on generalized (formal) wage relations
	Operationalization	
	(1) Chávez' government maximized its oil resources since it carried out the oil reform in 2001	(1) Correa's government maximized its oil resources since it carried out the oil reform in 2001
	(2) The moderate decrease of the labor informality since 2001 did not bring about the expansion of the corporative associational and the political associational power resources of the labor unions and the working class political parties	(2) The moderate decrease of the labor informality since 2001 did not bring about the expansion of the corporative associational and the political associational power resources of the labor unions and the working class political parties
"What" question	*Contextualization*	
	The power struggles over the social security system reform revolved around:	The power struggles over the social security system reform revolved around:
	(1) The introduction of individual capitalization pension funds managed by private administrators	(1) The continuity of the existing special social security regimes of the military and police forces
	(2) The continuity of the existing collective capitalization pension funds known as "special pension regimes"	(2) The orientation of the state contribution to the pension system

(continued)

Table 5.1 (continued)

	Venezuela	Ecuador
	Operationalization	
	The contending actors initially mobilized their corporative associational, political associational, and, to some extent, communicational power resources. If necessary, they subsequently mobilized their structural, mobilizational (including insurrectionary actions), and fully fledged communicational power resources	The contending actors initially mobilized their corporative associational, political associational, and, to some extent, communicational power resources. If necessary, they subsequently mobilized their structural, mobilizational (including insurrectionary actions), and fully fledged communicational power resources
"Who" question	*Contextualization*	
	(1) The actors involved in the struggles over the social security system reform commingled the government, political parties, labor unions, employers' organizations, professional associations, lobby groups, and nongovernmental organizations (2) The stances of the contending actors regarding the social security system reform did not necessarily correspond with their positions in the productive process as presupposed by the political class struggle approach (3) The government represents an extraordinary social, economic, and political actor due to its prerogative over the oil sector	(1) The actors involved in the struggles over the social security system reform commingled the government, political parties, labor unions, peasant and indigenous organizations, and police and military forces (2) The stances of the contending actors regarding the social security system reform did not necessarily correspond with their positions in the productive process as presupposed by the political class struggle approach (3) The government represents an extraordinary social, economic, and political actor due to its prerogative over the oil sector

(continued)

Table 5.1 (continued)

Venezuela	Ecuador
Operationalization	
The government fell back upon structural, corporative associational, political associational, mobilizational, and communicational power resources. The political parties comprised corporative associational, political associational and, to a lesser extent, mobilizational power resources. The labor unions fell back upon structural, corporative associational and mobilizational power resources. The employers' organizations comprised corporative associational, mobilizational, communicational, and structural power resources. The professional associations fell back upon corporative associational power resources. The lobby groups and nongovernmental organizations comprised corporative associational power resources	The government fell back upon structural, corporative associational, political associational, mobilizational, and communicational power resources. The political parties comprised corporative associational, political associational and, to a lesser extent, mobilizational power resources. The labor unions fell back upon corporative associational and mobilizational power resources. The peasant and indigenous organizations comprised corporative associational, and mobilizational power resources. The police and military forces mobilized corporative associational and mobilizational (insurrectionary) power resources

(continued)

Table 5.1 (continued)

"How" question	Venezuela	Ecuador
	Contextualization	
	(1) The struggles over the social security system reform were not dissociated from the general struggles for hegemony, which came about in manifold ways	(1) The struggles over the social security system reform were not dissociated from the general struggles for hegemony, which came about in manifold ways
	(2) The struggles over the social security system reform were not exclusively determined by the corporative associational and political associational power resources of the contending actors, as reckoned by the class center approach, but they additionally comprised structural, mobilizational, and communicational arenas in which the participating actors mobilized their power resources	(2) The struggles over the social security system reform were not exclusively determined by the corporative associational and political associational power resources of the contending actors, as reckoned by the class center approach, but they additionally comprised structural, mobilizational, and communicational arenas in which the participating actors mobilized their power resources
	(3) The radicalization of the hegemonic struggles between government and opposition initially brought down the obstacles to the sanction of the social security system reform since it took down the internal opposition to the reform from within the government and the government party. However, the hegemonic struggles subsequently brought about the establishment of a parallel structure of social policy (including social security), which eventually precluded the implementation of the system of social security prescribed by the LOSSS sanctioned in December 2002	(3) The hegemonic struggles between government and opposition did not bring about a final defeat of the opposition. Correa's government maximized its power resources since 2007, but the insurrectionary police revolt perpetrated in September 2010 brought out the potential insurrectionary power of some sectors of the opposition which repudiated the social security system reform intended by government. In this context, the government determined to carry out a stepwise strategy, even though it could have autonomously brought out its initially intended law for the social security system reform after taking over the absolute majority of the national assembly in 2013

(continued)

Table 5.1 (continued)

	Venezuela	Ecuador
	Operationalization	
	(1) The government and the government party accumulated extraordinary structural, corporative associational, political associational, mobilizational, and communicational power resources	(1) The government and the government party accumulated substantial structural, corporative associational, political associational, mobilizational, and communicational power resources
	(2) The political parties allied with the government either preserved their limited power resources or decreased them, as they could not successfully materialize as autonomous alternatives of power. The political parties which initially accompanied Chávez' government but later abandoned it did not advance their power resources either	(2) The political parties allied with the government either held back their limited power resources or decreased them, as they could not successfully materialize as autonomous alternatives of power, with the only exception of the AV. The political parties which initially accompanied Chávez' government but later abandoned it did not advance their power resources either
	(3) The labor unions allied to the government diminished their power resources as well, in line with the general weakening of all labor unions	(3) The labor unions allied to the government diminished their power resources as well, in line with the general weakening of all labor unions
	(4) The social, economic, and political actors opposed to Chávez' government conglomerated substantial power resources, including remarkable mobilizational power resources. However, the power resources of the political parties, labor unions, and employers' organizations opposed to the government drastically decreased after their total defeat in 2004, which culminated the all or nothing struggles for hegemony initiated in December 2001 between government and opposition	(4) The social, economic, and political actors opposed to Correa's government conglomerated substantial power resources, including remarkable mobilizational power resources, especially after 2014

Source Prepared by the author

established substantial resemblances concerning their largely rent-based economic structures and their highly informal labor markets. Precisely because of these common characteristics, the governments of Chávez and Correa brought forward the reforms of the existing social security systems which purposed to establish universal social security systems beyond the limits of formal employment.

Additionally, the comparative analysis made out considerable parallelisms regarding the changes occurred in the economic structures and labor markets of both countries since the left-wing governments took over power. In both cases, the governments could successfully carry through exhaustive reforms of the oil sectors, which maximized their possession and control of the oil resources. However, they could not bring about substantial reductions in labor informality.

In the case of the "what" question, the comparative analysis of the power struggles over the post-neoliberal social security system reforms in Venezuela and Ecuador brought out extensive similarities concerning the points of contention around which the struggles revolved. In both countries, the points of contention were associated with the defense of the existing prerogatives of particular social groups, which contravened the establishment of a universal and unified social security system as proposed by the governments of Chávez and Correa. As explained above, the fact that the introduction of individual capitalization pension funds administered by private administrators represented the bone of contention in the struggles over the reform in Venezuela but not in the struggles over the reform in Ecuador was basically predicated on the historic context in which the struggles came about. When the struggles over the post-neoliberal reform promoted by Correa's government started out in Ecuador in 2007, the contention over the privatization of social security had already settled down.

Similarly, the comparative analysis determined that the power resources mobilized by the contending actors in Venezuela corresponded to the power resources mobilized by the contending actors in Ecuador, comprising corporative associational, political associational, structural, mobilizational, and communicational power resources in both cases.

In the case of the "who" question, the comparative analysis of the power struggles over the post-neoliberal social security system reforms in Venezuela and Ecuador established considerable resemblances concerning the complex arrays of social, economic, and political actors involved in the struggles over the reforms, their positioning with regard to the social security system reforms and the power resources at their disposal. In both countries, the actors involved in the struggles over the reforms were not circumscribed to the labor unions and the class political parties, as presupposed by political class struggle approaches, but they concatenated manifold and interrelated social, economic, and political actors, including the government, (class and nonclass) political parties, labor unions, employers' organizations, military and police forces, peasant and indigenous organizations, professional associations, lobby groups, nongovernmental organizations, and associations of social security beneficiaries. This ascertainment corroborated the criticism regarding the restricted analytical focus of the political class struggle approach and substantiated the capacity of the theoretical approach of this research to acknowledge the multiplicity of social, economic, and political actors involved in the struggles over social policy. Likewise, the positions of the contending actors in Venezuela and Ecuador regarding the reforms divaricated from the positions assumed by the political class struggle approach, according to which the labor unions and labor parties would essentially advocate the development of social policy aimed at decommodification. As matter of fact, the positions of the largest Venezuelan and Ecuadorian labor unions regarding the reforms correlated their positions within the struggles for hegemony between government and opposition, because of which they repudiated the reforms aimed at the universalization of social security promoted by the left-wing governments. The power resources at disposal of the contending actors brought out substantial similarities in both countries, including corporative associational, political associational, structural, mobilizational, and communicational power resources.

In addition, the comparative analysis brought out the extraordinary importance of the Venezuelan and Ecuadorian governments as social, economic, and political actors, which in both cases was associated with their prerogative over the oil sector. Because of this, Venezuelan and Ecuadorian governments have historically taken over a structuring role in the economy and the society, both as the main economic drivers, and as the exclusive interlocutors of the socially and economically excluded groups.

In the case of the "how" question, the comparative analysis determined that the power struggles over the post-neoliberal social security system reforms in Venezuela and Ecuador were profoundly correlated with the struggles for hegemony which came about in both countries. However, this common element actually brought about divergent outcomes of the social security system reforms in Venezuela and Ecuador, as the different development of the hegemonic struggles generated opposite effects on the social security system reforms in both countries.

In the case of Venezuela, the radicalization of the hegemonic struggles between government and opposition initially brought about the sanction of the social security system reform in December 2002 because it brought down the opposition to the reform within the government party. However, after the total defeat of the opposition in 2004, the government undertook the development of the parallel system of social policy based on the Misiones Bolivarianas and Grandes Misiones, later called Sistema Nacional de Misiones y Grandes Misiones Socialistas (SNMGMS), which was clearly superimposed upon the Sistema de Seguridad Social (SSS) devised in the LOSSS. The SNMGMS and the SSS did not essentially divaricate in terms of the social services provided, as the missions included in the SNMGMS corresponded with the contingencies usually associated with social security such as disease, maternity, invalidity, old age, family, unemployment, etc. However, the SNMGMS brought about two political advantages over the SSS for the government. First, it was not institutionally established as a universal state social security system, but it was politically associated with the government. Accordingly, the continuance of the missions included in the SNMGMS was subordinated to the continuance of the government. Second, the SNMGMS was not financially established as a unified social security system, in which the affiliates of the contributory social insurances and the state co-participated in the funding. Instead, the missions included in the SNMGMS were completely subsidized by the national government through ad hoc foundations funded by PDVSA. Based on this, the government could discretionally determine the development of the missions based on its political convenience without any accountability.

In the end, the parallel system of social policy based on the Misiones Bolivarianas and Grandes Misiones accomplished its two main objectives. On the one side, it clearly ameliorated the socioeconomic situation of the historically excluded social groups. On the other side, it maximized the political base of the government in the context of the hegemonic struggles between government and opposition. However, at the same time, the development of the SNMGMS relegated the implementation of the institutional structure of social security prescribed by the LOSSS, in spite of the extraordinary structural, corporative associational, political associational, mobilizational, and communicational power resources accumulated by the government since its coming to power.

In the case of Ecuador, where the power resources of Correa's government did not measure up to the extraordinary power resources controlled by Chávez' government, the hegemonic struggles brought out the potential insurrectionary power of some sectors of the opposition which repudiated the post-neoliberal social security system reform. Because of this, the government was to restructuralize its strategy regarding the reform, even though it could have autonomously carried through its original reform law after taking over the absolute majority of the national assembly in 2013. Accordingly, the government countenanced the demanded continuity of the special social security regimes of the police and military forces, superseded its originally intended thoroughgoing reform with subsequent partial reforms of the existing social security system, and correlated the creation of a special social security regime for the homemakers with the reorientation of the state contribution of 40% to the pensions of the existing general pension regime, thereby counterbalancing the opposition of the affiliates of the general pension regime with the support of the homemakers. Based on this stepwise strategy, Correa's government successfully brought about a substantial part of its originally intended reform.

The extraordinary expansion of social policy carried out by Correa's government since its coming to power undoubtedly represented a fundamental factor in its relation with the socially and economically excluded groups, which materialized a central part of its political base. However, as the government essentially maximized the magnitude and the scope of the previously existing social programs, especially the conditional cash transfer known as Bono de Desarrollo Humano (English: Human Development Voucher), the expansion of social policy came about in the context of the preexisting social institutions. For this reason, in contrast to Venezuela, no parallel structure of social policy was established in Ecuador.

All in all, the comparative analysis determined that the struggles over the social security system reforms in Venezuela and Ecuador corresponded with one another with regard to their structural conditions (the "where" question"), their points of contention (the "what" question), and their contending actors (the "who" question). In contrast, the comparative analysis established substantial divergences with respect to the ways in which the struggles over the reforms came about (the "how" question) due to the divergent development of the hegemonic struggles between government and opposition in both countries. These divergences finally determined the indefinite stagnation of the post-neoliberal social security system reform in Venezuela and brought about the advancement of subsequent partial reforms aimed at the universalization of social security in Ecuador.

5.6 Prospects of the Complementary Approach for the Analysis of Social Policy in Latin America and the Global South

In terms of theory, this research came out from two interrelated starting points. The first was associated with the shortcomings of political class struggle approaches when confronted with social policy in the Global South. The second was predicated on the reconceptualization of social policy in the Latin American academia initiated during the 2000s, which established the focus on the economic and political determinants of social policy and consequently advocated its universalization.

Against this background, this research brought forward a theoretical approach to social policy which basically undertook two goals: (1) deracinating the shortcomings of political class struggle approaches when confronted with social policy in Latin America and (2) acknowledging the economic and political determinants of social policy at the same time. In a nutshell, this approach commingled the Poulantzian and the political class struggle approaches into a complementary approach which capitalized on their analytical strengths while circumventing their analytical weaknesses. The "compatibility" between both approaches was substantiated by their common theoretical premise, according to which social policy represented the outcome of power struggles among contending social groups.

Based on the results of this research, the complementary approach to social policy accomplished its two main. First, it effectively deracinated the aforementioned flaws of political class struggles approaches when taking up social policy in Latin America. Second, it successfully puzzled out the economic and political determinants of social policy in the context of the post-neoliberal social security system reforms in Venezuela and Ecuador.

The incorporation of the Poulantzian approach represented the key for both achievements, as it brought about the theoretical framework to associate the power struggles over the social security system reforms with the historical, social, economic and political conditions in which they came about. In the end, the analysis corroborated that the power struggles over the reforms in Venezuela and Ecuador were profoundly correlated with the hegemonic struggles between government and opposition. Moreover, it established that the struggles for hegemony finally determined the failure or success of the post-neoliberal social security system reforms in both countries.

In view of the foregoing, the theoretical approach to social policy introduced in this research brings about promising prospects regarding its application to the comparative study of social policy in Latin America and the Global South. The fact that this approach predicates on extensive and detailed knowledge of its research cases does not deteriorate its potential for comparative analysis at all. As George and Bennett point out, case studies can be concatenated into comparative studies with ease inasmuch as their analytical categories are carried over (George and Bennett 2005).

Future research based on the complementary approach could branch out its analytical scope in order puzzle out the concealed power struggles over the implementation of social policy within the state apparatus. Though concealed, these struggles determine the way in which social policy is effectively carried out in practice, and they can even bring about the complete non-implementation of social policy despite the government's directives. To this aim, future research based on the complementary approach might break down the institutional and operational dimensions associated with the implementation of social policy. Even though this task would necessarily have to circumvent the wall of secrecy which characterizes the power struggles within the state apparatus, it would certainly bring about fascinating results.

Reference

George A, Bennett A (2005) Case studies and theory development in the social sciences. The MIT Press, Cambridge

Notes

Interviews

Venezuela

Absalón Méndez Cegarra, Investigador de la Universidad Central de Venezuela. Interview conducted on 19/03/2013 in Caracas, Venezuela

Ana Mercedes Salcedo, Investigadora de la Universidad Central de Venezuela. Interview conducted on 05/04/2013 in Caracas, Venezuela

Arturo Tremont, Funcionario de la Comisión Permanente de Desarrollo Social Integral de la Asamblea Nacional de Venezuela. Interview conducted on 11/02/2014 in Caracas, Venezuela

Aurelio Concheso, Presidente de la Comisión de Asuntos Laborales de la Federación de Cámaras y Asociaciones de Comercio y Producción. Interview conducted on 29/05/2013 in Caracas, Venezuela

Carlos Aponte Blank, Investigador de la Universidad Central de Venezuela. Interview conducted on 27/05/2013 in Caracas, Venezuela

Christian Colombet, Investigador de la Universidad de Carabobo. Interview conducted on 04/04/2013 in Valencia, Venezuela

Daniel Santolo, Secretario general de La Causa Radical. Interview conducted on 27/05/2013 in Caracas, Venezuela

Fernando Barrientos, Asesor de la Confederación de Trabajadores de Venezuela. Interview conducted on 05/04/2013 in Caracas, Venezuela

Fernando José Bianco Colmenares, Presidente del Colegio de Médicos de Caracas. Interview conducted on 02/04/2013 in Caracas, Venezuela

Jorge Díaz Polanco, Investigador de la Universidad Central de Venezuela. Interview conducted on 04/04/2013 in Valencia, Venezuela

Julio César Alviárez, Superintendente del Sistema de Seguridad Social. Interview conducted on 01/04/2013 in Valencia, Venezuela

León Arismendi, Coordinador del Instituto de Altos Estudios Sindicales, Asesor de la Confederación de Trabajadores de Venezuela. Interview conducted on 04/04/2013 in Valencia, Venezuela

Leticia Barrios, Investigadora de la Universidad de Carabobo. Interview conducted on 04/04/2013 in Valencia, Venezuela

Manuel Cova, Secretario General de la Confederación de Trabajadores de Venezuela. Interview conducted on 10/02/2014 in Caracas, Venezuela

© Springer Nature Switzerland AG 2019
E. L. Bistoletti, *The Power Struggles over the Post-neoliberal Social Security System Reforms in Venezuela and Ecuador*, The Latin American Studies Book Series,
https://doi.org/10.1007/978-3-319-98168-0

María de Esperanza Hermida Moreno, Coordinadora de Seguridad Social en el Programa Venezolano en Educación-Acción en Derechos Humanos. Interview conducted on 28/05/2013 in Caracas, Venezuela

Orlando Chirino, Ex Secretario General de la Federación Unitaria de Trabajadores del Petróleo, Gas, Similares y Derivados de Venezuela. Interview conducted on 11/02/2014 in Caracas, Venezuela

Oscar Figuera, Secretario General del Partido Comunista de Venezuela. Interview conducted on 10/02/2014 in Caracas, Venezuela

Rafael Ríos, Tesorero del Sistema de Seguridad Social. Interview conducted on 03/04/2013 in Caracas, Venezuela

Tirso Silva, Ex Asambleísta del Partido Socialista Unido de Venezuela. Interview conducted on 01/04/2013 in Caracas, Venezuela

Williams Aranguren, Investigador de la Universidad de Carabobo. Interview conducted on 28/03/2013 in Caracas, Venezuela

Yudi Chaudary, Investigadora de la Universidad Central de Venezuela. Interview conducted on 02/04/2013 in Caracas, Venezuela

Ecuador

Alejandro Vela Loza, Subdirector del Instituto de Seguridad Social de las Fuerzas Armadas. Interview conducted on 28/03/2014 in Quito, Ecuador

Ana Lucía Torres, Asesora del Ministerio de Salud Pública. Interview conducted on 03/05/2013 in Quito, Ecuador

Carmen Corra Ponce, Ex Intendenta de la Intendencia Nacional de Seguridad Social de la Superintendencia de Bancos y Seguros. Interview conducted on 28/03/2014 in Quito, Ecuador

David Alomía, Ex Vicedirector del Programa de Protección Social. Interview conducted on 19/04/2013 in Quito, Ecuador

Diego Martínez, Ex director del Programa de Protección Social. Interview conducted on 22/04/2013 in Quito, Ecuador

Emma Rosana Palacios, Presidenta de la Unión Nacional de Educadores. Interview conducted on 25/03/2014 in Quito, Ecuador

Jorge Granda, Investigador de la Facultad Latinoamericana de Ciencias Sociales. Interview conducted on 29/04/2013 in Quito, Ecuador

José Chávez, Presidente de la Confederación Ecuatoriana de Organizaciones Sindicales Libres. Interview conducted on 06/05/2013 in Quito, Ecuador

Juan Javier Silva, Director Nacional de Bienestar Social de la Policía Nacional del Ecuador. Interview conducted on 24/03/2014 in Quito, Ecuador

Luis Alfredo Muñoz Neira, Abogado. Interview conducted on 29/04/2013 in Quito, Ecuador

María Quishpe, Coordinadora Nacional de la Asociación Nacional de Mujeres por la Vida. Interview conducted on 30/04/2013 in Quito, Ecuador

Nivea Vélez, Asambleísta de la Asamblea Nacional del Ecuador. Interview conducted on 30/04/2013 in Quito, Ecuador

Paulina Guerrero, Vocal del Consejo Directivo del Instituto Ecuatoriano de Seguridad Social. Interview conducted on 06/05/2013 in Quito, Ecuador

Pedro Montalvo, Investigador de la Facultad Latinoamericana de Ciencias Sociales. Interview conducted on 18/04/2013 in Quito, Ecuador

Rosa Argudo Coronel, Secretaria General Nacional del Sindicato Nacional Único de Obreros del Instituto Ecuatoriano de Seguridad Social, Presidenta de la Confederación Ecuatoriana de Trabajadores y Servidores de la Seguridad Social. Interview conducted on 25/03/2014 in Quito, Ecuador

Osvaldo Santana, Secretario de la Confederación Nacional de Jubilados. Interview conducted on 19/03/2014 in Quito, Ecuador

Wilson Oswaldo Rivadeneira Ruiz, Presidente de la Confederación Nacional de Jubilados. Interview conducted on 19/03/2014 in Quito, Ecuador
Ximena Ponce, Asambleísta de la Asamblea Nacional del Ecuador. Interview conducted on 22/04/2013 in Quito, Ecuador

Newspapers, Magazines and Electronic Resources

Cobertura 09/2002: "Seguridad social venezolana entre dos visiones"
Correo del Orinoco 29/10/2015: "Primero Justicia afirmó tener 1 millón de voluntarios registrados para el 6-D". http://www.correodelorinoco.gob.ve/nacionales/primero-justicia-afirmo-tener-1-millon-voluntarios-registrados-para-6-d/
Diario Opinión 09/02/2013: "Falso proyecto de ley remitido a policías y militares es otro intento desestabilizador contra Gobierno". http://www.diariopinion.com/nacional/verArticulo.php?id=846717
Ecuadorinmediato 16/07/2010: "Incremento de 57 dólares mensuales a pensiones jubilares sería retroactiva y obligatoria, anuncia Nivea Vélez". http://ecuadorinmediato.com/index.php?module=Noticias&func=news_user_view&id=130324&umt=incremento_57_dolares_mensuales_a_pensiones_jubilares_seria_retroactiva_y_obligatoria_anuncia_nivea_velez_audio
Ecuadorinmediato 09/05/2015: "'Fondo de Cesantía del Magisterio era caja chica del MPD', denuncia el presidente de Ecuador". http://www.ecuadorinmediato.com/index.php?module=Noticias&func=news_user_view&id=2818781001
Ecuavisa 13/04/2015: "Jubilados y miembros del FCME rechazan cese de pago de prestaciones jubilares". http://www.ecuavisa.com/articulo/noticias/actualidad/105628-jubilados-miembros-del-fcme-rechazan-cese-pago-prestaciones
El Comercio 08/03/2010: "'Banco del IESS solo debe ser de inversiones'". http://www.elcomercio.com/actualidad/negocios/banco-del-iess-debe-inversiones.html
El Comercio 01/09/2014: "En dos meses, Alianza País entregó 161913 carnés". http://www.elcomercio.com/actualidad/alianza-pais-carnes-militancia.html
El Comercio 17/02/2015: "La UNE perdió 80000 aportantes en ocho años". http://www.elcomercio.com/actualidad/une-aportantes-meryzamora-ecuador-maestros.html
El Mundo Economía y Negocios 14/08/2013: "¿Quién es José "El Chino" Khan?, el nuevo presidente de Cadivi". http://www.elmundo.com.ve/noticias/actualidad/ noticias/las-claves-de-jose–el-chino–khan.aspx
El Mundo Economía y Negocios 30/09/2013: "Solo 9% de la masa laboral venezolana está afiliada a sindicatos". http://www.elmundo.com.ve/noticias/economia/laboral/solo-9-de-la-masa-laboral-venezolana-esta-afiliad.aspx
El Telégrafo 26/09/2012: "Más de 2 millones de afiliados tienen los grupos políticos". http://www.telegrafo.com.ec/noticias/informacion-general/item/mas-de-2-millones-de-afiliados-tienen-los-grupos-politicos.html
El Telégrafo 08/02/2013: "Ministros denuncian intento desestabilizador en la fuerza pública". http://www.telegrafo.com.ec/noticias/informacion-general/item/ministros-denuncian-intento-desestabilizador-en-la-fuerza-publica.html
El Telégrafo 27/05/2013: "Fractura del sindicalismo ecuatoriano". http://www.telegrafo.com.ec/economia/masqmenos/item/el-reto-de-los-sindicatos-en-la-transformacion-productiva.html
El Telégrafo 10/04/2015: "La reforma laboral garantiza el pago de las pensiones jubilares por parte del Estado". http://telegrafo.com.ec/politica/item/la-reforma-laboral-garantiza-el-pago-de-las-pensiones-jubilares-por-parte-del-estado.html
El Universal 13/12/1998: "Comisiones de enlace tienen diez días para entregar informe a Hugo Chávez". http://www.eluniversal.com/1998/12/13/pol_art_13116DD
El Universal 31/01/1999: "Comisión de enlace rechaza ley de salud". http://www.eluniversal.com/1999/01/31/ccs_art_31180AA

El Universal 26/07/1999: "Victoria aplastante en todas la regiones". http://www.eluniversal.com/1999/07/26/pol_art_26104AA

El Universal 23/03/2000: "El gobierno prepara ley de AFP privadas". http://www.eluniversal.com/2000/03/23/eco_art_23204CC

El Universal 07/08/2000: "Urge proteger a las prestaciones de la inflación". http://www.eluniversal.com/2000/08/07/eco_art_07201AA

El Universal 10/08/2000: "Es excesiva presencia bancaria en comisión de seguridad social". http://www.eluniversal.com/2000/08/10/eco_art_10204EE

El Universal 10/08/2000: "Estructuras de seguridad social costarán 4,5 millardos". http://www.eluniversal.com/2001/06/06/eco_art_06202AA

El Universal 04/09/2000: "Se cambiará la estructura económica". http://www.eluniversal.com/2000/09/04/eco_art_03201AA

El Universal 15/06/2001: "Sistema de seguridad social es inviable". http://www.eluniversal.com/2001/06/15/eco_art_15201AA

El Universal 02/08/2001: "Asamblea entregará otra ley marco de seguridad social". http://www.eluniversal.com/2001/08/02/eco_art_02202HH

El Universal 13/10/2001: "Pensar para toda la población". http://www.eluniversal.com/2001/10/13/apo_art_13202CC

El Universal 07/11/2001: "Sin considerar recomendaciones aprobaron ley de hidrocarburos". http://www.eluniversal.com/2001/11/07/eco_art_07201BB

El Universal 12/11/2001: "Reforma previsional requiere cambios en el área fiscal". http://www.eluniversal.com/2001/11/12/eco_art_12201CC

El Universal 19/11/2001: "La seguridad social es un problema técnico". http://www.eluniversal.com/2001/11/19/apo_art_19201CC

El Universal 01/12/2001: "Preocupa a sector privado reforma previsional". http://www.eluniversal.com/2002/12/01/eco_art_01207AA

El Universal 29/11/2001: "Cerrada ovación ratifica la protesta". http://www.eluniversal.com/2001/11/29/pol_art_29102AA

El Universal 05/12/2001: "CTV también irá al paro". http://www.eluniversal.com/2001/12/05/pol_art_05102AA

El Universal 23/01/2002: "Opositores unidos". http://www.eluniversal.com/2002/01/23/apo_art_23106FF

El Universal 10/03/2002: "Grupo Garibaldi en repliegue". http://www.eluniversal.com/2002/03/10/pol_art_10104AA

El Universal 05/04/2002: "Paro petrolero indefinido". http://www.eluniversal.com/2002/04/05/pol_art_05102AA

El Universal 03/07/2002: "Proponen que trabajadores decidan régimen de pensiones". http://www.eluniversal.com/2002/07/03/eco_art_03202GG

El Universal 17/07/2002: "Aporte al régimen de pensiones será 12,76 %". http://www.eluniversal.com/2002/07/10/eco_art_10205AA

El Universal 06/11/2002: "Diputados analizan mantener el seguro social". http://www.eluniversal.com/2002/11/06/eco_art_06201CC

El Universal 14/11/2002: "El Estado administrará régimen de pensiones". http://www.eluniversal.com/2002/11/14/eco_art_14202FF

El Universo 31/12/2002: "Sociedad Patriótica quiere fortalecerse". http://www.eluniverso.com/2002/12/31/0001/8/9C0375E84CA844C1842676FA60975353.html

El Universo 04/11/2006: "Noboa dice que seguirá la receta del ex presidente Ronald Reagan". http://www.eluniverso.com/2006/11/03/0001/8/8366E35D1CDC4A708B45DA62F4A1F08A.html

El Universo 04/11/2006: "El futuro del IESS no ha sido un tema de actual campaña electoral". http://www.eluniverso.com/2006/11/04/0001/9/E889327EAF98461DBF4B78D66ACB87FC.html

El Universo 17/02/2009: "J Polémica por eliminación de aporte a pensiones". http://www.eluniverso.com/2009/02/17/1/1355/11CD228D6F384336908EE01226CFFA52.html

El Universo 18/02/2009: "Jubilados amenazan con sus votos a Correa si quita aporte". http://www.eluniverso.com/2009/02/18/1/1356/E274B5B9DEE74B7C99BD168A817A3048.html

El Universo 02/03/2009: "Congresillo con 8 leyes este mes". http://www.eluniverso.com/2009/03/02/1/1355/06B07A39833F4A348E4D4997DE25B3D4.html

El Universo 30/03/2009: "Gobierno se reúne con jubilados para explicar Ley de Seguridad Social". http://www.eluniverso.com/2009/03/30/1/1356/C52A433376DF47209A6F881B2F6A006C.html

El Universo 20/01/2010: "Jubilados piden mejor aumento en pensiones". http://www.eluniverso.com/2010/01/20/1/1356/jubilados-piden-mejor-aumento-pensiones.html

El Universo 04/08/2010: "Régimen piensa redireccionar aporte del 40 % de pensiones". http://www.eluniverso.com/2010/08/04/1/1356/regimen-piensa-redireccionar-aporte-40-pensiones.html

El Universo 16/08/2010: "Alza espera el regreso de la Asamblea". http://www.eluniverso.com/2010/08/16/1/1356/alza-espera-regreso-asamblea.html

El Universo 06/08/2010: "Pedido de subir $ 57 a pensiones no tiene apoyo". http://www.eluniverso.com/2010/08/06/1/1356/hay-consenso-monto-incremento-pensiones.html

El Universo 05/10/2010: "Gobierno aumentará sueldos a oficiales de Policía y FF.AA.". http://www.eluniverso.com/2010/10/05/1/1355/retroactivo-sube-salario-mandos-medios-fuerza-publica.html

El Universo 22/10/2010a: "Fue aprobada el alza a jubilados de $40 a $60". http://www.eluniverso.com/2010/10/22/1/1356/asamblea-aprobo-subir-pensiones-jubilados.html

El Universo 22/10/2010b: "Aumento de pensiones no tendrá veto presidencial". http://www.eluniverso.com/2010/10/22/1/1356/aumento-pensiones-tendra-veto-presidencial.html

El Universo 13/01/2014: "Oficialismo definirá esta semana la agenda de la Asamblea". http://www.eluniverso.com/noticias/2014/01/13/nota/2025421/dos-meses-comenzara-trabajo-fuerte-comisiones

El Universo 26/03/2015: "Rafael Correa dice que IESS tiene superavit por lo que 'no tiene sentido' darle el 40 % para pensiones". http://www.eluniverso.com/noticias/2015/03/26/nota/4704431/correa-dice-que-iess-tiene-superavit-que-no-tiene-sentido-darle-40

El Universo 14/04/2015: "Aprobada la Ley de Justicia Laboral, que reforma la seguridad social". http://www.eluniverso.com/noticias/2015/04/14/nota/4770421/aprobada-ley-justicia-laboral-que-reforma-seguridad-social

El Universo 15/05/2015: "El BIESS ya administra el Fondo del Magisterio Nacional". http://www.eluniverso.com/noticias/2015/05/15/nota/4874096/biess-administra-hoy-fondo-magisterio-nacional

El Universo 05/10/2015: "Unidad Popular se constituyó como partido nacional". http://www.eluniverso.com/noticias/2015/10/05/nota/5168492/unidad-popular-se-constituyo-como-partido-nacional

Hoy 24/02/1999: "IESS Tres años para reforma". http://www.explored.com.ec/noticias-ecuador/iess-tres-anos-para-reforma-104578.html

Hoy 12/07/2001: "Concluye la reforma del IESS". http://www.explored.com.ec/noticias-ecuador/concluye-reforma-del-iess-122151.html

Hoy 03/06/2005: "Rafael Correa, opuesto a devolver los fondos". http://www.explored.com.ec/noticias-ecuador/rafael-correa-opuesto-a-devolver-los-fondos-206203.html

Hoy 23/07/2005: "El IESS respalda el veto parcial del Ejecutivo". http://www.explored.com.ec/noticias-ecuador/el-iess-respalda-el-veto-parcial-del-ejecutivo-210179.html

Hoy 02/11/2006: "Planes opuestos para la seguridad social". http://www.explored.com.ec/noticias-ecuador/planes-opuestos-para-la-seguridad-social-249606.html

La Hora 08/03/2009: "Policías y militares en servicio pasivo anuncian protestas a nivel nacional para próximo 26 de marzo". http://www.lahora.com.ec/index.php/noticias/show/847898/-1/Polic%C3%ADas_y_militares_en_servicio_pasivo_anuncian_protestas_a_nivel_nacional_para_pr%C3%B3ximo_26_de_marzo.html#.VbeGPFLimzk

La Hora 27/03/2009: "Jubilados protestan contra Banco del IESS". http://www.lahora.com.ec/index.php/noticias/show/856378/-1/Jubilados_protestan_contra_Banco_del_IESS.html#

La Hora 14/05/2015: "Policía anti motines toma oficinas del Fondo de Cesantía del Magisterio". http://www.larepublica.ec/blog/politica/2015/05/14/policias-anti-motines-toma-oficinas-fondo-cesantias-magisterio/

Notitarde 19/10/1998: "Henrique Salas Römer propone renegociar la deuda pública". http://historico.notitarde.com/1998/10/19/economia/economia1.html

Tal Cual 07/03/2001: "Empleadores fuera del sistema de salud". http://www.talcualdigital.com/ediciones/2001/03/07/f-p11s2.htm

Tal Cual 13/06/2001: "Una prórroga de $1.600 millones". http://www.talcualdigital.com/ediciones/2001/06/13/f-p13s1.htm

Tal Cual 16/11/2001a: "La novela rosa del MVR". http://www.talcualdigital.com/ediciones/2001/11/16/f-p3s1.htm

Tal Cual 16/11/2001b: "Talibanes del MVR al asalto de la inteligencia". http://www.talcualdigital.com/ediciones/2001/11/16/f-p2s2.htm

Tal Cual 21/11/2001a: "La reforma es demasiado débil". http://www.talcualdigital.com/ediciones/2001/11/21/f-p13s1.htm

Tal Cual 21/11/2001b: "Seguro está el infierno". http://www.talcualdigital.com/ediciones/2001/11/21/f-p3s1.htm

Tal Cual 01/07/2002: "El pote versus capitalización individual". http://www.talcualdigital.com/ediciones/2002/07/01/f-p16s1.htm

Youtube 08/02/2013: "Versión oficial ISSPOL y cesantía". https://www.youtube.com/watch?v=FVAO4uAEiFg

Youtube 06/04/2013: "ISSFA e ISSPOL no desaparecerán". https://www.youtube.com/watch?v=bGs1YL4Y-5U

References

Books, Journals and Documents

Althuser L (1971) "Lenin and philosophy" and other essays. Monthly Review Press, New York

ACE (Asamblea Constituyente de Ecuador) Actas. http://montecristivive.com/category/archivo-constitucional/constituciones-del-ecuador/constitucion-2008-asamblea-constituyente-de-monte cristi/actas-de-la-asamblea-de-montecristi/

ANCV (Asamblea Nacional Constituyente de Venezuela) Actas. https://carloseramos.wordpress.com/tag/asamblea-nacional-constituyente-1999

Arkonada K (2015a) ¿Fin del ciclo progresista o reflujo del cambio de época en América Latina? 7 tesis para el debate. In: Rebelión. http://www.rebelion.org/noticia.php?id=203029

Arkonada K (2015b) ¿Fin de ciclo? La disputa por el relato. In: MDZ. http://www.mdzol.com/opinion/646979-fin-de-ciclo-la-disputa-por-el-relato/

Bachrach P, Baratz M (1962) Two faces of power. Am Polit Sci Rev 56(4) (Menasha)

Barnett M, Duvall R (2005) Power in international politics. Int Organ 59(1) (Cambridge University Press, Cambridge)

Bäcker G, Naegele G, Bispinck R, Hofemann K, Neubauer J (2008) Sozialpolitik und soziale Lage in Deutschland. Band 1: Grundlagen, Arbeit, Einkommen und Finanzierung. VS Verlag für Sozialwissenschaften, Wiesbaden

Borón A (2016) ¿Estancamiento, retroceso, involución?. In: Rebelión. http://www.rebelion.org/noticia.php?id=209555

Carranza Barona C, Cisneros MV (2014) Hacia un sistema de protección social más inclusivo en el Ecuador: seguimiento y desenlace de un proceso de construcción de consensos en la búsqueda del buen vivir. Comisión Económica para América Latina y el Caribe, Santiago de Chile

CND (Consejo Nacional de Desarrollo) (1993) Agenda para el desarrollo: plan de acción del gobierno 1993–1996. Consejo Nacional de Desarrollo, Quito

Dahl R (1957) The concept of power. Behav Sci 2(3) (Wiley, New Jersey)

Dahl R (1968) Power. In: Sills D (ed) International encyclopedia of the social sciences, vol XII. Macmillan, New York

Díaz LE (2008) Concepto y aplicación de la seguridad social en Venezuela. In: Cuestiones Políticas, vol 24, no 41. Facultad de Ciencias Jurídicas y Políticas, Universidad del Zulia, Maracaibo

Digeser P (1992) The fourth face of power. J Polit 54(4) (Cambridge University Press, Cambridge)

Fernández ME (2003) Comentarios a la Ley Orgánica del Sistema de Seguridad Social. In: Gaceta Laboral, vol 9, no 2. Facultad de Ciencias Jurídicas y Políticas, Universidad del Zulia, Maracaibo

Fuentes Hernández W (2009) Apuntes sobre la seguridad social y el sistema de previsión venezolano. Ediciones Liber, Caracas

© Springer Nature Switzerland AG 2019

E. L. Bistoletti, *The Power Struggles over the Post-neoliberal Social Security System Reforms in Venezuela and Ecuador*, The Latin American Studies Book Series, https://doi.org/10.1007/978-3-319-98168-0

Granda D (2012) El hiperpresidencialismo en el Ecuador. Universidad Central del Ecuador, Quito

Gudynas E (2015) La indentidad de los progresismos en la balanza. In: América Latina en Movimiento, vol 39, n 510. Agencia Latinoamericana de Información, Quito

Hegel G (2005) [1821] Philosophy of right. Dover Publications, Mineola

Hobbes T (1929)[1651] Leviathan or the matter, forme and power of a common wealth ecclesiastical and civil. Oxford University Press, London

Jessop B (1990) State theory: putting the capitalist state in its place. Polity Press, Cambridge

Korpi W (1989) Social policy and distributional conflict in the capitalist democracies: a preliminary framework. West Eur Polit 3(3) (Routledge, London)

Lander LE, López Maya M (1999) Venezuela. La victoria de Chávez. El Polo Patriótico en las elecciones de 1998. In: *Nueva Sociedad*, no 160. Friedrich Ebert Stiftung, Buenos Aires

Lasswell H, Kaplan A (1950) Power and society: a framework for political inquiry. Yale University Press, New Haven

Lenin V (1972)[1919] Collected works, vol XXIX. Progress Publishers, Moscow

Lockwood D (1981) The weakest link in the chain? Some comments on the Marxist theory of action. In: Simpson R, Simpson I Research in the sociology of work. JAI Press, Greenwich

Lukes S (1983) Macht und Herrschaft bei Weber, Marx, Focault. In: Matthes J (ed) Krise der Arbeitsgesellschaft? Verhandlungen des 21. Deutschen Soziologentages in Bamberg 1982. Campus Verlag, Frankfurt am Main

Martínez Franzoni J, Castro M (2007) Régimen distributivo en Costa Rica: límites del desencuentro entre mercado laboral y política social. International Labour Organization, Geneva

Marx K (1887)[1867] Capital: a critique of political economy, vol I. Progress Publishers, Moscow

Méndez Cegarra A (2008) Origen, desarrollo, crisis y reforma de la seguridad social en Venezuela. Instituto Latinoamericano de Investigaciones Sociales, Caracas

Nettl JP (1968) The state as a conceptual variable. World Polit 20(4) (Cambridge University Press, Cambridge)

Nuñez González C (2008) El sistema de seguridad social en la República Bolivariana de Venezuela. Universidad Bolivariana de Venezuela, Caracas

Offe C (1972) Strukturprobleme des kapitalistischen Staates. Suhrkamp Verlag, Frankfurt am Main

Ospina P (2011b) La CONAIE. In: La Línea de Fuego. Pensamiento Crítico. http://lalineadefuego.info

Ospina P (2016) El agotamiento del progresismo. In: Nueva Sociedad: democracia y política en América Latina. http://nuso.org/articulo/el-agotamiento-del-progresismo/

Penfold Becerra M (2008) Clientelism and social funds: evidence from Chávez's misiones. Lat Am Polit Soc 49(4) (University of Miami, Miami)

Penfold Becerra M (2010) La democracia subyugada: el hiperpresidencialismo venezolano. In: Revista de Ciencia Política, vol 30, no 1. Pontificia Universidad Católica de Chile, Santiago

Poulantzas N (1978) State, power, socialism. New Left Books, London

Rauber I (2015) Gobiernos populares de América Latina, ¿fin de ciclo o nuevo tiempo político? La clave del protagonismo popular. In: América Latina en Movimiento, vol 39, no 510. Agencia Latinoamericana de Información, Quito

Recalde P (2007) Elecciones presidenciales 2006: una aproximación a los actores del proceso. In: Íconos. Revista de Ciencias Sociales, no 27. Facultad Latinoamericana de Ciencias Sociales Sede Ecuador, Quito

Roig AA (2008) El pensamiento latinoamericano y su aventura. El Andariego, Buenos Aires

Sader E (2015) ¿El final del ciclo (que no hubo)?. In: América Latina en Movimiento Online. http://www.alainet.org/es/articulo/172389

Sader E (2016) La izquierda del siglo XXI. In: Página/12. http://www.pagina12.com.ar/diario/elmundo/4-289505-2016-01-04.html

Salcedo González (2008) Ana Mercedes: Los servicios sociales en Venezuela: retos y perspectivas. Comisión de Estudios de Postgrado, Facultad de Ciencias Económicas y Sociales, Universidad Central de Venezuela, Fondo Editorial Tropykos, Caracas

Schimitt C (2008)[1932] The concept of the political. University of Chicago Press, Chicago

Schulze R (1961) The bifurcation of power in a satellite city. In: Janowitz M (ed) Community political systems. The Free Press of Glencoe, New York

Therborn G, Kjellberg A, Marklund S, Ohlund U (1978) Sweden before and after social democracy: a first overview. In: Acta Sociologica, no 21 (supplement). Nordic Sociological Association, Oslo

Weber M (1978)[1922] Economy and society: an outline of interpretive sociology. University of California Press, Berkeley